Public Values, Private Schools

3 day
loan

The Stanford Series on Education and Public Policy

General Editor: Professor Henry M. Levin, School of Education, Stanford University

The purpose of this series is to address major issues of educational policy as they affect and are affected by political, social and economic issues. It focuses on both the consequences of education for economic, political and social outcomes as well as the influences of the economic, political and social climate on education. It is particularly concerned with addressing major educational issues and challenges within this framework, and a special effort is made to evaluate the various educational alternatives on the policy agenda or to develop new ones that might address the educational challenges before us. All of the volumes are to be based upon original research and/or competent syntheses of the available research on a topic.

School Days, Rule Days: The Legalization and Regulation of Education *Edited by David L. Kirp, University of California, Berkeley, and Donald N. Jensen, Stanford University.*

The Incompetent Teacher: The Challenge and the Response *Edwin M. Bridges, Stanford University.*

The Future Impact of Technology on Work and Education *Edited by Gerald Burke, Monash University, Australia and Russ W. Rumberger, University of California, Santa Barbara.*

Comparing Public and Private Schools: Volume 1 Institutions and Organizations *Edited by Thomas James, Brown University and Henry M. Levin, Stanford University.*

Comparing Public and Private Schools: Volume 2 School Achievement *Edited by Edward H. Haertel, Stanford University, Thomas James, Brown University and Henry M. Levin, Stanford University.*

Managing Educational Excellence *Thomas B. Timar, Harvard Graduate School of Education and David Kirp, University of California, Berkeley.*

The Changing Idea of a Teachers' Union *Charles T. Kerchner, Claremont Graduate School, California and Douglas Mitchell, University of California.*

Academic Labor Markets and Careers *Edited by David W. Breneman, Kalamazoo College and Ted I.K. Youn, State University of New York at Albany.*

Inside Schools: A Collaborative View *J. Myron Atkin, Donald Kennedy and Cynthia L. Patrick, Stanford University.*

Public Values, Private Schools

Edited by

Neal E. Devins

 The Falmer Press

(A member of the Taylor & Francis Group)
London • New York • Philadelphia

UK   The Falmer Press, Falmer House, Barcombe, Lewes, East Sussex, BN8 5DL

USA The Falmer Press, Taylor & Francis Inc., 242 Cherry Street, Philadelphia, PA 19106–1906

First published 1989

Library of Congress Cataloging-in-Publication Data

Public values, private schools/edited by Neal E. Devins.
  p. cm. — (Stanford series on education and public policy)
  Bibliography: p.
  Includes index.
  ISBN 1–85000–342–4: $36.00. — ISBN 1–85000–347–5 (pbk.): $18.00
  1. Private schools — United States. 2. Private schools — Law and legislation — United States. 3. Discrimination in education — United States. 4. Education and state — United States. 5. Church schools — United States. 6. Values — Study and teaching — United States.
  I. Devins, Neal E. II. Series.
  LC49.P838 1989
  371.02 0973 — dc19

British Library Cataloguing in Publication Data

Public values, private schools — (The stanford series on education and public policy).
1. United States. State schools compared with independent schools.
I. Devins, Neal E. II. Series
379.73

ISBN 1–85000–342–4
ISBN 1–85000–347–5 pbk

Typeset in 11/13 Bembo by
Alresford Typesetting & Design, New Farm Road, Alresford, Hants.

Printed in Great Britain by Taylor & Francis (Printers) Ltd, Basingstoke

Contents

Dedication

For Deborah with love and thanks

Acknowledgments

The idea of a book on public values and private schools occurred to me five years ago when I directed a project on religious liberty and private education for the Vanderbilt Institute for Public Policy Studies. It seemed to me then (as it does today) that private school controversies were decided by public school values, e.g., Christian evangelicals succeeded in challenging programmatic teacher certification and curriculum requirements because students in fundamentalist academies tested as well as their public school counterparts; a nineteenth century civil rights statute protecting the freedom to contract was interpreted to prohibit discriminatory admissions policies in private schools because such practices undermined the public value of school desegregation. With the publication of this collection of essays, this conception has at last borne fruit.

Over these past few years, numerous people have helped the process move along. Henry Levin, editor of the Stanford Series, was more than kind in encouraging me to pursue the project and then substantiating that encouragement with a book contract. Malcolm Clarkson of Falmer Press likewise offered much appreciated encouragement. Special thanks are also owed to Michael Greve, who held me and this project by the hand during its early stages.

In completing this project, I have benefited from numerous sources at the Marshall-Wythe School of Law, College of William and Mary. Several law students have assisted me in copy-editing, cite-checking and proof-reading the various essays in this collection. They are David Watson, Rob McDowell, Jeanne Swanick, Stephen Lauer and especially Tad Pethybridge. Working alongside these students and myself has been a first-rate support staff headed by Della Howard and Betty Abele. The exceptional and timely work of these individuals contributed substantially to the final product. Financial support has come, in part, from the law school.

Finally (but most significantly), the contributors to this volume have

Acknowledgements

amazed and humbled me by their generosity and good works. When they were first approached by me, the publication of this collection seemed anything but definite. Yet, through a series of leaps of faith, a book has emerged.

Williamsburg, Virginia
July 1988

1
Introduction:
Private Schools and Public Values

Neal E. Devins

Private Schools and Public Schools

Private school controversies, for the most part, are public school controversies. We care about the racial composition of private schools because it tells us something about the racial make-up of public schools. Similarly, student performance in private schools serves as a gauge for the quality of instruction in public schools. Finally, the Supreme Court's recognition in *Pierce v. Society of Sisters* that parents have a right to send their children to private schools hinges on the public schools' value inculcation function.[1]

The essays in this collection highlight this public-private connection. Each of the essays ultimately asks one of two questions: how much unlike public schools can private schools be? How much like private schools should public schools be? In answering these questions, the authors explore compulsory education's role as value inculcator and education provider, as well as the duty of educational institutions to conform to constitutional norms.

These explorations are framed around narrower concerns, e.g., government authority to insist that private schools adopt nondiscriminatory practices or inculcate nondiscriminatory values; the nexus between private schools and the nondiscrimination objectives of public schools; and the legality of equality-based regulation of private schools. Each of these concerns is given extensive treatment.

Values

Several of the essays consider the appropriateness of value-based instruction and regulation. Michael Rebell utilizes *Pierce*'s acceptance of private schools as an escape-hatch for value dissenters to understand recent litigation over the public schools' role as value inculcator. For Rebell, the proliferation of law suits challenging the public schools' failure to accommodate religious value dissenters exemplifies the larger failure of public schools to take a leadership role in the inculcation of shared community beliefs. Stephen Arons offers an alternative interpretation of *Pierce* and with it a much different conception of the schools' role as value inculcator. Reading *Pierce* as a broad declaration of parental authority to determine their children's upbringing, Arons advocates the adoption of a voucher scheme allowing all parents to search out schools whose values and objectives match their own. A third approach to the value inculcation question is provided by Robert Fullinwider. Rejecting Rebell's 'family state' and Arons' 'state of families', Fullinwider argues that value inculcation should be limited to the instilling of the virtues of mutual respect and the duty to participate, the two tools necessary to a democracy.[2]

Fullinwider also argues that the instillation of these democratic tools necessitates the extension of nondiscrimination requirements to private schools. Erwin Chemerinsky extends this proposition beyond nondiscrimination, arguing that private schools must conform to *all* constitutional norms if they are to advance democratic values. For Chemerinsky, associational preferences and religious liberty must give way to the larger mission of constitutional self-government.

Henry Levin also calls into question the ability of private schools to serve the commonweal. Levin argues that private schools cannot produce essential public goods such as religious and racial tolerance; these schools' *raison d'être* is to further the self-selected values of a discrete portion of the community. Consequently, private schools are only able to serve the private ends of improving the lives of students and their families. Since the production of these public goods is an integral component of schooling, Levin contends that private schools cannot serve the public by providing students with a common set of values and knowledge. While not advocating the abolition of private schools,[3] Levin argues that the public schools' production of private goods should be the focus of educational reform. John and Shirley Lachs advance a similar argument. For them, education is truly effective only when there is a sense of common enterprise among teacher, student, and parent. In their view, private schools can only serve narrow constituent interests, and therefore sap the vitality and openness necessary to truly worthwhile education. Although quite critical of public education, the Lachs contend that meaningful reform can occur only in the public schools.

In stark contrast, Stephen Arons posits that public schools' leadership caters to a narrow class of well-to-do parents, thereby undermining the public schools' ability to advance nondiscrimination objectives. Under this conception, civil rights objectives may well be enhanced by the privatization of the school's value inculcation function.

An interesting twist to these wide-ranging concerns over value inculcation is provided by Tyll van Geel. In considering the validity of an imagined mandate that private schools inculcate nondiscrimination, van Geel concludes that neither case law nor jurisprudential models provide a solution. He therefore reasons that personal preferences will determine the legality of such regulations.

Nondiscrimination Objectives

The impact of private schools on the universalistic value of equal educational opportunity is considered by most of the authors. For some, private schools pose a significant threat to this value. Erwin Chemerinsky's proposal to constitutionalize private schools, for example, is rooted in his belief that private schools often serve as havens for whites fleeing school desegregation obligations. Empirical support for this proposition can be drawn from Christine Rossell and Robert Crain's study on segregation levels in private schools. Rossell and Crain — based on their investigation of Catholic school enrollments in Boston, Chicago, and Cleveland — conclude that private schools are highly segregated and therefore undermine public school desegregation.

Stephen Arons' and Jeremy Rabkin's essays cast a different light on this subject. Arons argues that the *Brown* mandate has been made meaningless by the Supreme Court's insistence that proof of intentional discrimination precede a school desegregation remedy. Questions about the impact of private school enrollment on desegregation have little relevance under this formulation. Instead, as Arons advocates, the appropriate inquiry concerns the utilization of funding devices that ensure racial balance.[4] Rabkin likewise feels that private schools should not be blamed for the failure of public school desegregation. Suggesting that most white flight is to suburban public schools, Rabkin views as controlling the Supreme Court's refusal to extend urban school desegregation into neighboring suburbs. Unlike Arons, Rabkin — pointing to political realities and possible nonracist motives of whites — endorses the Court's action.

Rabkin also offers another vantage to the private school and equality question. In considering the controversy over whether private schools should demonstrate their commitment to racial equality, Rabkin claims that this controversy is not just about the threat of private schools undermining school desegregation. The symbolism of government assistance to racial discrimination also played a large role in this matter. Thus recast, *Brown*'s universalistic demand stands independent, thereby undercutting arguments that private schools (even religious ones) be exempt from nondiscrimination enforcement. At the same time, Rabkin criticizes overreliance on the tax code to enforce nondiscrimination in education. In his view, rather than obfuscate the meaning of *Brown* in the private sector through indirect measures undertaken by administrators and the courts, Congress — if it truly cares — should enact legislation that speaks directly to the responsibility of private schools in this area.

Finally, John Chubb and Terry Moe consider lessons that public schools can learn from private schools in their efforts to advance equal educational opportunity. Chubb and Moe's study of educational outcomes reveals that the private school model can substantially benefit disadvantaged youth. Determining that the existing public school bureaucracy scraps the vitality and malleability necessary to the effective education of disadvantaged students, Chubb and Moe advocate the deregulation of public education through a voucher-finance scheme.[5]

Legality of Regulation

Nondiscrimination regulation of private schools is given extensive treatment in several of the essays. On one issue all of the authors are in agreement: government may insist that private schools adopt racially nondiscriminatory admissions.[6] Beyond consensus on this universalistic demand, there is sharp disagreement. On one side of the argument, Carl Esbeck argues that church-affiliated schools are immune from all other categories of nondiscrimination regulation. Esbeck concludes that the first amendment places such a high value on religious self-determination that government regulation cannot extend beyond race and minimal academic criteria. Robert Fullinwider echoes Esbeck's sentiment that religion has a special place among liberties. Fullinwider, however, argues that government seeks to penalize religious discrimination indirectly through the tax system.[7]

William Marshall and Joanne Brant offer yet another view. The critical inquiry for Marshall and Brant is whether government action threatens the church-affiliated schools' essential sectarian character. Consequently, while recognizing that schools can prefer church members over nonmembers, the government is empowered to prohibit exclusionary practices that limit the rights of minorities, women, etc. on religious grounds. Erwin Chemerinsky is less solicitous of the religion clauses. For Chemerinsky, speech, due process, and equality all override religious liberty.

The range of views expressed in these papers is not surprising. The contributors come from varying disciplines (economics, political science, law, education, philosophy). They also bring to the book varying perspectives on such matters as parental rights, the purposes of education, and state authority in the private sector. Indeed, the contributors were selected with an eye towards their differences.

What is surprising is the areas of commonality among the authors. The public-private connection turned out to be the focal point of many essays ostensibly about private education. A second area of agreement concerned the primacy of *Brown*'s universal ideal. *Brown* envisioned that 'once racial barriers were lifted . . . there would exist neither white schools nor black schools, but "just schools".'[8] None of the authors questions this aspiration. Interwoven through all of the essays is intolerance towards private schools that serve whites fleeing from public school desegregation — the so-called segregationist academies.

At first, the authors' separation of equality from other concerns made me pause. Yet, it is a typical division. In the balance of this essay, I will address the sharp differences between equality and other pedagogical concerns in public and private education.

Government Regulation and Resistance

Private school controversies in recent years have centered on governmental efforts to ensure that private schools abide by public school norms. These governmental demands have involved programmatic concerns, such as the certification of teachers and school curriculum, and equality measures prohibiting race and gender-based discrimination. Resistance to these demands has come from Christian educators who argue that compliance with these regulations would make the state 'lord over their schools'.[9] A review of these battles reveals a remarkable phenomenon — Christian educators ultimately prevail on programmatic matters; the state ultimately prevails on nondiscrimination matters.

The success of Christian educators in their challenges to programmatic regulations is surprising. Although the 1925 *Pierce* decision spoke broadly of the rights of parents to direct their children's destiny, the case did not abridge the authority of the state to make reasonable regulations governing nonpublic schools. To the contrary, the Court recognized that

> no question is raised concerning the power of the State reasonably to regulate all schools, to inspect, supervise and examine them, their teachers and pupils; to require that all children of proper age attend some school, that teachers shall be of good moral character and patriotic disposition, that certain studies plainly essential to good citizenship must be taught, and that nothing be taught which is manifestly inimical to the public welfare.[10]

More recently, in the 1976 decision *Runyon v. McCrary* the Court observed that parents 'have no constitutional right to provide their children with private school education unfettered by reasonable government regulation.'[11] In other words, 'if the State must satisfy its interest in secular education through the instrument of private schools, it has a proper interest in the manner in which those schools perform their secular educational function.'[12]

With Supreme Court decisions seemingly on the side of the regulators, how is it that the fundamentalists prevail in these battles? The answer, of course, is that the success of Christian education is not contingent on favorable court rulings. Although regulations may ask too much of private schools and therefore be found unreasonable, the state most often suffers political defeats. In the end, rather than jail parents and ministers for noncompliance, state officials shy away from *High Noon*-style showdowns with the fundamentalists.[13]

In Nebraska, for example, in 1984, the state ended a ten-year controversy with Christian educators by deregulating private schools. Despite a Nebraska Supreme Court ruling upholding teacher certification and other regulations, the state legislature invalidated this regulatory regime for fear that it was an unconstitutional infringement on religious liberty. The root of this contradictory behavior is the embarrassment Nebraska suffered when it sought to enforce the state court ruling by the jailing of ministers and parents, the padlocking of churches, and the prospect of the state taking custody of the affected children. Newspaper stories, visits to the padlocked church by Jerry Falwell and Jesse Jackson, and threats of federal investigation accompanied these state actions.

What happened in Nebraska can happen elsewhere, for Christian educators would rather go to jail than comply with expansive state regulations. Nebraska is not an isolated incident. In North Carolina, the state legislature rendered moot legal proceedings against several Christian schools by effectively deregulating religious education. In Maine, the state failed to appeal a trial court decision that held that the state was without authority to shut down unapproved private schools. Finally, Kentucky and Ohio have failed to respond legislatively or administratively to state supreme court decisions of the late 1970s that invalidated state approval procedures.

The fundamentalists' success here speaks to public doubts over the efficacy of programmatic regulation, not widespread support for the evangelical movement. Fundamentalist children perform at least as well as their public school counterparts on nationally recognized achievement tests. Moreover, Christian schools are largely free of many of the problems that beset the public schools, such as discipline, violence, and drugs. Finally, while many people are skeptical of the fundamentalists, few doubt either the sincerity of their beliefs or their dedication toward their children. When it comes to programmatic matters, Christian educators will ultimately win in a game of 'chicken' with the state, for whatever wrong they might be guilty of, it is a wrong that does not justify the padlocking of churches, the jailing of ministers and parents, or the state's assuming custody of children.

When it comes to civil rights conflicts, however, Christian fundamentalists are frequently losers before both the courts and the public.[14] Whereas Christian schools can forcefully advocate that their students can read, write, and compute as well as public school students, it cannot be seriously argued that discrimination has a place in their education. The 1983 *Bob Jones University* decision exemplifies this situation.[15] In affirming an IRS ruling that denied tax exemptions to racially discriminatory private schools, the Court emphasized that these schools cannot serve a public function: 'The legitimate educational function [of such private schools] cannot be isolated from discriminatory practices. . . . Discriminatory treatment exerts a pervasive influence on the entire educational process';[16] 'it cannot be said that educational institutions that, for whatever reasons, practice racial discrimination, are institutions exercising "beneficial and stabilizing influences in community life."'[17] This language extends to private schools the universal principle of *Brown* 'that a stable, just society, without violence, alienation, and social discord, must be an integrated society.'[18] Consequently, although Bob Jones University's prohibition of interracial dating was rooted in 'sincere religious belief', the Court held that the government's interest in eradicating racial discrimination was a 'fundamental, overriding' one and consequently, '*substantially* outweighs *whatever* burden denial of tax benefits places on [the school's] exercise of their religious beliefs.'[19]

In contrast to teacher certification and other programmatic regulations, Bob Jones University could not seek vindication in the court of public opinion. Quite the contrary. When the Supreme Court decided *Bob Jones University*, Congress, the press, the National Association of Independent Schools, and other mainstream private school interests joined with civil rights groups in condemning the university's discriminatory practices. This opposition movement was precipitated by the Reagan administration's ill-conceived initiative to restore the tax-exempt status of admittedly discriminatory private schools. This initiative took *Bob Jones University* — a case about the rights of a handful of private schools that engaged in discrimination as a matter of belief — and tranformed it into a public hearing on the nation's commitment to nondiscrimination in education.

A similar episode was recently precipitated by the Supreme Court. In the spring of 1988, the Court took the unusual step of seeking re-examination of a 1976 decision, *Runyon v. McCrary*, which prohibited commercial private schools from denying admission to qualified minority students.[20] Like the Reagan tax-exemption initiative, this decision was greeted with a firestorm of criticism. Indeed, while the Court was flooded with *amicus* briefs on this question, every brief advocated the preservation of *Runyon* (including briefs by forty-seven states, numerous private school groups, 200 members of Congress, and over 100 civil rights and civic organizations). The number of briefs filed and unanimity of opinion in this case are unprecedented.

Bob Jones University and the *Runyon* re-examination both demonstrate this nation's commitment to *Brown*'s universal value of nondiscrimination in education. Racially discriminatory private schools strike at the heart of this value and therefore must be prohibited. Under this formulation, it is irrelevant that discriminatory schools can advance strong legal arguments on their behalf. As stated in *Norwood v. Harrison*, a 1973 Court decision striking down state textbook assistance to discriminatory private schools,

> Under *Brown*, discriminatory treatment exerts a pervasive influence on the entire educational process. The private school that closes its door to defined groups of students on the basis of constitutionally suspect criteria manifests, by its own actions, that its educational processes are based on private belief that segregation is desirable in education.... Such private bias...[cannot] call on the Constitution for material aid from the State.[21]

Private schools, rather than being immunized from *Brown*, are fully accountable for simple nondiscrimination.

The extension of *Brown* to private education does not mean that private schools must further numerical equality. Just as the public desegregation value is muddied when it comes to busing, efforts to ensure state-prescribed levels of minority enrollment in the private schools have failed, the most notable example being the defeat of Carter administration proposals to deny tax-exempt status to private schools that have a disproportionately low number of minority students. A public outcry followed this proposal, prompting Congress to delay implementation of this procedure by withholding appropriations for its formulation and enforcement.[22]

The Carter administration's failure is not surprising. If school desegregation obligations do not extend to nondiscriminating schools in the surrounding suburbs, there is little reason to hold nondiscriminating private schools to a higher standard. In other words, since it is the public value of nondiscrimination — not racial balance — that encompasses both private and public schools, the Carter administration erred in demanding that private schools conform to values that cannot garner public support. By the same token, the Reagan administration committed error when it sought to excuse private schools from their *Brown* obligations.

Why *Brown*'s nondiscrimination mandate is inviolable while programmatic regulations remain vulnerable is a more complex question. Yet, as the next section establishes, equality's special status is also revealed in legislative and judicial approaches toward public school governance.

Legislative and Judicial Approaches

Over the past decade, a substantial gulf has emerged in the Supreme Court regarding equality and school governance matters. On school governance questions, the school board prevails because of its presumed expertise.[23] On equality questions, little deference is accorded official decision-making; consequently, the school board frequently loses.

Beginning with its approval of corporal punishment in 1977, the Court has taken a hands-off approach on school governance issues.[24] It is the Court's view that the 'education of the Nation's youth is primarily the responsibility of parents, teachers, and state and local school officials, and not of federal judges.'[25] This extraordinary deference is best seen in the Court's most recent handiwork in this field.

In 1985, the Court ruled in *New Jersey v. T.L.O.* that the fourth amendment prohibition of unreasonable search and seizures has only limited applicability to the public schools.[26] Consequently, a 14-year-old high school student's rights were not violated when an assistant principal searched her purse for marijuana without either a search warrant or probable cause to believe that the purse contained evidence of some illegality. For the Court, 'maintaining security and order in the schools requires a certain degree of flexibility in school disciplinary procedures.'[27] The Court, moreover, felt that such a result was sensible since the relationship between student and teacher is 'rarely adversarial', characterized instead by a 'commonality of interests.'[28]

Bethel School District v. Fraser, decided in 1986, is more striking.[29] In *Fraser*, the Court upheld on free speech and due process grounds the suspension of a student who delivered a sexually provocative — but not obscene — speech before a student assembly. The Court reasoned that school boards are empowered to determine standards of civility in the schoolhouse, for 'schools must teach by example the shared values of a civilized social order.'[30] Consequently, by endorsing local control, the school's value inculcation role of 'prepar[ing] pupils for citizenship in the Republic'[31] takes precedence over the first amendment and due process rights of students. In a telling passage, the Court recognizes the propriety of the school 'disassociat[ing] itself' from the speech, since the Constitution does not require 'teachers, parents, and elected school officials to surrender control of the American public school system to public school students.'[32] In short, while the Constitution may not be shut out at 'the schoolhouse gate', student rights give way to the inculcation of state-selected values.

This subordination of student rights in favor of local control was recently reaffirmed in the 1988 decision *Hazelwood School District v. Kuhlmeier*.[33] *Hazelwood* involved a high school principal's censorship of a student newspaper. Noting that a school should be able to '"disassociate itself". . . from speech that is ungrammatical, poorly written, inadequately researched, biased or prejudiced, vulgar or profane, or unsuitable for immature audiences,'[34] the principal's conduct was upheld. 'Otherwise, the schools would be unduly constrained from fulfilling their role as "a principal instrument in awakening the child to cultural values, in preparing him for later professional training, and in helping him to adjust normally to his environment."'[35] Like *Bethel* and *T.L.O.*, *Hazelwood* emphasizes that the appropriate locus of educational decision-making is the public school system.

The Supreme Court's equality decisions stand in sharp contrast to these cases. When a school system denies educational services to a discrete group of students or discriminates on the basis of race or gender, the courts are willing to intervene.[36] In fact, school desegregation decisions are notorious for riding roughshod over local prerogatives. Over the years, courts have intervened in virtually all facets of school operations to remedy illegal discrimination.

Platitudes about the propriety of local control cannot be found in school desegregation opinions. The emphasis, instead, is the equality norm. While this focus is appropriate, the Court could well have gone down another road, one much more in line with its school governance rulings. Former Justice Powell's school desegregation opinions emphasize this other road. For Powell, 'the primary and continuing responsibility for public education, including the bringing about and maintaining of desired diversity, must be left with school officials and public authorities.'[37] In extolling the virtues of neighborhood schools, Powell elaborates upon this position:

> Public schools have been a traditional source of strength to our Nation, and that strength may derive in part from the identification of many schools with the personal features of the surrounding neighborhood. Community support, interest, and dedication to public schools may well run higher with a neighborhood attendance pattern.[38]

In cases where actionable discrimination is found, Powell's view is in the minority. A majority of the justices are willing to pay a high price for desegregation 'that promises realistically to work *now*.'[39] When it first approved of busing in *Swann*, for example, the Court recognized that desegregation remedies might have to be 'administratively awkward, inconvenient, and even bizarre.'[40]

This high price has its limits, however. Indeed, Powell's concerns might help explain severe judicially imposed restrictions in this area.[41] School desegregation remedies require proof of pernicious intentional discrimination. A school board is not subject to a court order if it merely applies a neighborhood school policy the foreseeable effect of which is racial isolation. Desegregation remedies, moreover, apply only to a single school system. Surrounding schools whose enrollments are boosted by students fleeing desegregation are immune from liability.

Court actions here certainly send a mixed message: busing is appropriate, but interdistrict remedies not permissible; black-white population ratios define the school district's obligation, but intent is prerequisite to any remedy. The Court, apparently, is caught between two poles. On the one hand, simple nondiscrimination is unsatisfactory. Neighborhood schools and freedom of choice do not shake dual school systems at their core. On the other hand, effects-based proofs of discrimination and/or the extension of school desegregation obligations to nonculpable suburban schools would be politically unacceptable social engineering.

Congressional action is less varied.[42] Although it failed to ratify proposed constitutional amendments to prohibit forced busing, Congress has not embraced expansive desegregation remedies. Federal desegregation assistance, for example, cannot be used to defray busing costs. While greatly concerned with the *Brown* mandate, Congress does not support court orders that force public school students to attend schools outside their neighborhoods.

Congress' role in school desegregation, despite this hesitancy, should not be underestimated.[43] Prior to *Swann*, Congress set the stage for federal enforcement of the *Brown* mandate by enacting Title VI of the Civil Rights Act of 1964. Title VI prohibits recipients of federal financial assistance from engaging in purposeful discrimination. Armed with the power to cut off federal education funds, by the end of the 1960s the efforts of the federal government had dramatically eroded southern school segregation. For example, between 1965 and 1968 the percentage of black children confined to all-black schools in the South dropped from 98 per cent to 25 per cent. As described by David Kirp, 'During the mid-1960s, Congress, the executive branch, and the courts acted in concert, exercising extraordinarily effective leadership.'[44]

These congressional efforts parallel the resolution of the private school tax exemption affair. Opposition to numerical equality was exemplified there by the rejection of the Carter initiative; steadfast adherence to simple nondiscrimination is demonstrated by the repudiation of Reagan administration arguments. While there is no private school counterpart to mandatory busing, the private school experience clearly reflects a growing recognition of government's authority and responsibility to ensure some form of nondiscrimination in education.

The public school experience also parallels private education in the contrasting treatment accorded equality and school governance concerns. Just as programmatic regulation governing the content of education gives way to the religious liberty interests of Christian educators, speech, due process, and the fourth amendment give way to the public school's interest in controlling the school environment. By the same token, religious liberty and school governance interests are volatile when placed against equality concerns. To be sure, there are limits here, but basic equality clearly predominates.

Private Schools, Equality and Pedagogy

This phenomenon is readily understandable. Equality is at once more quantifiable and more abstract than either school governance or effective education. These two dimensions of equality secure its hegemony over other educational concerns.

Equality can be measured by student population ratios, dissimilarity indexes, and the like.[45] More significant, our nation's commitment to *Brown* is universal. While educational outcomes are capable of measurement through achievement tests, there is a raging debate on what makes for an effective education. Consequently, when Christian school students test at least as well as their public school counterparts, it is difficult for the educational bureaucracy to demand that regulations of questionable effect be put into place. When it comes to equality, however, there is no dispute as to the meaning of pernicious discrimination. If 'in the field of education, separate cannot be equal,'[46] schools that insist upon separatist practices have no place educating our youth for citizenship.

Equality is also more abstract. Rather than a living, breathing concern with virtues and pitfalls, equality often seems a normative aspiration. Aside from Justice Powell's talk of resegregation, immediacy in education, and educational outcomes, Supreme Court public school equality rulings seem removed from the day-to-day operations of the schools. In sharp contrast, the Court's recent school governance casework pays close attention to the conjunction of local control and effective education.

The justices consider school governance an issue of pedagogy and are therefore willing to sacrifice student rights in the name of educational effectiveness. Equality of educational opportunity is not considered a 'schools' issue, however. There is an element of foolishness here. Student rights clearly implicate more general free speech and due process concerns; court equality rulings have a great impact on school effectiveness. Yet, equality as an issue — except among those whose lives are affected by school desegregation — is removed from the schools. On the other hand, since we have all been to school, student rights are widely understood as an educational issue.

That this equality-pedagogy disjunction extends similarly to public and private schools is not at all surprising. Legislative and judicial actions tend to be driven by public values. At this level, equality can be separated from school governance or programmatic regulation. A similar separation between public and private schools does not exist, for public and private schools both share in the enterprise of educating youth. The seriousness of this enterprise defines the nexus between public and private schooling.

Education is a public good of fundamental importance. As stated in *Brown*,

> Compulsory school attendance laws and the great expenditures
> for education both demonstrate our recognition of the

importance of education to our democratic society . . . It is the very foundation of good citizenship. Today it is a principal instrument in awakening the child to cultural values, in preparing him for later professional training, and in helping him to adjust normally to his environment.[47]

Education, under this formulation, is too important to allow private schools to be freed from public school concerns.

But what are these concerns? Clearly, private schools can be required to offer competent instruction in reading, writing, and arithmetic. Private schools also can be made to conform to the *Brown* mandate. These conclusions tell us very little, however. The conflict between the fundamentalists and the regulators is not about the need for competent instruction; instead, the conflict concerns the *definition* of competency. Likewise, the conflict between the Carter and Reagan administrations on the tax-exemption issue was not about the propriety of *Brown*. The conflict, rather, involved differing views of the role of government in regulating private behavior.

This problem is intractable, and I offer no magic solution. It is my opinion, however, that private schools should never be held more accountable for attaining the goals of compulsory education than are public schools. In short, if the public schools' desegregation obligation is not measured by numerical equality, private schools should also be free of such standards. For identical reasons, if students in Christian academies test as well as their public school counterparts, the state cannot demand that such schools change their methods of instruction.

From the standpoint of private schools, this formulation seems satisfactory, at least at present. Unless there is a considerable change in the educational outcomes of public school students, private schools should be able to match these outcomes without altering their preferred methodology.[48] Furthermore, compliance with simple nondiscrimination places few burdens on private schools — even those religious schools which believe in the separation of the races. Under current standards, the only absolute limitation on such a school is the requirement of racially nondiscriminatory admissions.

Were public school standards to change, however, private schools might be asked to bear a greater burden. This prospect is troublesome, for it may interfere with parental prerogatives in education. While these prerogatives do not mandate abandonment of either competence in core subjects or simple nondiscrimination, real limits should be placed on state authority. As John Garvey has written, 'family members are likely to be more capable than the state of providing the kind of continuing understanding and care necessary after any decision has been made that affects the long-term welfare of the child.'[49] Substantial judicial authority backs up this proposition.[50]

Determining where to draw the line between parental rights and educational necessities is, of course, the issue and the problem.[51] The balance of this volume should help in the resolution of this question. Not only are powerful arguments advanced on both sides, but suggestions are also made for new ways of thinking about the public and private roles of compulsory education. These essays show that a private education focus is extremely useful in considering the central problems of educational reform. In thinking about appropriate state authority over private schools, we must confront our aspirations for compulsory education.

Notes

1 268 US 510 (1925).
2 For an extensive and insightful treatment of democracy enhancing education, see A. GUTMANN (1987) *Democratic Education*, Princeton, N.J., Princeton University Press, pp. 19–48.
3 Levin does advocate that efforts be made to decrease market demand for private education.
4 For Arons, vouchers are such a device. In contrast to Arons, Michael Rebell's voucher scheme is not driven by equality concerns. At the same time, Rebell's proposal safeguards against value dissenters utilizing their vouchers at racist private schools.
5 John and Shirley Lachs also advocate the debureaucratization of education. In their view, rules and regulations create harmful distance between school officials, parents, and children.
6 Ironically, in April 1988, the Supreme Court — on its own motion — decided to reconsider its 1976 ruling that federal civil rights legislation prohibits such discrimination. *Patterson v. McLean Credit Union*, 108 S. Ct. 1419 (1988).
7 The perils of such indirect regulation are discussed at length in Jeremy Rabkin's essay.
8 D. KIRP (1982) *Just Schools: The Idea of Racial Equality in American Education*, Berkeley, Calif., University of California Press, p. 6.
9 See N. DEVINS (1983) 'State Regulation of Christian Schools', *Journal of Legislation*, 10, p. 351. Mainstream private school interests, such as Catholic schools, generally support programmatic and equality regulation. This support, in part, is explained by the desire of these groups to receive governmental assistance. Moreover, these schools are truly committed to public school norms. *Amicus* briefs filed by these groups in cases such as *Bob Jones Univ. v. United States, Ohio Civil Rights Comm'n v. Dayton Christian Schools*, and *Patterson v. McLean Credit Union* demonstrate this commitment.
10 268 US at 534.
11 427 US 160, 178 (1976).

12 *Board of Education v. Allen*, 392 US 236, 247 (1968).

13 See N. DEVINS (1986) 'Nebraska and the Future of State Regulation of Christian Schools', in D. KELLEY (Ed.), *Government Intervention in Religious Affairs*, New York, Pilgrim Press, p. 107.

14 Two of these episodes are given extensive treatment in this volume. In 'Taxing Discrimination', Jeremy Rabkin provides a detailed history and analysis of the government's demand that private schools eligible for tax-exempt status not discriminate on the basis of race. William Marshall and Joanne Brant, in 'Employment Discrimination in Religious Schools: A Constitutional Analysis', review the issues presented to the Supreme Court in *Dayton Christian Schools*, a case concerning a religious school's obligation to conform to state gender nondiscrimination requirements.

15 461 US 574 (1983).

16 *Ibid.* at 593–94 (quoting *Norwood v. Harrison*, 413, US 455, 468–469 (1973)).

17 *Ibid.* at 595 (quoting *Walz v. Tax Comm'n*, 397 US 664, 673 (1970)).

18 M. YUDOF (1973) 'Equal Educational Opportunity and the Courts', *Texas Law Review*, 51, p. 457.

19 461 US at 604 (emphasis supplied). For an extended discussion of the case's religious liberty issue, see D. LAYCOCK (1982) 'Tax Exemptions for Racially Discriminatory Religious Schools', *Texas Law Review*, 60, p. 259.

20 *Patterson v. McLean Credit Union*, 108 S. Ct. 1419 (1988) (calling for the re-examination of *Runyon v. McCrary*, 427 US 160 (1976)).

21 413 US 455, 469 (1973).

22 See N. DEVINS (1987) 'Regulation of Government Agencies through Limitation Riders', *Duke Law Journal*, 6, pp. 488–99.

23 This phenomenon is given considerable treatment in Michael Rebell's essay, 'Values Inculcation and the Schools: The Need for a New *Pierce* Compromise'.

24 *Ingraham v. Wright*, 430 US 651 (1977). Prior to 1977, the Court was frequently a forceful advocate of student rights. See, for example, *Goss v. Lopez*, 419 US 565 (1975) (due process); *Tinker v. Des Moines Indep. Community School Dist.*, 393 US 503 (1969) (free speech).

25 *Hazelwood School Dist. v. Kuhlmeier*, 108 S. Ct. 562, 571 (1988).

26 469 US 325 (1985).

27 *Ibid.* at 340.

28 *Ibid.* at 340; *ibid.* at 350 (Powell, concurring).

29 106 S. Ct. 3159 (1986). An extensive discussion of this case can be found in Michael Rebell's essay.

30 *Ibid.* at 3165.

31 *Ibid.* at 3164.

32 *Ibid.* at 3166 (quoting *Tinker v. Des Moines*, 393 US 503, 526 (1969) (Black, dissenting)).

33 108 S. Ct. 562 (1988).

34 *Ibid.* at 570.

35 *Ibid.* (quoting *Brown*, 347 US at 493).

36 As the balance of this section makes clear, intervention is not automatic; rather, it is considered appropriate when the state action is considered truly offensive. Compare, for example, *San Antonio Indep. School Dist. v. Rodriguez*, 411 US 1 (1973) (when basic education is provided to all, a state finance

scheme that encourages disparities in spending among school districts is permissible) with *Plyer v. Doe*, 467 US 202 (1982) (fee-based finance scheme that denies basic education to illegal aliens is unconstitutional).

37 *Columbus Bd. of Educ. v. Penick*, 443 US 449, 489 (1979) (Powell, dissenting).
38 *Keyes v. Denver School Dist. No. 1*, 413 US 189, 246 (1973) (Powell, concurring and dissenting).
39 *Green v. County School Bd.*, 391 US 430, 439 (1969) (emphasis in original).
40 *Swann v. Charlotte-Mecklenburg*, 402 US 1, 28 (1971).
41 For further discussion of this concern, see in this volume S. Arons, 'Educational Choice as a Civil Rights Strategy'.
42 The following description is too general. For a more complete treatment, See N. Devins and J. Stedman (1984) 'New Federalism in Education: The Meaning of the Chicago School Desegregation Cases', *Notre Dame Law Review*, 59, pp. 1243–57.
43 *Ibid.*, pp. 1246–9.
44 D. Kirp (1977) 'School Desegregation and the Limits of Legalism', *Public Interest*, 47, Spring, p. 101.
45 See, for example, in this volume R. Crain and C. Rossell, 'Catholic Schools and Racial Segregation'.
46 Paraphrasing *Brown v. Board of Educ.*, 347 US 483 (1954).
47 *Ibid.* at 493.
48 There is good reason to think that the educational outcomes of private schools will be higher than those of public schools. See in this volume J. Chubb and T. Moe, 'Effective Schools and Equal Opportunity'.
49 J. Garvey (1978) 'Child, Parent, State and the Due Process Clause: An Essay on the Supreme Court Court's Recent Work', *Southern California Law Review*, 51, p. 817.
50 See, for example, *Parnham v. J.R.*, 442 US 584 (1979); *Santosky v. Kramer*, 455 US 745 (1982).
51 Another consideration here is the school's role as value inculcator. This essay has steered clear of this question, but it is given ample consideration throughout the volume. *Cf.* in this volume H. Levin, 'Education as a Public and Private Good' (in understanding the government's role in private education, consideration must be given to education's public function as value inculcator).

Part I
Private Schools and the Purposes of Compulsory Education

2
The State's Interest in Racially Nondiscriminatory Education

Robert K. Fullinwider

The state's proper role in our children's education remains a source of enduring social debate. Why should the state be involved at all? What interests — and whose — does its involvement serve? As a context for answering these questions, I focus in this essay on a more specific controversy. What are the state's interests in racially nondiscriminatory education? How far do those interests justify state intrusion into private schools? I do not try to answer these questions in detail because many other essays in this book treat problems of law and policy. Instead, I explore the general framework of values and principles within which specific problems of law and policy can be illuminated. I give a positive, though not uncritical, account of the state's place in education. Other essays in this book will balance my account with a more skeptical and negative view of the state.

Introduction

Plato twice turned his hand to describing an ideal society, first in *The Republic* and later in *The Laws*. As much as the two descriptions differed, one feature remained constant: the most important function of the state is to control education. Plato blamed all state pathologies on educational failure and rested the success of his two ideals on a correct and common education. One threat to proper education is the family. 'In the privacy of family life,' he noted, 'a great many trivial activities never get [public attention], and...they can all too easily fly in the face of the lawgiver's recommendations and produce citizens whose characters are varied and conflicting, which is a social evil.'[1] The education of children must not be left to the whims of their parents, for the children 'belong to the state first and their parents second.'[2]

No community that wants to survive can afford to ignore Plato's concerns. It must ensure the transmission of its culture, language, practical skills, and religion to succeeding generations. In the past, this transmission could be largely an informal affair, incidental to family and village life. Formal education — what little there was of it — was controlled by the church.

But in modern complex states, education is a deliberate and regulated activity, for two reasons. First, modern economies put a premium on the widest diffusion of very sophisticated skills — on literacy, computational abilities, and a command of information once solely the possession of an elite few. Second, modern democracies require a level of informed participation made possible by extensive, common schooling. The social integration once achieved by rigid hierarchies and static social roles must now be performed by government coordination.

These facts of modern life fuel a three-way struggle among the state, the family, and the church to determine primary influence on children. Formal education is compulsory and provided largely by public schools, and public authority constrains in many ways the operations of private schools, most of which are religious.[3] This milieu provides fertile soil for conflict. The parents of public school children complain about the curriculum: sex education should be taught; sex education should not be taught; the textbooks contain foul language, or teach secular humanism, or leave out positive accounts of minorities; there are not enough basics; and so on. Parents of children in private schools complain that the state's refusal to subsidize their costs is unfair. Private schools themselves chafe under government regulation and frequently take their complaints to court, as do parents, whether their schools are public or private. Churches enter the fray, jealously guarding religious liberty from any public limitation.

Adding a special dimension to the struggle and discord are native strains of anti-statism. American suspicion of government encompasses a number of distinct, but seldom clearly disentangled, ideas. There are two grounds for resisting government regulation of an activity. We can argue that the government has no legitimate interest in regulating it, or we can argue that the government cannot be trusted to regulate it. Overlaying these two grounds is a different pair of ideas: centralism versus localism. When people say that government has no legitimate interest in some activity or cannot be trusted to regulate it, they may mean to direct that charge at *certain* governments, or governments at a certain *level*. They may mean that control of education, for example, ought to remain in the hands of local or state governments but not the federal government.

In contrast, others may hold that *no* government at any level can be trusted to control education, or that *no* government at any level has any legitimate interest in such control. Anti-statist rhetoric often is elusive because it fails to be clear about which claim it wants to make.

The proposition that government, at whatever level, has no legitimate interest in overseeing education would seem hard to sustain. For example, one vehement anti-statist asserts the *sole* right of parents to direct the education of their children and denies *any* legitimate oversight by the state, only to concede that in cases of great abuse of children we must take recourse to 'the ultimate power in us all, as a society, to utilize the law to restrain great and manifest evil.'[4] Another, who argues adamantly against majority control over the content of schooling, acknowledges that some values may be so basic to the community's life that they can be imposed through education.[5]

We certainly do not have to embrace Plato's view that children belong to the state first and parents second to see education's undeniable importance to community well-being. Three obvious and extraordinarily important state interests come immediately to mind. First, in a highly integrated society, education is a public good. The costs of bad education are not borne just by those who are badly educated but by everyone else as well. Children who do not learn to function in the economy and who do not learn basic moral control burden all of us with their subsequent failures and delinquencies. Second, in a democracy ignorance and delusions born of ignorance undermine political deliberation. Plato was extremely wary of democracy because he saw the power of the demagogue as a menace to governmental stability. That power feeds off ignorance and excitability. Third, the state has an interest in the regulation of education because children have rights. Children are not mere extensions of their parents, nor property, but human individuals with rights of their own, including the right not to be physically or educationally crippled by being denied the nurture, protection, and training that will enable them as adults to form and carry out decent and rewarding life plans.[6] Proper care of children is a parental duty, and the state has a legitimate interest in seeing the duty fulfilled. Thus, it creates laws against physical abuse, neglect, abandonment — and for the provision of a basic training.

A more plausible anti-statist line urges that the state cannot be *trusted* to oversee education because it is hostile to families, unwilling to 'tolerate any rival to itself for the loyalty and obedience of its subjects', or because it is incompetent, always doing badly what families do better.[7] The editors of a recent book on families and the state push such a position by counterposing to the artificial, coercive, and planned order of the state the 'natural', 'spontaneous', and 'voluntary' order of the family.[8]

The family is, in fact, none of these things. It has always been a form of life carefully controlled by law and custom, allowing little variation and no competition. Until recently marriage was the only socially legitimate form of intimate and procreative association, a form whose terms, though contractual, remained relatively fixed and immutable. The only option in marriage lay in the choice of a marriage partner, and even this feature is of recent vintage.

Family law establishes who and what the family is. It defines property holdings; assigns duties to protect and support; provides immunities against breach of confidentiality; regulates inheritance; secures the earnings of minor children to parents; authorizes parental control over children, including choice of domicile, regulation of movement, and limitation of privacy; specifies the terms of dissolution; and many other things.[9] The anti-statist editors mentioned above no doubt regret such contemporary legal entanglement in the family, and they look for support in Robert Nisbet's observation that 'family and state wax and wane inversely to each other.'[10] Nisbet contrasts the decline of the family under late Roman bureaucratic statism with the flourishing of the family during the politically fragmented Middle Ages. But this fact, if it is one, does not show the family to be natural, spontaneous, or voluntary. While the state was weak in the Middle Ages, the church was not; it developed an elaborate canon law of family and marriage, setting out the conditions for permissible and valid marriages, including limitations on age, consanguinity, notice, sexual performance, and inheritance, with a detail rivaling modern legal codes.[11] At best, Nisbet's observation supports the idea that the family flourishes under one sort of legal regime rather than under another. It does not support the idea that the family flourishes in the absence of law.

In fact, the best argument for limiting the state's interference in family affairs stems not from nature or natural rights, or from the voluntariness of contract, but from the very fact that the family *is* a creature of law. Our law and custom lodge vast autonomy in the family, permitting parents extensive discretion in shaping their children's lives. Minor children are deprived by law of any independent standing to govern their own affairs. If they are discontented with their parents, they lack independent standing to sue for their own emancipation. If they are harmed by their parents, they cannot bring legal actions for breach of contract, battery, or any number of torts one adult can plead against another. With few limitations, parents may determine the education, religion, and culture of their children. They are protected against outside interference in passing on to their children a preferred morality and way of life.

The broad immunities and liberties that attach to the family are not without independent justification. They allow family life to be constituted of deep and enduring intimacies, a form of association central to human good. We do not find the deepest values of our lives in commercial transactions and arms-length associations but in personal unions in which we share with others bonds of mutual caring and affection. The family is the central and most ubiquitous such union. Children grow up within a network of family relationships and, as adults, re-create such relationships by forming their own families. Whatever alternative social arrangements might in the abstract provide both children and adults lives centered on intimate and loving commitments, in practice there is no alternative to the family and the functions it provides.

Guiding their children's development lends an irreplaceable significance and meaning to parents' lives, and guidance by adults who love them is vital to children's development. Consequently, freedom from outside control is among the most important liberties a family can possess and one the state itself has a vital interest in respecting and protecting. The argument for noninterference does not arise from some innate opposition between law and the family but from a recognition of the *nature* of the institution that law has created. Having established the family as the principal institution for raising children, the state must take care not unnecessarily to undermine or interfere with family relationships. The notions of state hostility and state incompetence are best interpreted by reference to the nature of those relationships: the state's impersonal rule versus the family's personal and intimate order, the inflexibility and uniformity of bureaucratic regulation versus the variety and particularity of family circumstances.

This argument for general noninterference, however, is not inconsistent with regulation of the family's form and does not deny to the state ultimate oversight for the care and education of children. If for no other reason than that its law has rendered children dependent on their parents' authority, the state cannot disengage itself from responsibility for what happens in families. Unregulated parents are not always more trustworthy than government in looking after the community's children. Experience shows us enough dismal and destructive parental failure to make us skeptical that children's rights can safely be left in parents' hands without *any* formal community oversight.

In theory, the choice about community oversight need not be between unregulated parents and regulating governments. Some third institution might discharge the community's interest in the education of children. As noted earlier, the church once provided most formal education. Where there is a single, established church, the state might feasibly rely on it to oversee education. Religiously directed education could be expected to represent the collective interest in education and to support, rather than undermine, civic virtue. But in our contemporary world, such reliance is no longer an option. With the proliferation of religions and sects, and the absence of formal or informal controls on theology and practice, the range of churches is as great as the range of parents, from the most responsible to the most irresponsible. Wholly unregulated religious education could not now express and represent our collective interest in education. Only the state can serve this role.[12]

Thus, profoundly important state interests weigh both for and against the regulation of children's education. The nature of these interests justifies state oversight but limits its reach. Working out the details and boundaries of the oversight is a matter of politics. The opposition between state and families should not be understood as a contest between an alien force (the state) and us (the people). The opposition is within ourselves, between ourselves as private individuals and ourselves as a public. The state is simply the institutional form of our collective interest in seeing that children are brought up in ways that do not harm them or us.

The foregoing remarks, sketchy and abstract as they are, map out in a rough way the terrain on which the perpetual tension among state, family, and church is played out. I want to consider in greater detail one of the contemporary contests on that terrain, the problem of racial integration of schools. In particular, I want to assess the strength of the state's interest in regulating private schools in the name of racial nondiscrimination. As other essays in this book will exhibit, this is a nettlesome and contentious use of state power, confronting us with conflicting values, unsettled legal doctrine, and divided public opinion.

In what follows, I want to locate our nation's interest in nondiscriminatory education in a particular history and in a particular theory about the nature of discrimination. Because of our history and because of the nature of discrimination, our social interest in nondiscriminatory education may justify intrusions into private education we would not otherwise support. My goal is to identify the actual point of dispute about schools and nondiscrimination.

Nondiscrimination versus Associational Preferences

Plato contended that children must be raised to have the special virtues and abilities required for life in the state. What are the special virtues and abilities upon which a thriving democratic state depends? Unlike the Platonic state, which must be modeled by its founders upon philosophical truth and then kept static and unchanging, the democratic state is one in which citizens shape the society itself to permit the flourishing of different ways of life. Not only will this state contain 'citizens whose characters are varied and conflicting', its educational practices will produce such diversity in character and interests. If this is not to be the social evil Plato feared, democratic citizens must be able to transcend their varied and conflicting characters through self-government. Consequently, children prepared to live in a democracy must be given the *ability to participate* and the *virtue of mutual respect*.[13]

The democratic goal of participation requires universal *access* to a decent education. Adults whose inadequate education has deprived them of the common stock of skills and knowledge will be handicapped as democratic citizens. Access is not enough, however. Unless well-educated adults also respect each other and the different communities to which they belong, popular participation in a democracy will degenerate into incessant power struggles or a tyranny of the majority. The democratic goal here is to instill appropriate *attitudes* of tolerance and acceptance. A democratic society has to ensure against education that leaves citizens fearful of and hostile to one another and their differences.

Racial discrimination hinders both goals. Excluding people from a good education because of their race violates universal access. Fostering the attitudes of racial contempt and fear that emerge from and undergird such exclusion undermines mutual respect. Consequently, a democratic society has a powerful reason to ensure nondiscrimination in education.

This we could say about *any* democratic society, but much more needs to be said about our own. For us, racial discrimination is special. It is special because of its long history, a history of deliberate, systematic, all-pervasive oppression, first in the form of slavery and then in the form of despised and segregated caste. Under the laws and social conventions that prevailed until recently, the lives of blacks were not blighted by occasional episodes of discrimination but by permanent channeling into the backwaters of American society. Denied any but a marginal role in the economy, education, culture, and government, the very identities of blacks were defined by their race — as beings not fit for association with whites. Apart from its victims' personal costs, racial discrimination has deeply distorted social and political life in the United States.

Consequently, the extirpation of racial discrimination is paramount in our society, especially in education. The urgency of this goal derives not only from general moral strictures against discrimination but from the special role of race in our own history.[14]

What we think necessary for extirpation will depend on how we understand the nature of discrimination. For twenty years, the United

States has pursued aggressive nondiscrimination policies in the public schools that reflect a conception of discrimination as a deeply rooted way of life, woven into the very fiber of society. Discrimination is *habitual*. It happens even when we oppose it and resolve to be fair and unbiased. It happens because for 200 years the social environment has been perfected to produce it.

Conceiving of discrimination this way suggests an approach to its elimination: alter the social environment by distributing blacks into those parts of it from which they always have been absent. Thus, the law has sought vigorously to integrate schools. Children must be bused so that schools will reflect a mixture of black and white, and school boards must take affirmative action to make sure blacks are significantly represented in teaching and administrative roles. Once the environment is fixed with blacks in it, according to this conception of discrimination, old habits — both institutional and personal — will fade and new ones emerge that support the environment of their own accord. *Nondiscrimination* will become habitual.[15]

Many people oppose busing and affirmative action. Parents are rightfully concerned, for example, that in being bused to distant schools their children are put at greater risk of danger or inferior schooling. But if busing is designed to ensure reasonable quality schooling and reasonable safety, then the resistance to busing must stem from either of two grounds. Some opponents may view it as unnecessary because they reject such a conception of discrimination.[16] They may believe that discrimination is not a deep or pervasive phenomenon and can be overcome without the races being educated together. They may believe that discrimination is a matter of bad will, rather than bad habits, and that schools effectively can teach students to have good will toward other races, even if the schools are monoracial.

Some parents do not have any special conception of discrimination but, out of simple fear or uncertainty, just do not want their children associating with another race. The fear of other races is what integration is supposed to overcome. If the state has good reasons to believe that measures that leave the races largely separated and isolated from one another will perpetuate the attitudes and habits upon which racism feeds, vigorous pursuit of public school integration is warranted.[17] Parents who conceded the state's good reasons but resisted integration anyway would be arguing, in effect, that their associational preferences ought to be honored even at the cost of social health.

Do associational freedoms take on greater weight in connection with *private* schools? Is the state prevented from imposing on them the policies it imposes on public schools? Posed in the abstract, these questions do not invite a single answer. The liberty to choose their children's associates and to shape the environment of their children's development is fundamental to the good of families, as observed earlier in this essay. But associational preferences must be balanced against the importance of securing for every child democratic abilities and virtues. There is no a priori reason to expect the balance always to tip in favor of freedom of association. The state must honor, as far as it can, the arrangements parents make in the choice of their children's schoolmates, but at the same time it must not abdicate its responsibility to see that education supports rather than undermines democratic abilities and virtues.

The state has three options when deciding upon direct intervention in private schools. First, it can simply take no action, leaving private schools to discriminate or not, as they choose. Second, it can require that private schools not discriminate, but otherwise leave them undisturbed. Or, third, it can require that private schools take positive action to integrate racially, as must public schools.

The viability of each option is largely a matter of circumstances. For example, if private schools were few and their effect on society negligible, then letting them go their own way might be a reasonable way to balance associational freedom against the state's interest in nondiscrimination. Their discriminatory policies would not significantly degrade universal access to good education, and although such policies teach students racial disrespect, the number of students affected would be too small to register a noticeable impact on the quality of democratic deliberation. Little would be gained in forcing parents of children in discriminating private schools to act against their wishes or beliefs.

Striking the balance in favor of the schools would not be reasonable in different circumstances, say, those that prevailed in the American South in the 1960s and 1970s. Private academies proliferated there as a response to federally imposed public school integration. A hands-off approach to private school discrimination would have encouraged this development. The public school system virtually might have disappeared in some states, or become a grotesquely underfunded repository for blacks. (The modest government efforts against private school discrimination that did occur have left many areas in the South with two de facto school systems: one white and private, the other public and black.) Where a hands-off attitude to private schools results in widespread denial of access and in widespread diffusion of racial disrespect, the two democratic goals are defeated. The balance between associational freedom and the state's interest in nondiscriminatory education must be struck against the private school.

Similar considerations apply in the other choices. Should the state be content merely to require nondiscrimination, or may it require private schools to take measures to integrate? Again, the answer must look to circumstances. If a policy of nondiscrimination leaves most private schools segregated and if private schools play a large educational role in the society, then given the conception of discrimination sketched above, the state may have good reason to force integrative policies on private schools. When the question about state policy is posed in the abstract, the public/private distinction does not count heavily in deciding how the balance between associational freedom and the two democratic goals ought to be struck.

But the question is not posed in the abstract. In the United States, the question is posed against the backdrop not only of our particular history of racial injustice and the urgency of transforming social habits but of our specific constitutional order as well. Two facts change the equation. The first is that the First Amendment to the Constitution gives a privileged place to religious freedom. The second is that most private schools in the United States are religious.

Government interference with religious schools must bear a considerable justificatory burden. Policies requiring religious schools actively to integrate almost certainly will not meet this burden. In fact, it is not likely that policies requiring simple nondiscrimination can meet the burden.[18] Thus, the government's pursuit of nondiscrimination, and of a social climate that fosters nondiscrimination, is importantly constrained by freedom of religious association, even to the detriment of the two democratic goals.

The special status given to religious association may seem straightforwardly warranted. Religious beliefs and worship — for which a community of believers is usually essential — are at the core of people's lives. Nothing could be more crucial or central than an individual's relationship with God. Religious liberty is so valuable that it must be protected unyieldingly from the state's interference. So runs the argument.

This argument, however, does not fully succeed in explaining why religious freedoms should have a privileged legal status. Secular associational preferences can play the same central role in people's lives as religious ones. Moral and philosophical beliefs can be as much at the core of a person's life as belief in God. Even so, our fundamental law has special solicitude for religious freedom.

A corollary to religious freedom is the right to discriminate. Churches must be free to admit or exclude whomever they want into membership. A forced fellowship of worship is as much an intrusion on religious freedom as a forced confession of faith. Consequently, where admittance into the religious school shares characteristics of church membership, the state is barred from prohibiting school discrimination in the same way it is barred from dictating church membership. The kinship between the 'fellowship of learners' and the 'fellowship of worshippers' is especially intimate in a small, closed sectarian school where the learning of worship and doctrine is pervasively intermixed with the other lessons of the curriculum. Thus, admission to such a school must be a matter over which it has unfettered control. This interpretation seems the most natural reading of religious liberty if it is to be given a special place among liberties.[19]

Indirect Influence on Religious Schools

The discrimination of private religious schools is not beyond all government influence, however. If direct regulation of religious schools is barred to the government, indirect means of affecting their discriminatory behavior are not.

Government policy has long given tax-exempt status to nonprofit institutions, including private schools. This valuable status allows donors to deduct their contributions from their income taxes. In recent years, the Internal Revenue Service has ruled that private schools, including religious schools, are not entitled to the status if they practice racial discrimination. By this means, at least, government can pressure discriminating religious schools.

Tax exemption is a gift from government: no one has a right to be free from the state's taxation. Withdrawing the exemption from schools that practice racial discrimination serves the distinct public interest in promoting the two democratic goals.[20] Although the withdrawal burdens certain religious practices, it does not constitute direct regulation of admissions. The government does not single out discriminating religious schools for hostile treatment. Its exemption policy applies to all schools alike, religious or nonreligious, and to noneducational institutions as well as schools.

In this indirect way, then, our government acts against discrimination in religious schools. Can it use the same indirect strategy to promote integration in religious schools? Suppose Congress enacted legislation conferring tax benefits only on schools that actively pursued racial integration. Religious schools, then, would have to take 'affirmative action' to avoid losing their tax exempt status.[21] Would this be unfair to them?

The answer suggested by the argument of this essay is, it depends. Is religious education pervasively segregated, and is the segregation so extensive that it threatens the two democratic goals? In such circumstances, the legislation may be warranted. At least it would not be ruled out by religious liberty.

Religious liberty is expressed in two principles, one negative, the other positive. The negative principle tells us not to violate religious freedom. We must not prevent, forbid, or penalize religious practices and beliefs even when they are socially harmful. The positive principle tells us actively to promote religious freedom, to facilitate, encourage, and assist people's exercise of religious practice. *This* principle, however, is subject to limitations imposed by other values, such as realizing the two democratic goals. Every religion has the right not to be interfered with in its practices; no religion has the right that it be benefited for its practices.[22] The indirect 'affirmative action' policy imagined above does not interfere in a church's practices except to *refuse* to provide state *benefits* to its socially harmful educational policies.

I am not arguing that this 'affirmative action' policy be actual law. Policies that give tax benefits to actively integrating religious schools, but not to others, may run afoul not of the 'free exercise' clause of the First Amendment but of the 'no establishment' clause. Moreover, an 'affirmative action' policy applied to *all* tax-exempt institutions might outrun the state's legitimate interest in nondiscriminatory education; yet a policy applied only to educational institutions might seem an abuse of tax policy.

The point of discussing this 'affirmative action' policy is to show the pivotal issues in our assessment of the state's interest in nondiscriminatory education in circumstances where the two democratic goals are threatened. The present accommodation between church and state in the United States probably would not permit the sort of 'affirmative action' policy just described. This accommodation seems acceptable to us, I suggest, because we believe that the two democratic goals *are* being served tolerably well. We believe that enough access to decent education exists and that enough students are being taught sufficient racial respect so that the two democratic goals do not require going beyond the present indirect pressure on religious schools' discriminatory policies. Despite the social harm of discriminatory policies and segregated education, church schools do not contribute enough to that harm to warrant further action against them, in light of the high value we place on religious freedom, in its positive as well as negative dimensions. We would be forced to see the present accommodation differently if we viewed racial discrimination as ineradicable except by the most extensive integration of education, and if we saw segregated religious schools as a significant barrier to achieving this integration.

Conclusion

The import of the foregoing discussion has been to emphasize four main points. First, the state must, consistent with its other duties, honor associational preferences and protect parental liberties. One of its other duties, however, is to assure children a decent education, especially a nondiscriminatory education.

In the abstract, there is no necessary weighting that makes the second duty defeat the first. There is no a priori reason why associational preferences and parental liberties must give way to nondiscriminatory education. Rather — and this is the second point — what gives *our* state's interest in nondiscriminatory education particular urgency and priority is not so much principle as history. It is the specific nature of our past racial oppression and its enduring legacy, rather than the bare principle of nondiscrimination, that gives paramount weight to enforcing nondiscrimination and to creating the conditions that allow it to flourish.

Third, this special weight supports extensive efforts by the state to integrate education, even private education, given these two facts: (1) racial discrimination is a deeply habitual and ingrained practice that will not yield to simple admonitions or prohibitions, and (2) integration of schools, including private ones, is an effective way to undermine discriminatory habits and practices, and to promote the two democratic goals.

Fourth, the special status of religious liberty complicates the picture. It means that the state cannot interfere directly with religious schools — as it might with nonreligious private schools — even to prevent racial discrimination. But other avenues of state influence remain available, such as denial of tax exemption to discriminating religious schools, and these may be used.

Precisely because the democratic state violates Plato's first rule and encourages the creation of 'varied and conflicting characters', it must rely for its stability on the ability and willingness of its citizens to govern themselves and the community for the good of all. Consequently, its educational system must, above all, protect the two democratic goals. In our time and place, that means our educational system must serve racial nondiscrimination.[23]

Notes

1 PLATO, *The Laws*, trans. by T. Saunders (1970) New York, Penguin Books, p. 271.

2 *Ibid.*, p. 293.

3 Governments constrain private education directly by establishing minimum curriculum standards, health and safety regulations, and teacher qualifications. They also constrain private education indirectly through their control of accreditation and certification processes. Entrance into higher education and into most occupations or professions often depends upon passing special tests or possessing special certificates or degrees, and the state either sets the test or certification requirements or enforces the requirements of private associations. Consequently, private schools cannot deviate markedly from the standard public curriculum without depriving their students of a meaningful opportunity to participate in the economy or to enter higher education. Thus, private schools will provide curricular variety only at the margins.

4 W. BALL (1984) 'Parental Rights in Schooling', in C. MARSHNER (Ed.) *A Blueprint for Education Reform*, Chicago, Ill., Regnery/Gateway, p. 11.

5 S. ARONS (1984) 'Pluralism, Equal Liberty, and Public Education', in MARSHNER, *op.cit.*, pp. 39–47.

6 William Bentley Ball argues that 'by virtue of parentage, one's child is one's *own*, to nurture and to guide' (MARSHNER, p. 12; emphasis added). Roger Arnold, arguing from a libertarian position, claims that children *are* property of their parents ('Marriage, Divorce, and Property Rights: A Natural Rights Framework', in J. PEDEN and F. GLAHE (Eds) (1986) *The American Family and the State*, San Francisco, Calif., Pacific Research Institute for Public Policy, p. 213). For a libertarian position denying that children are property, see R. NOZICK (1974) *Anarchy, State, and Utopia*, New York, Basic Books, pp. 38–9, 48–51, 287–91.

Arnold's position seems the most direct challenge to my contention that children are not property, but his argument is too confused to be taken seriously. According to Arnold, a person is free to do as he pleases with his property 'as long as he does not infringe on the natural rights of others' (p. 211). Are children property? Yes (pp. 213, 223). Thus, parents 'can do with the child as they see fit, as long as they do not infringe upon his or her natural rights' (p. 213). Now this last clause is puzzling; how can property have natural rights? Natural rights presuppose self-ownership, and 'children, up to a certain age, cannot own themselves the way adults can own themselves' (p. 223). Up to that 'certain age', children have no natural rights that impede parental choice; so parents can do as they will with their children, even abuse or destroy them. (No owner violates anybody's natural rights by deciding he does not like the shrubs in front of his house and ripping them out.)

That Arnold adds the qualifying clause about infringing on the child's natural rights suggests that he is not prepared to live with the conclusion that follows from taking children *literally* to be property. It is reasonable that he is not, for only a monster would be. In fact, Arnold's reasons for saying that small children do not own themselves are quite beside the point. Children are too young to have their own voice, he says, too young to form a conception of their own purposes (pp. 213, 223). These facts of youth show not that children lack self-ownership but that they lack the capacity to exercise it in their own best interests. Thus, a parent must act as the *agent* of her children and as the *guardian* of their rights, not as the owner and possessor of chattels and goods.

7   J. PEDEN and F. GLAHE (1986) 'Introduction: The American Family in a Free Society', in PEDEN and GLAHE, *op.cit.*, pp. 3, 7–8.

8   PEDEN and GLAHE, *op.cit.*, pp. 3–9.

9   See W. O'DONNELL and D. JONES, (1982) *The Law of Marriage and Marital Alternatives*, Lexington, Mass., D.C. Heath and Company; and J. GOLDSTEIN and J. KATZ (1965) *The Family and the Law*, New York, Free Press.

10 R. NISBET (1986) 'Foreword', in PEDEN and GLAHE, *op.cit.*, p. xxiii.

11 H. BERMAN (1983) *Law and Revolution: The Formation of the Western Legal Tradition*, Cambridge, Mass., Harvard University Press, pp. 224–37.

12 In making this claim, I do not presuppose very much about the nature of the state. The claim is compatible with various ways of organizing and channeling state power. The core idea is expressed in the next paragraph below.

13 See A. GUTMANN (1987) *Democratic Education*, Princeton, N.J., Princeton University Press, pp. 44–5. My argument here and throughout the next several paragraphs is indebted to Gutmann's work. See also N. DEVINS (1983) 'State Regulation of Christian Schools', *Journal of Legislation*, 10, pp. 352, 353 (emphasis on ability to participate and to think critically about society).

14 The point here is that general moral principles are not applied in a vacuum. For example, in the United States, our law tolerates public displays of swastikas and other symbols of Nazism. However ugly the swastikas and hateful their symbolism, our commitment to toleration of political expression in general gives Nazis as much latitude as Democrats. However, in West Germany, it is against the law to display the swastika. This is not because West Germany is less committed to free expression than we are; it is because of Germany's special history. Treating the swastika like any other ugly symbol would, in Germany, be treating Nazism and World War II like any other unfortunate and regrettable national episode, not the special horrors that they were. Germany history demands that it treat displays of the swastika differently than we do. American history demands that we deal more forcefully with our racial discrimination than does, say, Canada.

15 A fuller statement of this conception of discrimination would root discrimination in the psychology and sociology of institutions rather than individuals. It would emphasize the role of institutional organization and culture in structuring individual perception: what people see is a function of what they expect to see, and their surrounding institutional framework supplies the expectations of what is normal and natural.

16 On differing conceptions of discrimination, see W. B. REYNOLDS (1986) 'Stotts: Equal Opportunity, Not Equal Results'; R. WASSERSTROM (1986) 'One Way to Understand and Defend Programs of Preferential Treatment'; and R. FULLINWIDER (1986) 'Achieving Equal Opportunity', in R. FULLINWIDER and C. MILLS (Eds) *The Moral Foundations of Civil Rights*, Totowa, N.J., Rowman and Littlefield, pp. 39–45, 46–55, 99–114.

17 Of course, the experience of busing may show that bringing blacks and whites together fuels rather than undermines racial stereotyping and hostility. For a survey of the literature on busing, see J. HOCHSCHILD (1984) *The New*

American Dilemma: Liberal Democracy and School Desegregation, New Haven, Conn., Yale University Press.

18 See *Runyon v. McCrary*, 427 US 160 (1976), whose ruling against a school's discriminatory policies was carefully tailored to apply to nonsectarian private schools. For sectarian schools, the issue of the right to discriminate remains legally undecided; see *Brown v. Dade Christian Schools*, 556 F.2d 310 (1977), *cert. denied*, 434 US 1063 (1978), and *Fiedler v. Marumsco Baptist Church*, 486 F. Supp. 960 (1979). See below, note 20.

19 See B.N. BAGNI (1979) 'Discrimination in the Name of the Lord: A Critical Evaluation of Discrimination by Religious Organizations', *Columbia Law Review*, 79, December, pp. 1539–43.

20 M. BRAITERMAN and D.M. KELLEY (1982) 'When Is Governmental Intervention Legitimate', in D.M. KELLEY (Ed.) *Government Intervention in Religious Affairs*, New York, Pilgrim Press, deny that tax exemptions are privileges or that they are limited by 'public policy' considerations (p. 191). But see *Bob Jones Univ. v. United States*, 461 US 574 (1983). The Court there argued that the common law notion of 'charitable institution' means an institution that provides a public benefit. Since discrimination in education violates a basic national policy, discriminating schools fail to qualify as publicly beneficial and, thus, charitable under the tax law (at 592–95). The right of schools to receive tax exemptions is, according to the Court's analysis of the relevant legislation and common law, conditioned on acting in accord with public policy. But the constitutional right of churches and church schools to act on their religious beliefs is not similarly conditioned on conforming to established public policy. Consequently, the reach of the *Bob Jones* ruling, in which public policy trumps the school policy, does not settle the question, discussed in note 18 above, about the right of sectarian schools to discriminate. See also *Walz. v. Tax Comm'n*, 397 US 664 (1970).

21 This legislation would be like rules proposed in 1978 by the IRS to establish that a private school's policies were nondiscriminatory. Under the guidelines, schools with 'insignificant numbers' of minority students would have the burden of proving, by affirmative steps such as active minority recruitment programs, that they were in compliance with IRS policy. The rules have never been put into effect. See P. SKERRY (1980) 'Christian Schools Versus the IRS', *The Public Interest*, 61, Fall, pp. 31–2.

22 The reason tax exemptions for churches should be viewed (contra BRAITERMAN and KELLEY, note 20, above) as privileges, not rights, is because they fall under the *positive* principle of religious liberty. They are devices to help religious institutions flourish. Just as groups 'fostering national or international amateur sports competition', granted tax exemptions in 1976 (see *Bob Jones Univ. v. United States* at 616–17), have no *right* that the public make it easy for them to flourish, religious institutions have no such right.

23 I am grateful to Neal Devins, Henry Shue, and Claudia Mills for their comments on earlier versions of this essay.

3
Values Inculcation and the Schools: The Need for a New *Pierce* Compromise

Michael A. Rebell[1]

The Supreme Court's most recent decisions on education matters seem to deal with relatively minor discipline and curriculum issues. The main education law decisions of the past three Supreme Court terms were *Bethel School District v. Fraser*,[2] a case that upheld the disciplining of a high school student who delivered a 'lewd' speech at an assembly, *Edwards v. Aquillard*,[3] a decision that invalidated a Louisiana statute requiring equal time for instruction in 'creation science' in all classes in which evolution was taught, and *Hazelwood School District v. Kuhlmeier*,[4] a decision that upheld school officials' authority to censor high school newspapers.

The seemingly limited significance of *Fraser*, *Edwards*, and *Hazelwood*, however, masks a fundamental legal and public policy issue at the root of all three cases, an issue that may be the most perplexing problem affecting public education in the United States today. This is the dilemma of how to reconcile the schools' responsibility for inculcating the 'fundamental values necessary to the maintenance of a democratic political system'[5] with the critical need in a liberal democratic society not to have the state impose values that 'may conflict with the private beliefs of the student and his or her family.'[6]

The Supreme Court confronted this fundamental value conflict more than sixty years ago in *Pierce v. Society of Sisters*.[7] There, the Court established the right of parents who objected to the values being taught in the public schools to enroll their children (at their own expense) in private schools. This compromise allowed public schools to inculcate cohesive community values while, at the same time, providing dissenters with an option to avoid such socialization by attending a private school of their choosing. At the time, the *Pierce* compromise appeared to resolve nicely the value inculcation dilemma. But under the contemporary stresses of urbanization, centralization and individual rights assertion, the strings holding together the *Pierce* package are beginning to unravel.

As illustrated by *Fraser, Edwards,* and *Hazelwood,* and also by a number of lower court cases involving fundamental religious values, there is growing dissatisfaction with the *Pierce* compromise. Little consensus exists concerning the values that public schools should properly convey. At the same time, the private school option is not providing a satisfactory escape valve for dissident pressures. It is likely, therefore, that the Supreme Court will soon face again the fundamental value clash that seemingly was resolved by *Pierce.* This chapter will discuss the reasons why a contemporary reconsideration of the *Pierce* compromise is imperative, and will then offer suggestions for achieving a satisfactory new resolution of the fundamental values conflict. In so doing, this chapter will demonstrate that the propriety of state control over private schools goes hand-in-hand with one's perception of the public school's value inculcation function.

Pierce in Historical Perspective

In colonial days, and through much of the nineteenth century, schools were essentially extensions of churches, families and local communities; they were expected to transmit the values held by these institutions to the next generation. Since towns, villages and other local communities tended to be conglomerations of like-minded citizens, differences on fundamental values tended to be rare — or at least rarely articulated. Moreover, since, in early days, neither the federal constitution nor most state constitutions contained any provisions entitling youngsters to a free, public education, a would-be dissident had no legal basis upon which to challenge the content of the local school curriculum.

The advent of the common school movement in the mid-nineteenth century dramatically altered this situation. As its name implied, the common school movement was an attempt to bring together in one educational milieu all children living in a particular geographic area, whatever their class or ethnic backgrounds. Thus, in place of the prior variegated pattern of elitist academies for the rich and shanty schools — or no schools — for the poor, the common school crusade sought both to democratize and to standardize American education.[8]

The common schools were also clearly intended to undertake an enhanced value inculcation role. Thus, Horace Mann, their prime advocate, proclaimed in millenial terms the movement's potential for uplifting the character of the coming generation:

Let the common school be expanded to its capabilities, let it be worked with the efficiency of which it is susceptible, and nine-tenths of the crimes in the penal code would become obsolete; the long catalog of human ills would be abridged; men would walk more safely by day; every pillow would be more inviolable by night; property, life and character held by strong tenure; all rational hopes respecting the future brightened.[9]

The value inculcation role inherent in the common school movement was complicated, however, by the concomitant trends toward consolidation of school districts and statewide supervision of schooling practices that occurred in its wake. Moreover, the concept of compulsory education implicit in the notion of the common schools — which became a legal mandate in most states by the beginning of the twentieth century — put additional stress on the traditional value transmission role. In short, the combined effects of consolidation, urbanization, and compulsory education brought together under the jurisdiction of a single educational authority a heterogeneous amalgam of school children of differing class, ethnic, and cultural backgrounds. Under such circumstances, how could the schools continue to transmit a cohesive set of communal values?

Like most other fundamental social conflicts in American society, this problem was eventually brought before the Supreme Court for principled resolution. The issue came to a head in 1925 in the form of a challenge in the Oregon Compulsory Education Act, which held parents criminally liable for any failure to enroll children under the age of 16 in a *public* school. This Act had been adopted as a result of a referendum campaign with strong anti-Catholic overtones, organized and promoted primarily by the Ku Klux Klan and Oregon Scottish Rite Masons, as part of a strategy to 'Americanize' the schools.[10] Not surprisingly, therefore, the constitutional challenge was brought by the Society of Sisters, a Catholic group that ran a number of parochial elementary and high schools, as well as a military academy, that would have been put out of business if the Act were to take effect.

The case presented the Supreme Court with a difficult dilemma. On the one hand, the state clearly had a legitimate interest in acclimatizing newly arrived immigrant groups to the majoritarian political culture. A proliferation of separate private schools, some of which carried out their instruction in languages other than English, threatened to impede substantially this socialization process. On the other hand, if Catholics or other minorities felt that separate schooling was necessary to maintain the integrity of their religious and other fundamental beliefs, how could their request be denied under the First Amendment?[11]

The Court discussed the issue largely in terms of a soon-to-be-outdated 'substantive due process' right of private schools, as business entities, not to have their 'liberty' undermined by the state. At one point, however, the Court did directly focus on the schooling values dilemma, reaching a Solomonic conclusion: it upheld the right of parents to send their children to private schools, but at the same time served notice that the state could impose basic regulations on such schools that 'certain studies plainly essential to good citizenship must be taught.'[12] In short, *Pierce* set forth a well balanced, subtle compromise that

> represents a reasonable, if imperfect, accommodation of conflicting pressures. The state may promulgate its messages in the public school, and parents are free to choose private schools with different orientations. The state must tolerate private education, but need not fund it. The state may make some demands of private schools in satisfaction of compulsory schooling laws, but those demands may not be so excessive that they transform private schools into public schools managed and funded by the private sector. The integrity of the communications and socialization processes in private school and families remains intact, while the state's interest in producing informed, educated and productive citizens is not sacrificed.[13]

The *Pierce* compromise requires a number of factors to remain in equilibrium if its delicate balance is to be maintained. First, the overwhelming majority of parents and children must be satisfied with the education being provided in the public schools, and specifically with the values that are being inculcated there; otherwise, there will be too much resistance and too much flight from the public schools for the state to be able to carry out its socialization function. Second, the small minority strongly opposed to the values being transmitted in the public schools must have access to a private school alternative; otherwise, the constitutional right to maintain the integrity of each individual's personal beliefs will have been undermined. Finally, the state's right to regulate private schools in order to maintain minimal adherence to good citizenship values must remain a background pressure, subtly influencing the minimal values content of private school curricula, but rarely being exercised in fact, since each actual exercise of the state's regulatory authority threatens to upset the precarious *Pierce* equilibrium.

For most of the decades since 1925, the *Pierce* compromise retained its vitality because these three conditions were met. Except for among Catholics, who had organized their own alternative parochial school system,[14] there was general acceptance of the values orientation of the public schools. Moreover, state education departments, whether from satisfaction with the education being offered in the alternative Catholic school system or as a tacit political compromise, seldom exercised the regulatory power authorized by *Pierce*.[15]

In recent years, however, each of the constituent segments of the *Pierce* compromise has come under pressure. Public school students and parents express increasing dissatisfaction with aspects of the education they are receiving. At the same time, the private school option, *Pierce*'s 'escape valve' for the release of such pressures from the public school system, is in danger of becoming clogged by the massive number of students preferring alternative education,[16] and by a change in the traditional laissez-faire approach to state regulation of the private schools.[17] In other words, the *Pierce* compromise is unraveling because both the public schools' exercise of their traditional socialization function and the availability of private schooling for the dissenting minority are becoming less viable under contemporary circumstances.

The necessary prerequisite for unabashed exercise of the schools' traditional socialization function, i.e., a coherent set of local community values, is fast disappearing under the continuing pressures of centralization and urbanization. The rural to urban (or suburban) population shift in most parts of the country means that most local school districts now serve culturally diverse student populations. Moreover, urban, suburban, and the remaining rural school district inhabitants are part of a national 'community' whose often inconsistent values are influenced by the pervasive national media.[18] In the schooling context, accelerating doses of state regulation and federal mandates further undermine the cohesion of the local community's value stock.[19] In short, a critical underlying premise of the *Pierce* compromise, that there is a cohesive majoritarian values consensus of the local community that can be transmitted through the public schools, is no longer true.

Contemporary social and political developments have also affected the workings of the private school options, the other pole of the *Pierce* compromise equation. Increasing dissatisfaction with the public schools (perhaps in part resulting from the schools' perceived inability to inculcate firm values), individualistic trends, and diverse lifestyles have expanded interest in alternative private education. The extensive debate on educational vouchers and tuition tax credits that has dominated much educational policy analysis in recent years reflects this trend.[20]

Pierce allowed a private school option as an abstract constitutional right, but did not mandate or authorize public funding to subsidize private education for those who could not otherwise afford it. The result has been that with the exception of Catholic schools, which have had a broad independent funding base, private schooling has been available primarily for the rich. This inequity has been exacerbated in recent years by the 'white flight' exodus to private schools of many affluent students during desegregation conflicts. The desire of parents of more limited means to seek private schooling is a major factor behind the extensive recent interest in vouchers and tuition tax credits.

Vouchers and tax credits are not consistent, however, with the limited 'escape valve' role for private schools contemplated by *Pierce*. Although voucher schemes — or at least those versions that assure access for racial minorities and the economically disadvantaged — might rectify the inequity in access to private schools today, they would also encourage massive withdrawals from the public school system. Such an exodus would further undermine the public schools' ability to serve as transmitters of majoritarian cultural values.

In short, the tenuous balance of the *Pierce* compromise is tottering because of contemporary trends that are undermining both of its fundamental tenets, the public school socialization process and the private school escape valve. The magnitude and significance of the growing values crisis in the schools are evidenced by the rising number of cases reflecting these problems that are being brought before the courts. *Fraser*,[21] which dealt with the enforcement of 'civility values', *Edwards*,[22] which focused on curriculum values issues, and *Hazelwood*,[23] which was concerned with the schools' authority to influence the articulation of values in school publications, all demonstrate this trend. The most dramatic illustration of the value conflicts confronting the schools, however, is the recent litigation involving fundamentalist religious objections to elementary school readers, *Mozert v. Hawkins County Public Schools*.[24] *Mozert* also brings into focus the difficulties of implementing the *Pierce* private school 'opt out' remedy under contemporary circumstances. For these reasons, the next section will analyze the implications of *Mozert*, before our discussion returns to a consideration of how the *Pierce* compromise might be restructured to meet contemporary needs.

Mozert v. Hawkins County: 'Opting Out' While Staying In

The *Mozert* litigation was initiated by parents of several Tennessee public school children who objected to a mandatory elementary school reading series. The parents claimed that the books were offensive to their fundamentalist religious beliefs. Several of the stories were said to 'teach witchcraft', demean traditional family roles, imply that values are relative, or suggest that one can achieve salvation by having faith in the supernatural without necessarily believing in Jesus.

After an extensive trial, federal district judge Thomas G. Hull determined that plaintiffs' religious objections to the books were sincere and that the school board's insistence on uniform use of these books infringed on their right to 'free exercise' of their religion. Applying the relevant constitutional standard, the court then considered whether the state had a 'compelling interest' that could not be satisfied by a less restrictive means of accommodating the plaintiffs' needs and the school board's prerogatives. Under this standard, the district court decided that the children's needs could be accommodated 'less restrictively' by permitting them to 'opt out' of reading classes and be taught at home by their parents.[25]

This ruling, in essence, stood the *Pierce* compromise on its head. In *Pierce*, the Supreme Court implied that the public schools could transmit cultural values in a thorough going, cohesive manner to all students enrolled in the schools because of the availability of an 'escape valve' in the form of a right to attend private school, for those few who could not accept these values. The *Mozert* district court opinion, by way of contrast, ignored the escape valve approach and sought to compel the public schools to modify or fragment their curricular approach to meet the objections of the dissenting minority.

Allowing a few students to study reading at home may seem a relatively minor challenge to the integrity of the school system's instructional methodologies and curricular content. It is likely, however, that Judge Hull's decision would allow religious parents to assert objections to the content and value implications of virtually all social studies texts, English readers or other curriculum materials — and probably also to lectures or oral statements teachers make every day in class.[26] At that point, 'if we are to eliminate everything that is objectionable to any of [the religious bodies existing in the United States] or inconsistent with any of their doctrines, we will leave public education in shreds.'[27]

Judge Hull's 'opt-out' ruling was unanimously reversed by the appeals court for the Sixth Circuit. However, through a narrow reading of the free exercise clause of the First Amendment,[28] the appelate court ducked the core *Pierce* issue. In its view, since the students were not required to affirm or act on the objectionable ideas presented in the Holt readers,[29] there was no constitutional infringement on religious belief.[30] In short, although the lower court's opt out remedy was clearly unacceptable, the *Mozert* appeals court opinion has not satisfactorily resolved the underlying value conflict issues.

A possible alternative to the individual opt out remedy that would meet fundamentalist objections to the content of school curriculum materials would be simply to ban the use of the controverted texts. This was precisely the tack taken by a federal district court in *Smith v. Board of School Commissioners*,[31] a case pressed by a religiously oriented group of parents and teachers who objected to the values content of public school curriculum materials. The specific holding in *Smith* was that the forty-four textbooks under consideration (most of which were social studies or home economics texts) systematically promoted the 'religion' of 'secular humanism' in violation of the establishment clause of the First Amendment.[32]

The Court's depiction of the secular values being conveyed by the contested texts as a 'religion of secular humanism' was clearly strained. The appeals court for the Eleventh Circuit did not, however, reverse the decision on this ground.[33] Rather, it held that the textbook materials to which plaintiffs objected did not have as their primary effect the advancement of religion, since 'none of these books conveys a message of governmental approval of secular humanism or governmental disapproval of theism.'[34]

Thus, the narrow holding of the appellate court decision in *Smith*, like that in *Mozert*, avoided the fundamental issue of the culture clash 'between views of Biblical literalists and our modern society.'[35] This clash will, however, need to be addressed if the critical problems of the schools' value inculcating mission discussed in the preceding section are to be resolved. The wholesale judicial book-banning approach of *Smith*, like the opt out mechanism of *Mozert*, clearly is an unacceptable remedy. Is there any feasible way that courts faced with these issues can ameliorate the contemporary value clashes in the public schools?

It is puzzling that neither the parties nor the courts in either of the fundamentalist litigations looked to the Supreme Court's historic *Pierce* compromise for a solution to these problems. Despite the contemporary strains on the *Pierce* compromise, the concepts behind that historic case remain highly relevant. Logically, the notion of offering dissenting students a separate schooling environment where their own religious preferences can be exercised freely without underming the public schools' socialization mission would seem the obvious 'opt out' solution. How the *Pierce* compromise can be reoriented to serve both of these functions under modern conditions will be the subject of the next two sections.

Revitalizing the Public Schools' Value Inculcating Role

The Supreme Court's decision in *Bethel School District v. Fraser*,[36] which permitted a school board to censor lewd references in a student's assembly speech, may have major precedential implications for a revitalization of the schools' traditional value inculcating role. *Fraser* was the first recent education law decision to explicate and uphold a school board's values mission.[37] The fact that the decision reflected a near-unanimous agreement of the Court's liberal and conservative wings[38] — and that its value inculcating themes were reiterated in the recent *Hazelwood* decision[39] — adds to its significance.

The core issue in *Fraser* was whether a school district's interest in maintaining a level of civility in school affairs justified regulation of student speech that was considered a part of the school curriculum.[40] The court below had emphatically rejected the suggestion that school officials have a right to inculcate standards of 'civility' or 'decency':

> we fear that if school officials had the unbridled discretion to apply a standard as subjective and elusive as 'indecency' in controlling the speech of high school students, it would increase the risk of cementing white, middle-class standards for determining what is acceptable and proper speech and behavior in our public schools.[41]

The proposition that social authorities may not impose 'white, middle-class standards' is extraordinary. As indicated above, inculcation of basic social values has always been assumed to be a fundamental function of the schools. Although the perjorative term, 'white, middle class standards,'[42] is being used here in the context of values such as 'decency', the reference really is to the broad majoritarian values that the locally elected school board believes should be transmitted to the younger generation. Certainly, any attempts to inculcate majoritarian values in a manner which would stigmatize or discriminate against members of minority groups or cultures would be inconsistent with the American educational tradition, and with contemporary constitutional precepts. But the avoidance of invidious discrimination or the desirability of sensitizing the curriculum to our pluralistic society does not require complete abandonment of the local school boards' traditional value inculcation authority.

It was in this context that the Supreme Court considered the value inculcation issues raised by *Fraser*. In response to the appellate court's undermining of the schools' traditional socialization function, the high court went out of its way to emphasize the centrality to the educational process — and to the nation's democratic culture — of the school's traditional value transmittal role:

> The role and purpose of the American public school system... [is to] 'prepare pupils for citizenship in the Republic.... It must

inculcate the habits and manners of civility as values in themselves conducive to happiness and as indispensable to the practice of self-government in the community and the nation'....
The process of educating our youth for citizenship in public schools is not confined to books, the curriculum and the civics class; schools must teach by example the shared values of a civilized social order.[43]

Applying that standard to the facts of the case before it, the Court concluded that it would not read the First Amendment to interfere with the local school board's determination that Fraser's speech was lewd and vulgar.[44]

Moreover, by reiterating that 'schools must teach by example the shared values of a civilized social order', the Court indicated that certain majoritarian values — at least those such as civility and 'sensitivity', which do not have obvious racial implications — can properly be put forth as standards of propriety for school children. In other words, the Supreme Court's reversal of the Ninth Circuit on these points can be seen as a statement to the lower courts — and to the nation's students and school boards — that its prior invalidation of school board actions that occurred in the context of heated national, political controversies[45] was an exceptional judicial intervention in schooling affairs; such decisions were not meant to recast fully the traditional value inculcating role of local educational authorities.

Fraser's focus on the schools' fundamental value inculcation role is, to some extent, a re-establishment of past tradition. From a larger perspective, however, *Fraser* highlights the need for new approaches to the schools' values mission. Although the Supreme Court in *Fraser* indicated that the Ninth Circuit had gone too far in its attempt to preclude the school board from transmitting 'white, middle-class' values, the extent to which the majority can press its values in the heterogeneous environment of most modern school districts remains an open question. The free expression issue here is analogous to the religious expression issue in *Mozert* and *Smith*: how can individual rights be reconciled with the school's vital value inculcation role?

Fostering such a reconciliation is a major responsibility and a major challenge for the federal courts.[46] In order to accomplish this task, courts need to distinguish explicitly between those fundamental individual value issues that warrant consistent judicial protection and other value issues that do not have substantial constitutional dimensions. Generally speaking, this distinction could be expressed in terms of basic 'national' constitutional values and other local 'community' values. Such a delineation would acknowledge the reality that many contemporary educational value issues have moved to the national policy and legal arena, but that nevertheless, certain core educational and value inculcation functions should remain rooted in the local communities. Judicial clarification of the proper spheres for national value assertions and local community value formulation would remove the cloud of confusion that has immobilized effective value articulation at both levels in recent years.

'National value' issues would mean, at the least, the right to speak freely on important political controversies, like the Vietnam War protests, fundamental equity issues, like the right to desegregated schooling articulated in *Brown v. Board of Education*,[47] and basic church/state separation matters, like the prohibition against school prayer.[48] Each of these issues raises fundamental constitutional questions that require a uniform, national resolution of the underlying value issues. Local community values, by way of contrast, would include such matters as notions of civility and decency, sexual mores, and curriculum priorities. The range of issues encompassed by 'local community values' and the degree of controversy they engender obviously are vast. That is precisely why these issues, on which there is no clear constitutional mandate and no clear national consensus, should be left to the discretion of the local school authorities.

The line between national values and local community values will not, of course, be easy to draw in many specific situations.[49] Nevertheless, the attempt is of critical significance. A forthright values clarification approach by the courts is necessary not only to uphold individual constitutional rights, but also to promote a more active assertion by local school boards of their value inculcating role. A judicial focus on these issues, and the delineation of parameters for the exercise of school board prerogatives on values issues, is likely to galvanize interest and activity on these questions by local school boards and local communities. Such an enhancement of the value formulation process is likely to result in a higher degree of consensus on local value issues.[50]

This does not mean, of course, that resolutions of value issues by local communities today will replicate the cohesive value formulations of traditional communities. Nevertheless, focused dialogues on these issues would be a significant improvement over the adversarial value confrontations that predominate in many local communities today, and agreements reached through such a process are likely to gain more broad-based communal support. Indeed, the communal stimulus of participating in a dialogue on values issues, in and of itself, is likely to render the public schools more dynamic and appealing communal institutions. Such participation should create a positive socialization process that will feed upon itself. As the public schools come to confront directly important values issues, more members of the community will be drawn into the process, and this, in turn, will render the participation more inclusive and the process even more appealing. As the community comes closer to achieving full participation, the schools will, in turn, become more confident in asserting the community's values.

In sum, a forthright focus on value clarification processes by courts and local school boards gives promise of revitalizing the public school socialization pole of the *Pierce* compromise.[51] National and local values will be delineated, and communities will be motivated to promote intensive community dialogues leading to greater consensus on values issues. No matter how appealing the public school setting may become to the majority of the population in any given community, however, there will always remain a minority whose values cannot be reasonably accommodated by participation in a 'melting pot' community culture. For such a minority, *Pierce*'s private school option must be retained — both to allow them to pursue their strongly held value choices, and to maintain the integrity of the public school system itself. How this second prong of the *Pierce* equation can be revitalized to meet contemporary needs will be explored in the section that follows.

Revitalizing the Private School Option

One of the main defenses of the school board defendants in *Mozert* was that if the plaintiffs had strong objections to the texts in general use, their children should not remain in the public schools.[52] This position was in keeping with the decades-old *Pierce* resolution of school-based value clashes, which offered religious dissenters the option of educating their children in their own private schools. In 1986, however, the *Mozert* plaintiffs did not consider this option adequate, either because they could not afford private schooling or because their sense of entitlement led them to claim a right to public support for their children's education equivalent to that provided to other children in the community.[53]

In short, the major contemporary problem with the *Pierce* private school option is that it offers a right to attend a private school, but no right to a public subsidy to pay for it. Given the political and legal climate of 1925, the parents of the students involved in the original *Pierce* controversy[54] were apparently satisfied to receive constitutional support for their right to attend separate schools and not be coerced to remain in an inhospitable state school setting. In the contemporary climate of individual entitlement, however, many fundamentalist parents are unwilling to remain in the back of the bus: as *Mozert* and *Smith* demonstrated, if they are not given public support to attend schools that are consistent with their values, they will seek to impose their values on the public schools that they by right may attend. Consequently, in order to promote the enhanced value inculcation role of the public schools advocated in the previous section, an effective escape valve that will release this dissenting pressure to an outside environment also needs to be created.[55] It is necessary to confront today the issue of public funding of private school tuition left open by the *Pierce* decision.

A state inclined to provide such tuition subsidies — or a court inclined to order them — must overcome two major problems, one practical and one legal. The practical problem is how to expand the scope of the *Pierce* escape valve to provide tuition subsidies for the non-affluent without encouraging a massive exodus from the public schools. Since almost half of all public school parents would prefer to see their children in private schools,[56] would not a publicly funded *Pierce* escape valve empty the public schools and/or deplete the state's coffers? The broad-based values consensus advocated in the previous section, if achieved, would presumably enhance the attractiveness of the public school setting and reduce the number who would seek a private school option. Even so, if private school tuition were free, larger numbers than the public fisc — or the need for a broad-based values consensus within the public schools — could accommodate are likely to seek this alternative. Is there any way to limit these numbers and still meet the contemporary *Pierce* needs?

Students who might choose a free private schooling option would have a variety of reasons for their preference, ranging from more desirable instructional methodologies and perceived quality differentials, to elitism and racism. The type of value conflict that *Pierce* seeks to address is only one of the motivating factors for private schooling — and there is some evidence that it is a relatively minor one.[57] Most voucher schemes would offer subsidies to all students who prefer private schooling for any of these reasons; indeed, competition with the monopolistic public school, rather than value differences, is the main rationale for most of the voucher schemes.[58] If the purpose of a voucher scheme is to rectify inequities under the original *Pierce* holding, however, only those who have substantial conflicts with the values being inculcated in the public schools, and seek access to private schooling for that reason, should have a right to call on the public fisc.

Thus, the practical problem of limiting a potentially open-ended drain on public funds can be solved, at least theoretically, by restricting a '*Pierce* voucher' to legitimate values dissenters. Ironically, however, this solution to the practical problem of limiting public subsidies may exacerbate the second area of concern: the legal hurdle. This is because the smaller number of students who would qualify under a values dissenting criterion are likely to consist largely of students asserting religious values, but accommodating these values raises a serious separation of church and state issue under the federal constitution.[59]

The Supreme Court has repeatedly struck down, under the establishment clause of the First Amendment, attempts to provide financial assistance to institutions with a religious affiliation. Legal doctrine in this area is, however, far from clear. Although direct subsidies to private schools and reimbursements for activities such as teacher salaries,[60] state mandated testing,[61] or instructional materials and equipment[62] have been invalidated, the Court has permitted states to reimburse parents for expenses incurred in transporting their children to religious schools,[63] and to loan secular textbooks to all school children within the state, including those attending religious institutions.[64]

The Court's case-by-case treatment of aid to religious schools has been frustratingly inconsistent. There is, however, a principled approach, consistent with the general thrust of the Supreme Court's past decisions, that could be applied in this area. This approach would be to invalidate state funding schemes that directly benefit religiously affiliated schools (such as construction grants or teacher salary subsidies), but to permit schemes that provide financial benefits to individual parents (such as transportation or textbook subsidies), even if religiously affiliated schools would indirectly benefit thereby.

Such a distinction finds support in *Mueller v. Allen*,[65] a 1983 decision upholding Minnesota's scheme for tax deductions for tuition payments. Distinguishing an earlier decision,[66] that rejected a New York tuition subsidy scheme, the Court in *Mueller* emphasized that the Minnesota statute permitted the deduction to be taken by parents of both private and public school students, in contrast to the subsidy in the New York case, available only to private school students. The distinction was obviously strained, however, since few public school students in Minnesota would incur sufficient school expenses to allow them to take advantage of the deduction.[67] The majority opinion in *Mueller*, authored by Justice Rehnquist, expressed clear sympathies for the financial burdens of parochial school students,[68] and at times came close to adopting forthrightly the individual subsidy doctrine.[69] The court, in its next deliberation on these issues, may be prepared to take a direct unqualified stance.[70]

If a more strongly stated *Mueller* doctrine should eliminate establishment clause objections to publicly funded tuition subsidies, further consideration of the implications of recent Supreme Court holdings on the free exercise aspect of the First Amendment[71] might make such subsidies not only constitutionally acceptable, but even constitutionally mandated in certain circumstances. In other words, free exercise doctrine, which has developed significantly since 1925, might provide a basis for upholding a claim for a right to a public tuition subsidy for religious dissenters in a contemporary *Pierce*-type litigation.

The Court has held in recent decades that governmental benefits cannot be denied those who seek to exercise their religious convictions, where there is a substantial burden on a sincerely held religious belief and the government cannot demonstrate a compelling reason to deny the religiously-based claim.[72] This does not mean, of course, that any denial of a government benefit by a uniformly applicable statute will be considered unconstitutional.[73] One factor that weighs heavily in the constitutional calculus in this area is whether participation in the governmental program at issue is voluntary or involuntary:

> We conclude then that government regulation that indirectly and incidentally calls for a choice between securing a governmental benefit and adherence to religious beliefs is wholly different from governmental action or legislation that criminalizes religiously inspired activity or inescapably compels conduct that some find objectionable for religious reasons.[74]

This doctrine was applied to the school setting in *Wisconsin v. Yoder*,[75] where the Supreme Court held that Wisconsin's compulsory school law, which would require Amish children to attend secular high schools whose values undermined their religion and way of life, violated their free exercise rights. The Amish children were therefore exempted from the compulsory education requirements. In *Yoder*, the Supreme Court emphasized the unique 300-year history of the Amish Order, with the obvious intent of narrowing the precedential implications of that case.[76] Nevertheless, one cannot reasonably assume that the way of life of a fundamentalist religious community is not also substantially threatened if their children are compelled to attend public schools whose values conflict with theirs. At the least, the *Smith* and *Mozert* litigations established the incompatibility of the plaintiffs' beliefs with the 'secular humanist' curriculum materials. It would be disingenuous to deny that continued exposure of impressionable children to such incompatible materials in an authoritative school setting must detrimentally affect their commitment to their parents' beliefs. These cases, therefore, call for a reconsideration, and prudent extension, of the *Yoder* doctrine.

Combining *Yoder* and the recent free exercise analysis discussed above, the Supreme Court might approve a limited 'opt out' remedy through public subsidies for private school tuition for dissenting students. Such a holding concededly would broaden the Court's past statements concerning the extent of the *Pierce* doctrine,[77] but such a reconsideration would not be inconsistent with the trend in recent cases permitting a greater degree of accommodation of religious values in public institutions.[78] Providing an avenue of accommodation through an appropriate 'escape valve' for those with irreconcilable religious views might also have the indirect salutary effect of expanding the scope of the values consensus in the public schools to encompass a broader range of nonsectarian values.[79]

A free exercise doctrine upholding the right to public tuition subsidies for the *Mozert* and *Smith* plaintiffs, and those similarly situated, need not be open-ended. The Court in *Yoder* explicitly declined to include secular value dissension within the scope of its free exercise protection from compulsory schooling, holding that 'the claims must be rooted in religious belief.'[80] Reiteration of this limitation in a holding limited to other sincere religious dissenters beyond the Amish would constitute a reasonable, confined extension of this doctrine. Of course, other individuals holding conscientious objections to values being inculcated in public schools based on sincerely held secular beliefs would argue for similar treatment. From a constitutional view, such dissent, if 'secular', does not raise basic free exercise claims and would not be entitled to the same degree of protection. On the other hand, since the Court has never defined the term 'religious' for constitutional purposes, arguably many of those with strong nonmajoritarian value beliefs that are not rooted in traditional religious institutions could be included in the ambit of the free exercise voucher program.[81] From a prudential perspective, it is important that the parameters of any extension of the *Yoder* doctrine be limited to avoid opening a voucher option to an unmanageable number of students and undermining efforts to promote consensus on local community values. Thus, at least initially, *Pierce* vouchers should be available only to those whose values dissent is based on a (broadly defined) religious belief cognizable under the free exercise clause.[82]

In order to implement a *Pierce* voucher scheme for religious values dissenters, a mechanism would need to be established to distinguish those with sincere, deep-seated value conflicts from students with other motives for seeking a private school tuition subsidy. An administrative process that would require those seeking a subsidy to file a statement setting forth their religious principles or tenets that differ substantially from the goals and objectives of education set forth in the public school curriculum could accomplish this end.[83] If such filings are not clear and convincing, parents or students might also be required to justify the requested eligibility status before an administrative tribunal. Moreover, to prevent private schools from undermining the *Brown* mandate of nondiscrimination in education, the *Pierce* voucher scheme would also require protection to assure that any private schools accepting public subsidy students would be free of racial or ethnic discrimination.[84]

Since only those with strong, deep-seated values objections that cannot be accommodated within the public schools could meet this test,[85] presumably relatively few students would be eligible for the *Pierce* vouchers. Moreover, if, like conscientious objector status, the subsidy program were perceived as a limited status, available only on an exceptional basis — and if the public schools were to become sufficiently appealing in their own right — few students would be motivated to make public declarations and seek such value dissenter status.

In essence, the proposal suggested here is to reconstitute the *Pierce* compromise to reflect current conditions by encouraging the courts to revitalize the value inculcating role of the schools and by refashioning the private school escape mechanism into an equitable, but little used constitutional option. Such a reconstituted *Pierce* compromise, like the original version, would remain a tenuous equilibrium, liable at any moment to disintegrate if the public schools' socialization function should become overbearing or if the private school escape mechanism should become clogged. Such a tenuous balance is, however, probably an inevitable — and highly desirable — tension within any attempt to carry out a socialization process in a democratic society.

Notes

1 I would like to thank Stephen Arons, John E. Coons, Jacklyn Frankfurt, Roberta Koenigsberg, Burke Marshall, Anne Murdaugh, Keith Roberts, Rhoda Schneider, Sharon Rebell, Melicent Rubin, and Marc C. Yudof for their comments on prior drafts of this article.
2 106 S. Ct. 3159 (1986).
3 107 S. Ct. 2573 (1987).
4 108 S. Ct. 562 (1988).
5 *Fraser, supra* note 2, 106 S. Ct. at 3164.
6 *Edwards, supra* note 3, 107 S. Ct. at 2577.
7 268 US 510 (1925).
8 For insightful discussions of values issues related to the common school movement, see D. TYACK (1985) *Toward a Social History of Law and Public Education*, in D. KIRP and D. JENSEN (1985) *School Days, Rule Days: The Legalization and Regulation of Education*, Philadelphia, Pa., Falmer Press; and P. PETERSON (1985) *The Politics of School Reform 1870–1940*, Chicago, Ill., University of Chicago Press.

9 H. Mann (1841) *Common School Journal*, 3, 15, quoted in L. Cremin, *American Education: The National Experience 1783–1876*, New York, Harper and Row, p. 137.

10 For a discussion of the background events in the Oregon initiatives, see D. Tyack *et al.* (1986) *Law and the Shaping of Public Education, 1785–1954*, Madison, Wisc., University of Wisconsin Press, Ch. 7.

11 Interestingly, constitutional systems in other societies have accepted each of these polar positions. Compare B. Stenholm (1984) *The Swedish School System*, pp. 19–20 (most forms of private schooling prohibited) with S. Abramov (1979) *Perpetual Dilemma: Jewish Religion in the Jewish State*, Rutherford, N.J., Farleigh Dickenson Press (state funding provided to religious and ethnic groups to run separate education systems). See generally S. Sherman *Public Finance of Private Schools: Observations from Abroad* in T. James and H. Levin (Eds) (1983) *Public Dollars for Private Schools*, Philadelphia, Pa., Temple University Press, p. 71.

12 268 US at 534.

13 M. Yudof (1982) *When Government Speaks*, Berkeley, Calif., University of California Press, p. 230. See also *Abington School Dist. v. Schempp*, 374 US 203, 242 (1963) (Brennan, J. concurring) (First Amendment forbids restricting liberty of private schools to inculcate sectarian values or jeopardizing freedom of public schools to resist sectarian pressures).

14 For discussions of the origins of the separate Catholic school system in the city of New York, see D. Ravitch (1974) *The Great School Wars*, New York, Basic Books; and in California, see D. Tyack, *supra* note 10 at 90–91.

15 But see *Farrington v. Tokushige*, 273 US 284 (1927) (detailed regulatory scheme on foreign language schools operating in Hawaii declared unconstitutional).

16 A recent Gallup survey asked the following question: 'Suppose you could send your oldest child to a private school, tuition free, which would you prefer — to send him or her to a private school or a public school?' The response of present public school parents was: Private school 45%, Public school 47%, Don't know 8%. (1982) 'Gallup Poll of Public Attitude toward the Public Schools', *Phi Delta Kappan*, 64, September, p. 47. A follow–up poll the next year found 51% of a national total, including 48% of public school parents, favored an educational voucher system. (1983) *Phi Delta Kappan*, 65, September, p. 38.

17 In the past ten years, there has been a growing number of challenges to curriculum content, teacher certification, building code violations, and other aspects of the operations of fundamentalist academies and other religious private schools. See, e.g., *Fellowship Baptist Church v. Benton*, 815 F.2d 486 (8th Cir. 1987); *New Life Baptist Church Academy v. Town of East Longmeadow*, 666 F. Supp. 293 (D. Mass. 1987); *Kentucky State Bd. for Elementary and Secondary Educ. v. Rudasill*, 589 S.W.2d 877 (Ky. 1979).

18 For an insightful discussion of television and democratic education, see A. Gutmann, *Democratic Education*, Princeton, N.J., Princeton University Press, Ch. 8.

19 For a detailed discussion of why 'public schools as presently organized chill the traffic in ideas...[and why] the system is tuned to keep the message mellow', see J. Coons (1985) 'Intellectual Liberty and the Schools', *Notre Dame Journal of Law, Ethics & Public Policy* 1, pp. 515–16. It is also not

coincidental that the advent of large-scale standardized testing in the schools has coincided with these centralization trends and the concomitant de-emphasis on local curriculum and local values. See W. HANEY (1984) 'Testing Reasoning and Reasoning about Testing', *Review of Educational Research*, 54, p. 597.

20 The voucher concept, which would provide public tuition subsidies for students attending private schools, has a wide range of particular forms. The purpose of most of these proposals is to challenge the public schools' monopoly over education and to promote more initiative and creativity. For a summary of various voucher proposals, see M. REBELL (1982) 'Educational Voucher Reform: Empirical Insights from the Experience of New York's Schools for the Handicapped', *Urban Law*, 14, p. 441. For an overview of tuition tax credit plans, see T. JAMES and H. LEVIN (Eds) (1983) *Public Dollars for Private Schools: The Case of Tuition Tax Credits*, Philadelphia, Pa., Temple University Press.

21 See *supra* note 2.

22 See *supra* note 3.

23 See *supra* note 4.

24 647 F. Supp. 1194 (E.D. Tenn 1986), *rev'd sub nom. Mozert v. Hawkins County Bd. of Educ.*, 827 F.2d 1058 (6th Cir. 1987), *cert. denied*, 108 S. Ct. 1029 (1988).

25 647 F. Supp. at 1203.

26 Defendants strongly pressed the precedential implication point in *Mozert*. 647 F. Supp. at 1202. The trial court summarily rejected defendants' fears of pedagogic chaos by asserting that 'such a scenario seems unlikely to occur.' This cavalier stance ignores the realities of the broad impact of court decisions on educational value issues. See JENKINSON, E. (1987) 'The Significance of the Decision in Scopes II', *Phi Delta Kappan*, 68, p. 445. An opt out solution would be especially problematic in large urban settings with diverse student populations, where school officials may be faced with a 'myriad number of possible requests for religious accommodations concerning the curriculum.' Brief *Amicus Curiae* of the New York State School Boards Association at 17, *Mozert v. Hawkins County Public Schools*, 827 F.2d 1058 (6th Cir. 1987).

  Courts have in the past upheld state laws or regulations permitting students to opt out of mandatory 'family life' or sex education courses: see, e.g., *Smith v. Ricci*, 446 A.2d 501 (N.J. 1982); or physical education classes calling for 'immodest dress': see, e.g., *Moody v. Cronin*, 484 F. Supp. 270 (C.D. Ill. 1979). Since the subjects from which the religious students were excused in these cases were electives, or at least not core curricular instructional subjects, the integrity of the basic school curriculum was not at stake in these instances, as in *Mozert*.

27 *McCollum v. Board of Educ.*, 333 US 203, 235 (1948) (Jackson, J. concurring).

28 See discussion *infra* p. 10.

29 827 F.2d at 1064. Judge Lively's majority opinion held that exposure to objectionable ideas, without compulsion to affirm or act on them, is not constitutionally significant. This holding is not only inconsistent with most learning theory (see, e.g., R. DAWSON *et al.* (1977) *Political Socialization: An Analytical Study*, 2nd ed., Boston, Mass., Little Brown, but it is also belied

by the opinion's own admission that 'public schools serve the purpose of teaching fundamental values essential to a democratic society.' *Id.* at 1068.

30 Judge Kennedy's concurring opinion, which discussed at some length the reasons why the 'opt out' remedy was unworkable and how the State had a 'compelling interest' in inculcating a uniform set of values and a uniform pedagogic approach, provided a stronger basis for reversing the district court's ruling. In any event, from a *Pierce* perspective, 'the extent to which school systems may constitutionally require students to use educational materials that are objectionable, contrary to, or forbidden by their religious beliefs is a serious and important issue.' *Id.* at 1074 (Boggs, J. concurring). Judge Boggs also disagreed with the majority's holding on the free exercise issue, but concurred in the result because he believed that under existing Supreme Court doctrine, school boards are given wide latitude on curriculum matters and that any 'significant change in school law and expansion in the religious liberties of pupils and parents should come only from the Supreme Court itself, and not simply from our interpretation.' *Id.* at 1081.

31 655 F. Supp. 939 (S.D. Ala. 1987), *rev'd* 827 F. 2d 684 (11th Cir. 1987).

32 655 F. Supp. at 988.

33 The court held that the Supreme Court has never established a test for defining 'religious belief' for First Amendment purposes. It determined that it need not reach this issue in this case because the immediate matters could be decided on the 'primary effect' grounds discussed in the text. Cf. Note (1986) 'Secular Humanism, The Establishment Clause and Public Education', *New York University Law Review*, 61, p. 1149 (arguing that courts should not decide whether secular humanism is a religion).

34 827 F.2d at 690.

35 655 F. Supp. at 948. The extensive interest in the *Mozert* and *Smith* cases, evidenced by the fact that thirty-three separate briefs *amicus curiae* were filed with the Eleventh Circuit in the later case, is reflective of the significance and profundity of the value clash.

36 See *supra* note 2.

37 The Supreme Court had previously noted, but not explicated, the value inculcating role of the schools. See, e.g., *Ambach v. Norwick*, 441 US 68, 76–77 (1979); *Board of Educ., Island Trees Union Free School Dist. v. Pico*, 457 US 853, 864 (1982) (plurality opinion) ('there is a legitimate and substantial community interest in promoting respect for authority and traditional values, be they social, moral or political'); *Plyler v. Doe,* 457 US 202, 221 (1982) ('the pivotal role of education in sustaining our political and cultural heritage'); *Brown v. Board of Educ.,* 457 US 483, 493 ('[Education] is the very foundation of good citizenship. Today it is a principal instrument in awakening the child to cultural values...').

38 Eight of the nine justices — all but Justice Marshall — agreed, despite several separate opinions, on the basic issue of a school district's right to preclude 'lewd' speech from school assemblies. Compare *Board of Educ., Island Trees Union Free School Dist. v. Pico, supra* note 37 (school board authority to remove books from school library with seven separate opinions being issued); *New Jersey v. T.L.O.,* 105 S.Ct. 733 (1985) (school system's right to conduct reasonable searches upheld by 6–3 majority); *Goss v. Lopez,* 419 US 565 (1975) (student's right to fair notice and hearing prior to suspension upheld

by 5–4 majority); *Ingraham v. Wright*, 430 US 651 (1977) (school system's right to impose corporal punishment upheld by 5–4 majority).

39 'A school must also retain the authority to refuse to sponsor student speech that might reasonably be perceived to advocate drug or alcohol use, irresponsible sex, or conduct otherwise inconsistent with the "shared values of a civilized social order".' *Hazelwood*, 108 S. Ct. at 570 (quoting *Fraser*, 106 S. Ct. at 3165). Justice Brennan's dissent in *Hazelwood* was partially based on his view that the *Fraser* precedent was being misapplied in extending it to permit censorship of school publications. *Id.* at 576–77.

40 The Ninth Circuit had viewed *Fraser* as fundamentally a case involving application of the First Amendment free speech doctrine of *Tinker v. Des Moines Independent School District*, 393 US 503 (1969), the famous Vietnam War protest case. Applying *Tinker's* 'material disruption' standard, the Ninth Circuit did not consider evidence of some 'hooting and yelling' in response to Fraser's lewd remarks, and even some simulated sexual movements, factors 'material enough' to warrant interference with the exercise of the student's First Amendment freedoms.

41 755 F.2d at 1363.

42 For an insightful discussion of sociological attempts to distinguish a 'lower-class' culture from a 'middle-class' culture, see D. RAVITCH (1983) *The Troubled Crusade: American Education 1945–1980*, New York, Basic Books, pp. 156–7.

43 106 S. Ct. at 3164–65.

44 Chief Justice Burger concluded that:

> A high school assembly or classroom is no place for a sexually explicit monologue directed towards an unsuspecting audience of teenage students. Accordingly, it was perfectly appropriate for the school to disassociate itself to make the point to the pupils that vulgar speech and lewd conduct is wholly inconsistent with the 'fundamental values' of public school education.

Id. at 3166. Chief Justice Burger believed that the verbal content of speech here was 'acutely insulting to teenage girls', and that it 'could well be seriously damaging to its less mature audience, many of whom were only 14 years old and on the threshold of awareness of human sexuality.' *Id.* at 3165. Justice Brennan, in his concurring opinion, took less umbrage at the speech and stated that 'there is no evidence in the record that any students, male or female, found the speech "insulting".' *Id.* at 3168 n.2. Whichever Justice's view of the level of sophistication or exposure to lewd language of 14-year-olds in the State of Washington is correct, the important point for present purposes is that both Chief Justice Burger and Justice Brennan upheld the discretion of the school authorities to inculcate civility values.

45 The Court explicitly distinguished between the political message of the anti-war protest arm bands in *Tinker v. Des Moines Independent School District, supra* note 41, and the sexual content of the speech at issue here. 106 S. Ct. at 3166. See also *Hazelwood, supra* note 41 at 569. Cf. BLASI, V. (1985) 'The Pathological Perspective and the First Amendment', *Columbia Law Review*, 85, p. 449 (arguing for judicial recognition of special factors influencing constitutional issues during certain historical periods).

46 Judicial intervention in education cases has been a topic of substantial controversy in the legal literature. For an overview of the arguments concerning 'judicial activism' in this context, as well as empirical data on the impact of court intervention in school affairs, M. REBELL and A. BLOCK (1982) *Educational Policy Making and the Courts*, Chicago, Ill., University of Chicago Press. It is significant that even the more conservatively oriented Supreme Court of recent years has maintained an activist role in education cases. This may be because the same modernizing trends and pressures which have created a values formulation void and complicated the schools' socialization function have also led parents and students to bring values oriented issues before the Courts for authoritative, principled resolution. See M. REBELL (1982) 'Judicial Activism and the Court's New Role', *Social Policy*, 25, Spring; L. FRIEDMAN (1985) *Total Justice*, New York, Russell Sage Foundation; J. LIEBERMAN (1981) *The Litigious Society*, New York, Basic Books; G. CLARK (1985) *Judges and the Cities*, Chicago, Ill., University of Chicago Press.

47 347 US 483 (1954).

48 See *Abington School Dist. v. Schempp*, 374 US 203 (1963); *Engel v. Vitale*, 370 US 421 (1962).

49 The attempt by a local school board to remove certain controversial books from the school library, considered recently by the Supreme Court in *Board of Education v. Pico, supra* note 37, illustrates these difficulties. Justice Brennan's plurality opinion in *Pico* recognized a fundamental distinction between competing types of values similar to the national/local value categorization being advocated here. See 457 US at 870–871. He held that if the school authorities removed the library books because of partisan political motives, 'national values' of interference with free speech would be raised and court intervention would be warranted. On the other hand, if the books were removed for reasons related to curriculum content or offensiveness to local mores, then local community values, with which the federal courts should not interfere, would be at issue. The case was remanded to the lower courts to consider these issues. In *Hazelwood, supra* note 4, a majority of the Court ruled, in essence, that local community values on issues of teenage pregnancy and divorce could be enforced by regulation of articles in student publications.

50 In a recent poll, a vast majority (79%) of the American public said they favor moral education of children in the public schools. GALLUP (1980) 'The 12th Annual Gallup Poll of the Public's Attitudes towards the Public Schools', *Phi Delta Kappan*, 62, p. 39. For arguments for the need to promote meaningful dialogues on values issues from both a liberal and a conservative direction, see B. BARBER (1984) *Strong Democracy*, Berkeley, Calif., University of California Press; and G. WILL (1983) *Statecraft as Soulcraft*, New York, Simon and Schuster.

51 Admittedly, the perspective set forth in the text may be describing a model of communal cohesiveness that is, in reality, not fully attainable. Other analysts of *Pierce's* contemporary challenge have argued for wide-ranging voucher schemes, seemingly without regard for their impact on overall communal values. See e.g., S. ARONS (1983) *Compelling Belief*, New York, McGraw Hill. This call amounts to a position of values anarchy that has

grave implications for the future of American democracy. Another approach advocates a voucher scheme that would allow each group to strengthen its particular values. J. COONS and S. SUGARMAN (1978) *Education by Choice: The Case for Family Control*, Berkeley, University of California Press pp. 91–108. That engaging prospect is, however, even less likely than the community dialogue approach advocated in the text. Given the implausibility of attaining any of the ideal goals, perhaps the real question is which model is likely to promote the greatest degree of actual value cohesion in practice. Even if imperfectly realized, the public school revitalization approach is likely to move us further toward a values consensus than the pure voucher model, since the latter's basic methodology is to foster fragmentation.

52 827 F.2d at 1074 (Boggs, J. concurring).

53 See Letter to the editor from MARGARET G. KLEIN, *New York Times*, 20 September, 1987, Section E, at 26, col. 3.

54 Note, of course, that the named plaintiffs in *Pierce* were the private schools whose financial needs apparently were being met by privately paid tuitions or church subsidies, rather than the individual parents or students.

55 One recent analysis of the *Mozert* case argued that public schools should 'respond to the new textbook litigation by seeking to make the curriculum more fair to the convictions of millions of American parents who are religiously conservative' by implementing a 'more truly comprehensive curriculum'. C. GLENN (1987) 'Religion, Textbooks and the Common School', *Public Interest*, 88, 28, p. 46. The argument in the text assumes that although a broader consensus on value issues can be achieved in local communities, a dissenting minority will inevitably remain outside the widened mainstream. To the extent that the majoritarian values consensus is strengthened, the need for a viable escape valve for this minority becomes even more compelling.

56 See *supra* note 16.

57 According to the 1980 Gallup poll, *supra* note 51, only 5% of present public school parents favoring a private school option did so for 'religious/moral reasons'. The overwhelming motivations for preferring private schools were higher standards of education: 28%; better discipline: 27%; and more individual attention: 21%.

58 See e.g., M. FRIEDMAN (1962) *Capitalism and Freedom*, Chicago, Ill., University of Chicago Press.

59 Others who have argued for a reconsideration of *Pierce's* failure to provide private school tuition subsidies have avoided this constitutional problem by focusing on the educational needs of minority groups and political dissenters, rather than religious dissenters. See S. ARONS (1976) 'The Separation of Church and State: Pierce Reconsidered', *Harvard Education Review*, 46, 76 (arguing that free speech guarantees of the First Amendment entitle those rejecting majoritarian values to private school funding). This approach, even if constitutionally viable, does not, however, confront the practical need to limit the numbers involved in a *Pierce* voucher scheme and would undermine the public school socialization function being advocated herein.

60 *Lemon v. Kurtzman*, 403 US 602 (1971).

61 *Levitt v. Committee for Pub. Educ. and Religious Liberty*, 413 US 472 (1973).

62 *Meek v. Pittenger*, 421 US 349 (1975).

63 *Everson v. Board of Educ.,* 330 US 1 (1947).

64 *Board of Educ. v. Allen,* 392 US 236 (1968).

65 463 US 388 (1983).

66 *Committee for Pub. Educ. v. Nyquist,* 413 US 756 (1973). Former Chief Justice Burger's dissent in Nyquist, joined by the present Chief Justice Rehnquist and Justice White, explicitly advocated an individual subsidy doctrine: 'the Establishment Clause does not forbid governments, state or federal, to enact a program of general welfare under which benefits are distributed to private individuals, even though many of those individuals may elect to use those benefits in ways that "aid religious instruction or worship".' *Id.* at 799.

67 Indeed, this fact was pressed by the petitioners in *Mueller,* who presented a statistical analysis of those who actually claimed the tax deduction. The Court, however, refused to engage in 'the type of empirical inquiry into those persons benefited by state law which petitioners urge.' 463 US at 402.

68 See 463 US at 402 ('parochial schools, quite apart from their sectarian purpose, have provided an educational alternative for millions of young Americans; they often afford wholesale competition with our public schools; and in some States they relieve substantially the tax burden incident to the operation of public schools').

69 It is noteworthy that all but one of our recent cases invalidating state aid to parochial schools have involved the direct transmission of assistance from the State to the schools themselves. The exception, of course, was *Nyquist,* which, as discussed previously, is distinguishable from this case on other grounds. Where, as here, aid to parochial schools is available only as a result of decisions of individual parents no 'imprimatur of state approval,' *Widmar, supra,* at 274, can be deemed to have been conferred on any particular religion, or on religion generally. 463 US at 399.

70 The unconvincing public/private tuition holding may well have been adopted to obtain the swing vote of Justice Powell for the slim 5–4 *Mueller* majority. Justice Powell authored the *Nyquist* opinion and at one point indicated that a tuition tax subsidy applicable to both public and private school students might be acceptable to him. See 413 US at 782, n. 38.

71 The First Amendment provides, in relevant part, that 'Congress shall make no law respecting an establishment of religion, or prohibiting the free exercise thereof....' First Amendment doctrine involves an inherent tension between the two clauses since satisfaction of one raises spectres of violating the other. See *Tilton v. Richardson,* 403 US 672, 677 (1973); L. TRIBE (1988) *American Constitutional Law,* 2nd ed., Mineola, N.Y., Foundation Press, Ch. 14. The proposal in the text could satisfy both elements.

72 See, e.g. *Sherbert v. Verner,* 374 US 398 (1963) (denial of unemployment compensation benefits to Seventh Day Adventist who refused to seek work on Saturdays held to violate her right to free exercise of her religion); see also *Hobbie v. Unemployment Appeals Comm'n,* 107 S. Ct. 1046 (1987) (same); *Thomas v. Review Bd.,* 450 US 707 (1981) (denial of unemployment benefits to Jehovah's Witness who voluntarily quit job because of pacifist religious beliefs held to violate free exercise rights).

73 See, e.g., *Bowen v. Roy,* 106 S. Ct. 2147 (1986) (welfare applicants required to obtain social security number despite claimed violation of religious beliefs);

Hamilton v. Regents of Univ. of Cal., 293 US 245 (1934) (university students required to take military courses despite claimed violation of religious beliefs). Cf. *Spence v. Bailey*, 465 F.2d 797 (6th Cir. 1972) (denial of high school diploma to student who refused to participate in ROTC program on religious grounds invalidated).

74 *Bowen, supra* note 73, at 2155.

75 406 US 205 (1972).

76 The Sixth Circuit emphasized these limits in its *Mozert* opinion, noting that the case rested on a singular set of facts. See 827 F.2d at 1067.

77 In *Norwood v. Harrison*, 413 US 455, 462 (1973), a case involving claims for public subsidies of segregationist academies, the Court explained the *Pierce* decision as affirming the right of private schools to exist but not to 'share with public schools in state largesse.' See also *Maher v. Roe*, 432 US 464, 477 (1977) ('*Pierce* casts no shadow over a State's power to favor public education by funding it').

78 See, e.g., *Lynch v. Donnelly*, 465 US 668 (1984) (government sponsored nativity displays held constitutional); *Marsh v. Chambers*, 463 US 783 (1983) (practice of permitting paid chaplains to lead state legislatures in prayer upheld). Compare *Grand Rapids School Dist. v. Ball*, 473 US 402 (1985) (public funding for remedial educational programs for disadvantaged students held on parochial school premises invalidated).

79 There are indications that the courts would be amenable to such a broadened consensus. See, e.g., *Wallace v. Jaffree*, 472 US 38, 67 (1985) (O'Connor, J. concurring) (moment of silent prayer statutes not 'entirely motivated by a religious purpose' likely to be held constitutional); *Stein v. Plainwell Community Schools*, 822 F.2d 1406 (6th Cir. 1987) (nonsectarian benedictions held permissible at high school commencement ceremonies); *Florey v. Sioux Falls School Dist. 49–5*, 619 F.2d 1311 (8th Cir. 1980) (singing of Christmas carols in schools consistent with guidelines drawn up by nondenominational committee held constitutional); *Grove v. Mead School Dist. No. 354*, 752 F.2d 1528, 1536 (9th Cir. 1985) (Canby, J. concurring) (arguing against tendency to divide the universe of value-laden thought into only two categories — the religious and the anti-religious); K. GREENAWALT (1985) 'Religious Conviction and Law Making', *Michigan Law Review*, 84, p. 352 (attempt to distinguish proper reliance on religious considerations in democratic decision-making); D. LAYCOCK (1986) 'Equal Access and Moments of Silence: The Equal Status of Religious Speech by Private Speakers', *Northwestern University Law Review*, 81, p. 1 (arguing for broad interpretation of 'neutrality' for religious speech in open forums created in public schools). See also *Note* (1976) 'Civil Religion and the Establishment Clause', *Yale Law Journal*, 75, p. 1237.

80 406 US at 215.

81 See, e.g., *United States v. Seeger*, 380 US 163, 188 (1965) (Douglas, J. concurring) (free exercise clause requires broad definition of 'religious'); L. TRIBE *American Constitutional Law, op. cit.,* § 14–6; Note (1978) 'Toward a Constitutional Definition of Religion', *Harvard Law Review*, 91, pp. 1072–5 (arguing for a definition of religion covering any individual belief system involving matters of ultimate concern).

82 At a later stage, after experience with the program has revealed the number

of dissenters who would qualify under a broad definition of religious belief, further consideration could be given to the need and the impact of extending eligibility for *Pierce* vouchers to 'secular' dissenters.

83 A similar procedure for implementing an 'Amish exemption' from Iowa's compulsory education law was recently discussed in *Fellowship Baptist Church v. Benton*, 815 F.2d 485, 496 (8th Cir. 1987). If the *Yoder* doctrine is extended to include religious and/or values dissenters beyond the Amish, ipso facto, so should the procedures for defining *Yoder* eligibility. See also *Seeger, supra* note 81 (administrative hearing procedure for determining sincerity of conscientious objectors to military conscription).

84 See, e.g., *Bob Jones Univ. v. United States*, 461 US 574 (1983) (educational institutions practicing racial discrimination denied tax exemption).

85 In order to claim the entitlement to a private school tuition subsidy, students should also be required to show that all educational options within the public school system, not only those in the neighborhood school, would substantially interfere with their deeply held values. To the extent that a large public school system might offer options and alternatives within its bounds, the right to private schooling alternatives would be further constricted.

4
Educational Choice as a Civil Rights Strategy

Stephen Arons

Decisions of the United States Supreme Court during the past ten years have rendered the equal protection clause of the Fourteenth Amendment nearly useless for remedying school segregation in America. As a consequence, many middle-class whites have been able simultaneously to pursue quality education for their children and to tolerate, even take advantage of, housing and job discrimination in the suburbs. The Court's crabbed interpretation of the equal protection clause has made it possible for many American families to act this way without fear of legal recognition of, or metropolitan remedies for, the discriminatory consequences of their choices.

Outside the South, and especially in urban/suburban areas, American public schools in the 1980s have remained segregated, with Hispanics increasingly becoming the victims of an absence of equal educational opportunities.[1] With the failure of traditional desegregation tactics, the movement for educational choice may present a useful political and legal strategy for equalizing the availability of quality education regardless of race or wealth.

This chapter will evaluate some premises of the movement for increased school choice, especially the argument that such choices are First Amendment rights of expression and belief, to see whether a viable civil rights strategy may be contained in an idea traditionally associated with perpetuating racism in schooling. Racism is so thoroughly institutionalized in American culture, in spite of our best intentions, that it is not possible to reach a compelling answer to the question on the basis of legal analysis or political speculation alone. But the argument that an equality of school choice would increase the power of minority and poor families significantly does seem strong enough to suggest that civil rights advocates ought not dismiss school choice out of hand as a segregationist strategy. It may be that choice and racial equality can find common ground in carefully designed and monitored settings.

Since the early 1970s, when the federal Office of Economic Opportunity first seriously considered the idea of education vouchers, some advocates of choice have tried to design programs consistent with civil rights law and appealing to a skeptical civil rights community.[2] Two changes since then warrant re-examining choice as a strategy for reducing school racism. First, the Supreme Court has introduced into equal protection jurisprudence the idea that unless racial motivation or intent can be proven to have caused segregation, the courts may neither find a constitutional violation nor impose a legal remedy for plainly segregated conditions.[3] As the equal protection clause began to die in this area, civil rights advocates were deprived of their most powerful tool — one that an entire generation had sharpened sufficiently to yield the unanimous decision in *Brown*.

Second, other schooling conflicts have focused on issues of value socialization.[4] At the same time that segregated schools have been showing themselves unresponsive to the culture and concerns of African-American, Hispanic, and Asian families,[5] other families have insisted that their values be reflected in their children's schools. Books have been banned from high school libraries and fought over in statewide textbook commission hearings and federal courts because of their value content.[6] Home education has been restricted and private schools regulated or persecuted because they did not reflect majority values in their curricula.[7] Powerful legislative efforts have been made to elevate creationism to a science and to impede the teaching of evolution because it contradicts Christian fundamentalist beliefs.[8] Outside desegregation efforts, the common theme of school wars in this decade has become the preservation of religious, subcultural, and family heritage in the face of a school bureaucracy structurally unable to respect pluralism.

Taken together, the closing of one frontier of school litigation and politics and the opening of another suggest that it is appropriate to ask whether a little judo applied to the force of school choice might not yield a result beneficial to those frustrated by the impotence of equal protection arguments. In exploring this issue, it will be necessary to keep in mind that the process has generally worked in reverse. Historically, most gains in liberty for whites have come at the expense of African-Americans; and gains for minorities have often depended upon whites being able to gain still more from any proffered social change.[9] A healthy dose of skepticism should be taken internally before reading further.

The starting point must be a brief review of the way in which the Supreme Court has rendered the equal protection clause moribund in matters of race. The idea that 'proof of racially discriminatory intent or purpose is required to show a violation of the equal protection clause'[10] first appeared in the school context in *Keyes v. School District No. 1 Denver* in 1973.[11] In the process of granting the plaintiffs relief in Denver's massively segregated system, the Court articulated the so-called 'intent requirement' as part of a distinction between de jure and de facto segregation. By 1976 the standard found its first full-blown expression in the notorious employment discrimination case of *Washington v. Davis*,[12] in which the Court refused to find an equal protection violation in the segregated employment allegedly produced and maintained by a facially neutral test of verbal and written abilities. The Court reached its conclusion in spite of the fact that the civil service test in question was not clearly related to job performance for the Washington, D.C. police department promotions at issue, and in spite of the fact that four times as many blacks as whites failed this non–job-related exam. In the Court's view, the plainly discriminatory impact of the test was insufficient evidence in the absence of direct proof that its use by the Civil Service Commission was *intended* to produce these foreseeably segregative results. One key to the Court's reasoning in *Davis* and to the embedding of the intent requirement in equal protection clause cases since 1976 is the Court's fear that the alternative 'racial impact' test would operate to invalidate 'a whole range of tax, welfare, public service, regulatory and licensing statutes.'[13] To put the matter more honestly than the majority of the justices were willing to do, the creation of the intent requirement puts most institutional racism out of the reach of the Fourteenth Amendment.

At present, the intent requirement operates not only to make constitutionally adequate proof of plainly segregated schooling next to impossible to produce, but also to make metropolitan school desegregation remedies as rare as hen's teeth. Although a few metropolitan remedies have been approved,[14] plaintiffs must generally demonstrate racist intent *across* district lines in order to gain that approval,[15] and even then remedies will only be available to correct the segregation caused by the intent proved. These developments have slowed the move toward integrated education to a near standstill,[16] and have reinvigorated the idea that if schools are to remain racially separate, they ought at least to be made qualitatively equal.[17] There is power and ethical validity in the claim that minority children do not need to be physically mixed with white children in order to excel in school,[18] and that coercive integration may be as stigmatizing of minorities now as coercive segregation has been for the past century.[19] But the fact remains that the intent requirement has been a significant obstacle to minority families seeking integrated education, and has been of virtually no help to those seeking the material resources and political clout necessary to create quality education in the schools to which they are assigned.

The intent requirement has been the subject of vigorous attack by scholars and practitioners.[20] But given the increasingly conservative cast of the Court, these attacks are not likely to have much effect other than prodding the supporters of the doctrine to become more articulate, and further entrenching in the public mind the anachronistic idea that the absence of identifiable individual racial bigots means that segregation no longer exists in America. Racial violence in Howard Beach, New York, in the FBI, or at the University of Massachusetts at Amherst is condemned by virtually all Americans. But massive dropout and pushout rates among minority students and the failure of public schools to provide quality education to the children of poor families seem to be regarded simply as inconvenient blips on the public policy screen by all but the victims of institutional racism.

One scholar has attempted to deal forthrightly and creatively with the intent requirement by interpreting it consistently with modern psychology and cultural knowledge of human motivation. In a creative effort to bring the law into the twentieth century, Charles Lawrence III has argued that the only real problem with the intent requirement is that the Court has restricted its use to matters of conscious intent. Modernizing the legal understanding of motive in accordance with Freudian and other psychologies of the unconscious, Lawrence argues in 'The Id, the Ego, and Equal Protection: Reckoning with Unconscious Racism',[21] that if we pay attention to the cultural meaning of allegedly segregatory acts, the false dichotomy of intent and impact will dissolve, and equal protection jurisprudence will be able effectively to distinguish between those kinds of segregation that ought to be remedied and those that are rightfully beyond the reach of the Fourteenth Amendment. In the process, a pursuit of an increased quality of life for all (including in schooling) may replace the fixation on individual responsibility for racism and the sometimes counterproductive consequences and 'seductive power'[22] of the ideology of formal equal opportunity.

The very pragmatic transformation of world views that Lawrence urges upon Court and culture may come to pass eventually. But in the meantime, those who understand that racism is the most odious cultural inheritance of the American past and the most corrosive policy problem of the American present may want to examine other possible avenues for ending discrimination in schooling. We therefore turn to the issue of educational choice, its roots in the First Amendment, its history as a segregationist tactic, and its potential as a civil rights strategy.

First Amendment Principles and the Right of School Choice

An understanding of the legal and educational significance of family choice in schooling must begin with the simple fact that, according to the Supreme Court, no state has the power to require that a child attend a government school.[23] The state may require children to be educated or to attend school of some kind, but the Constitution preserves the parental prerogative of determining *how* a child shall be taught.

The same Constitution that forbids a government school monopoly also has been read to grant the state the power to make regulations affecting the various schools a parent may choose in satisfaction of a legitimate compulsory schooling statute. But considerable debate exists about the range of this power to regulate. There is also disagreement about whether the entitlement to choose a nongovernment school arises from individual substantive due process rights, the right of privacy, the First Amendment protection of conscience, or from an absence of government power. At the center of these controversies over the right to choose an alternative to government schooling lies one issue: what is the significance to individuals, family, and society of the right of educational choice?

The original holding in *Pierce* that 'the fundamental theory of liberty upon which all governments in this Union repose excludes any general power of the state to standardize its children by forcing them to accept instruction from public teachers only'[24] has been reaffirmed many times since it was handed down in 1925. Although the debate persists on its proper interpretation,[25] the ruling generally is understood as denying the state the power to dominate the socialization of children in school.[26] This school socialization, or value inculcation, is an important process by which the beliefs, values, and world view of the child are formed and reinforced. Whatever may be the importance of teaching such measurable skills as reading or computation, *Pierce* makes clear that the formation of character and beliefs that inevitably accompanies skill teaching must be left primarily to the influence of the family. 'The child', the Court held, 'is not the mere creature of the state.'

The *Pierce* Court's concern for value socialization in schools, and the value conflicts that since then have been brought yearly before the courts or injected into the political system, demonstrate the high stakes in the allocation of power over schooling. Individual conscience, the communication and transmission of culture, the formation of religious and secular beliefs, the maintenance of pluralism, the dignity of the individual, the health of the political system, and the protection of the process by which communities create and define cohesion all must be balanced when allocating power over school socialization. The First Amendment provides perhaps the most comprehensive and powerful tool for understanding the value socialization issue and for determining how a constitutional allocation of power should be arranged in the nation's school system.[27]

A First Amendment analysis of the power over value socialization also reflects the reality of schooling conflicts. Whatever may be their values, most parents and educators recognize that schooling is a part of child-rearing, that school is a social environment in which a child learns much more than is in the formal curriculum. In spite of the occasional claim that schooling can be a value-neutral marketplace of ideas, the reality is otherwise. Schooling is a major influence in the molding of children's consciousness, their conception of reality, their perception of and reaction to all things. The basic beliefs that eventually become part of individual conscience are formed in part at school. To leave significant power over the formation of conscience in the hands of a political majority governing state schools would be to sacrifice the dignity of the individual to a totalitarian conception of society.[28]

The Court's 1925 recognition of the primacy of family in conscience formation extends John Stuart Mill's 1859 statement that state-sponsored education 'is a mere contrivance for moulding people to be exactly like one another' that 'establishes a despotism over the mind.'[29] It also prefigures the 1946 statement in the United Nations Universal Declaration of Human Rights that 'parents have a prior right to choose the kind of education that shall be given to their children.'[30] If the individual is to retain any measure of dignity and autonomy in a complex and institutionalized society, substantial coercion in the formation of conscience must be denied the political majority, even in as apparently benevolent an institution as schooling.

The state's preclusion from prescribing the content of individual conscience in its formative stages is already in place as the primary regulator of the relationship between church and state.[31] This doctrine of state neutrality ought to apply to the formation of secular beliefs, just as it does to religious beliefs. When the religion clauses of the First Amendment were written, the great issues of conscience and meaning in life were fought under religious banners. Now that society — and schooling — is more secular, interpreting the First Amendment as a protector of belief formation in secular as well as religious matters has become necessary. To fail to modernize our understanding of the First Amendment would be to leave most conscience formation unprotected from the coercive encroachments of majoritarian politics.

A partial recognition of the importance of state neutrality toward secular value content has been achieved in the freedom of expression cases arising in public schools.[32] What has not been recognized is that belief *formation* is as important as belief *expression* in the inevitably value-laden context of schooling. Once the Court forthrightly re-examines the artificial distinctions between the rights of belief expression and formation, between skill teaching and value inculcation, and between secular and religious schooling, the unity of the five First Amendment clauses can be acknowledged.[33] It will then be clear that in school as in society the First Amendment can be an important protection for individual conscience whether religiously or secularly based. More important, the analogy between secular schooling and religious freedom can move us toward establishing a separation of school and state to parallel the separation of church and state.

If family choice of schooling is important to preserving the individual freedom of belief and conscience embedded in the First Amendment, it is no less important to the transmission of culture from one generation to the next. From this point of view, schooling may be understood as a process of communication between the culture and the individual, a process by which a pluralism of heritages is passed on to and modified by the rising generation. This is also an important part of the process by which the common heritage and shared values of American society are formed and communicated with the input of all citizens. Where there are differences among the values and traditions of American subcultures, and where compromise and community building are, for whatever reason, not possible, conflict arises. Under these circumstances, a majoritarian structure of schooling will require a destructive, zero-sum struggle among subcultures as to whose beliefs will determine the value content of school socialization.[34] Many of the recent struggles over school curriculum and texts can be read as just these kinds of conflicts. *Pierce* is itself such an example, for there a xenophobic and anti-Catholic political majority had legislated nongovernment schools out of existence in the name of 'Americanization' of immigrants and all those who were not white, Anglo-Saxon and Protestant. When the Supreme Court struck down this Oregon statute, it was, in essence, affording the communication of culture the same constitutional protections as other forms of communication receive.

The application of the comprehensive rights of freedom of expression to the system of public schooling is clearly seen in the 1943 case of *West Virginia v. Barnette*.[35] There the Court ruled that a compulsory pledge of allegiance and flag salute, even at the height of the fascist threat during World War II, invaded the plaintiff's 'sphere of intellect and spirit' protected by the First Amendment. Compulsory education, the Court ruled, must be neutral on such basic belief issues as patriotism, and may not in general create a 'compulsion of students to declare a belief.'[36] The government school had controlled not only the content of its own communication of culture to students, but also the content of the students' overt response, requiring a confession of belief from each.

In less obvious but more insidious ways, such requirements dominate the lives of school children today.[37] Not only does the hidden curriculum of role models, classroom structure, authority patterns, and student status pressure students to adopt identifiable beliefs that may be contrary to those of their families and subcultures, but constant testing, grading, and grade promotions amount to content control of communication, and often require that students adopt majority beliefs in order to succeed in school.[38]

That *Pierce* may be read as articulating a First Amendment principle of protecting the unencumbered communication of individual and subcultural values is reinforced by the Court's words in *Barnette*. Striking down the flag salute was very much like striking down the Oregon public-school-only law, especially when the *Barnette* Court considered the consequences of an opposite ruling:

> Free public education, if faithful to the idea of secular instruction and political neutrality, will not be partisan or enemy of any class, creed, party or faction. If it is to impose any ideological discipline, however, each party or denomination must seek to control, or failing that, to weaken the influence of the education system.[39]

The Court's opinion was not only an accurate statement of the kind of politics that had led to the Oregon law in 1922 and the West Virginia practice in 1943; it was a chilling prediction of the battles over control of school content and influence now being waged around the country.

The Court's constitutional conception of the value-neutrality required to avoid pitched battles over irresolvable issues of conscience was not satisfied merely by providing an 'escape hatch' for families seeking an alternative to the government school.[40] The *Barnette* ruling reversed the 1939 *Gobitis* case,[41] in which Justice Frankfurter upheld the flag salute and pledge on the grounds that *Pierce* guaranteed the right of dissenters to escape to a nongovernment school. Justice Frankfurter's argument that society 'may in self-protection utilize the educational process for inculcating those almost unconscious feelings which bind men together in a comprehending loyalty'[42] was thus rejected in favor of reaffirming a set of positive family rights of belief and expression and of communication of culture, to be vindicated within public schools by prohibiting an establishment of orthodoxy, as well as by securing the choice of attending private schools. As in matters of religious establishment within the public schools, the existence of an alternative to the government school did not satisfy the Constitution's requirements. Were it sufficient to regard the *Pierce* rights as no more than a guarantee of a hypothetical and reasonably regulated alternative to the government school, *Barnette* would not have invalidated the compulsory flag salute, nor would the Court have written,

> Probably no deeper division of our people could proceed from any provocation than from finding it necessary to choose what doctrine and whose program public educational officials shall compel youth to unite in embracing. Ultimate futility of such attempts to compel coherence is the lesson of every such effort.[43]

The consequences of denying to families the primary influence over value socialization in schools are not limited to matters of individual freedom and dignity or to the communicative rights of subcultures in a pluralistic society. Of equal and perhaps greater importance is the preservation of the process by which disparate individuals and groups arrive at compromise and consensus in the formation of our common culture. The principles of *Pierce*, of *Barnette*, and of the First Amendment in general should be read as protecting the group process of community-building, not only in the political arena but in schooling as well. In fact, in schooling the absence of equal and effective choice for families works against the very cohesion that restrictions on choice are meant to foster.

The *Barnette* Court pointed a prophetic finger at the kind of corrosive conflict that would result from the attempt to 'compel coherence' through value inculcation in majoritarian public schools. Cases in the past fifteen years have shown how divisive and unresolvable these conflicts can be.[44] But it remains clear that the constructive resolution of value conflicts in public schools is often possible and seldom reported. The dissonance between home and family that characterizes much schooling can proceed — through compromise, mediation, and reorientation of the parties, and through the formulation of inclusive rather than exclusive settlements — to a constructive resolution that builds common values and shared community standards.[45] But the sine qua non of such community building is every family's knowledge that if they are not satisfied with the substance of the compromises offered, they have the *equal right and ability* to send their children to another school more suitable in the family's judgment.

Without equal financial ability to exercise the *Pierce* right, a family is disempowered *within* the public school debate over value formation and community building. Having one's beliefs and values taken seriously becomes difficult and perhaps impossible within the school or district because dissenting families have no real choice but to accept what is imposed on them by the majoritarian process in which they are, perhaps, invited to participate. It is a short journey from the inability to choose another school to this lack of power within the public school. It is a shorter journey still from disempowerment to apathy and despair over schooling and family integrity.

For minority families, this disempowerment is harsher in its consequences simply because the values of those in the minority are seldom accommodated by the majority. Because of the imbalance of power resulting from inequality of choice — and because of the zero-sum nature of conflict in a majoritarian institution — the majority almost always succeeds in imposing its values upon dissenters within the public school system. This is the clear message of most conflicts over textbook content, curriculum, and even disciplinary policies. To argue, as some have, that a nongovernment school is unlikely to respect and reflect the values of minority families because minority families are not part of the nongovernment school constituency is to ignore the reality of public school policy-making. As long as minority families find themselves with unequal bargaining power and no school choice, majoritarian public school systems will continue to impose the ideology of the majority (or those in control in the majority's name) upon dissenters. Schooling — whether government or nongovernment in sponsorship — will become truly public only when choice and bargaining power are truly equal among all families.

The relationship of equal school choice to consensus building within schools can be seen more clearly with reference to the elements of mediation. It is a long-observed and easily reaffirmed truth that in any mediative process that seeks common ground rather than polarization, the parties to a conflict must be of roughly equal power and must voluntarily accept any conflict resolution they may craft. In the absence of these two factors, either there will be no settlement possible or the negotiated agreement will reflect the flaws in the process and be rendered useless. This is no less true in schooling, especially where basic values and matters of conscience are at stake. If the requisite voluntariness and rough equality of power are absent, the conflict easily can become destructive (as the Supreme Court saw in *Barnette*) or the resolution can become a repressive one reflecting the majority's power and the minority's lack of power, an outcome acceptable in the political realm but not in matters of conscience, belief, and expression. Under these circumstances, the dissenting family's First Amendment interests are destroyed, and the process of community building does not take place. For a real community of shared values respecting those differences that cannot be compromised, there is substituted an imposed, bureaucratic order devoid of substance and demoralizing to students, families, and educators alike. If the right of educational choice is not equally available to all regardless of wealth, the process of using universal, compulsory schooling as an arena for fashioning and refashioning the American consensus is crippled. It is this process — both in school and out — that it is among the fundamental purposes of the First Amendment to protect.

It has been argued here that social decisions about the distribution of power over value socialization in schools have enormous impact. These decisions affect the expression and formation of individual beliefs, opinions, and conscience; they influence the transmission of culture in a pluralistic society; and they determine the health of the political system and success of the primary means by which we form consensus and community. These issues of individuality and collectivity are at the core of the First Amendment, and indeed of an entire constitutional structure of government based on individual political sovereignty and the just consent of the governed. Conditioning these First Amendment rights of school choice upon the economic status of families violates the principles of the First and Fourteenth Amendments.

A considerable amount of research, writing, and litigation deals with the economic disparities that affect the quality of education available to American children.[46] Much of this work has focused on geographical differences in tax base, family differences in income, and the discriminatory allocation of school resources typical of segregated schooling. The effect of these economic disparities on the right of school choice is devastating, making wealth and race the primary determinants of which families are permitted to exercise their *Pierce* rights.

At the center of this web of economic and political considerations lies the present financial structure of American schooling. Taxes are collected universally to support the education of all children regardless of their needs, family values, backgrounds, or aspirations, but those tax dollars can be spent only in government operated schools, regardless of whether these schools are suitable for the individual child or family.[47] The system has two results. The family with substantial resources can leave a school it regards as unsuitable or insufficiently responsive to its interests either by moving to another district or by paying tuition at a private school.[48] The family likewise dissatisfied with the local school but that has few or no resources must abandon its values, beliefs, and judgments about good education as the price of receiving a 'free' public education. In sum, the result is freedom of choice for the wealthy, compulsory socialization for the rest.

The fundamental liberties that the First Amendment is designed to protect are, in effect, distributed according to economic status.[49] *Pierce* rights are denied to poor and working-class families by the financial structure of public education. The claim is not that government should subsidize choice for the poor, but that it should end a school finance scheme that discriminates against them in the exercise of their First Amendment rights. It should come as no surprise that minority families are vastly overrepresented among the poor and working class.[50] Nor is it unpredictable, given the history of racism in America, that it is the minority family that is most likely to read between the lines that the real cost of public education is the destruction of culture, the hobbling of family and individual dignity, and the dilution of opportunities to participate equally in the molding of the American consensus.[51]

In the sixty-three years since *Pierce*, schooling has increased so much in cost, pervasiveness, and importance, that what was once a right of meaningful choice abstractly available to all has now become the centerpiece of a profound system of invidious discrimination. Since the *Pierce* right cannot be taken from the wealthy, it must be made equally available to all families if the system of discrimination in First Amendment rights of conscience is to be remedied.

Educational Choice as an Element of Civil Rights Strategy

If the discriminatory financial structure of schooling denies large numbers of people the fundamental rights that flow from equal access to school choice, then the campaign for choice is itself an effort to restore civil rights. More importantly, if those who are the primary, though not the only, victims of unequal access to school choice are members of minority racial, ethnic, and linguistic groups, then these victims of discrimination will be the primary beneficiaries of a properly designed restoration of choice. If the Supreme Court has erected an intent requirement to block the equal protection path to desegregated schooling, perhaps the addition of a First Amendment claim to equal choice for minorities will help clear the way.

One of the significant advantages of using school choice arguments to achieve civil rights remedies is the degree to which whites can themselves find benefits in a fairly designed plan of equal choice. History makes clear that gains for blacks are most likely to be realized when whites also benefit from the proposed changes.[52] There may therefore be a possibility of making common cause and compromise in the interests of all the victims of an absence of equal choice, religious and secular, black and white, poor and middle-class. But the same history also makes clear that whites often have solved their own problems at the expense of minorities,[53] and that plans of choice designed through the political process are more likely to resegregate than to desegregate.[54] For these reasons, the use of school choice as a civil rights tactic requires careful and pragmatic evaluation.[55]

There are a number of school policy issues on which First Amendment school choice arguments can be brought to bear for the purpose of advancing civil rights. Legislative plans for increasing choice appear on both the state level (e.g., Minnesota's tuition voucher demonstration bill) and the federal level (e.g., the proposal to allocate Chapter 1 compensatory education funds through vouchers). These plans are generally supported by private school adherents and by those whose religious preferences for schooling are frustrated by the absence of equal choice. They are generally opposed by the public school establishment and by those who fear that choice will exaggerate rather than ameliorate segregation in schooling. The former may seem to have no real interest in the civil rights of minorities, while the latter, though appearing to support desegregation, may have nothing more than their own economic power and security in mind. Legislation being the quintessence of political struggle, the design and effectiveness of any voucher plan depends completely, from a civil rights perspective, upon the ability of minorities to generate their own political power and form reliable coalitions with unlikely allies. The legislative route remains an uncertain one that must be evaluated on a situation-by-situation basis. At present none of these political situations looks promising.

It is conceivable to mount a direct legal attack on the financial structure of schooling in a state and local district setting. This attack would involve a suit brought by minority families claiming that their First Amendment rights of school choice, their Fourteenth Amendment right to attend nonsegregated schools, and their Fourteenth Amendment right to be free of economic discrimination in the exercise of the fundamental freedoms of belief and expression are violated by the school expenditure mechanism created by the state. By combining a First Amendment argument with two Fourteenth Amendment arguments, litigation of this type might be substantially more powerful than current equal protection arguments alone. On the other hand, it must be recognized that the remedy sought in this case involves nothing less than the restructuring of a system of public schooling that has been entrenched for a century and constitutes a $150 billion industry. It is not likely that the Supreme

Court would order such a fundamental restructuring in the absence of a change in the public's conception of schooling or without broad support from all segments of the population.

A third, more promising possibility exists for employing school choice arguments in the service of civil rights gains, the creation of mechanisms of equal choice as part of remedies being sought in existing school desegregation litigation. Although some research and litigation has addressed the inclusion of choice mechanisms in desegregation litigation, few have attempted to include choice of nonpublic schools in their design. The pros and cons of this strategy are worth examining in some detail.

Intervening on Behalf of Minority Choice in Desegregation Litigation

The most likely scenario would begin with an urban school desegregation case in which the court already had found that the district in question had unconstitutionally created and perpetuated a segregated school system.[56] This would remove the need, but also the possibility, of testing the legal power of adding the First Amendment argument to the equal protection arguments to prove a constitutional violation, but it would leave intact the use of First Amendment arguments to gain a more meaningful remedy and to vindicate an independent right of choice.[57] The facts of such a case would also probably indicate that a high ratio of minority to white students in the school district would make traditional desegregation remedies, such as redrawn attendance zones, busing, and magnet schools, unavailing.[58] It should further be assumed that adjacent suburban school districts are predominantly white and could not legally be compelled to join a metropolitan desegregation remedy that called for reconfiguring suburban districts and policies. This is a situation similar to that of Detroit,[59] Kansas City,[60] and many other urban areas across the country.

Under these circumstances, a federal district court judge might fashion a remedy including some reshuffling of student attendance patterns, the expenditure of additional funds to upgrade the quality of education of schools that remained segregated, and changes in the hiring patterns of faculty and administrators in the system.[61] But these options are limited in their ability to satisfy plaintiffs' demands for vindication of their constitutional right to desegregated schooling. More important, without a First Amendment claim of a right to school choice, there may be little to convince a court to go beyond these limited desegregation remedies. Suppose, therefore, that some plaintiffs asked the court, based on a school choice argument, to grant interested members of the plaintiff class scholarships or vouchers to be paid for by the defendant school district and state. The vouchers would be usable in complete payment for attendance at any suburban public school, or at any district or suburban private school willing to accept plaintiff children and provide them with an education satisfying minimum standards set by the court[62] and the state's applicable statutes. Were such a motion to be granted, and assuming that it was accompanied by a carefully worked-out mechanism protecting and monitoring plaintiffs' educational rights, a school choice mechanism satisfying both equal protection and First Amendment rights would be in place. The results might be beneficial to the cause of both desegregated schooling and the right of educational choice for all, but especially for minority families.

It is also possible that the result might be a considerable worsening of segregation and a totally superficial provision of choice to only the most aggressive and well-to-do minority families. The freedom of choice plans that have come before the federal courts since *Brown* have been rejected precisely because they were subterfuges designed to appeal to the desire for educational choice, while perpetuating existing school segregation.[63] Professor Paul Gewirtz has provided a thoughtful and passionate analysis of the issue of choice and desegregation in 'Choice in the Transition: School Desegregation and the Corrective Ideal.'[64] In a particularly incisive section of the article, Gerwirtz provides a detailed analysis why the Supreme Court turned back a freedom of choice plan in *Green v. County School Board*. Gewirtz's analysis suggests that three factors made the board's freedom of choice plan unacceptable. First, the options available to parents in the school district were restricted in that they were 'tainted' by previous discrimination: 'choices are restricted to schools already having a racial identity caused by the defendant's discrimination...[which] not only limits the available choices but also *channels* them.'[65] Such restrictions might arise from racially identifiable schools, segregated faculties, or unequal resources.

The second factor in *Green*, and presumably in judging any choice plan, is 'duress'. The choices that might be made by minority parents would not be voluntary choices if there were 'reasonable fear of retaliation, or simply predictable discrimination within the traditional white school.'[66] These would be particularly powerful disincentives for minority parents to choose their preferred schools in view of the practices of discriminatory suspension and expulsion and of tracking and classification, not to mention the more subtle but insidious forms of racial hostility found even in apparently integrated public schools. The duress might also include disincentives such as extra transportation costs associated with a system of choice in a metropolitan area.

Gewirtz labels the third factor 'distorted attitudes'. It is at once the most subtle and the most troublesome of his warnings. The nub of the warning is 'the possibility that victims of discrimination may have internalized the perspective of the discriminator that they are unworthy and belong in a separate place; ...and that they will therefore "choose" to perpetuate their stigmatized role.'[67] The weakness in this part of the analysis, which Gewirtz appears to recognize himself, is that it risks assuming that any choice based on racial pride and solidarity among blacks is a mere gloss on internalized feelings of inferiority.[68]

Gerwirtz's argument for 'distrust' of choice mechanisms as a means of aiding desegregation of schools is powerful; it becomes even more convincing when he points out the ways in which the Reagan administration has used the choice argument in desegregation cases as a means of sidetracking the desegregation effort.[69] Still, the problem analysis contains the seeds of its own resolution, for it is arguably possible for the careful plaintiff class and federal judge to require changes in the defendant school district that will remove the taint from existing schools of choice, reduce the duress and disincentives in participating public and private schools, provide the information and support necessary to make choice universally meaningful, and monitor the educational results[70] of minority family choice of racially identifiable schools. What is more, Gewirtz states that even in the light of his mistrustful analysis of the likely results of choice, interdistrict choice mechanisms (such as the one here being discussed) 'have great potential.'[71]

There are other potential problems in combining the arguments for school desegregation with those for an equality of family choice in education: (1) the participation of nonpublic schools, many of which would undoubtedly be religious schools, would raise establishment clause questions;[72] (2) the autonomy of participating suburban public schools and of nonpublic schools would have to be guaranteed or increased lest the choices available to parents become meaningless or the schools decline to participate for fear of losing their identity and their freedom;[73] (3) the need for school autonomy and real choice would have to be balanced in part by a careful crafting of court requirements designed to prevent discriminatory admissions, suspensions, tracking, or other practices that might reinject racism into an apparently integrated school receiving plaintiff children;[74] (4) the right of choice in a nonsegregating context is a right of all families in the school district, not just of minority plaintiffs. It is possible, therefore, that defendants would seek to oppose the choice remedy for desegregation, on the grounds that it would require the restructuring of the entire school system along voucher lines, without input from the remainder of the class of persons aggrieved by an absence of school choice.

Against the problems enumerated here and those suggested by Gewirtz can be arrayed a number of positive consequences and reasons for articulating the First Amendment choice argument in the context of a desegregation suit. First, the fashioning of a mechanism of equal choice that respects the rights of those most injured by an absence of choice will be more principled in a court than in a legislature. The remedies ordered will be more likely to reflect constitutional rights and a careful analysis of consequences than merely a balancing of the political power that can be generated by competing interest groups. Second, because the basic premise of the litigation as it began was the protection of minority rights in education, all remedies will be scrutinized from this perspective; thus, the argument for choice will be less likely to be manipulated or misused to the disadvantage of minority families. The right-wing or strictly sectarian interests that lie behind some parts of the movement for school choice will have less influence in the context of a desegregation case than in other litigation or in legislative initiatives.

Third, and also arising from the fact that the issue is handled by a court hearing a desegregation case, the mechanism of choice ordered or approved by the court is subject to continuing scrutiny for its results. It is an experiment under the close supervision of a court constitutionally committed to an improvement in both desegregation and educational choice. In Gerwitz's argument against choice, he notes that 'the courts should be willing to give *some* kinds of choice remedies a chance — provided they are treated as an experiment and provided they contain specific features that make realistic the prospect of actually achieving the greatest possible degree of integration.'[75] The addition of the First Amendment school choice argument envisions an experiment that may vindicate not only the desegregation rights of minority families, but their independent and equally important right to choose an alternative to government schooling without the burden of financial restrictions imposed by that same government. The continuing jurisdiction of the court should make monitoring both sets of interests and results possible, while allowing corrections in the plan where indicated.

Fourth, the combining of First and Fourteenth Amendment arguments for remedies includes suburban public schools and nonpublic schools, and activates alternatives for desegregation where segregated residential patterns have seemingly reduced the possibilities for any meaningful desegregation. Advocates for choice in the white community can find satisfaction of their interests and needs insofar as they are willing to join the effort to desegregate schooling for all. It puts these advocates of choice to the task of demonstrating by their actions that their commitment to educational choice is not a mere pretext for further victimizing those who already suffer most from inequality of choice in schools.

Fifth, a court-approved mechanism for school choice that includes public and nonpublic schools, both within and without the defendant district, would make clear that a thoroughgoing desegregation plan has room for minority parents who voluntarily choose schools of racial solidarity. Racially identifiable schools[76] would not be condemned merely because they were inconsistent with the integration ideal, nor would minority families be coerced or stigmatized because of their educational preferences, their pride in their heritage, or their desire to be apart at times from a school culture they have every reason to distrust.[77]

Finally, restructuring school finance to make the *Pierce* right of school choice a reality for all families, regardless of wealth, race, and schools chosen, would greatly enhance community building, the formation of genuine social cohesion, and the reduction of irresolvable conflicts of conscience that threaten to paralyze school systems. Beginning in the context of an urban school desegregation case is modest, but it is a beginning. It is a way for us to understand from experience that real consensus is the voluntarily conceived child of equally empowered families and subcultures, not a commodity produced by bureaucrats and imposed by law.

To balance these and the many other pros and cons involved in applying a First Amendment school choice argument to the problem of school desegregation is a mammoth task that cannot be accomplished in the abstract. An effort must be made to deal with real problems in a controlled context, such as that provided by intervention in a desegregation suit.

The First Amendment argument for school choice is a powerful and significant one. It raises many dangerous possibilities for undoing what progress has been made in school desegregation. It also holds the possibility of succeeding where equal protection arguments and remedies have failed. Either way, equality of choice in schools is of independent and crucial importance to minority families. This is not the time for naivete about what may be destructive agendas among some supporters of educational choice. But it may be the time, even the best of times, to consider whether careful alliance among civil rights advocates and the proponents of school choice might produce a common good.

Notes

1 G. ORFIELD (1987) 'School Desegregation Needed Now', *Focus*, 17, 7, pp. 5–7. Orfield discovered, among other things, that while the percentage of black students in 90–100% minority schools declined in the South from 75% in 1968 to about 30% in 1984, in the Northeast the percentage in the same years increased from about 40% to 55%.

2 See G. LANOUE (Ed.) (1970) *Education Vouchers*, Cambridge, Mass., Center for Study of Public Policy, and C. JENCKS (1972) *Inequality*, New York, Basic Books.

3 See, e.g., *Keyes v. School District No. 1 Denver*, and *Washington v. Davis*, at notes 11 and 12, *infra*.

4 See, for example, S. ARONS (1983) *Compelling Belief*, New York, McGraw Hill, and E. JENKINSON (1979) *Censors in the Classroom*, Carbondale, Ill., Southern Illinois University Press.

5 See, for example, *Hawkins v. Coleman*, 376 F. Supp. 1330 (N.D. Tex. 1974) and *Ross v. Saltmarsh*, 500 F. Supp. 935 (S.D.N.Y. 1980), which demonstrate the possibility that discriminatory patterns of suspension and expulsion, like tracking and classification and some programs for minority-language students, may be based upon stereotyped reactions to students whose backgrounds are unfamiliar to teachers or school administrators. See also D. KIRP (1972) 'Schools As Sorters: The Constitutional and Policy Implications of Student Classifications', *University of Pennsylvania Law Review*, 121, p. 705.

6 The leading case on library bannings is *Island Trees v. Pico*, 102 S. Ct. 2799 (1982). People For the American Way in Washington, D.C. monitors and has been involved in a number of state-wide textbook selection controversies; a current list of book censorship cases is maintained by the Coalition Against Censorship in New York City.

7 See S. ARONS *Compelling Belief, op. cit.*, on both the home education movement and the regulation of private schools.

8 See *Edwards v. Aquillard*, 107 S. Ct. 2573 (1987) and *McLean v. Ark. Bd. of Educ.*, 529 F. Supp. 1255 (E.D. Ark. 1982).

9 See generally, D. BELL (1980) *Race, Racism, and American Law*, 2nd ed., Boston, Mass., Little Brown and Co., especially Ch. 1 and section 7.11.6, 'Racial Interest-Convergence Principles'.

10 *Hunter v. Underwood*, 471 US, 222, 226 (1985).

11 413 US 189 (1973).

12 *Washington v. Davis*, 426 US 229 (1976). The number of cases citing *Davis* in the process of applying the discriminatory intent requirement is massive. See C. LAWRENCE (1987) 'The Id, the Ego, and Equal Protection', *Stanford Law Review*, 39, p. 318 n. 2.

13 *Washington v. Davis*, 426 US at 248, n. 14 (1976).

14 See, for example, *Hoots v. Pa.*, 672 F.2d 1107 (3d Cir.), *cert. denied*, 459 US 824 (1982), and *Little Rock School Dist. v. Pulaski*, 597 F.Supp. 1220 (E.D. Ark. 1984).

15 *Milliken v. Bradley*, 418 US 717 (1974).

16 G. ORFIELD (1987) *School Segregation in the 1980s: Trends in the States and Metropolitan Areas*, A Report by the National School Desegregation Project to the Joint Center for Political Studies.

17 D. BELL *Race, Racism, and American Law, op. cit.,* section 7.10.

18 In fact, there is an element of white racism in the twin assumptions that blacks cannot become well educated outside integrated schools and that whites do not suffer educationally by attending all-white schools while blacks do suffer by attending all-black schools. The issue is discussed in D. BELL (Ed.) (1980) *Shades of Brown: New Perspectives on School Desegregation,* New York, Teachers College Press, Columbia University, and is painfully and elegantly stated by J. LESTER (1980) 'The Constitution and Racism', unpublished paper written for a faculty seminar on 'Teaching the Constitution', University of Massachusetts, Amherst, February. See also BELL, *supra* note 17, pp. 424–31.

19 Patricia Lines has made the argument that the denial of choice was at the heart of the *Brown* decision itself: LINES, P. (1987) 'The Denial of Choice and *Brown v. Board of Education',* in *Metropolitan Education,* 4, p. 108.

20 See the discussion in Lawrence, note 21 *infra,* generally.

21 *Op. cit.* Lawrence's article is completely devastating to the Court's nineteenth century view of motive. He puts in its place a reasonable and well informed understanding of racism, and suggests a means of identifying racial motive which is practical and will be acceptable to most people. The article should be required reading for the members of the bench, including the High Court.

22 *Id.* at 326.

23 *Pierce v. Society of Sisters,* 268 US 510 (1925).

24 268 US at 535.

25 See Michael Rebell's chapter in this book, for example.

26 The limitations on the state's power to control value socialization in schooling, whether understood as a First Amendment principle or a substantive due process right, extend to government regulation of private schools as well. Were this not true, the government could effectively eliminate choice by regulating private schools into virtual conformity with public schools. Such regulation, however, has been disapproved by the courts in such cases as *Farrington v. Tokushige,* 273 US 284 (1927) and *State v. Whisner,* 351 N.E.2d 750 (Ohio 1976). If the First Amendment interpretation of the right of school choice is accepted, as suggested by this article, the analysis of state regulation of private schools becomes fairly straightforward. As with other First Amendment rights, states may not regulate the *content* of private schools, but only the incidents (days/year, names of required courses, safety and health standards, etc.) of private school operation. Likewise, a state regulation of private school value content may be approved when it is justified by a compelling state interest, such as the elimination of racism. For further discussion of the private school regulation issue, see S. ARONS (1976) 'Separation of School and State', *Harvard Education Review,* 46, p. 76.

27 The argument that *Pierce* can fruitfully be understood as articulating First Amendment principles, and that were it to come before the Court now, it could be decided as a First Amendment case, was first broached in S. ARONS (1976) 'The Separation of School and State: *Pierce* Reconsidered', *op. cit.,* and is further discussed in ARONS, S. and C. LAWRENCE (1980) 'The Manipulation of Consciousness: A First Amendment Critique of Schooling', *Harv. Civil Rights/Civil Liberties Law Review,* 15, p. 309, and in ARONS, *Compelling Belief, op. cit.*

28 The best discussion of the meaning and significance of the First Amendment both politically and in terms of sanctity of the individual is still T. EMERSON (1966) *Toward a General Theory of the First Amendment*, New York, Random House.

29 Mill's statement was that state-sponsored education 'is a mere contrivance for moulding people to be exactly like one another; and as the mould in which it casts them is that which pleases the predominant power in the government, whether this be a monarch, a priesthood, an aristocracy, or the majority of the existing generation, in proportion as it is efficient and successful, it establishes a despotism over the mind.' J. MILL (1859) *On Liberty*, London, J.W. Parker and Son, pp. 190–1. Ivan Illich modernized this statement in 1969 when he said, 'The School has become the established church of secular times.'

30 International Bill of Human Rights (1946), Article 26, sec. 3 (3), Official Records of the General Assembly, 3rd session, part 1, pp. 71–9.

31 It was determined more than two centuries ago that the failure to separate church and state in the drawing of a substantial repression of individual freedom of religious conscience and in disabling conflict over religious establishment. Since then the separation of church and state has been carefully and exhaustively applied to schooling in order to prevent distortions of conscience and the endlessly destructive conflicts that would otherwise arise among religious sects vying for control of the content of government schools.

32 In a series of cases stretching from *Tinker v. Des Moines*, 391 US 963 (1968), to *Island Trees v. Pico*, 102 S. Ct. 2799 (1982) to *Hazelwood v. Kuhlmeier*, 108 S. Ct. 562 (1988), the Court has made it clear that students retain their right of free expression and free access to information even when the school administration is justified in placing some limitations on these rights. What has distinguished these cases from ones involving adults outside school has been not so much the differing standards of regulation applied within the school system as the Court's implied view that schools may inculcate majority values even though government may not similarly regulate belief formation among adults. This contradiction in the Court's view of the nature and purposes of public schooling is a major obstacle to dealing successfully with the issue of school choice and the First Amendment.

33 See A. MEIKLEJOHN (1953) 'What Does the First Amendment Mean?' *University of Chicago Law Review*, 20, p. 461.

34 However much we may rely upon the schools to help create or reinforce social cohesion, it must be remembered that the structure of our constitutional government withdraws coercive power over beliefs and opinions from the political majority. In this respect, a republican form of government requires that the First Amendment protections of belief and value formation and communication be applied to schooling precisely because it is an agency of socialization that, in the absence of such restrictions, would be in the position to turn the government into a political perpetual motion machine by manipulating the world views effectively enough to make control of their later expressions of opinion superfluous.

35 319 US 624 (1943).

36 *Id*. at 631.

37 See *Mozert v. Hawkins*, 647 F. Supp. 1194 (1986), and the reversal by the

Court of Appeals, 827 F.2d 1058 (1987), *cert. denied*, 108 S. Ct. 1029 (1988) The debate over the nature and legal significance of value inculcation and confession of belief in school curriculum has just begun. For an enlightening presentation of socialization through textbooks, see S. de CASTELL, A. LUKE and C. LUKE (1988) *Language, Authority and Criticism,* Philadelphia, PA., Falmer Press.

38 There has been considerable work on the ways in which ideology affects curriculum and is in turn affected by it. One of the most thoughtful writers in this area is Michael W. Apple, especially in (1982) *Education and Power,* Boston, Mass., Routledge and Kegan Paul. Teachers frequently complain about having to 'teach to the test', a comment that indicates that state prescribed testing may control school content regardless of local control or teacher professionalism. On testing as a means of controlling value inculcation, see S. ARONS and C. LAWRENCE 'Manipulation of Consciousness', *op. cit.,* text at notes 79–88 and note 23.

39 319 US at 637.

40 Although the Court did not discuss the escape hatch argument in *Barnette,* it seems plausible that they took account of the fact that the *Pierce* choice was financially unavailable to many families *and* of the basic thrust of the First Amendment as a principle that withdraws from the majority the power to impose its beliefs upon dissenters by establishing government-sponsored orthodoxy, whether religious or secular. The principle upheld in *Pierce* was thus to be viewed as broader than a mere escape-hatch — a principle as broad as that of the First Amendment itself.

41 *Minersville v. Gobitis,* 310 US 586 (1940).

42 *Id.* at 600.

43 319 US at 641.

44 The cases leading up to *Pico,* 102 S. Ct. 2799 (1982), are just the tip of the iceberg. But the Court has shown that it does not really understand the magnitude of the problem that *Barnette* discussed, as witness this dictum in *Pico:* 'We are therefore in full agreement with petitioners that...there is a legitimate and substantial community interest in promoting respect for authority and traditional values be they social, moral, or political.' 102 S. Ct. at 2807.

45 For an excellent discussion of school/faculty dissonance and of constructive versus destructive conflict, see S. LIGHTFOOT (1978) *Worlds Apart,* New York, Basic Books, p. 197.

46 The best work on the subject remains J. COONS, W. CLUNE and S. SUGARMAN (1970) *Private Wealth and Public Education,* Cambridge, Mass., Belknap Press of Harvard University Press.

47 State and federal laws requiring the provision of suitable education for special needs students open the possibility that educational services can be provided in nongovernment schools under limited circumstances.

48 See the statistics reported by D. LINES note 53 *infra,* pp. 112–13.

49 Economic disparities in the distribution of First Amendment rights are of a very different sort than differences in resources available to school districts because of their tax bases. In the former case, it is clear that money affects school quality because the absence of money restricts the choice and bargaining power by which families define and attain quality. In the latter

case, there is some debate over the apparent truth that the amount of money available to a school district affects the quality of education it can deliver. See *Serrano v. Priest*, 487 F.2d 1241 (1971), and (1986) 'Financing Public Schooling in Cal.: the Aftermath of *Serrano v. Priest* and Proposition 13', *University of San Francisco, Law Review*, 21, p. 1.

50 See the statistics reported by D. BELL (1987) *And We Are Not Saved*, New York, Basic Books, pp. 45–8. The number of whites who are also poor, while a smaller percentage of all white families, nevertheless is enormous. One possible conclusion is that but for racism these two groups would probably make a powerful force demanding an equal right of school choice with the well-to-do.

51 Slavery was based upon just such strategies, separating Africans from their culture and language, attempting to destroy the families of slaves by selling their members to distant owners, denying slaves access to the white world by, among other things, making it a crime to teach a slave to read, and dismembering the dignity of individual slaves through punishment and humiliation made possible by regarding African Americans as property rather than as persons.

52 See D. BELL *Race, Racism and American Law, op. cit.*

53 The Constitution is a prime example of this phenomenon. The 'three-fifths compromise' and the supports for slavery in the entire document allowed whites to reach an agreement on establishing a federal government by reading African Americans out of that government and out of the status of persons.

54 See, for example, *Griffin v. County School Board*, 377 US 218 (1964), and *Poindexter v. Louisiana Fin. Asst. Comm.*, 275 F. Supp. 833 (E.D. La. 1967), *aff'd per curiam*, 389 US 571 (1968), as well as *Green v. County Board*, 391 US 430 (1968). Freedom of choice plans of many types were tried by southern school districts in an attempt to undermine or delay court-ordered school desegregation.

55 The general problem of choice and race is considered in S. ARONS and C. LAWRENCE 'The Manipulation of Consciousness: A First Amendment Critique of Schooling', *op. cit.*; in D. LINES (1978) 'An Equal Choice Plan for Eliminating School Segregation', *Texas Law Review*, 56, p. 1245; in J. COONS and S. SUGARMAN (1977) 'Choice and Integration: A Model Statute', *Parents, Teachers and Children*, San Francisco, Institute for Contemporary Studies; and in ABRAMS, J. COONS and S. SUGARMAN (1988) 'School Integration through Carrots, Not Sticks', *Theory into Practice*, 27, p. 23.

56 For an early attempt at suggesting this strategy to a trial court, see the *amicus* brief of the Education Finance Reform Project submitted in May 1977 to the Superior Court of California for Los Angeles County in *Crawford v. Board of Education*.

57 There is a substantial difference between urging a choice mechanism on the court as a means of fostering desegregation, and arguing that in addition there is an affirmative right to school choice under the First Amendment (or substantive due process) that has been denied to minority plaintiffs by an economically discriminatory school finance and expenditure system.

58 Even where they are practical, some of these remedies have been misused. Magnet schools, for example, have been allowed to employ selective admissions criteria that result in locking out the very students whose right

to a desegregated education was to have been served by the creation of the magnet schools. On top of this, it has been suggested that the magnet school system is a system of choice and that its discriminatory impact proves that choice is once again a tool for the maintenance of segregation. Selective high schools that give all the choice to school admissions officers and none to families with school children do not deserve the label 'choice'. See, for example, W. SNIDER (1988) 'School Choice: New, More Efficient "Sorting Machine"?' *Education Week*, 7, 34, p. 1.

59 See *Milliken v. Bradley, supra* note 15.

60 It is reported that members of the minority plaintiff class in the Kansas City desegregation suit are currently considering intervening with a school choice argument. The facts appear to be very much like those described in the text.

61 These changes would be similar to those discussed by Gewirtz as needed to remove the continuing institutional expressions of a segregated system. See text at note 64 *infra*.

62 A careful and well informed court would assure that such mechanisms as tracking, disciplinary policies, or the absence of support and parental participation in schools of choice did not arise as de facto mechanisms for restoring segregated education.

63 See the cases on freedom of choice plans at note 54 *supra*.

64 (1986) *Columbia Law Review*, 86, p. 728.

65 GEWIRTZ, *op. cit.*, p. 743.

66 *Id.*, p. 744.

67 *Id.*, p. 746.

68 This point shades into a fourth that suggests that the limited experience and information of families in segregated school systems will lead them to choose against integrated alternatives. In either case, the problem is large numbers of minority families 'left behind' in inferior and underfunded city schools, while a smaller number of more aggressive, well informed, and perhaps middle-class minority families choose alternative schools. As the test suggests, there are ways, within the context of a desegregation suit, to prevent or ameliorate these effects.

69 GEWIRTZ, *op. cit.*, p. 771, n. 148.

70 According to the standards and values of the minority parents themselves.

71 GEWIRTZ *supra*, note 64, p. 778. See also the results of the Cambridge, Mass. controlled choice plan as reported in 'Family Choice and Public Schools: A Report to the State Board of Education', January, 1986. The article by M. ALVES 'Maximizing Parental Choice and Effective Desegregation Outcomes: The Cambridge Plan', at p. 39 of the report is especially interesting.

72 A thoroughgoing mechanism for school choice, which put the operative decision as to school chosen in the hands of individual families and offered no incentive to choose nonpublic over government schools, would in all likelihood pass constitutional muster. See *Mueller v. Allen*, 463 US 388 (1983).

73 See *Farrington v. Tokushige, supra* note 26. The First Amendment analysis would provide considerable leverage for resisting all but the most compelling regulations by the state. Some nonpublic schools already oppose participation in any form of voucher or tax credit plan because they see government regulation inevitably accompanying tax dollars. Nothing in the desegregation

choice plan would or could require nonpublic schools to participate if they did not wish to, and regulations effectively forbidding racism in schools of choice would have to be applied as part of any acceptable plan. Discriminatory and nonparticipating private schools may be able to be dealt with adequately through the tax code.

74 These requirements would have to be designed with real teeth, covering a wide range of possibilities. The mere recitation of compliance with Title VI of the Civil Rights Act would be insufficient. The whole matter may be thrown into doubt outside desegregation litigation because of the Supreme Court's willingness to review the private school discrimination case, *Runyon v. McCrary*, 427 US 160 (1976), in the forthcoming reargument of *Patterson v. McLean Credit Union*, 108 S. Ct. 1419 (1988).

75 GEWIRTZ, *op. cit.,* p. 767.

76 It is assumed that racially identifiable schools that restrict family choice because they continue to be identified as expressions of the previously segregated system would have to be changed before the choice plan went into effect. See GEWIRTZ, *op. cit.* For a description of an academically excellent and racially identifiable school, see, e.g., J. LIGHTFOOT (1983) *The Good High School*, New York, Basic Books, pp. 29–55. See also W.E.B. DuBOIS (1935) 'Does the Negro Need Separate Schools?' *Journal of Negro Education*, 4, 328.

77 While integration is the ideal, it is not viewed in this article as the only constitutionally and morally acceptable outcome. See GEWIRTZ, *op. cit.*

Part II
Law, Politics, and the Regulation of Private Schools

5
Employment Discrimination in Religious Schools: A Constitutional Analysis

William P. Marshall and Joanne C. Brant

The obligations imposed upon sectarian elementary and secondary schools derive from two sources. On the one hand, the schools serve the goals of their affiliated religion by passing on its tenets, doctrines, and values to their students. On the other hand, the schools serve the state purposes of educating children in secular knowledge and in the values of good citizenship. The dual and at times conflicting role of religious schools has long been recognized. In *Pierce v. Society of Sisters*,[1] the seminal case establishing the constitutional right of parents to educate their children in private and parochial schools, the United States Supreme Court expressly noted that the state has a concomitant right to impose standards upon those schools to ensure that the state's interest in education will be effectively served.[2]

Not surprisingly, the overlap between the interests of religion and state in parochial education has engendered bitter dispute. Since the minds of children are at the center of the controversy, the passions on both sides can be vehement, especially when the secular values of the state and the theological values of the religion are perceived to be in conflict. In some cases, accommodation has been accomplished through the legislature, since both state and federal laws frequently exempt religious schools from their regulatory requirements.[3] At other times, however, the government has actively and aggressively enforced regulatory enactments against parochial schools. In response, the schools have sought judicial relief from government regulations, arguing that the application of these regulations to them is unconstitutional on a number of grounds.

A particularly problematic example of this constitutional conflict involves state efforts to apply anti-discrimination laws concerning employment relations to religious schools. This issue not only raises the secular/sectarian value conflict noted above, it also directly pits the school's essential right of religious liberty against the equally fundamental right of equal protection. Thus, as one commentator has cautioned, the issue can have no truly satisfactory answer,[4] as the stakes on either side are far too great. Undaunted, we shall nonetheless posit in this chapter a way in which the issue may be resolved.

Our primary tool of analysis in this venture will be the jurisprudence surrounding the free exercise clause of the First Amendment. The free exercise clause provides the strongest constitutional basis for a religious school's right to be free of anti-discrimination regulations. Until recently, there had been some indication in the decisions of lower courts that the establishment clause of the First Amendment might also serve to invalidate anit-discrimination requirements. These decisions were primarily based on the theory that enforcement of anti-discrimination laws might lead to unconstitutional entanglement between church and state — which is arguably prohibited by the establishment clause.[5] However, recently in *Ohio Civil Rights Commission v. Dayton Christian Schools*,[6] the Supreme Court rejected the establishment clause argument.[7] In this the Court was surely correct.[8] As the word itself indicates, 'establishment' is concerned with state support of religion, not state regulation of it. Establishment clause analysis is therefore an inappropriate response to the issues surrounding state attempts to impose anti-discrimination requirements on religious entities.[9] Accordingly, the focus of this chapter will be on the free exercise concerns raised by the application of anti-discrimination laws to religious schools.[10]

At least on paper, free exercise analysis is not unduly complicated. As interpreted by the Supreme Court, the free exercise clause requires simply that a burden on religious exercise must be supported by a 'compelling' state interest in order to be sustained.[11] Thus, in our case the Court's test will require a balancing of the state anti-discrimination interests against the countervailing free exercise right.

Some guidance as to how the Court might resolve this balance does exist in the case law. The Court, using a similar methodology, has upheld state anti-discrimination requirements against countervailing First Amendment claims (based primarily upon the right of free association) in matters involving employment,[12] education,[13] and private club membership.[14] Indeed, in the celebrated *Bob Jones* case,[15] which did involve free exercise, the Court upheld the denial of tax-exempt status to two religious schools because of the schools' policy of racial discrimination, despite the claims of the religious schools that their policies were protected by the free exercise clause. Nonetheless, the Court's approach in these cases has made it clear that a 'right to discriminate' could be protected in some instances.[16] The question of when such a right will outweigh the state interest in uniform enforcement of its anti-discrimination laws depends on careful identification and analysis of the competing rights, a matter to which we now turn.

Title VII

Any understanding of the competing constitutional interests underlying the anti-discrimination/religious school employment issue must begin with Title VII of the Civil Rights Act of 1964, which is the primary federal legislation proscribing discrimination in employment. Included in its coverage, albeit with certain exemptions,[17] are religious entities and religious schools. Because of its scope, Title VII presents the primary battleground upon which this aspect of the church-state conflict is being decided. Indeed, not only has most of the litigation attacking discrimination by religious institutions been brought under Title VII, but most states have used the substantive provisions of Title VII, including its religious exemptions, as a model for their own anti-discrimination statutes.[18]

Title VII itself raises two issues. The first is the extent of its statutory coverage: to what extent did Congress intend religious employers to be subject to the provisions of Title VII, and to what extent did they intend religious employers to be exempt from its coverage?[19] The second issue is whether the first amendment prohibits the application of Title VII to religious employers in matters for which they are not statutorily exempt.[20]

The original version of Title VII in the Civil Rights Act of 1964 as passed by the House of Representatives[21] contained a broad exemption entirely excluding religious employers from coverage under the Act. Section 703 of that bill stated: 'This title shall not apply...to a religious corporation, association, or society.'[22] A substitute bill was then proposed by Senators Humphrey, Dirksen, and Mansfield, which limited the exemption to permit religious employers to employ only individuals of a particular religion to perform work connected with the employer's religious activities.[23] A return to the total exemption for religious organizations was later proposed by Senators Clark and Case,[24] but was rejected after extensive debate on the various proposals. The Senate eventually passed the Dirksen-Mansfield substitute, and this version was accepted by the House without amendment.[25]

During the debate on the 1972 amendments to Title VII, Senators Ervin and Allen again proposed a blanket exemption removing all employment practices of religious institutions from EEOC jurisdiction.

Again, the Senate rejected the option of a complete exemption.[26] Senator Ervin then proposed an amendment that provided a blanket exemption for discrimination based on religion, but did not exempt the religious employer from discrimination based on other grounds. This amendment was accepted, and the current version of Section 702 reads,

> This subchapter shall not apply...to a religious corporation, association, educational institution, or society with respect to the employment of individuals of a particular religion to perform work connected with the carrying on by such corporation, association, educational institution, or society of its activities.[27]

As the above account of the legislative history establishes, Congress affirmatively considered the possibility of a blanket exemption, and rejected it. Instead, Congress chose to grant a limited exemption for religious employers allowing discrimination on the basis of religious affiliation. It is thus appropriate to conclude, as many courts have done,[28] that Congress has demonstrated an intent to preclude religious employers from discriminating on the grounds of race, sex, and national origin.

Nevertheless, some courts have concluded that, because such code applications might be unconstitutional, Title VII was not intended by Congress to encompass employment decisions involving specific types of employees, such as ministers or ecclesiastical officers, even though no explicit exemption for those employees was provided by the statute.[29] The fact that the rationale of these courts was to avoid unconstitutional infirmity, however, suggests their 'statutory construction' was actually no more than a reformulation of the constitutional issue.

The question then becomes whether the application of Title VII to religious employers in situations where they have not been statutorily exempted may nonetheless be constitutionally proscribed under the free exercise clause. While the Supreme Court has never directly ruled on this question, a number of lower courts have; a brief review of their decisions is informative.

The initial reported decision in which a church sought a constitutionally-based exemption from Title VII was *McClure v. Salvation Army*.[30] *McClure* involved a claim by a female minister that she had been treated in a discriminatory manner, and eventually fired from her position because of her gender. In reviewing her claim of sex discrimination, the court observed that a 'minister is the chief instrument by which the church seeks to fulfill its purpose. Matters touching this relationship must necessarily be recognized as of prime ecclesiastical concern.'[31] Accordingly, the court held that the application of Title VII to a

religious group's selection of a minister would be unconstitutional and, for this reason, concluded that Congress must not have intended such an application.[32] For *McClure*, in short, there was a constitutionally compelling zone of institutional autonomy protecting the ministerial decision — a zone which the court read into the provisions of Title VII.[33]

The autonomy interest was not recognized as providing constitutional protection to employment relations between a church and its clerical employees in *Whitney v. Greater New York Corp. of Seventh-Day Adventists*.[34] In that case, a white typist-receptionist was discharged for maintaining a casual social relationship with a black man and brought a Title VII action alleging racial discrimination.[35] The church raised a first amendment defense, relying on *McClure*, in which it argued that the plaintiff's discharge was not subject to judicial review. The court rejected this argument, noting that *McClure* was expressly limited to the 'church-minister relationship', and did not apply to employees whose functions were purely clerical in nature. The court also rejected a doctrinal free exercise challenge, albeit on nonconstitutional grounds, since it found no indication in the record that the plaintiff's discharge was based on church doctrine or policy.[36]

In *EEOC v. Pacific Press Publishing Ass'n*,[37] on the other hand, a serious doctrinal interest was presented by the religious employer. In that case, an editorial secretary brought suit against a nonprofit religious publishing house, alleging violations of Title VII based on sex discrimination. The plaintiff alleged that she had been denied monetary allowances paid to similarly situated male employees, and that she had been terminated in retaliation for filing charges under Title VII.

The publishing house in question was affiliated with the Seventh-Day Adventist Church, and published religiously oriented material. All of its employees were required to be members of the church in good standing. The employer contended that the plaintiff had been terminated for failure to adhere to church authority and biblical teaching, specifically, because she had sued the church and was 'unresponsive to spiritual counsel'.[38]

The court acknowledged the presence of a substantial impact on the exercise of religious beliefs, since the plaintiff's employer had based her dismissal on church doctrine prohibiting lawsuits between church members.[39] However, the court found this burden to be justified by the government's compelling interest in eliminating all forms of discrimination. The court also rejected the employer's claim that the retaliatory dismissal was an unreviewable 'ecclesiastical decision', comparable to those made in intrachurch disputes over religious doctrines

and practices.[40] The court stated that this plaintiff was not seeking review of an ecclesiastical decision and the issue therefore was not reviewable.[41]

The applicability of the 'ministerial' exception in an educational setting was first addressed in *EEOC v. Mississippi College.*[42] In that decision, a part-time professor of psychology claimed that the school had refused to offer her an available full-time position because of her gender. The court reaffirmed the understanding of *McClure* that the exemption provided by Section 702 does not apply to all actions of a religious employer.[43]

On the constitutional issue, however, the court distinguished *McClure* on the grounds that the College was not a church, and its faculty and staff did not function as ministers. The court noted that

> The faculty members are not intermediaries between a church and its congregation. They neither attend to the religious needs of the faithful nor instruct students in the whole of religious doctrine. That faculty members are expected to serve as exemplars of practicing Christians does not serve to make the terms and conditions of their employment matters of church administration and thus purely of ecclesiastical concern.[44]

The court also rejected the college's claim that the application of anti-discrimination regulations would interfere with the school's doctrinal interests. The court noted that most of the employment practices that would be affected by Title VII were not clearly predicated on religious beliefs, and thus the burden on the school's free exercise was minimal. The court also noted that the government has a compelling interest in eradicating all forms of discrimination.[45] The court refused to broaden the Section 702 exemption on constitutional grounds, noting that religious educational institutions play a substantial role in shaping the values of society's young people. Balancing these interests, the court easily determined that the government's compelling interest was sufficient to justify the minimal burden imposed on the school's free exercise rights by the application of Title VII.[46]

Finally, in *EEOC v. Southwestern Baptist Theological Seminary,*[47] the court held that Title VII does not apply to the employment relations between a seminary and its faculty, where all of the teaching faculty qualified as ministers.[48] However, the court found that the application of Title VII's reporting requirements to the seminary's nonministerial employees (including the support staff and some administrative personnel) would not violate the First Amendment.

The court acknowledged its duty to determine independently which employees actually serve a ministerial function, and stated that a religious organization cannot control the legal status of its employees by designating them as ministers. In reaching its independent conclusion that seminary faculty were ministers, the court noted that the school valued religious commitment more highly than academic or teaching abilities, and that the faculty served as intermediaries between the Baptist Convention and the future ministers of many local Baptist churches. Further, the faculty instructed seminarians in 'the whole of religious doctrine', and only religiously oriented courses were taught in the college.[49] While admitting that the lines of demarcation can often be 'only dimly perceived',[50] the court concluded, based on these facts, that the entire faculty of the seminary were entitled to ministerial status and, following *McClure,* were ostensibly not intended by Congress to be covered by Title VII.

The court faced a different concern with respects to the nonministerial support staff of the seminary. After finding no autonomy interest applicable to these positions,[51] the court then addressed the claim that the seminary was entitled to exemption on the grounds that its religious beliefs conflicted with the anti-discrimination requirements. In reviewing this claim, the court found only a minimal burden on the beliefs of the school, since the seminary did not hold any religious tenets that required discrimination on the basis of sex, race, or national origin. The court then echoed the concern expressed in *Mississippi College* that an exemption for educational institutions would undermine the Congressional policy of eliminating discrimination because of the school's influence on the development of moral values in the young. Accordingly, the court held that an exemption was not compelled by the free exercise clause.[52]

Summary of Title VII Cases

As the above review of the law in this area indicates, neither the Supreme Court nor the lower federal courts have conclusively determined the boundaries of Title VII's application to religious employers. Nevertheless, there is widespread agreement on a number of basic principles. First, it is conclusively established that the statutory exemption to Title VII provided by Section 702 does not authorize a religious employer to discriminate with respect to the terms or conditions of employment on the grounds of race, sex, or national origin.[53] Both the literal language of the statute and its legislative history establish that Congress only intended to permit a religious employer to discriminate on the basis of religious affiliation.[54]

On the second and more important issue of constitutional exemption, the courts have held that the application of Title VII to employment relations between a church and its ministers violates the free exercise clause of the First Amendment.[55] Whether an employee can properly be classified as a minister is a question of law that cannot be resolved by the employer's designation, and does not depend on either the fact of ordination or whether the employer is a church.[56] Instead, the courts look to the function and duties of the employee, and determine whether the employee (1) serves as an intermediary between a church and its congregation, (2) attends to the religious needs of the faithful, or (3) instructs students in 'the whole of religious doctrine'.[57] Courts have also considered whether the employee's religious credentials are valued more highly by the employer than secular qualifications and, if the employer is an educational institution, whether secular as well as religious subjects are part of the curriculum.[58] In sum, if a religious employer can show that the challenged employment decision involved an employee whose function and duties were ministerial in nature, the courts will conclude that Title VII is not applicable.

Finally, it is interesting to note that if a religious employer is unable to invoke the 'ministerial exception', every court that has gone on to consider the constitutional issue has held that the application of Title VII to religious institutions does not violate the free exercise clause, even if such application conflicts with religious doctrine. The importance of this observation, however, should not be overstated. The statutorily-based Title VII exemption for discrimination based on religious affiliation coupled with the constitutionally-based ministerial exemption undoubtedly serves to protect most doctrinal matters.

The Title VII cases do contain some significant ambiguities that, for the moment, must remain unresolved. The first surrounds the application of Title VII itself. When is an employer's discriminatory conduct actually based upon religious affiliation appropriately entitled to exemption under the Act? If a religious group excludes all blacks from its polity, is its subsequent decision to deny a position of employment to a black on the grounds that he is not a member of its religion protected by the Title VII exemption? Similarly, when an employee who shares the religious beliefs of her employer allegedly deviates from church dogma (as the teacher allegedly did in *Pacific Press*), under what circumstances can the employer contend that the offender is no longer a member of the religion, so that any discrimination may then be characterized as discrimination based upon religious affiliation?

More importantly, is the constitutional understanding presented in the Title VII cases correct? Is the 'ministerial exemption' applicable to religious schools, and if so, is it defined broadly enough? Are there any other constitutional claims for exemption available beyond the ministerial exemption? We now turn directly to these constitutional issues.

Beyond Title VII: The Constitutional Framework

Nonexemption and Dayton Christian Schools

If Title VII, which allows a partial exemption for religious institutions, raises serious constitutional issues in its application to religious schools, the constitutional dilemmas are even more perplexing with respect to legislation like the Ohio Civil Rights Act,[59] which provides no such exemption. The Ohio Act, which was at issue in *Dayton Christian Schools,* presents the purest manifestation of the religious school/anti-discrimination issue precisely because it is uncompromising and clear in its application. The *Dayton Christian Schools* case thus provides an illuminating vehicle for the examination and analysis of the constitutional issues.

The controversy in *Dayton Christian Schools* arose when, Dayton Christian School (DCS) a religious school, refused to renew the contract of a pregnant teacher, because the religious doctrine of the school allegedly required mothers to stay at home with their pre-school age children.[60] The teacher consulted an attorney regarding the nonrenewal of her teaching contract. This action brought her into further confrontation with the school, since seeking legal advice apparently violated another religious tenet of the school, called the 'biblical chain of command'. This doctrine essentially holds that conflicts within religious institutions should be resolved internally and not by recourse to outsiders.[61] DCS then rescinded its initial nonrenewal letter, and issued a second letter suspending the teacher immediately for violation of the 'biblical chain of command' doctrine.

The teacher initiated an action with the Ohio Civil Rights Commission alleging sex discrimination and retaliatory discharge, and the Commission started an investigation and other preliminary proceedings.[62] While these administrative proceedings were pending, DCS brought a federal court action under 42 U.S.C. § 1983 seeking to enjoin the Civil Rights Commission proceedings on both free exercise and establishment grounds. The district court initially rejected the constitutional claims,[63] but was reversed by the Sixth Circuit on both free exercise and establishment grounds.[64] The Supreme Court, as mentioned previously, reversed again, without reaching the free exercise arguments.[65] It dismissed the case primarily on procedural grounds, and rejected the establishment argument as well.[66]

The free exercise argument presented by DCS was essentially composed of two parts. The first claim was that a decision forcing the school to rehire a teacher against its religious tenets (no pregnant teachers in the classroom, no employees who transgress the 'biblical chain of command') would be unconstitutional.[67] The second aspect of the free exercise claim, however, was more far-reaching. As the district court described this religious claim,

> every aspect of the school's operation is geared toward exposing and educating the students on how to lead a Christian life by understanding what the members consider to be the guidance and direction provided by the Bible...The teachers at DCS are selected because of their ability to blend their avowed religious beliefs into every lesson and school activity. Teachers are required to be born again Christians and to carry with them into their classes the religious fervor and conviction felt necessary to stimulate young minds into accepting Christ as savior. Because of the emphasis placed on the religious education of the students, the school demands that teachers conform both in thought and conduct to the tenets and principles felt essential to leading a Christian life. The belief system espoused by the members of DCS touches every aspect of their life: work, interpersonal relationships, family and recreational activities. Deviation in any way from what is felt to be the proper religious way of life may cast doubt on a teacher's ability to perform his or her critical role and may, therefore, be grounds for dismissal.[68]

In short, DCS argued that the entire school operation was part of their religious exercise in that it attempted to shape moral and religious values. Any incursion into this aspect of the school operation, of which teacher selection was a major part, was therefore an infringement upon religious exercise. Additionally, DCS argued that every aspect of a teacher's way of life was subject to church review, and potentially grounds for dismissal. The appropriate question then was whether the infringement presented by the Ohio Act amounted to a constitutional violation.

The Free Exercise Interest of the Religious Schools

There appear to be three distinct free exercise interests that may be harmed by the application of anti-discrimination laws to religious schools. The first is the right of the religious school to conduct its affairs in a manner that it deems consistent with its religious doctrine and tenets;[69] the second is the right of the religious school to preserve its essentially sectarian character;[70] and the third is the right to protect the institutional autonomy of the religious school.[71] As we shall see, these interests are not mutually exclusive; the applicability of each will vary depending upon the specific circumstances of the case involved. It is useful, then, briefly to examine each of these interests separately.

The protection of the religious school's right to conduct its affairs in a manner consistent with its religious doctrine and tenets is the interest most closely associated with traditional free exercise analysis. In most cases, the courts have not recognized the existence of a religious claim unless it is shown that the religious beliefs of the claimant are burdened by the challenged state requirements.[72] In order to raise this interest in the anti-discrimination context, the school would have to show that its discriminatory conduct was required by a religious principle.

The nature of this 'doctrinal' interest will vary substantially from case to case. In some circumstances, as the passage excerpted above from *Dayton Christian Schools* illustrates, it will be alleged that the entire operation of the school is based on religious tenets. Under this theory, the school's doctrinal interest is present in all its employment decisions. In other cases, the doctrinal interest is more limited, as in *Mississippi College,* where the school refused to hire a woman for a particular position on the grounds that its religious tenets required that position to be held by a man. *Dayton Christian Schools* also presented this more limited doctrinal concern, relying on tenets prohibiting pregnant teachers in the classroom and requiring absolute adherence to the 'biblical chain of command'. Finally, in some cases, a doctrinal interest may not be present at all. Even the decision of a school to hire only a member of its religion to teach religious courses would not raise the doctrinal interest unless that decision was based upon some tenet or dogma.

The second interest is the religious school's right to preserve its sectarian character. It could be argued that to prohibit a religious school from making the discriminatory choices in hiring that may be necessary to establish and maintain a suitably religious atmosphere is in effect to reject the school's right to maintain its essential identity. This position has surfaced to some extent in the Title VII cases, where the courts have recognized that the school has a legitimate interest in providing appropriate role models for its students. This interest also seems to be the essence of the school's complaint in *Dayton Christian Schools.* The argument that the entire school operation is religiously-based, although argued as a doctrinal point, seems at least equally well understood as an argument for the preservation of the sectarian character of the school

— the right of the school to maintain an internal atmosphere that is consistent with its essential purpose.

The third interest, which played a significant role in the Title VII cases, is the right of institutional autonomy. The applicability of this interest depends entirely on the job that is the target of the anti-discrimination effort, regardless of the presence or absence of a doctrinal basis for the discriminatory conduct. The proper scope of the 'autonomy' interest has been the subject of some debate. The Title VII cases, as we have seen, hold that the autonomy interest is essentially a 'ministerial' concern limited to those positions with significant ecclesiastical aspects, such as ministers, theology instructors, and so on.[73] It is not apparent under the Title VII understanding that the autonomy interest would have any place in the discussion of religious schools unless the schools were themselves seminaries, as in *Southwestern Baptist.* Indeed, that is the express holding of *Mississippi College.*

Others have argued, however, that autonomy protection should extend to all jobs within the religious school's internal organization;[74] before proceeding, it is necessary to address this contention. In fact, extending the autonomy protection to employment decisions of the religious school does not seem appropriate. First, the desire to avoid resolving ecclesiastical disputes that formed the basis for the ministerial exemption of *McClure* is not at issue in the religious school context. Certainly, for most positions, such disputes are unlikely: it will not require an interpretation of church doctrine to determine who is qualified to be a secretary, supervise the basketball team, or teach math.[75]

But the claim that all decisions are entitled to blanket exemption, as a mechanism to avoid state involvement in ecclesiastical disputes, is subject to dismissal on other grounds. Obviously, it is wholly inapplicable to decisions based on sex or skin color, even if those decisions are doctrinally-based. The issue here is not the determination of a theological position; the issue is whether that decision overrides the countervailing state concerns.[76] Even hiring decisions based on religious affiliation for teachers of religious courses cannot be justified as necessary to avoid judicial resolution of an ecclesiastical dispute. Perhaps some theological issues may arise in the evaluation of the manner in which a religious study course is taught, but it does not follow that the freedom to discriminate with respect to that position is necessary even along religious lines. A person who is not Jewish, for example, may be as qualified to teach Judaism as someone who is. Deference to the religious school, in short, is required only to the extent that the school bases its employment decision on qualification — not on a per se rule of religious allegiance. This is not, incidentally, as harsh a rule as it sounds. The Jewish school's decision to hire Jews for its religious study positions does implicate the constitutional concern noted earlier, the preservation of the essential character of the institution, and may be entitled to protection on that basis.[77]

Other autonomy rationales are similarly unpersuasive. It has been argued, for example, that institutional autonomy is necessary to further the process of theological development.[78] The difficulty with this position is twofold. First, any government action, from anti-discrimination regulation to foreign policy, may theoretically affect religious doctrine; to suggest that religion is entitled to be insulated from the effects of government action is simply unrealistic.[79] Second, the theological development notion artificially separates religious groups from other organizations staking a high claim to constitutional protection. Political parties, the press, and private associations also develop philosophies and ideas, yet are not freed from all strictures of state regulation in order to do so.[80]

Finally, the autonomy claim has been justified as necessary to ensure the continued separation of church and state.[81] The regulation of religious organizations, with its attendant investigations and enforcement proceedings, it is argued, violates the separation principle.[82] This argument, however, is essentially the establishment argument rejected in *Dayton Christian Schools*.[83] Suffice it to say that the rejection of this position is supported by sound policy considerations as well. Religious organizations are entitled to some constitutional protection but they are not as institutions immune from all regulatory aspects of the law. The conclusion is that only the first two interests that have been identified — the school's doctrinal interest and its interest in preserving its sectarian character — are at issue in the application of anti-discrimination requirements to religious schools.

The State's Interests

The state's interests in applying anti-discrimination requirements to religious schools are considerably easier to ascertain. The goal of eliminating discrimination in employment has long been viewed as a state interest of the most compelling magnitude, since it both promotes the economic well-being of those employed and benefits society at large by assuring that those qualified and competent to hold a particular job are allowed to do so.[84]

It is equally clear that the state has a compelling interest in eradicating the stigma that attends invidious discrimination. The creation and perpetuation of negative stereotypes of minority groups prevent full equality from ever being realized. Accordingly, as the Supreme Court has recognized, the state may act to redress this harm as well.[85]

Perhaps because it combines the interest in equal opportunity with the interest in eliminating stigma, it has further been recognized that the elimination of discrimination in education is also recognized as an interest of the highest order.[86] Not only is the state legitimately concerned with promoting opportunity for all citizens, but it also has an interest in promoting the value of nondiscrimination through the educative process. Indeed, as both *Mississippi College* and *Southwestern Baptist* held, the continued presence of discrimination in secondary and elementary education may be particularly harmful in perpetuating invidious prejudice in society.[87] Fighting discrimination in the elementary and secondary school arenas is thus at the heart of the state interest.

Applying the Balance

At this point, it might seem that regardless of how the interest of the religious school is characterized, the state should prevail. If the state interest is compelling under free exercise analysis, it will prevail over any countervailing considerations. Certainly there is Supreme Court precedent to support this result. In *Runyon v. McCrary*[88] the Court held that anti-discrimination requirements would prevail over a purported First Amendment associational interest advanced by a school and its students in maintaining an all-white private (nonreligious) school. Even more on point is the decision in *Bob Jones University v. United States*[89] which held in denying a tax exemption that governmental anti-discrimination interests are sufficiently compelling to override the interest of a private school whose policy prohibiting interracial dating and marriage was based upon religious doctrine.

There are other factors, however, that make the analysis much less straightforward. First, Supreme Court precedent indicates that the existence of an otherwise compelling state interest may not always lead to vindication of the governmental position. When the harm to the entity or individual asserting the constitutional claim is so severe that the government's action threatens virtually to extinguish the exercise of the constitutional right, an exemption from the state program may be constitutionally mandated.[90] Thus, if it could be shown that the application of anti-discrimination requirements to a religious school would effectively destroy the religious right, relief might be appropriate.

Let us suppose that the Ohio law at issue in *Dayton Christian Schools* prohibited the teaching of discrimination and that such teaching was required by church doctrine. In that situation, the state law clearly would burden the religious school's right to inculcate its doctrine. Moreover, since the teaching of discrimination need not entail the actual practice of employment discrimination, the state's interest in equal employment opportunity is likely to be absent. The state's only interests in this case would be promoting the value of nondiscrimination through the educative process and eliminating the stigma that results from negative stereotypes of minority groups.

While these state interests are clearly 'compelling',[91] the religious claim should prevail. The Supreme Court has indicated in other contexts that religious schools have the right to impart their doctrine.[92] Also, there is another First Amendment right at stake in this dispute — the right of free expression. If the state cannot eliminate controversial speech and unpopular ideas from the marketplace generally,[93] it is even less likely to be able to prohibit the teaching of a disfavored doctrine in a private religious school.

There are other instances where the state interest in applying its anti-discrimination requirements may be less weighty than in the normal case. One of the evils associated with discrimination is that it tends to demean or stigmatize its victims. This concern may be mitigated when the discriminatory decision is inclusionary (selecting from its own adherents), rather than exclusionary (aimed at an external group). There are, after all, differences between classifications drawn with 'a feeling of antipathy' against a specific group and those drawn without such invidious intent.[94] A religious school's decision, for example, to hire only from its associated faith does not stigmatize nonmembers in the way that another school's decision to refuse to hire the members of a minority group may be seen adversely to affect that group. One of the primary purposes behind anti-discrimination efforts, in short, is not implicated in inclusionary discrimination cases. When inclusionary discrimination is involved, the state's 'compelling' interest in economic opportunity and efficiency provides the sole factor to be balanced against the countervailing religious interest.

Surprisingly, recognition of this point makes some sense of the religious discrimination exemption within Title VII. Title VII, as we have seen, permits discrimination on religious grounds, but prohibits discrimination on the basis of race, sex, or national origin. In this respect, the statute accurately predicts that a religious group's decision to discriminate on religious grounds will most often not be viewed as 'invidious' to those excluded, but will instead be perceived as a measure of self-definition and reinforcement of its own membership. Yet Title VII apparently misses the mark in that it would allow exclusionary dissimination along religious lines. For example, it would apparently be permissible under Title VII for a religious school to refuse to hire Jews or Catholics to teach a certain course, even if the school were willing to hire teachers from other religious groups outside its associated faith to fill that position. There seems little reason why, in those circumstances, the group's discriminatory decision should be exempt from the anti-discrimination laws, while its equally exclusionary decision to discriminate against women or blacks would not be.

In any event, the foregoing suggests that despite the compelling nature of the state interest, the religious schools may prevail in some, albeit limited, circumstances. In order to determine which specific circumstances will lead to a vindication of the religious school's claim, one must re-examine the two free exercise interests previously identified in order to ascertain when the interest is threatened as opposed to simply burdened, and when the discrimination for which exemption is sought is inclusionary rather than exclusionary.

As applied to a school's doctrinal interest — that is, discrimination allegedly compelled by religious doctrine — the inclusionary/exclusionary distinction suggests that no claim for exemption would be recognized when the religious tenet in question required the school to discriminate on the basis of sex, race, or against a particular religious group. The sole candidate for exemption would be the school presenting a religious tenet that permitted only persons sharing their faith to hold a particular position. An example of this might be found in the *Dayton Christian Schools* case, if we assume that the teacher was terminated because her actions in proceeding outside the biblical chain of command, in effect, put her outside the faith. (Undoubtedly there are some perversities in this argument, since it suggests that a religious organization may be able to justify a discriminatory action by excommunicating the victim of its bias.)

Yet, even if this were the case, it does not appear that the effect on the religious school's doctrinal interests would be all that severe. In *Runyon v. McCrary,* the Court drew a sharp distinction between government regulation of curriculum content, including the teaching of segregationist dogma, and government regulation of discriminatory admission policies. The Court stated that the latter practice was entitled to no First Amendment protection, so long as the school remains free to teach or inculcate whatever values and standards it deems desirable.[95] This point was correctly made since, as the district court pointed out in *Dayton Christian Schools,* the remedy sought in most employment discrimination cases does not prohibit a religious school from teaching its doctrine. It follows from *Runyon* that a simple doctrinal interest would not be sufficient to sustain a constitutional objection to the application of anti-discrimination requirements.

Constitutional protection for the discriminatory conduct of religious schools may best be found in the school's interest in preserving its sectarian character. The school does have an interest in maintaining its essential religious character, and there is no question that interest could be destroyed if the school were not able to use employment decisions to further its basic purposes. A Christian school would hardly be a Christian school if all its teachers were Jews, Moslems, or Unitarians.

Even here, however, it must be emphasized that the presence of a significant burden on the constitutional right may not be sufficient. In the *Dayton Christian Schools* case, for example, although it may be that the school's interest in providing appropriate role models for its students would be undercut by the presence of a pregnant female teacher who might appear as a challenge to the desired archetype, it could hardly be contended that the presence of such a teacher would threaten the school's identity as a pervasively sectarian institution.

Scenarios in which the requisite harm could occur are, however, entirely possible. As we have stated, a religious school would clearly lose its identity if it were forced by the application of anti-discrimination laws to hire a majority of its teachers from outside its religion. At the least, if the school is to retain its sectarian character, its faculty must be pervasively sectarian. In order to provide the appropriate sectarian influence, particular accommodation may be necessary to have persons within the religion teach certain subjects highly tied to the identity of the institution, such as theology, catechism, and 'Christian living'. Anti-discrimination requirements prohibiting any discrimination in favor of particular religious adherents for these types of teaching positions may well be unconstitutional.

The problem, of course, is that a standard based on preserving the sectarian character of the institution does not lend itself to easy application. A helpful analogy may be found in the statutory defense of Bona Fide Occupational Qualification found in Title VII. Under this provision, an employer may discriminate according to religion, sex, or national origin 'when reasonably necessary to the normal operation of that particular business or enterprise.' The recent application of this provision in a religious educational setting is illuminating.

In *Pime v. Loyola University of Chicago*,[96] a Jew denied a tenure-track position in the philosophy department of a Catholic university brought a Title VII action against the university, contending that it had discriminated against him by reserving its tenure-track vacancies for Jesuits. The university contended that the purpose of its hiring decision was to increase the 'Jesuit presence' in the philosophy department. (Filling the three vacancies in question with Jesuits would have resulted in seven of the thirty-one philosophy positions in the department being held by Jesuits.) The court held that discrimination on this basis was appropriate: 'it seems to us that here the evidence supports the more general proposition that having a Jesuit presence in the philosophy faculty is "reasonably necessary to the normal operation" of the enterprise, and that fixing this number at 7 out of 31 is a reasonable determination.'[97]

Prime, of course, does not establish a mathematical formula. Loyola of Chicago was satisfied with seven out of thirty-one of its philosophy teachers being of a certain religious denomination, but the percentages involved in that case will not be universally applicable. Rather, the exact amounts should be adjusted as the circumstances warrant, depending upon such factors as whether the character and mission of the school are predominantly secular or sectarian, and whether the employment position sought relates to a religious or secular subject.

There are, however, two definitive conclusions. Purely exclusionary employment decisions in religious schools will not be protected, because of the increased strength of the state interest, and the tenuous relation between employment decisions and the preservation of the school's essential sectarian character. Moreover, a requirement that one or two imperfect role models serve on the school's faculty will not be sufficient to violate a school's constitutional rights under the free exercise clause.

Conclusion

The protectable constitutional interest that a religious school asserts when it seeks exemption from anti-discrimination requirements in employment is its right to preserve its essential sectarian character. Accordingly, when the religious school relies on this interest, it must be able to show that anti-discrimination enforcement seriously threatens its pervasively sectarian character. Reference to the bona fide qualification defense available under Title VII offers a helpful analogy in applying this standard to particular cases. The important conclusion, however, is that although some religious discrimination may be tolerated, the Constitution does not support the assertion that religious teaching can only be accomplished when the religious faith of all those associated with the institution is ideologically pure.

Notes

1 268 US 510 (1925).
2 *Id.* at 534.
3 For example, most state civil rights acts contain a provision similar to section 702 of Title VII, which exempts religious employers with respect to discrimination on religious grounds. Some, however, contain no such exemption. The state statutes are summarized in *Dayton Christian Schools v. Ohio Civil Rights Comm'n*, 766 F.2d 932, 941 n. 18 (6th Cir. 1985), *reversed*, 106 S.Ct. 2718 (1986).
4 B. WOLMAN (1986) 'Separation Anxiety: Free Exercise versus Equal Protection', *Ohio State Law Journal*, 47, p. 453. See also D. LAYCOCK, (1982) 'Tax Exemptions for Racially Discriminatory Religious Schools', *Texas Law Review*, 60, p. 262.
5 See *Lemon v. Kurtzman*, 403 US 602 (1971).
6 106 S. Ct. 2718 (1986).
7 *Id.* at 2724. The Court did not explicitly refer to the establishment clause in its holding.
8 The argument in favor of establishment clause limitations on government regulation of religious organizations, however, has been strongly asserted in C. ESBECK, (1984) 'Establishment Clause Limits on Governmental Interference with Religious Organizations', *Washington and Lee Law Review*, 41, Spring, p. 347.
9 The weakness of the establishment clause has been addressed at length in W. MARSHALL, and D. BLOMGREN, (1986) 'Regulating Religious Organizations under the Establishment Clause', *Ohio State Law Journal*, 47, p. 293.
10 This issue was raised but not reached in *Dayton Christian Schools*, when the action was dismissed on procedural grounds.
11 *Hobbie v. Unemployment Appeals Comm'n*, 107 S. Ct. 1046, 1049 (1987).
12 *Hishon v. King and Spalding*, 467 US 69 (1984).
13 *Runyon v. McCrary*, 427 US 160 (1976).
14 *Board of Directors of Rotary Int'l v. Rotary Club of Durate*, 107 S. Ct. 1940 (1987).
15 *Bob Jones Univ. v. United States*, 461 US 574 (1983); see also *Norwood v. Harrison*, 413 US 455 (1973).
16 See W. MARSHALL, (1986) 'Discrimination and the Right of Association', *Northwestern University Law Review*, 81, p. 68.
17 See *infra* notes 27–78.
18 *Dayton Christian Schools v. Ohio Civil Rights Comm'n*,766 F.2d 932, 941, n. 18 (6th Cir. 1985), *reversed* 106 S. Ct. 2718 (1986).
19 *N.L.R.B. v. Catholic Bishop*, 440 US 490 (1979).
20 *Catholic Bishop* teaches that when the proposed application of a federal statute raises serious constitutional questions, courts should find the statute inapplicable unless there is an 'affirmative intention of Congress clearly expressed' to so apply it. 440 US at 501.
21 H.R. 7152.
22 H.R. Rep. No. 914, 88th Cong., 1st Sess. 10 (1963), reprinted in 1964 US Code Cong. and Admin. News 2355. 2402.
23 110 Cong. Rec. 12812.
24 110 Cong. Rec. 12864.

25 See Title VII, Section 702, 789 Stat. 255 (1964) (current version at 42 U.S.C. 2000e-1).

26 118 Cong. Rec. 1982.

27 42 U.S.C. 2000e-1, Pub. L. 88–352, Title VII, Section 702, 2 July, 1964,d 78 Stat. 255; Pub. L. 92–261, Section 3, 24 March, 1972, 86 Stat. 103. See 1972 U.S. Code Cong. and Admin. News 2137. The Supreme Court has recently held that Section 702 does not violate the establishment clause by informally shielding some activities of religious employers while not exempting secular organizations. See *Corporation of Presiding Bishop v. Amos,* 55 U.S.L.W. 5005 (24 June 1987).

A second provision expressly applying the religious exemption to religious schools also appears in Title VII, directly following the bona fide occupational qualification exemption. This provision states that

> (2) it shall not be unlawful employment practice for a school, college, university, or other educational institution or institution of learning to hire and employ employees of a particular religion if such school...is, in whole or in substantial part, owned, supported, controlled, or managed by a particular religion or by a particular religious corporation, association, or society, or if the curriculum of such school...is directed toward the propagation of a particular religion.

42 U.S.C. 2000e-2(e)(2). Since the scope of this exemption appears to be identical to that provided by Section 702 to religious employers generally, it does not require independent consideration.

28 See *supra* text accompanying notes 54–59.

29 *McClure v. Salvation Army,* 460 F.2d 553 (5th Cir.) *cert. denied,* 409 US 896 (1972); *EEOC v Southwestern Baptist Theological Seminary,* 6151 F.2d 277 (5th Cir. 1981), *cert. denied,* 456 US 905 (1982).

30 460 F.2d 553 (5th Cir.), *cert. denied,* 409 US 896 (1972).

31 *Id.* at 559.

32 The court based its stretched reading of Title VII on the 'cardinal principle' that statutory construction should be utilized, wherever it is fairly possible to do so, to avoid finding a statute unconstitutional. See *N.L.R.B. v. Catholic Bishop,* 440 US 490 (1979).

33 The recognition of a right of autonomy as the basis for constitutional protection of church decisions involving employees in ecclesiastical positions did not begin with *McClure.* In concluding that the First Amendment required a 'ministerial' exemption to Title VII, *McClure* relied heavily on a pair of Supreme Court cases taken from outside the civil rights context, in which the Court had indicated that the First Amendment limits the role of both the courts and the legislature in resolving intra-church disputes. For example, *Gonzales v. Roman Catholic Archbishop,* 280 US 1 (1929), held that a court could not question a religious employer's decision, based upon a disputed point of religious law, to refuse to hire a person for the position of chaplain. While *Gonzales* itself is explicable on the grounds that secular courts have no authority to adjudicate the correctness of a decision interpreting religious law, its suggestion of a zone of autonomy for decisions involving certain religious positions was subsequently expanded in *Kedroff v. St. Nicholas*

Cathedral, 344 US 94 (1952). In that case, the Court struck down a state law that interfered with the authority of the Patriarch of Moscow of the Russian Orthodox Church to appoint clergy for Russian Orthodox churches in North America. Although *Kedroff*, as well, can be explained as simply a constitutionally mandated abstention from determinations of ecclesiastical law, the language employed by the Court in reaching its decision was broad: 'legislation that regulates church administration, the operation of the churches [or] the appointment of clergy...prohibits the free exercise of religion.' *Id.* at 107, quoted in *McClure*, 460 F.2d at 559.

34 401 F. Supp. 1363 (S.D.N.Y. 1975).

35 The court rejected the argument that the plaintiff lacked standing to raise a claim of race discrimination since she was white, noting that since her complaint alleged unlawful discharge because she, a white woman, associated with a black man. The court found that plaintiff's allegations fell within the statutory language relating to discrimination based on race. The court distinguished prior cases in which white employees were found to lack standing to charge their employers with racial discrimination against minorities, since those plaintiffs had not alleged that they personally had been subject to discriminatory treatment on account of their race. 401 F. Supp. at 1366–67.

36 *Id.* at 1368.

37 676 F.2d 1272 (9th Cir. 1982).

38 The plaintiff did, however, remain a member of the Adventist church in good standing throughout the litigation. *Id.* at 1275.

39 *Id.* at 1280.

40 See *Serbian E. Orthodox Diocese v. Milivojevich*, 426 US 696 (1976); *Presbyterian Church v. Mary Elizabeth Blue Hull Presbyterian Church*, 393 US 440 (1969).

41 676 F.2d at 1281.

42 626 F.2d 477 (5th Cir. 1980), *cert. denied*. 453 US 912 (1981).

43 The court cautioned, however, that if a religious institution presented convincing evidence that the challenged employment practice resulted from discrimination on the basis of religion, then Section 702 would deprive the EEOC of jurisdiction to investigate further and determine whether the religious discrimination was in reality a pretext for some other form of discrimination. 626 F.2d at 484. Presumably the court's basis for this holding was that investigation of the basis for a religious belief might be unconstitutional. The holding of the Court in *Dayton Christian Schools*, however, apparently rejects this position. 106 S. Ct. at 2724. See also W. Marshall and D. Blomgren, *supra* note 9.

44 626 F.2d at 485.

45 *Id.* at 488, citing *Brown v. Dade Christian Schools*, 556 F.2d 310, 323 (5th Cir. 1977) (*en banc*) (Goldberg, J., concurring), *cert. denied*, 434 US 1063 (1978).

46 626 F.2d at 489.

47 651 F.2d 277 (5th Cir. 1981), *cert. denied*, 456 US 905 (1982).

48 651 F.2d at 284, 285.

49 *Id.* at 283–84.

50 *Id.* at 284, citing *Lemon v. Kurtzman*, 403 US 602, 612 (1971).

51 The court noted that whether the claim was based on establishment or free exercise was not entirely clear. *Id.* at 285 n. 5.

50 *Id.* at 284, citing *Lemon v. Kurtzman*, 403 US 602, 612 (1971).

51 The court noted that whether the claim was based on establishment or free exercise was not entirely clear. *Id.* at 285 n. 5.

52 The court also noted that the state interest in the case was not overly weighty, since the EEOC had sought only to enforce reporting requirements against Southwestern Baptist, and not to ensure substantial compliance. *Id.* at 287.

53 *EEOC v. Southwestern Baptist Theological Seminary*, 651 F.2d 277 (5th Cir. 1981), *cert. denied*, 456 US 905 (1982); *EEOC v. Mississippi College*, 626 F.2d 477 (5th Cir. 1980), *cert. denied*, 453 US 912 (1981); *EEOC v. Pacific Press Publishing Ass'n*, 676 F.2d 1272 (9th Cir. 1982); *Rayburn v. General Conference of Seventh-Day Adventists*, 772 F.2d 1164 (4th Cir. 1985).

54 *EEOC v. Southwestern Baptist Theological Seminary*, 651 F.2d 277 (5th Cir. 1981), *cert. denied*, 456 US 905 (1982); *McClure v. Salvation Army*, 460 F.2d 553 (5th Cir.), *cert. denied*, 409 US 896 (1972).

55 *McClure v. Salvation Army*, 460 F.2d 553 (5th Cir.), *cert. denied*, 409 US 896 (1972); *EEOC v. Mississippi College,* 626 F.2d 477 (512 Cir. 1980) cert. denied, 453 US 912 (1981).

56 *Rayburn v. General Conference of Seventh-Day Adventists*, 772 F.2d 1164 (4th Cir. 1985); *EEOC v. Southwestern Baptist Theological Seminary*, 651 F.2d 277 (5th Cir. 1981), *cert. denied*, 456 US 905 (1982).

57 *EEOC v. Mississippi College*, 626 F.2d 477, 485 (5th Cir. 1980), *cert. denied*, 453 US 912 (1981).

58 *EEOC v. Southwestern Baptist Theological Seminary*, 651 F.2d 277 (5th Cir. 1981), *cert. denied*, 456 US 905 (1982).

59 Ohio Revised Code 4112.02(A). The distinction between the Ohio Act and Title VII was noted by the Sixth Circuit in *Dayton Christian Schools*, 766 F.2d at 942 n. 18.

60 *Dayton Christian Schools*, 106 S. Ct. 2718, 2721 (1986).

61 *Id.*

62 *Id.*

63. 578 F. Supp. 1004 (S.D. Ohio 1984).

64 766 F.2d 932 (6th Cir. 1985).

65 106 S. Ct. 2718 (1986).

66 *Id.* at 2724–26.

67 The Sixth Circuit expressly agreed with this claim. 766 F.2d at 951.

68 578 F. Supp. at 1018–19.

69 *Dayton Christian Schools* 766 F.2d 932 (6th Cir. 1985), *reversed,* 106 S. Ct. 2718 (1986); *EEOC v. Pacific Press Publishing Ass'n*, 676 F.2d 1272 (9th Cir. 1982).

70 *Dayton Christian Schools*, 766 F.2d 932 (6th Cir. 1985), *reversed,* 106 S. Ct. 2718 (1986); *EEOC v. Mississippi College*, 626 F.2d 477 (5th Cir. 1980), *cert. denied,* 453 US 912 (1981).

71 *EEOC v. Southwestern Baptist Theological Seminary,* 651 F.2d 277 (5th Cir. 1981), *cert. denied,* 456 US 905 (1982).

72 *Braunfeld v. Brown*, 366 US 599 (1961); *Sherbert v. Verner*, 374 US 398 (1963).

73 *McClure v. Salvation Army,* 460 F.2d 553 (5th Cir.), *cert. denied,* 409 US 896 (1972); *EEOC v. Southwestern Baptist Theological Seminary*, 651 F.2d 277 (5th Cir. 1981), *cert. denied,* 456 US 905 (1982).

74 D. Laycock (1981) 'Towards a General Theory of the Religion Clauses: The Case of Church Labor Relations and the Right to Church Autonomy', *Columbia Law Review,* 81, p. 1373.
75 I. Lupu (1987) 'Free Exercise Exemption and Religious Institutions: The Case of Employment Discrimination', *Boston University Law Review,* 67, p. 437.
76 *Id.*
77 See *supra* text accompanying note 72.
78 D. Laycock *supra* note 74.
79 W. Marshall and D. Blomgren, *supra* note 10.
80 *Id.* See also Lupu, *supra* note 74.
81 C. Esbeck *supra* note 8.
82 D. Laycock *supra* note 73.
83 See W. Marshall, and D. Blomgren, *supra* note 9.
84 W. Marshall (1986) 'Discrimination and the Right of Association', *Northwestern University Law Review,* 81, Fall, p. 98; 'Developments — Religion and the State', (1987) *Harvard Law Review,* 100 p. 1606.
85 *Roberts v. United States Jaycees,* 468 US 609 (1984).
86 *Brown v. Board of Educ.,* 347 US 483 (1954); *Bolling v. Sharpe,* 347 US 497 (1954); *Bob Jones Univ. v. United States,* 461 US 574 (1983).
87 *EEOC v. Mississippi College,* 626 F.2d 477 (5th Cir. 1980), *cert. denied,* 453 US 912 (1981); *EEOC v. Southwestern Baptist Theological Seminary,* 651 F.2d 277 (5th Cir. 1981), *cert. denied,* 456 US 905 (1982).
88 427 US 160 (1976).
89 461 US 574 (1983).
90 W. Marshall *supra* note 84, p. 103 n. 201; G. Stone, and W. Marshall, (1983) '*Brown v. Socialist Workers:* Inequality as a Command of the First Amendment', in P. Kurland, *et al.* (Eds.) *Supreme Court Review,* Chicago, Ill., University of Chicago Press, p. 610.
91 *Roberts v. United States Jaycees,* 468 US 609 (1984).
92 *Meyer v. Nebraska,* 262 US 390 (1923); *Pierce v. Society of Sisters,* 268 US 510 (1925); *Runyon v. McCrary,* 427 US 160 (1976).
93 *Terminiello v. Chicago,* 337 US 1 (1949); *Cohen v. California,* 403 US 15 (1971); *Collin and Nat'l Socialist Party v. Smith,* 578 F.2d 1197 (7th Cir. 1978). *cert. denied,* 439 US 916 (1978); *Hess v. Indiana,* 414 US 105 (1973).
94 *New York City Transit Auth. v. Beazer,* 440 US 568, 595 n. 40 (1979).
95 427 US at 177.
96 803 F.2d 351 (7th Cir. 1986).
97 *Id.* at 354.

6
The Establishment Clause as a Limit on Governmental Regulation of Religious Schools

Carl H. Esbeck

Federal, state, and local governments seek to implement within private schools a variety of behaviors and values that can rightly be characterized as 'mildly coercive socialization' when such ideas are advanced by force of law. Besides the more familiar proscriptions against discrimination in the treatment of students, teachers, and school staff, possible additions to such a state determined agenda abound. These possibilities include procedural safeguards for teachers and students facing academic or disciplinary sanctions; free speech rights for teachers and students when criticizing the private school or its creed or participating in theatrical productions or the student newspaper; requiring classes and information on human sexuality and the prevention of sexually transmitted diseases; and control of curriculum by standardizing course content or subject matter requirements, approved textbook lists, and mandatory uniform testing for student advancement and the conferring of diplomas or degrees.

The authority to enact laws that have as their purpose the penetration of state selected values into the private school has two sources: the direct application of police power to promote the general social welfare, enforced by the threat of legal coercion for those who are noncompliant, and the indirect means of utilizing the taxing and spending powers to promote the desired conduct by attaching conditions of compliance to the receipt of funding and tax benefits. Any realistic hope that private schools might successfully resist in the courts (as distinct from marshaling public opinion in their favor) the reach of these legislative powers turns on the schools being able to invoke a countervailing liberty found in the federal or state constitutions. The scope of this chapter is to explore the extent to which the religious liberty guarantees found in the First Amendment's establishment clause, embodying the mutual freedom intrinsic to the separation of the two institutions of church and state, attenuate these governmental powers should they be invoked to alter the basic nature of private religious schooling.

At the outset, it is useful to note that no credible claim of complete autonomy can be made for the private religious school. Indeed, a host of local, state, and federal laws already bear upon these schools.[1] While the legislation has provoked litigation by those concerned for the educational freedom of religious schools, nevertheless, to the extent that government selected values are propagated in independent schools by force of the state's power, the primary judicial vehicles are nondiscrimination laws and requirements promulgated to assure general standards of school and teacher competence. The mechanism of interest in this chapter is nondiscrimination legislation.

The intent here is to state what the law 'is', as applied in the United States Supreme Court, rather than to argue what the law 'ought' to be, based on certain stated or unstated sociological or philosophical presuppositions. The first part of this chapter briefly addresses why the free exercise clause does not comprise the totality of the First Amendment's protection of religious liberty. The establishment clause, embodying as it does the dualistic notion of a 'free church in a free state',[2] also safeguards the doctrinal purity of the churches from state involvement. The second part explores the Supreme Court's case law, which suggests that — aside from limiting state aid to religious schools — the establishment clause prevents state entanglements with religious schools that risk thwarting their central purposes.

The thesis in this chapter is that the First Amendment cases presuppose a freedom of thought and open inquiry that amply allows for governmental regulation of private schooling directed at health, safety, and employee welfare concerns, and the minimal academic competence of young pupils.[3] Beyond the most exigent of societal needs, however, a state can never require independent schools, whether sectarian or not, to inculcate behaviors and ideas fairly disputed within society. Clearly there is a compelling state interest in eradicating racial discrimination in the treatment of students and school employees.[4] However, that aspect of religious liberty assured by church-state separation through the avoidance of undue entanglement between religious schools and government calls for a unique treatment of parochial schools when it comes to other bases of discrimination such as homosexuality, marital status, sex, and religion.

Why the Establishment Clause Must Be Considered

In considering the autonomy of religious schooling from state regulation, it is woefully inadequate to regard the free exercise clause as the sole source of religious liberty in the First Amendment.[5] Some discussion of the Supreme Court's case law contrasting the free exercise and establishment clauses, as well as a brief examination of the history concerning the theological motivations for disestablishment, are required to dispel widely held misconceptions about the establishment clause.

Reconciling the Religious Clauses

Rather than being in 'tension' or at odds with one another, the free exercise and establishment clauses each in their own way work to advance religious liberty. The free exercise clause protects an individual's religious conscience.[6] Concomitantly, like other structural provisions in the Constitution, the establishment clause imposes an ordering of the institutions of church and state that inures to the benefit of religious freedom: institutional separation ensures that a believer's religious organization is free of the state's influence or control and, in turn, that a believer's (or nonbeliever's) government does not promote a creed that he or she does not share.

As interpreted by the Supreme Court, the religious interests protected by the free exercise clause focus exclusively on the individual claimant, not on a church qua church or a religious school qua school. Whereas a violation of the free exercise clause is predicated on coercion of the claimant's religiously informed conscience, the establishment clause allows for attending to the religious integrity of the parochial school without any required showing of a burden on the individual conscience of students or their parents.

Wisconsin v. Yoder[7] is most in point in helping to explain the limited reach of free exercise claims as a bar to state regulation of religious schools. Consistent with the individualistic nature of the free exercise clause, the claimants in *Yoder* were parents who refused to enroll their children in any school, public or private, after the age of 16 years. The evidence showed that the parents believed, in accordance with the tenets of the Old Order Amish sect, that their children's attendance at high school would expose the children to ideas and a social environment that would undermine the ascetic and agrarian ways of life of the sect. While the Supreme Court sustained the free exercise defense of the Amish parents to their prosecution for having truant children, the Court limited the reach of the defense to rather discrete and isolated religious sects with a long history of a socially beneficent if aberrant way of life. Thus, the facts in the case of the Amish were unique.[8] In the more ordinary instance where religious schools resist government intrusion, the parochial school's objection is not so much that the regulations will burden the religious consciences of pupils or their parents, but that the state's interference measurably compromises the school's ability to pursue its religious purposes and maintain uncompromised allegiance to its affiliated church.

In contrast to the free exercise clause, with its focus on coercing individual conscience, the establishment clause shields the religious school as an institution from excessive entanglements with the state. But before turning to establishment clause cases, a brief examination of early America's movement toward disestablishment will give assurance that the Supreme Court's case law is on a firm foundation.

Colonial Beginnings

It is now generally acknowledged that the separation of church and state was the result of an alliance between two quite diverse schools of thought: one philosophical and the other theological.[9] The philosophical influence was rationalism, characterized by the deism and skepticism of the Enlightenment. The religious view arose from new theological perceptions of the church and the necessity to ensure its vitality and integrity by shunning ties with the state.

Certainly Enlightenment rationalism, best epitomized by the writings of John Locke, heavily influenced American statesmen such as James Madison, Thomas Jefferson, and George Mason. Locke reasoned that religious belief was a matter of opinion, by nature consigned to the inward persuasion of the mind.[10] In Locke's words, 'the care of souls is not committed to the civil magistrate'[11] because, in striking the social compact, the people never consigned religious matters to the state. Locke's argument leads to the recognition of religious conscience as a civil right, requiring toleration by the state.

Disestablishment thinking out of theological concerns began in the seventeenth century, when, under the press of religious persecution, the argument developed for a theology of church–state separation to honor the right of human belief in religious matters. This movement often is identified with Roger Williams, the founder of Rhode Island, and to a lesser extent with the Quakers of Pennsylvania and the early efforts by

Lord Baltimore in Maryland. For dissenters such as Williams, the case for separation was twofold.[12] First, separation was best for the state because conformity in religious matters was impossible because of religion's personal nature, and state attempts to compel conformity would lead only to repression and civil discord. Second, separation was best for religion because it sealed the church from usurpation by the state and left it free to pursue its mission, however perceived. Williams believed that the civil government should deal only with temporal affairs, and that the government operated through the consent of the people. Civil government, therefore, must not meddle in church affairs.

Historians of the pre-Revolutionary period have also cited the profound influence of the widespread pietistic revival, the Great Awakening (1720s–1750s), in several of the colonies, as having prepared the American soil for disestablishment.[13] The leaders of the movement insisted 'that the Church should be exalted as a spiritual and not a political institution.'[14] Revivalism produced a religion which was 'individualistic, voluntaristic, enthusiastic: the act of faith was a quite particular matter for each individual.'[15] The religion of the Awakening 'challenged all notions of hierarchical society and exalted the voluntary church. Establishment of religion, even a "general" one, would have been quite antithetical to its spirit.'[16]

Churches newly formed as a result of the Awakening quickly acted as a counterpoint to the established church, and inevitable struggles ensued, first for toleration and later disestablishment. Importantly, these dissenting churches did not seek establishment themselves because they believed that union with the state debased the church. These churches saw true religion and the church as thriving only under conditions of disestablishment, eschewing any compromising liaison with government.

The Great Awakening and its resulting concern for the purity of religious societies have been trumpeted by several historians as a principal reason that separation was achieved.[17] As Professor Howe summarizes the matter, the separation principle is 'generally understood to be more the expression of Roger Williams' philosophy than that of Jefferson's.'[18] Separation arose from an 'American opinion in 1790 [that] accepted the view that religious truth is identifiable and beneficient.' The present view that separation is peculiarly appropriate to safeguard religious truth 'from the rough and corrupting hand of government' soon followed.[19]

The thinking thus developed along a two-step pattern: first religious toleration and then disestablishment. The natural consequence of religion redefined as voluntaristic was that government had no competence in the matter. Therefore, the state should not become an agent for achieving sectarian propagation and inculcation. Religious groups were left to attract members by force of persuasion and the appeal of their doctrine, not by force of law.

By the same token, if churches were to operate in a 'free market' environment, a prerequisite was that churches have independence from governmental control, not just independence from governmental support. If churches were to draw upon their own resources and pursue their calling as they understood it, the government should not unduly impede those efforts. To have free churches meant to be free of both government's help and hindrance. To be an independent church and to be a voluntaristic church was a unitary concept. One implied the other, and both were derived from the principle of institutional separation.

From the rationalist's view, volunteerism was desirable because it fostered liberal government by lessening sectarian strife that disrupted the civil peace. The sheer pragmatics of the situation required separation, for early America had many diverse sects. From the theological viewpoint, institutional separation was mandated by the very understanding of religion and the necessity of churches free of the state to protect their vitality and doctrinal purity. Because separation went beyond mere religious toleration, it required the state to be neutral in matters of religious doctrine and practice, even when a nonneutral stance by government did not burden the conscience of individuals in the practice of their religion.

The Supreme Court, in its search for the objectives that underlie the establishment clause, harks back to the early struggle for disestablishment in the states. The Court has found the pertinent history to be the slow but steady acceptance of the separation principle. This long span of history has been gathered by the Court and compressed into the foundational meaning of the establishment clause. If the Court has adopted the separation theory held by the rationalists and those of the theological view, logic and consistency require adopting the motives of both. If the separation of church and state were to inure to their mutual benefit, then governmental regulation of religious organizations, including religious schools, should be given the same strict scrutiny as governmental aid to religion.

The Establishment Clause in the Supreme Court

The Establishment Clause

The wall of separation erected by the establishment clause, although not impermeable, theoretically screens out undue traffic originating from either side. Supreme Court opinions are replete with statements that the establishment clause filters out improper involvement traveling in either direction.[20] Consequently, while the result in many of the Court's cases is to strike down a state funding plan directly to aid parochial schools, the language of the Court often states a rationale of *protecting* the religious schools, not preventing their *advancement*. For example, in *Lemon v. Kurtzman*, the Court emphasized that the religion clauses's 'objective is to prevent...the intrusion of *either* [state or religion] *into the precincts of the other.*'[21]

The Supreme Court has been active in establishment clause cases that have severely restricted state aid to religious schools. The Court, however, has avoided opportunities to hold squarely that the clause also prohibits governmental intrusion into the operation of religious schools. *NLRB v. Catholic Bishop* is a prime example.[22] While clearly raising the establishment issue — for the broad language in the National Labor Relations Act included religious schools within its scope — the Court dodged the question by fashioning a new rule of statutory construction. Pointing to the high stakes of an explicit constitutional ruling, the Court held that it would not assume that Congress intended to regulate parochial schools unless it specifically stated the intent to include them in the act. *Catholic Bishop* nevertheless suggests that the prospect of National Labor Relations Board (NLRB) jurisdiction over lay parochial school teachers poses 'difficult and sensitive questions' and a 'significant risk' that the separation principle would be infringed.[23] The establishment clause problems anticipated by the Court in *Catholic Bishop* concerned material involvement by government employees in religious affairs. The opinion gave two examples. The first was an unfair labor practice charge defended on the basis that the practice was required by religious faith. Such a charge would engage the NLRB in a determination of the good faith of the defense and its relationship to the religious mission of the school. Second, the National Labor Relations Act makes all terms and conditions of employment subject to mandatory collective bargaining. The all-inclusive scope of the act necessarily 'implicate[s] sensitive issues that open the door to conflicts' between organized religion and government.[24] Since the Roman Catholic schools resisting federal regulation in *Catholic Bishop* were the very entities the Court deemed too religious to be proper recipients of state aid in numerous cases, it is understandable that the Court would not be so double-minded as to permit parochial schools to be regulated by the NLRB. Nonetheless, the hesitation to ground the holding squarely on the establishment clause is puzzling.[25]

The Supreme Court's failure to extend its establishment analysis into the regulatory context calls for a brief review of Court parochial aid decisions.

The rationale of these decisions speaks to the forcefulness of establishment-based objections to excessive regulation. Most significant, these cases demand that there be an injunction against excessive entanglement between religious organizations and government.

In its 1971 decision in *Lemon v. Kurtzman*, the Supreme Court first stated the nonentanglement concept as a facet of the Court's establishment clause test.[26] *Lemon* found unconstitutional a Pennsylvania statute that provided direct monetary aid to parochial schools and a Rhode Island statute that provided salary supplements to parochial school teachers. No actual advancement of religion was shown, but the mere presence of this hazard was sufficient to raise constitutional concerns. To prevent aiding religion, Rhode Island had provided for 'comprehensive, discriminating, and continuing state surveillance' over the activities of qualified teachers. The textbooks and other materials had to be those used in the public schools. In certain events, the statute called for examination of school records to determine amounts spent on secular as opposed to religious education, thus causing state evaluation of the religious content of a church-related program. The Pennsylvania statute shared many of the entanglement problems of the Rhode Island statute. Additionally, it provided direct monetary aid to parochial schools with the attendant post-audit inquiries to ensure that no cash was spent on subjects of religion, morals, or forms of worship. To prohibit these interactions between the state and the schools was in part, said the Court, to *protect* the religious school from state regulation.[27]

Two years later, in companion parochial aid cases, *Levitt v. Committee for Public Education*[28] and *Committee for Public Education v. Nyquist*,[29] the Supreme Court invalidated several New York funding provisions. Specifically, the *Levitt* Court held unconstitutional the reimbursement of the cost of state required testing and record keeping. No attempt was made in the statute to ensure that the teacher prepared tests were free of religious instruction and inculcation of religious precepts, and none could be fashioned that would not become excessively entangling.[30] In *Nyquist*, the Supreme Court — among other things — disallowed state reimbursement for building maintenance.[31] Since nothing in the statute barred a school from diverting these funds for a religious purpose, the state would have had to conduct frequent audits and make other incursions into a church school's financial matters.[32] Such controls, of course, were not possible without violating the entanglement criteria.[33]

The 1985 *Aguilar v. Felton*[34] decision is the Court's most recent look at entanglement in religious schools. *Aguilar* struck down a federal education program that paid the salaries of public school employees who taught low-income, educationally deprived children enrolled in public or private schools. In order to insure that public funds not aid religion, the educational law adopted a system of monitoring in the parochial schools. In avoiding the result of aiding religion, however, the monitoring thereby created an unconstitutional permanent and pervasive state presence in the sectarian schools receiving the aid. The prohibition on excessive entanglement was said to be rooted in two concerns: freedom of religious belief for those not aided by the state, and an equal concern to safeguard 'the freedom of even the adherents of the denomination [aided by the state from being] limited by the governmental intrusion into sacred matters.' The Court in *Aguilar* thus reiterated that the church–state separation embodied in the establishment clause is for the mutual benefit of both the religious school and the state's citizens. In the absence of compelling reasons, such as eradicating racism, the same clause would shield religious schools from laws that attempt to turn these schools into instruments for the socialization of students in state determined values and ideas.

The Court has directed attention to three factors in these parochial aid cases. The first factor concerns the purposes of the organization that is benefited or inhibited. If the religious organization is 'pervasively sectarian'[35] — and parochial schools are — it is unlikely that much governmental contact is permissible. Second, courts are to examine the nature of the aid provided or the regulations imposed by the government. If the regulations provide public officials with sufficient discretion to trespass upon sectarian concerns, the involvement is likely to be prohibited. Third, the Court has focused on the resulting relationship between government and religious authorities. If that relationship is one requiring continued surveillance by public officials, the entanglement is likely to be excessive. Concerning all three factors, the overriding principle is to avoid governmental involvement where there is an 'appreciable risk' that the contact will be 'used to transmit or teach [or inhibit] religious views.'[36]

Each of these factors is applicable in a claim of undue regulatory interference. With the exception of compelling justification, such as the need to eradicate racial discrimination, parochial schools should be exempt from intrusive government regulation. Such exemption is not religious favoritism. Rather, it is a constitutionally mandated recognition of the separate spheres of church and state.

In a similar vein, the Supreme Court, in *Siberian E. Orthodox Diocese v. Milivojevich*,[37] has ruled that intrafaith church disputes are not subject to judicial review. Otherwise, courts would run the risk of impermissibly 'delv[ing] into the various church constitutional provisions' relevant to 'a matter of internal church government, an issue at the core of ecclesiastical affairs.'[38] The enforcement of terms in controlling church documents could not be accomplished 'without engaging in a searching and therefore impermissible inquiry into church polity.'[39] In short, civil authorities must always forgo questions that are essentially religious as a matter of noninterference in the affairs of religious associations, including, presumably, parochial schools. Among such matters are doctrine, discipline, church polity, internal administration, religious practices, and the appointment and removal of religious personnel, including teachers.

While nonentanglement and the avoidance of the civil resolution of intrafaith disputes are often viewed as distinct case law developments, they spring from the same underlying principle: government must avoid any involvement with pervasively sectarian societies, such as religious schools, that may touch upon matters central to their religious identity and mission. These matters are so highly reactive when placed in contact with civil authority that religious liberty requires that, in the absence of state interests of the highest order, any appreciable risk of interference be avoided.

Reconciling Civil Rights 'Exemptions' for Religious Schools with the Establishment Clause

Some litigants have objected when plenary governmental regulation does not apply to churches and religious schools, characterizing such a state of affairs as a 'privilege' or 'favoritism' towards religion and thereby violative of the establishment clause. Such objections demonstrate a woeful misunderstanding of the establishment clause and have been repeatedly rejected by the Supreme Court.

Unlike the other provisions of the First Amendment, which protect individual liberties, the establishment clause focuses on a structural concern; namely, mediating the relationship between the institutions of government and the institutions of religion. Government must not favor any particular religious organization or creedal teaching over another; nor may it favor the religious as a class over those who profess no religious beliefs. In order to maintain this neutrality, the establishment clause regiments the nature and degree of involvement between government and religious organizations, including parochial schools. There are no organizations in all of society — other than pervasively religious institutions — from which government must keep its distance in two respects. That is, unlike all other voluntary associations, religious organizations may neither enjoy government's 'benefits' in the form of funding or other largess, nor may they suffer the state's 'burdens' in the form of pervasive regulation. Neutrality by the state (i.e., neither advancing nor inhibiting religious organizations) means leaving the churches alone. When a government's plenary legislation leaves religious organizations alone by 'exempting' them, it thereby promotes the desired separation of church and state and thus the neutrality of government towards religious organizations.

Perhaps the best known of these 'exemption' cases is *Walz v. Tax Commission*.[40] *Walz* upheld the constitutionality of property tax exemptions for religious organizations. Not only did the Court find that the tax exemptions were compatible with the establishment clause, but stated that the exemptions actually fostered the desired noninvolvement of government with religious organizations. Elimination of the exemption, for example, would necessitate property valuation by local authorities, tax liens, and nonpayment foreclosures.

In its 1987 decision, *Corporation of the Presiding Bishop v. Amos*,[41] the Court returned to the question whether statutory 'exemptions' for religious organizations violated the establishment clause. Title VII of the Civil Rights Act of 1964, which prohibits employment discrimination, exempts religious employers that discriminate on religious grounds, regardless of whether the job is characterized as religious or nonreligious. A nonprofit gymnasium operated by the Mormon Church dismissed one of its janitors because he failed to qualify for a certificate indicating that he was a member of the church in good standing. The Supreme Court upheld the exemption over the janitor's claim that it violated the establishment clause. Like the property tax exemptions in *Walz*, the exemption was 'not unconstitutional simply because it *allows* churches to advance religion, which is their very purpose.' For a law to have 'forbidden "effects" under *Lemon*, it must be fair to say that the *government itself* has advanced religion through its own activities and influence.'[42] Accordingly, any 'benefits' to religion achieved by the gymnasium's control over selection of its janitor resulted from efforts of the church and could not be fairly attributed to the government. Moreover, the exemption decreased the opportunities of impermissible entanglement between church and state; thus, 'the statute effectuates a more complete separation of the two and avoids the kind of intrusive inquiry into religious belief' that the establishment clause seeks to avoid.

What the exemption did was return the relationship between church and state to the status quo prior to the enactment of the Civil Rights Act of 1964. That is, prior to 1964 the government in no way regulated alleged or actual religious discrimination by religious employers. Government neutrality is leaving churches and other religious employers alone. Leaving them alone cannot be 'favoritism' violative of the establishment clause.

In contrast to the exemptions at issue in *Walz* and *Amos*, accommodations that favor a limited set of religious beliefs may violate the holding in *Estate of Thornton v. Caldor*.[43] In *Thornton*, the Supreme Court invalidated a Connecticut statute providing employees of private employers with an absolute right not to work on their Sabbath. The law altered the status quo in favor of certain religious practices, for it had the effect of singling out a particular class of religious practices (i.e., Sabbath observance) for favorable treatment, thereby implicitly endorsing a particular set of religious beliefs. While the establishment clause does prohibit legislation that favors a particular denomination or class of religious practices, the clause does not prohibit government's avoiding involvement with religious organizations in its effort to remain neutral concerning their activities and affairs.[44]

Only a little reflection is needed to understand that all statutory classifications concerning religion cannot violate the establishment clause. Indeed, the First Amendment itself makes a classification as to religion, requiring the preservation of religious exercise. Statutory 'exemptions' for religious organizations from plenary regulatory schemes are really the legislature's way of saying that the status quo is to be maintained as to the activities of religious bodies. While the legislature chooses to regulate the activities of other organizations and individuals, the statutory 'exemption' for religion is not a legislative 'benefit' but an acknowledgment that the state should not interfere with the affairs of religious organizations and, without compelling reasons, does not intend to do so in the present statute. Exempting religious schools from nondiscrimination legislation is not only permissible within the establishment clause, but actually fosters the governmental noninterference and neutrality that the clause requires.

Conclusion

Private schools cannot claim complete autonomy from the reach of government's power. Nonetheless, the First Amendment harbors several rights (parental rights, freedom to believe, speak, acquire knowledge, teach, and enter into private associations) safeguarding the private school from the use of state power to interfere materially with educational philosophy, pedagogy, or curriculum content. These rights obtain whether the private school is sectarian or nonsectarian. They are rooted in two fundamental principles: (1) parents are to direct the upbringing of their children; and (2) concerning ideas that are ultimately matters of religious opinion, the state — in the absence of the most compelling of societal reasons — should not control the private school so as to propagate government determined beliefs.

The eradication of racially segregated schools is such a compelling societal reason. Indeed, few religious schools would today object on creedal grounds to prohibitions on racial discrimination. But employee relations and student behavior restricted on the basis of sex (including availability of abortion as a health-related benefit), marital status (including out-of-wedlock pregnancy, adultery, and fornication), handicap (including alcoholism, drug addiction, and sexually transmitted disease), homosexuality, and religion all touch matters of greater sensitivity to religious schools. To state the more obvious conflicts, many religious bodies (and thus any school associated with them) differentiate on the bases of sex and marital status in the appropriate role of women and ecclesiastical offices they may hold, as well as condemn premarital, extramarital and homosexual relations, and strongly counsel against abortion and chemical addiction. There is some justification, as well, in their distinguishing between prohibiting discrimination directed at students and discrimination in the selection and supervision of teachers. This is because a school's faculty is at the core of an institution's essential religious character and doctrinal integrity, and teachers model the adults these schools would like their students to aspire to become.

As discussed in the first part of this chapter, the free exercise clause has been limited to the task of preventing undue burdens on the religious beliefs and actions of individual pupils, their parents, and teachers. In comparison, the history of disestablishment evidences an intent to separate religious organizations from the state, to the mutual benefit of both. Thus, the two clauses are complementary, each in its own way working to ensure religious liberty.

The second part discussed whether private schools of a religious character enjoy rights under the establishment clause as construed by the Supreme Court. It appears that they do, at least if they are 'pervasively sectarian' as the Court has defined that term. Primary and secondary parochial schools are 'pervasively sectarian'. The applicable principle is that the separation of pervasively religious organizations from government prohibits any excessive entanglement between the two. This separation is required both to prevent the state from *advancing* a particular religion and to *protect* the religious school from the state and its 'corrosive secularism'.[45]

Religious liberty must, of course, be counterbalanced by societal imperatives, such as eradicating racially segregated schools. But differential treatment on the basis of sex, marital status, or homosexuality should not be regulated, given the right of First Amendment religious liberty. The First Amendment's religious liberty guarantee is preferred here. Unlike race, classifications on the basis of sex, marital status, and homosexuality are not suspect. Therefore, while the state may have a strong interest in preventing these forms of discrimination, religious liberty concerns only give way to the state's overriding interest in the eradication of race discrimination.

The times in which the state and lower federal courts have resisted egalitarian pressures by upholding religious liberty defenses raised by religious schools may have been mixed. Collected in the notes are discrimination claims lodged against religious schools at both the primary and secondary levels[46] and in higher education.[47] When two fundamental precepts of our law — liberty and equality — are set one against the other, as in these cases, the temptation to 'balance interests' and attempt to accommodate both precepts is great. Of course, such compromises satisfy neither the proponents of equality nor those of liberty. However, where the liberty claim is explicitly stated in the religion clauses of the First Amendment, and the equality claim is of legislative origin, the decision to side with liberty should be clear and uncompromising. Consider this analogy. While obscenity is not protected by the First Amendment, our courts have given vigorous First Amendment protection to pornography, not because it has intrinsic social value or is harmless, but because it is a form of speech and we do not want to travel too far down the slippery path of judicial exceptions to the freedom of speech. The same must be said for discrimination (other than racial) by religious schools. While we may agree that other bases of discrimination are of little social value, even harmful, because the discrimination is an exercise of religious liberty we do not want judge-made exceptions to First Amendment liberties, except in the most clear and compelling of cases.

Notes

1 Any attempt at a comprehensive list of such regulations would include the following: (1) fiscal accountability and tax reporting requirements; (2) health and safety controls; (3) zoning, land use and environmental ordinances; and (4) employee welfare legislation.
2 P. SCHAFF (1888) *Church and State in the United States*, Salem, N.H., Ayer, p. 9.
3 Dicta in several Supreme Court cases state that the regulation of religious schools to assure the minimal academic competence of these schools and their teachers does not violate religious freedom. *Wisconsin v. Yoder*, 406 US

205, 213 (1972) ('There is no doubt as to the power of a State, having a high responsibility for education of its citizens, to impose reasonable regulations for the control and duration of basic education.'); *Board of Educ. v. Allen*, 392 USA 236, 245–46 (1968) ('A substantial body of case law has confirmed the power of the States to insist that attendance at private schools, if it is to satisfy state compulsory-attendance at private schools, if it is to satisfy state compulsory-attendance laws, be at institutions which provide minimum hours of instruction, employ teachers of specified training, and cover prescribed subjects of instruction.'); *Prince v. Massachusetts*, 321 US 158, 166 (1944) ('Acting to guard the general interest in youth's well being, the state as *parens patriae* may restrict the parent's control by requiring school attendance....').

4 In *Runyon v. McCrary*, 427 US 160 (1976), black parents successfully sued several private, nonsectarian schools for excluding qualified children from enrollment solely because of their race. The Court distinguished between the right, protected by the First Amendment, to teach and to learn in the classroom of a private school the idea that the races should be segregated, from the asserted right to put that idea into practice. See also *Bob Jones Univ. v. United States*, 461 US 574 (1983) (federal tax-exemption denied to private school whose discriminatory practices are rooted in religious belief).

5 Entirely apart from whether the character of a private school is sectarian, an amalgamation of liberties found in the First and Fourteenth Amendments acts to safeguard the educational philosophy and pedagogy of the institution from unreasonable governmental interference. These constitutional rights have been given several doctrinal labels: parental rights, freedom of belief, freedom of expression including freedom to acquire knowledge, freedom to pursue the vocation of teaching, academic freedom, and freedom of association. The triad of *Meyer v. Nebraska*, 262 US 390 (1923), *Pierce v. Society of Sisters*, 268 US 510 (1925), and *Farrington v. Tokushige*, 273 US 284 (1927), are the usual starting point for a discussion of these rights. While acknowledging the powers to inspect private schools for compliance with reasonable standards, to examine their teachers and pupils, and to specify 'that certain studies plainly essential to good citizenship must be taught, and that nothing be taught which is manifestly inimical to the public welfare' were expressly acknowledged to be within the state's authority, *Pierce*, 268 US at 534, these cases also endorse rights of parents to direct the upbringing of their children. Private schools therefore cannot be co-opted to advance the aims of the general society as defined by the state.

6 See, e.g., *Abington School Dist. v. Schempp*, 374 US 203, 223 (1963) (necessary in a free exercise case for claimant to show coercive effect of state's action, but not so with establishment clause claim); *Board of Educ. v. Allen*, 392 US 236, 248–49 (1968) (no free exercise violation in absence of claim by plaintiffs that statute in question coerced them as individuals in the practice of their religion).

7 406 US 205 (1972).

8 Consequently, other courts have had little difficulty distinguishing *Yoder*. See, e.g., *Duro v. District Attorney*, 712 F.2d 96 (4th Cir. 1983), *cert. denied*, 465 US 1006 (1984); *Mozert v. Hawkins County Pub. Schools*, 827 F.2d 1058 (6th Cir. 1987), *cert. denied*, 108 S. Ct. 1029 (1988).

9 See generally L. Pfeffer (1967) *Church, State and Freedom*, Rev. ed., Boston, Mass., Beacon Press, pp. 103–4; Miller (1981) 'The American Theory of Religious Liberty', in H. Clark, (Ed.) *Freedom of Religion in America*, New Brunswick, N.J., Transaction Books, pp. 138–9; R. Bellah (1981) 'Cultural Pluralism and Religious Particularism', in Clark, *supra*, p. 36; T. Derr (1981) 'The First Amendment As a Guide to Church-State Relations', in J. Hensel (Ed.) *Church, State and Politics*, Washington, D.C., Roscoe Pound-American Trial Lawyers Foundation, pp. 75, 76–8.

10 J. Locke (1800) *A Letter Concerning Toleration*, London, Crowder.

11 *Id.* at 13.

12 3 *The Complete Writing of Roger Williams* (Bartlett ed. 1963).

13 See generally A. Stokes (1950) *Church and State in the United States*, New York, Harper and Row, 1, pp. 240–4; W. Gewehr (1930) *The Great Awakening in Virginia, 1740–1790*, Gloucester, Mass., P. Smith pp. 167–218; S. Cobb (1970) *The Rise of Religious Liberty in America*, New York, B. Franklin, pp. 484–9.

14 Stokes, *supra*, at 241.

15 Miller, *supra*, at 139.

16 Derr, *supra*, at 76.

17 W. Marnell (1964) *The First Amendment: The History of Religious Freedom in America*, Garden City, N.Y., Doubleday, pp. xi–xiii, 91–104; Gewehr, *supra*, pp. 187–8; Cobb, *supra*, pp. 484–9; Stokes, *supra*, pp. 240–4.

18 M. Howe (1965) *The Garden and the Wilderness: Religion and Government in American Constitutional History*, Chicago, Ill., University of Chicago Press, p. 19.

19 Howe, *supra*, p. 19.

20 Consider, for example: 'To withstand the strictures of the Establishment Clause there must be...a primary effect that neither advances *nor inhibits* religion.' *Abington Township School Dist. v. Schempp*, 374 US 203, 222 (1963) (emphasis added). 'The purposes of the First Amendment guarantees relating to religion were twofold: to foreclose *state interference with the practice of religious faiths,* and to foreclose the establishment of a state religion familiar in other Eighteenth Century systems. Religion and government, *each insulated from the other,* could then co-exist.' *Larkin v. Grendel's Den*, 459 US 116, 122 (1982) (emphasis added). See also *Walz v. Tax Comm'n*, 397 US 664, 669–70 (1970); *Engel v. Vitale*, 370 US 421, 431 (1962).

21 403 US 602, 614 (1971) (emphasis added).

22 440 US at 490 (1979).

23 *Id.* at 507, 502.

24 *Id.* at 503.

25 See also *St. Martin Evangelical Lutheran Church v. South Dakota*, 451 US 772, 788 (1981) (interpreting statute so as to circumvent the establishment clause question that would arise if unemployment taxes were assessed against church-affiliated schools).

26 403 US 602, 612–13 (1971). The current test of the establishment clause is (a) the law must have a secular legislative purpose; (b) the principal or primary effect of the law must be one that neither advances nor inhibits religion; and (c) the law must not foster excessive governmental entanglement with religion.

27 In *Tilton v. Richardson*, 403 US 672 (1971) decided the same day as *Lemon*, the Supreme Court upheld public construction grants for college and university facilities. Although the colleges assisted by the grants were church-affiliated, the *Tilton* Court found no impermissible entanglement. The Court distinguished *Tilton* from *Lemon*, holding that the aid in the form of capital improvements was religiously neutral, therefore not requiring surveillance to prevent diversion to sectarian use. Further, the grant was a one-time, single-purpose event, which engendered no continuing church-state relationship. Finally, the institutions involved, being colleges rather than primary and secondary schools, were considerably less permeated with sectarian purpose.

28 413 US 472 (1973).

29 413 US 756 (1973).

30 *Levitt*, 413 US at 479–80. The *Levitt* Court made no findings that the funds were actually used to teach religion but found a 'substantial risk' sufficient to violate the establishment clause. *Id.* at 480.

In a sequel to *Levitt*, the case of *New York v. Cathedral Academy*, 434 US 125 (1977), turned back an attempt to reimburse parochial schools for testing and record-keeping expenses incurred between the time of the enactment of a state-aid statute and the time it was struck down in *Levitt*. The prospect of even a one-time audit to determine if the expenditures were utilized for sectarian purposes would entangle the state and the civil courts in an 'essentially religious dispute'. In essence, the audit would compel the state auditors to pry into possible religious content of classroom examinations written by parochial school teachers. *Id.* at 132–33.

31 The *Nyquist* Court also disallowed provisions for tuition reimbursement and income tax credits to parents of parochial school children.

32 In *Meek v. Pittenger*, 421 US 349 (1975), a state law providing aid to church-related schools was again before the Court. The Court continued to uphold the lending of secular textbooks, but it rejected the provision of counseling, remedial classes, and therapy by public school professional staff on the parochial school campus. Surveillance would be required to ensure that religious instruction not become part of the professional's activity, and such surveillance would constitute impermissible entanglement. *Id.* at 369–72. The *Meek* Court also noted the potential for conflict between the public employees and religious authorities. *Id.* at 372 n. 22.

33 In *Roemer v. Board of Public Works*, 426 US 736 (1976) (plurality opinion), the Court continued its practice of permitting aid to church-related colleges, upholding noncategorical grants in the form of annual subsidies. A plurality of the Court held that aid did not foster an entanglement with religion because the colleges in question performed essentially secular educational functions; the annual payment did not alone implicate excessive entanglement; and the possibility of occasional audits was not likely to be more entangling than inspections and audits involved in the course of normal college accreditation inspections by the state. The case draws a sharp distinction between the 'pervasively sectarian' primary and secondary parochial schools, such as those in *Lemon*, and the church–affiliated colleges in *Tilton, Hunt,* and *Roemer*.

In the next two pronouncements by the Supreme Court on the continuing parochial aid controversy, the church-related schools were more successful. In *Wolman v. Walter*, 433 US 229 (1977), the Court upheld therapeutic, remedial, and guidance counseling held at sites away from the parochial school campus, diagnostic services provided at the parochial school campus, and standardized tests and test scoring provided by nearby public schools. The Court rejected as unconstitutional the financing of field trips and the provision of classroom educational equipment. In *Committee for Public Education v. Regan*, 444 US 646 (1980), the Court upheld state reimbursement of the costs for the administration by parochial schools of state prepared tests and the keeping of official records. In *Regan* the state had avoided the entanglement pitfalls by directing its aid to secular services that are 'discrete and clearly identifiable' so as to permit straightforward and routine reimbursement with little danger of excessive entanglement. *Id.* at 660–61. In *Wolman* the services for which the court prohibited state aid could be diverted to sectarian use. Any administrative controls to prevent improper use of the aid would be too entangling. 433 US at 254.

34 473 US 402 (1985).

35 *Roemer*, 426 US at 758. The elementary and secondary schools in *Committee for Public Education v. Nyquist*, 413 US 756, 767–68 (1973), will help to clarify the term 'pervasively sectarian'. The parochial schools in *Nyquist*, found to be pervasively sectarian, conformed to the following profile: the schools placed religious restrictions on student admissions and faculty appointments, they enforced obedience to religious dogma, they required attendance at religious services, they required religious or doctrinal study, they were an integral part of the religious mission of the sponsoring church, they had religious indoctrination as a primary purpose, and they imposed religious restrictions on how and what the faculty could teach. The state aid in *Nyquist* was held to be prohibited by the establishment clause. *Accord Grand Rapids School Dist. v. Ball*, 105 S. Ct. 3216, 3223 n. 6 (1985); *Aguilar v. Felton*, 105 S. Ct. 3232, 3238 and n. 8 (1985). But *cf. Bowen v. Kendrick*, 1085. Ct. 2582, 2585–87 (1988). (Blackmun, J. dissenting) (majority's refusal to follow profile of 'pervasively sectarian' organizations concerning federally funded teenage counseling centers operated by religious organizations.)

36 *Committee for Pub. Educ. v. Regan*, 444 US 646, 662 (1980). See *Grand Rapids School Dist.*, 105 S. Ct. at 3225 ('Respondents adduced no evidence of specific incidents of religious indoctrination in this case.... But the absence of proof of specific incidents is not dispositive.').

37 426 US 696 (1976).

38 *Id.* at 721.

39 *Id.* at 723.

40 397 US 664 (1970).

41 107 S. Ct. 2862 (1987).

42 *Id.* at 2868–69 (emphasis added).

43 472 US 703 (1985).

44 Churches and other pervasively sectarian organizations are to be distinguished from those that are primarily commercial in nature, even if connected to a religious organization. See *Alamo Foundation v. Secretary of Labor*, 105 S. Ct. 1953 (1985) (rejecting a First Amendment challenge to the application of federal minimum wage and maximum hour legislation

to the business operations of a nonprofit religious organization).

45 The term is Justice Brennan's. See *Grand Rapids School Dist. v. Ball*, 105 S. Ct. 3216, 3224 (1985).

46 Discrimination claims in which the parochial school won include: *Bennett v. Department of Fair Employment and Housing* and *Van Scoyk v. St. Mary's Assumption Parochial School*, 224 Kan. 304, 580 P.2d 1315 (1978) (religious discrimination; parochial school is not an 'employer' for purposes of state statute). Cases in which the claimant prevailed include: *Dolter v. Wahlert High School*, 483 F. Supp. 266 (N.D. Iowa 1980) (firing by Catholic high school based on unmarried teacher's pregnancy is not exempt under Title VII); *Brown v. Dade Christian Schools*, 556 F.2d 310 (5th Cir. 1977) (*en banc*), *cert. denied*, 434 US 1063 (1978) (church-operated school held liable under 42 USC § 1981 for race discrimination notwithstanding segregation claimed to be religious tenet); *EEOC v. Fremont Christian School*, 781 F.2d 1362 (9th Cir. 1986).

47 Discrimination claims in which the church-affiliated school won include: *Merrill v. Southern Methodist Univ.*, 806 F.2d 600 (5th Cir. 1986) (no sex discrimination found in denying tenure to female professor); *EEOC v. Mississippi College*, 626 F. 2d 477 (5th Cir. 1980), *cert. denied*, 453 US 912 (1981) (Title VII has no application to employment practices of religious educational institutions which discriminate on basis of religion); and *Pime v. Loyola Univ.*, 803 F.2d 351 (7th Cir. 1986) (denial of employment to Jewish professional applicant upheld as necessary to protect normal operation of Jesuit university). A case in which the claimant prevailed is *Ritter v. Mount St. Mary's College*, 495 F. Supp. 724 (D. Md. 1980) (female teacher denied tenure stated sex discrimination claim under Title VII, since § 702 only exempts religious institutions from religious discrimination).

7
Taxing Discrimination: Federal Regulation of Private Education by the Internal Revenue Service

Jeremy A. Rabkin

In the field of education, the main regulatory role of the federal government has centered on the enforcement of civil rights guarantees. But federal civil rights legislation prohibits discrimination only by institutions 'receiving federal financial assistance' — and few private schools, at least at the elementary and secondary level, receive direct federal grants. By default, therefore, the major federal regulatory role in private education (below the college level) has devolved on the Internal Revenue Service (IRS). The IRS can exercise regulatory leverage on private schools by granting or withholding tax-exempt status. Tax-exempt status is potentially a very valuable benefit, because it not only exempts a school's own direct income from taxation, but it may also help to increase private contributions to the school by making these contributions tax deductible for the donors. Since 1970, the IRS has exercised this leverage to discourage private schools from practicing racial discrimination. But there is still no consensus on the ultimate aims or the proper scope of this regulatory effort.

The lack of consensus undoubtedly reflects the touchiness of some of the underlying policy issues in this field — issues that have twice triggered major national controversies in the past decade. But the lack of consensus surely owes much, as well, to the fact that policy in this field has developed in an unusually indirect manner. In this field the most active policy-makers have been judges, but judicial interventions have been even more impulsive and inconsistent than is usual in 'civil rights' policy.

Yet there are serious policy issues at stake. One is the question whether and to what degree the federal government should seek to standardize the social character of private education. Another is whether the federal government has an obligation to ensure that private schools do not undermine public school integration by drawing off white students. Finally, there is the question whether tax-exempt status should be taken to imply federal endorsement of all practices of a tax-exempt institution. Existing policy gives ambiguous or inconsistent answers to all these questions, because that policy has emerged from successive controversies that have rarely addressed these questions directly.

Historical and Constitutional Background

Schools teach not only skills and facts but also attitudes and beliefs. That is why, with the advent of mass education, governments in most countries were anxious to assert public control over education. In Western Europe during the nineteenth century, many countries experienced bitter conflicts between aggressive national governments and traditional religious authorities seeking to maintain their own hold on education.

In America, where there was no established church, the issue was at first more readily compromised, but in time the United States experienced its own conflicts between education and religion. The first state systems of public education, developed in the northern states in the decades before the Civil War, were avowedly nonsectarian. But they were supported by most clergymen, because they employed Bible readings and general prayers to inculcate a common 'Protestant morality'. Almost from the outset, however, this pattern was viewed with some suspicion and resentment by Catholics.

The response of American Catholic leaders was to organize separate Catholic schools almost everywhere their numbers allowed. They then urged state authorities to supply public funding for such schools. Such pleas, which seemed like simple justice to Catholics — who were already paying taxes to support implicitly Protestant schools — were viewed with great alarm by many Protestants, who saw them as sinister maneuvers to extend the Roman Church's power over its adherents. It did nothing to allay this fear when Catholic bishops, on a number of occasions, delivered united voting blocks to candidates pledged to support public aid for church schools.

Concerns reached such a pitch that in 1876 President Grant urged Congress to supplement the other post-Civil War 'civil rights' amendments with a new constitutional amendment, requiring the states to 'forever maintain free public schools' for 'all the children...irrespective of sex, color, birthplace or religion', to guard against manipulation by 'priestcraft', and at the same time to prohibit the expenditure of any public school funds for religious schools. To complete the guarantee, Grant also urged that the amendment prohibit the states from according tax exemption to church property.[1]

Though this amendment failed to win a majority in Congress, the concerns behind it certainly did not die out with the nineteenth century. In this century, however, the main lines of policy have been set by the Supreme Court, without waiting for new constitutional amendments. Among the first and most important principles in the modern settlement was laid down in 1925, when the Supreme Court struck down an Oregon law requiring all students to attend public schools. 'Children are not mere creatures of the state', it declared, in affirming the right of parents to send their children to nongovernment schools.[2] The decision came in an era when the Court was unusually intent on limiting government efforts to standardize private activity. The year before it invoked similar reasoning to strike down a state law prohibiting the teaching of the German language.[3]

In more recent decades, while the Supreme Court has come to be much more accepting of government regulation in economic affairs than it was before the 1930s, it has, if anything, become more insistent about the constitutional guarantee of 'free exercise of religion'. In the late 1960s for example, the Court ruled that a Seventh-Day Adventist could not be considered 'voluntarily' unemployed for refusing to accept a job requiring work on Saturday; state unemployment insurance would have to 'accommodate' the distinctive religious needs of such a person.[4] Even more remarkably, the Court ruled in 1972 that a state could not require secondary school attendance of any kind for Amish children, if their parents claimed religious objections to schooling beyond the elementary level.[5]

On the whole, however, the modern Court has sought to maintain a sharp separation between church and state. In the early 1960s, it declared a constitutional prohibition on Bible reading and prayer in the public schools. In later years, it made even more restrictive rulings, culminating in a 1980 ruling that public schools could not display the Ten Commandments without violating the separation of church and state.[6] At the same time, however, the Court began to enforce increasingly rigorous restrictions on public aid to parochial schools, even when aid was made available to all other private schools.[7]

But the Court remained unwilling to follow the full logic of President Grant's proposed amendment. In several cases, it cautioned against a view of the separation of church and state that would burden or inhibit religion in the name of separation. In a 1970 challenge to tax exemption for churches, it insisted that this practice was not an improper public endorsement or form of assistance to religious institutions. Instead, the Court depicted tax exemptions as a reasonable device for avoiding excessive government 'entanglement' with religion, and elevated the goal of 'nonentanglement' to the status of separate criterion for acceptable government postures toward religion.[8]

By the early 1970s, therefore, the Supreme Court had sketched the outlines of a comprehensive constitutional settlement of disputes over education and governmental authority. Many aspects of this settlement remained quite controversial, since most Americans did not (and do not, even today) favor such a sharp separation between government and religion. But the Court's conception of government 'neutrality' always has had at least one saving grace: it seemed to promise religious institutions broad freedom from governmental interference, by forcing government to disclaim any general public policy responsibility for religion.

If the Court's constitutional framework had been maintained, there would have been no further debate about government regulation and religious schools. There almost certainly would have been no further dispute about the tax status of religious schools, since the Court had identified tax exemption as a neutral device for avoiding entanglement rather than a public endorsement. But the Court itself could not stick to this settlement when its notions about how to handle religious strife came into conflict with its ambitions for reforming American race relations.

Race Relations and Judicial Policy

In the aftermath of the Civil War, Congressional Republicans failed in their bid to contain Catholic separatism with a constitutional amendment, but they were at first more successful in their efforts to wield federal power against a different separatist menace — the emerging patterns of racial exclusion in the South. But the changing response of the Supreme Court left an equally confusing pattern in this area for the twentieth century.

The Civil Rights Act of 1875 prohibited racial discrimination by operators of hotels, restaurants, theaters, and other 'public accommodations'. In 1883, however, the Supreme Court struck down this measure as an unwarranted federal intrusion. The Court insisted that the guarantee in the Fourteenth Amendment — prohibiting any 'state' from denying the 'equal protection of the laws' — must be read literally as a restriction on the *state governments*; congressional authority to enact legislation enforcing this guarantee could not therefore reach discrimination by private businesses.[9]

This ruling seemed to leave room for the states to prohibit racial discrimination by private businesses, if their own legislatures wished to enact such measures. But for many decades thereafter, none of them did. Indeed, when Southern states proceeded to enact laws *requiring* segregation in privately operated facilities, the Supreme Court gave its constitutional blessing to such laws on the strained theory that, binding blacks and whites alike, they could not be a threat to the 'equal protection of the laws'.[10]

It was not until the mid-twentieth century that the Supreme Court finally began to take a more concerned and generous view of the treatment of blacks. It did not, however, explicitly repudiate either the 'state action' doctrine of 1883 or the 'separate but equal' doctrine of the nineteenth century. Beginning in the late 1940s, the Court sought ways to combat private discrimination, while still honoring the principle that the Constitution only prohibited invidious discrimination by the states. It did this by finding elements of state involvement in seemingly private activity. In 1963, for example, in one of the culminating cases in this trend, the Court ruled that a privately owned and operated restaurant was required to serve blacks under the Fourteenth Amendment because it rented space in a building operated by a state agency with a state flag on its roof.[11]

In relation to restaurants and hotels, such strained constitutional rulings were made unnecessary by the broad prohibition of discrimination in 'public accommodations' included in the 1964 Civil Rights Act — which was promptly endorsed by the Supreme Court as a regulation of 'interstate commerce' rather than an enforcement of equality guarantees in the Constitution. Even in housing, a 1968 federal enactment — again justified as a regulation of commerce — did away with the compulsion to extend state responsibility, by providing a simple statutory prohibition of private discrimination. In the field of private education, however, no federal statute was enacted, and the ambiguities in the old 'state action' doctrine remained to bedevil public law.

In the meantime, even the status of public obligations in education had become rather confusing. The historic decision in *Brown v. Board* had refused to say that the 'separation of equal' doctrine was wrong from the start. Rather, it stressed that public education had become far more important by the mid-twentieth century than it had been in earlier times. It then asserted that educational opportunities for black students could not be 'equal' if they were educated separately from whites, because 'in the field of education, separate is inherently unequal.'[12]

At the time it was made, the implications of this ruling remained somewhat obscure. But one thing at least had become clear by the end of the 1960s. Whatever else it meant, the obligation to 'desegregate' public schools would not be interpreted as a merely formal requirement to cease assigning students by race. By the mid-1960s, most Southern states and school districts had abandoned outright defiance of desegregation orders and had begun to rely instead on evasive maneuvers to avoid the logic of compliance. Prodded by civil rights advocacy groups as well as federal enforcement officials, federal courts, in turn, extended their doctrines to block such maneuvers. Thus when school districts allowed black students 'freedom of choice' in deciding which schools to attend, but then subjected them to various forms of harassment when they chose to attend white schools, federal courts began demanding that school officials simply assign students to schools on a racially integrated basis. In 1968 the Supreme Court firmly endorsed this rejection of 'freedom of choice' desegregation plans, thus shifting the emphasis of desegregation toward statistical results.[13] By 1972, the Supreme Court was endorsing compulsory busing plans as a device to ensure statistical integration.[14]

By then, it no longer seemed to matter whether all or even most of the 'racial imbalance' in particular schools — which busing plans were designed to 'remedy' — had actually been caused by deliberate school policies: statistical integration for its own sake seemed to be the aim. Hence by the early 1970s, desegregation suits — with consequent busing orders — were successfully waged against northern school districts where there was no history of official segregation, but where school authorities had avoided decisions that might have encouraged greater statistical integration.[15] Though the Supreme Court never explicitly articulated a simple right to integrated schooling per se, the drift of cases in the twenty years after *Brown* certainly lent itself to this view — a view eagerly expounded by integration advocates.

There could not be statistical integration, however, without a sufficient number of white students. In some areas, white students began to leave the public schools in such large numbers that the threat to integration was very real. Civil rights advocates accordingly turned their attention to private schools as a threat to integration. They had the precedents of 'state action' cases in other fields to work with. As in the struggles over integration in public schools, the courts were drawn into a deepening involvement by their initial eagerness to combat transparent government stratagems to evade the force of desegregation.

In the five years following the enactment of the 1964 Civil Rights Act — the period when desegregation first began to be systematically enforced in the South — enrollment in private elementary and secondary schools in the Southern states jumped tenfold. Almost all of those leaving the public schools were white. In some areas, this pattern of 'white flight' was directly facilitated by public authorities hostile to integration. In some districts, school authorities went so far as to close down formerly 'white' schools and transfer them to 'private' control — under which they proceeded to operate with the same teachers and the same all-white student bodies. Less blatantly, but evidently with the same intent, several state governments sought to ease the transition to private education with tuition grants, textbook loans, and other subsidies to private education. Civil rights lawyers had little difficulty persuading federal judges to order the termination of such state programs on the grounds that they constituted 'state action' denying the 'equal protection of the laws'.[16] The Supreme Court eventually offered emphatic endorsement to this line of cases, holding in 1974 that Mississippi could not loan textbooks to students in schools established to evade desegregation — even though it had earlier held that textbook loans to parochial school students in New York did not constitute government endorsement of, or excessive entanglement with, religion.[17]

But experience with lower court rulings in this area had already made it clear to civil rights advocates that denying private schools such direct state assistance would not be sufficient to safeguard public school integration. Most private schools continued to operate even without such public assistance, and where large numbers of white students had fled the public schools, even such court victories for the civil rights advocates did not lead many white students to return. Civil rights advocates thus looked for stronger leverage against the unsettling trend toward private education in the South. They came to believe that the federal Internal Revenue Service might provide it.

Initial Court Rulings on Tax Exemption

As early as 1967, the US Civil Rights Commission — an advisory body with no enforcement power — had urged that the federal government deny tax exemption to discriminatory private schools.[18] But even under the Johnson administration, which was eager to demonstrate support for desegregation efforts, the Internal Revenue Service declined to adopt this policy. The Service maintained that it could not deny tax exemptions, even to schools explicitly avowing a policy of racial segregation, because racial discrimination by private schools was not in itself illegal.

Civil rights advocates did not seek to have Congress enact a law prohibiting racial discrimination in private education or limiting their eligibility for tax exemption. Instead, they turned to the courts. In the spring of 1969, lawyers for the Washington-based Lawyers Committee for Civil Rights, assisted by the NAACP Legal Defense Fund, filed suit against the Internal Revenue Service in D.C. District Court. The suit was brought in the name of William Green, a black parent of school-age children in Mississippi, and named the then Secretary of the Treasury, David Kennedy (with departmental authority over the IRS), as principal defendant. *Green v. Kennedy* was framed as a class action suit, but was directed only at private schools in the state of Mississippi, where recent litigation against direct state support for 'segregation academies' had identified a large number of such schools.

The ultimate targets of this litigation were characterized at the outset, and through many subsequent controversies, as strongholds of Southern racism. But it is important to be clear on the real thrust of the litigation. While many of the newly created private schools in the South openly asserted racial exclusion policies, most did not. It probably would not have mattered if they all professed a nondiscriminatory admissions policy. In 1976, in the unrelated case of *Runyon v. McCrary*, the Supreme Court ruled that an obscure 1866 statute, prohibiting racial discrimination in the authority to make contracts, should now be read as prohibition on decisions by private business operations (including private schools) to refuse to contract with blacks.[19] It was surely a strained and improbable reading of the statute, but the ruling aroused little controversy. Nor did it put a stop to agitation over the tax status of private schools.

William Green's children had never, in fact, applied to any private school in Mississippi, and had no desire to attend one. The suit argued that Green had been denied his 'rights' because his federal tax dollars had been used to 'support' racial discrimination — and the suit insisted that tax exemption was equivalent to 'federal financial assistance', as prohibited by Title VI of the 1964 Civil Rights Act, or at least as prohibited by the more general reasoning of the 'state action' doctrine. Government attorneys pointed out that these legal arguments were irrelevant to this suit, since William Green had been too poor to pay any federal income tax. But the civil rights lawyers also advanced the less vulnerable — and certainly more pertinent — argument that Mr Green or his children were, in any case, denied their constitutional rights by existing IRS policy because this policy had the effect of 'denying the opportunity of a desegregated education.'[20]

The suit faced a variety of other technical objections, such as an explicit statutory measure limiting tax litigation to suits for a refund of disputed taxes by the payer and otherwise prohibiting 'any suit for the purpose of restraining the assessment or collection of tax...in any court by any person...'[21] The three-judge panel convened to decide the Green suit brushed aside all these technicalities, however, in an initial ruling in January 1970, which emphasized 'the substantiality of the grave constitutional issues presented' by the case. While the court did 'take note' of the problem of allowing the nontaxpaying plaintiffs to litigate the rights of 'taxpayers', it endorsed the notion that, as parents of 'Negro school children in Mississippi', Green and his fellow plaintiffs should still be allowed to 'attack the constitutionality of...[a] system of benefits and matching grants that fosters and supports a system of segregated private schools as an alternative available to white students seeking to avoid desegregated public schools.'[22]

While the court's initial decision only resulted in a preliminary injunction, freezing *future* applications for tax-exempt status for Mississippi private schools, the IRS took this initial loss as a strong indication that it could not defend its existing policy in arguments over a permanent injunction. Accordingly, after extensive consultations in the highest levels of the Nixon administration in the late spring of 1970, the IRS agreed to suspend all its past recognitions of tax-exempt status for private schools in Mississippi, unless it could determine that a school was not 'part of the system of private schools operated on a racially segregated basis as an alternative to white students seeking to avoid desegregated public schools.' But it did not say how this status would be 'determined'. Shortly thereafter, the IRS announced a general policy, applicable to the whole nation, of denying tax-exempt status to 'private schools which practiced racial discrimination...'[23] But this general policy said nothing about the effects of private school enrollment on public school desegregation.

Even this step by the IRS provoked a good deal of protest from Republican politicians in the South. But it did not satisfy civil rights organizations. At a congressional hearing in the summer of 1970, liberal senators expressed open distrust of IRS intentions, and a prominent civil rights advocate urged that the IRS 'put the burden on the [segregation] academies, the same way the Supreme Court has now put the burden on public school officials with the "integrate now, litigate later" approach.'[24] The civil rights lawyers in *Green* pressed for a more vigorous policy, urging the court to impose a permanent injunction denying tax-exempt status for any Mississippi school 'operated on a racially segregated basis for the purpose or *with the effect* of providing an alternative to white students seeking to avoid desegregated public schools.' To satisfy this standard, the *Green* lawyers urged, the IRS should require that tax exemptions be withheld from any private school that did not have a racially integrated faculty, a 'significant number of black students', or at least a documented record of efforts to increase black enrollment through specially targeted recruitment drives and scholarship programs for minority students.[25] The IRS balked at such an intrusive and burdensome program, insisting that it could not do more than check on whether schools refused to admit black students.

When the *Green* court issued a permanent injunction to the IRS in June 1971, it seemed to endorse the concerns of the civil rights advocates, without really constraining the IRS to satisfy them.[26] The IRS had offered, as the rationale for its new policy, the claim that the tax code, in granting tax exemption to charitable institutions, must be presumed to be limited to charities not acting in disregard of 'public policy'. Where the IRS had identified the relevant public policy as simple opposition to race discrimination, the court, in endorsing this position, invoked the far more ambiguous and open-ended 'public policy against support for racial segregation of schools, public or private.' The court, moreover, seemed to emphasize its concerns about the *effects* on public school desegregation by ordering the IRS to collect data not only on the actual racial composition of private schools and their faculties, but also on the political leanings or affiliations of their 'founders, board members, and principal donors....' Yet in professed deference to 'the scope of the administrative discretion that properly belongs to the Commissioner' of the IRS, the court declined to specify the precise standards for tax exemption or to tell the IRS precisely how to evaluate the information it was ordered to collect about the background and character of private schools.

Evidently content with this ambiguous outcome, the IRS did not appeal this decision.[27] Nor did it pursue its new mandate very rigorously. The *Green* court had stressed that it should 'not be misunderstood as laying down a special rule for schools located in Mississippi' but rather an 'underlying principle' applicable throughout the country. In practice, the IRS treated its own 1970 policy announcement as the norm and the more detailed requirements of the 1971 *Green* injunction as merely involving an extra paperwork burden. Thus in the fall of 1970, on its own initiative, it launched a survey of all separately incorporated private schools throughout the nation that were already tax-exempt — some 5000 in all. But the IRS simply asked these schools to certify that they maintained a racially nondiscriminatory admissions policy and to provide evidence that they had given public notice of this fact. Only in Mississippi did the Service collect data on the actual racial character of student enrollments and faculties, and only in Mississippi did it inquire into the political affiliations of school officers and donors. Even then, it did not make much use of these data. By the end of 1973, the IRS had denied tax exemptions to thirty-three Mississippi schools, but all of them were schools that had expressly refused to provide notice of a nondiscriminatory admissions policy. Only another fifty-nine schools throughout the rest of the country had their tax exemptions revoked — all on the same basis.[28] With this, as IRS officials soon after informed the Civil Rights Commission, the Service considered that it had 'eliminated almost all the schools which discriminate on the basis of race', and accordingly concluded that 'little additional enforcement is necessary.'[29] In fact, only another fourteen schools throughout the entire country were denied tax-exempt status through the end of the decade.[30]

This did not at all satisfy civil rights advocates. The IRS made several efforts to placate their protests over the following years. Most notably, it issued a ruling in 1975 that 'church-related' schools (those receiving tax-exempt status by virtue of their organizational connection with an already tax-exempt church) would be equally subject to nondiscrimination requirements. According to IRS estimates, this would bring some 12,000 additional private schools under its standards (well over twice the number of independently incorporated schools in its initial 1970 survey).[31] Civil rights advocates still protested, however, that the IRS paid no attention to the circumstances in which schools were founded, or to the effects of the private schools on public school desegregation. In the summer of 1976, therefore, the Lawyers Committee for Civil Rights filed for further relief in *Green*, charging that IRS actions had 'treated both the letter and spirit' of the 1971 injunction 'with contempt'. A week later, they also filed a national class action suit, styled *Wright v. Simon*, seeking to enjoin more demanding IRS enforcement standards against private schools throughout the country.

Six months after the filing of this national suit, a new administration took control of the executive branch. Among President Carter's new appointees were several lawyers who had co-signed the initial brief in the *Wright* suit.[32] The new administration proceeded to try to settle the case on favorable terms for the civil rights advocates. After eighteen months of negotiation with outside civil rights lawyers — during which no other private interests or advocates were consulted — the IRS announced a new policy. It was this policy that first catapulted a fairly specialized Washington policy dispute to national attention.

Political Explosions

The IRS's proposed new regulations for tax-exempt private schools were published for comment in the *Federal Register* in August 1978.[33] The regulations essentially adopted the policy perspective urged by civil rights lawyers from the outset of the *Green* suit. Under the proposed new standard, any private school established or substantially expanded during the period of public school desegregation in its area would be presumed ineligible for tax exemption unless it had at least a specified quota of minority students (set at one-fifth the percentage of the local area's minority school-age population). The presumption of 'discrimination' for schools that did not meet the quota could be rebutted only by showing that the school had undertaken 'active and vigorous recruitment' of minority students and teachers by such devices as 'publicized offering of tuition waivers, scholarships or other financial assistance for minority students', or 'special minority-oriented curriculum or orientation programs.'

Both IRS officials and civil rights lawyers were astonished at the response. The IRS received over 150,000 letters in response to this single, technical notice in the *Federal Register* — and almost all of the letters were bitterly hostile. By comparison, the Department of Health, Education and Welfare had taken it as a sign of intense public controversy when it received 10,000 letters, a few years earlier, in response to its proposed regulations on sex discrimination and intercollegiate sports. The deluge of hostile comment on the new IRS regulation was largely the result of a campaign organized by the Christian Action Coalition, an obscure sectarian school lobby. Christian Action, it turned out, had solicited letters from a mailing list of contributors supplied by a television evangelist — the then little known Rev. Jerry Falwell. Inspired by the success of this effort, Falwell and the director of the Christian Action Coalition, Warren Billings, proceeded a few months later to organize a new national political advocacy organization called 'The Moral Majority'.[34]

The new IRS regulations were a rather apt rallying point for resentments and frustrations of this newly aroused political constituency. Throughout the 1960s and 1970s, fundamentalist Christian schools — often styled 'Bible academies' — had been springing up throughout the country. By the end of the 1970s, the fundamentalist 'Christian schools' movement boasted over 900,000 elementary and secondary school students, or about one-fifth of all students in private schools throughout the country. Though this movement was concentrated in the South and may have benefited somewhat from resistance to public school integration, it was undeniably connected with a larger pattern of fundamentalist or conservative religious rebellion at the trends in public education. The era of school desegregation, after all, was also the era in which courts were seeking to suppress prayer, Bible readings, and even the most indirect or symbolic indications of respect for religion in public schools. It was also an era in which public school authorities — often under the prodding of civil liberties lawyers — abandoned dress codes and other disciplinary standards, and an era in which drug abuse, vandalism, and sexual promiscuity reached alarming heights in many public schools. To many religious conservatives, the new IRS regulations implied that the federal government viewed all objections or alternatives to public education as implicitly racist. Even worse, the new regulations seemed to view private schools as merely one more forum for government social engineering schemes, concocted by civil rights lawyers in distant Washington. The constituency of the new Christian schools — generally people of limited means, who had to make considerable financial sacrifices to afford even the limited tuition costs of shoe-string 'Bible academies' — were shocked to be told that their schools must alter their curriculum or provide special scholarships for minorities to avoid government harassment.[35]

The IRS tried to placate this uproar by proposing a scaled back version of the new requirements in the spring of 1979. But by then it was too late to calm its conservative critics. After a series of angry congressional hearings that spring, Congress voted appropriation riders to the IRS budget, prohibiting the agency from enforcing its proposed new regulations, and from developing any alternative new requirements in this area. These prohibitions were routinely re-enacted each year thereafter. For a time, it seemed that even the courts had absorbed the message of this protest. In the fall of 1979, the D.C. District Court dismissed the *Wright* suit and announced that it was not, after all, sufficient to claim status as a black parent to invoke judicial supervision of a national enforcement program of the IRS.

In the meantime, however, the original IRS policy had come under legal challenge from a different direction. Bob Jones University, a small and very strange fundamentalist college in South Carolina, had sought to challenge the IRS nondiscrimination policy when it was originally issued. After an initial procedural setback — having been treated with much more procedural rigor than the *Green* plaintiffs — it had actually won a district court ruling in 1978 that the IRS had no authority at all to impose nondiscrimination requirements under existing law. When the IRS appealed, a three-judge panel of the Fourth Circuit Court of Appeals issued a split decision, two judges voting to uphold the district court and one dissenter agreeing with the district judge.[37] The Supreme Court agreed to hear the appeal of Bob Jones in the fall of 1981, but by then a new set of appointees at the Justice Department had begun to have second thoughts about defending even the modest IRS policies of the early 1970s.

Perhaps it should not have been surprising that the new Reagan administration was prepared to rethink IRS policy. As the Carter era appointees had close ties to civil rights advocacy groups, the Reagan administration had various political ties to the defenders of the Christian schools movement. But like their predecessors, the Reagan officials underestimated the latent strength of their opposition. In early January 1982, the IRS announced that it would no longer impose racial policy restrictions of any kind on tax exemptions for private schools, and the Justice Department then asked the Supreme Court to vacate the *Bob Jones* case as no longer involving any substantive dispute between the government and the school. These steps unleashed a torrent of protest, magnified much beyond the controversy over the 1978 regulations by the sensationalist coverage of the mainstream news media and the eagerness of congressional Democrats to charge the Reagan administration with racism and lawlessness.

The Reagan administration sought to resolve this public relations nightmare by insisting that it was only opposed to IRS policy in this area because it was not authorized by statute — and that the administration was eager to have Congress enact specific legislation that would authorize a clear anti-discrimination policy for the future. But a subsequent administration proposal for such a measure was indignantly spurned by congressional Democrats, who were eager to fix the administration with continuing blame for overturning what they insisted was a perfectly valid and legal policy. For their part, civil rights advocates in Washington seemed eager to avoid opening the larger issues to more extended congressional debate. Congress ultimately failed to vote on or debate even the nonbinding resolution on the subject that had been promised at the outset of the controversy. Revelling in pious rhetoric and expressions of outrage at the Reagan administration, Congress declined to take any action to clarify legal requirements in this area.

The Supreme Court finally reached out to shape its own compromise. In an astonishing legal maneuver, it agreed to hear arguments on a hypothetical dispute between Bob Jones University and the Justice Department on whether the school *might* invoke First Amendment objections to a nondiscrimination policy *if* the IRS ever again asserted the policy it was now disavowing. Then the Court appointed its own advocate, Washington lawyer William Coleman, to offer arguments on why the IRS was already obliged to adopt such a policy. In the confusing legal posture of the case by then, Coleman did not represent any actual party in any actual suit. His role was essentially to offer arguments the Court wished to hear. Not surprisingly, the Court proceeded to endorse the argument that IRS was indeed obliged under existing law to deny tax exemptions to schools practicing racial discrimination. Schools that claimed religious scruples about compliance would simply have to forgo tax exemption, the Court further ruled, because the 'public policy' of opposition to racial discrimination must in these circumstances override any First Amendment claims to religious autonomy.[38] The following year, however, the Court turned around and ruled that the *Wright* case, reinstated in the meantime by the D.C. Court of Appeals, must be dismissed, because it would be improper for courts to interfere with the discretion of the IRS in determining how to enforce a national program.[39]

Neither Supreme Court decision is a model of clear legal logic — as powerful dissents in each case demonstrated. But taken together, they effected a compromise that endured through the 1980s. There could no longer be any question of allowing avowedly racist schools to retain tax exemptions. But there would also be no further legal pressure on the IRS to scrutinize the tax exemptions of private schools merely because they failed to attract black students or drew white students away from public schools. Even a further order in the *Green* case, requiring the IRS to re-examine tax-exempt schools denied participation in a state aid program, did not produce any significant number of new revocations.[40] No other schools lost their tax-exempt status in the 1980s. In general, public school integration levels did not rise above the levels achieved by the mid-1970s.[41]

Policies and Principles, Conflicts and Confusions

In its simplest terms, the dispute over federal tax policy toward private schools has pitted demands for the suppression of racism on the one side against claims to the toleration of diversity on the other. In crude political terms, it might be described as a struggle between racial minorities and religious minorities. When it has broken into national politics, it has been a contest of competing imageries, a contest over which side has the more compelling symbolism. At the level of imagery and symbolism, the civil rights lawyers have generally prevailed. They have been able to invoke vivid, living memories of Martin Luther King and the great struggles of the 1960s, while religious conservatives have been far less successful in associating their claims with the distant causes of Roger Williams or Thomas Jefferson.

In policy terms, however, the controversy over tax exemption and private schools looks somewhat different. As a practical matter, it has been a contest between those seeking to harness federal controls to ambitious public policy goals and those seeking to resist federal interference in order to pursue their own ends. In these terms, the advantage has gone to those seeking to pursue their own private ends. Perhaps this is the usual fate of federal regulatory programs and reflects, in part, some endemic weaknesses in American government. But in this instance, the limited impact of federal regulation might be more directly attributed to confusion of aims and the unsuitability of the method of control involved.

The one clear achievement of the civil rights advocacy groups has been in establishing the 'principle' that racist schools should not receive the benefits of federal tax exemption. This 'principle' has now been judged so important as to override contrary claims to religious autonomy. Perhaps this result provides continuing satisfaction to many people as a gesture of official disapproval toward racism. But civil rights advocates had already ceased to be concerned with mere official gestures or abstract principles by the time they began litigating over the issue of tax exemptions for discriminatory schools. If abstract principle had been the only issue, the courts might have resolved the whole matter at the outset by simply reaffirming that a tax exemption does not imply governmental endorsement — as the Supreme Court had affirmed in 1970 that the tax-exempt status of churches does not imply government approval of particular religious practices or theological doctrines. If a more emphatic gesture were required, the civil rights advocacy groups might have stopped with the initial program of the IRS to require that schools receiving tax exemptions publicly disavow racial discrimination.

But the civil rights lawyers who filed the *Green* suit sought something more from the beginning. They sought to exert actual regulatory leverage to bolster public school integration. In this effort, they were almost entirely unsuccessful. Private schools that affirmed a policy of nondiscrimination were never finally required to secure — or to try to secure — integrated enrollments. If private schools remained all-white, and for this reason particularly attractive to white parents opposed to integration in the public schools, they were never penalized by the IRS for this reason alone.

It is important to recall, however, that the tax status of private schools has only a limited bearing on the problem of white flight from the public schools. In northern cities, where public school systems came to be overwhelmingly dominated by minority enrollments in the course of the 1970s, more white parents deserted the public schools for the suburbs than for private schools. Resistance to school integration may have been a motive for many parents, but racism was surely not the only conceivable reason why parents preferred the greater security, affluence, and tranquility of suburban neighborhoods. At any rate, if integration were the overriding goal, busing into the suburbs would have been required to achieve it. But in 1974, the Supreme Court firmly repudiated the notion that interdistrict busing could be a constitutional requirement in ordinary circumstances. Given the intensity of anti-busing sentiment in the country, a ruling to the contrary might well have provoked a direct confrontation with Congress, forcing the Court to retreat from ambitious interdistrict busing requirements.[42] But if the Court was unwilling or unable to pursue the ultimate logic of integration in public education, it should not be surprising, after all, that private schools continued to be treated very cautiously.

In fact, regulation of private schools presents awkward problems. This is so even if the more ambitious goal of stemming white flight from public schools is discounted in favor of a more modest focus on assuring fair treatment of minorities within private education itself. Bob Jones University, which may seem an especially easy target for regulation, offers a revealing example of the difficulties. Following the *Runyon* decision in 1976, Bob Jones did agree to admit minority students. It lost its tax exemption because it insisted on maintaining a ban on dating between students of different races. The IRS ruled that this was discriminatory, even if not clearly forbidden by the statute invoked in *Runyon*. School officials, however, claimed that this rule was mandated by biblical authority. Assuming the government had been able to force Bob Jones to abandon this rule as official school policy, should the government then have taken the next step and forbidden Bob Jones from instructing students in the very bizarre and offensive interpretation of the Bible from which the rule was ostensibly derived? No doubt, the government would have hesitated to interfere with free speech or religious freedom. But if the school continued to teach such doctrines, how many black students was it likely to attract? If the government allowed Bob Jones to continue teaching such manifestly insulting doctrines, how could it ask other schools to alter their less overtly offensive curricula or their scholarship policies simply to make them more congenial to black students?

In its 1982 decision in *Bob Jones v. Regan*, the Supreme Court dismissed the school's First Amendment arguments on the grounds that denial of tax exemption is not the same threat to religious autonomy as direct coercion. Other cases, however, have held that the 'free exercise' clause of the First Amendment does require government benefit programs to accommodate the special religious obligations of religious claimants.[43] The conditional nature of the constraints in this case may not have been crucial to the result. The Court certainly gave no clear indication that First Amendment objections would have been more successful if the nondiscrimination standard had been an unconditional or universally binding rule. But if the Court's emphasis on the voluntary nature of tax-exemption standards in this case made it easier to dismiss the First Amendment issues, it also highlighted the central difficulties with tax exemption as a regulatory control mechanism.

Bob Jones University — like most of the private schools in Mississippi that had their tax exemptions revoked in the early 1970s — decided to forgo the benefits of tax exemption rather than change its objectionable policies.[44] If operated on a nonprofit basis — as almost all are — few schools would be liable for direct federal income taxes, in any case. The deductibility of private donations is only a concern for large donors seeking itemized deductions — and neither the segregation academies nor the fundamentalist Bible academies seem to have had very many large donors.[45] Under these circumstances, it was at best highly 'speculative' — as the Supreme Court noted in dismissing the *Wright* case in 1983 — whether even the more rigorous IRS enforcement policy demanded by civil rights groups would have achieved much more integration in private or in public schools. But if so, this conclusion made the demand for more rigorous enforcement seem reducible to the mere petulant desire to punish or harass what the government could not actually control.

This embarrassment could be avoided by de-emphasizing practical regulatory objectives, and refocusing instead on the symbolism of tax exemptions. If the principal evil is defined, in other words, as public endorsement or governmental complicity with tax-exempt institutions, then it may seem quite logical to insist on removing tax exemptions from discriminatory institutions, even if this does not force the institutions themselves to desist from objectionable practices. This line of argument was tempting to courts from the outset of the controversy, since it was always part of the rationale for the 'state action' doctrine in constitutional law. Thus, in justifying its preliminary injunction in 1970, the D.C. District Court noted that tax exemptions were a more indirect form of assistance than direct grants, but still insisted on characterizing this distinction as 'only a difference in degree that does not negative our essential finding...that the tax benefits...mean a substantial and significant support by Government to the segregated private school pattern.'[46] The argument was invoked with particular vehemence during the partisan uproar over the Reagan administration's decision to restore tax-exempt status to discriminatory institutions — as when the chairman of the Democratic National Committee charged that this new policy 'effectively made every American taxpayer a forced contributor to segregationist schools.'[47]

But if they prove anything, such appeals probably prove too much. It is merely scratching the surface of the difficulty to note that by such reasoning 'every American taxpayer' is already a 'forced contributor' to churches and synagogues and a vast number of other sectarian institutions. For once the distinction between direct grants and tax exemptions is treated as a mere 'difference of degree' — a difference that does not affect the underlying 'principle'. It is hard to attribute any greater constitutional or symbolic importance to the difference between complete tax exemption and favorable deductibility or accounting rules. Following such logic, one could readily demonstrate that constitutional restrictions applying to government entities must be extended to every corporation, every organization, every entity in the land that does not pay the maximum conceivable tax — and finally conclude that a private homeowner should be denied the standard deduction for mortgage payments if he refuses to entertain black guests in his home.

The inescapable truth is that taxes are framed and distributed for a variety of reasons, including administrative convenience and ease of collection. A decision not to tax, after all, is fundamentally a decision not to intervene, and in the nature of things, decisions not to intervene need not be so well considered or clearly articulated as direct government actions. To determine which tax 'benefits' are constitutionally improper, courts would have to elaborate a highly artificial and dubious set of doctrines to identify the private wealth that should most properly be taken by the government. Leading tax scholars had warned in the mid-1970s against the rigidities and confusions entailed in such efforts to 'constitutionalize' the Internal Revenue Code.[48] Their criticisms remain quite compelling, though they could scarcely be heard or recalled amidst the torrents of rhetoric provoked by the Reagan administration's attempted change of policy toward tax exemptions for private schools.

Concluding Assessments

Compared with the confusions in the contemporary debate over tax exemptions for private schools, there was much more logic in the arguments of nineteenth century critics of tax exemption for church property. Reconstruction Era Republicans did not waste much argument on the symbolism of tax exemption, but focused instead on its projected economic consequences in concentrating property in ecclesiastical hands — particularly in the hands of the much feared and resented hierarchy of the Roman Catholic Church.[49] Today such morbid suspicions of Catholic separatism have largely vanished from American life. The United States is in many ways a more securely homogeneous country than in the nineteenth century. We can afford to be much more tolerant of diversity and deviance than the generation that fought the Civil War over slavery and Southern secession, and struggled to assimilate a swelling tide of immigrants from strange and distant places.

Institutions like Bob Jones University — which have thankfully become quite rare — may or may not mark the limits of acceptable diversity in our time. It is at least arguable that neither racial minorities nor the country at large any longer need to force the remaining handful of such places to conform to national standards of fair treatment. This thought may have animated those Supreme Court justices who voted in the spring of 1988 to reconsider whether *Runyon v. McCrary* was correctly decided or whether its strained extension of the 1866 Civil Rights Act to govern private decision-making ought now to be abandoned.[50] The argument for a hands-off policy in private education may draw more support from the reflection that controversial affirmative action programs — often denounced by critics as 'reverse discrimination' and occasionally entangled in legal challenges by white or male claimants — are vastly more common today than the kind of racism displayed by a Bob Jones. An overly standardized approach to 'discrimination' may thus stifle valuable or at least potentially promising affirmative action experiments by private institutions, with little compensating gain.

It is certainly arguable, on the other hand, that even isolated instances of racial exclusion or old-fashioned discrimination are an intolerable affront to racial minorities, and an unacceptable threat to the moral consensus of the country. If this is so, however, the most appropriate policy response is to enact direct statutory prohibitions on discrimination in private education, rather than merely imposing financial disincentives to discrimination through the tax code. There may be constitutional questions on the margin concerning the permissible reach of such regulation. But the Supreme Court's decision in *Bob Jones University v. Regan* does not suggest that these limits are an insurmountable obstacle to some form of direct and substantial controls. In general, religious objections are not sufficient to claim exemptions from important legal obligations — as the Court refused to exempt Amish dissenters from paying Social Security taxes.[51] Similarly, the Court has repeatedly upheld the authority of states to impose nondiscrimination standards on private clubs, dismissing First Amendment 'freedom of association' claims as insufficient to withstand governmental authority to suppress discrimination.[52]

It is sensible to rely on tax-exemption standards to control objectionable conduct only where we are not sufficiently committed to the desired standard to enforce it directly and fully. That is the most plausible argument for taking this approach with outright segregation academies or with institutions like Bob Jones University — namely, that their discriminatory practices are morally repellant but may not be sufficiently dangerous or harmful to justify direct constraint. It is no great concession to tolerance or diversity to insist on penalizing and stigmatizing such institutions through the tax code, while still allowing them to follow their strange convictions if they insist upon doing so. For people who find this a reasonable compromise between public morality and civil liberty, the resolution effected by the Supreme Court in the early 1980s may seem to provide, after all, a reasonably happy ending to a tangled and troubling policy struggle.

The manner in which this result was achieved, however, should still give some pause. The Supreme Court's decision in *Bob Jones* managed to avoid ruling that tax exemptions are the constitutional equivalent of direct subsidies, and thereby avoided any direct holding that tax-exempt institutions must comply with all constitutional constraints now binding on the government. Nonetheless, the Court's construction of the Internal Revenue Code has disturbing implications. Adopting the reasoning advanced by the IRS itself in 1970, the Court held that when Congress authorized tax exemptions for nonprofit 'charitable' and 'educational' organizations in Sec. 501 (c) (3) of the tax code, it had implicitly intended to limit this benefit to organizations acting in accord with 'public policy'.

But all previous holdings applying a 'public policy' limitation to tax benefits dealt with actual illegality — such as the ruling that a truck company could not deduct highway fines as a 'business expense'.[53] The *Bob Jones* rationale suggests that what is not illegal may still be contrary to 'public policy'. Given the plethora of laws against sex discrimination, it would hardly be stretching the *Bob Jones* precedent at all for the IRS to declare that Catholic seminaries must be denied tax-exempt status for violating the general 'public policy' against sex discrimination — even though no law at present actually prohibits the practice of excluding women from training for the priesthood. Given the plethora of laws against religious discrimination, it would hardly be stretching the *Bob Jones* precedent much further to deny Catholic seminaries their tax-exempt status for violating the general 'public policy' against religious discrimination. Nor did the Supreme Court really lay to rest many doubts by emphasizing that, in this case, Congress had been aware of the basic IRS policy on private schools for many years and might thus be understood to have endorsed the policy by refusing to amend or suspend it. If legislative silence can be taken for legal authorization, then legal constraints on bureaucratic power will mean much less than we have previously supposed. It is usually much easier, after all, for legislators to remain passive than to build the broad consensus required for new enactments.

Yet from beginning to end, the story of tax policy toward private schools has been a story of policy-making in the absence of broad consensus or well defined aims. At various points, the issue has stirred strong feelings among significant political constituencies, and these feelings have been strongly sounded in Congress. But feelings are not policies, and Congress has been content to leave the policy-making in this area to judges and bureaucrats. Looking back over two decades of their maneuverings in this area, it would be hard to argue that the judges and the bureaucrats have displayed any more logic or consistency than what is normally expected of politicians. Instead, judges have repeatedly pushed the bureaucrats toward ambitious policy initiatives, then allowed them to settle for disconnected 'principles' when the policies went sour.

Perhaps the ultimate result does now symbolize a ripened moral consensus in the country. But even the symbolic value of the current policy must be discounted somewhat by the manner in which it was achieved. It is hard to feel much confidence or enthusiasm for a moral consensus that has only been articulated by unelected officials and unaccountable judges and never squarely endorsed by the elected representatives of the nation. Given the high feelings and conflicting sensitivities in this debate, congressional enactments might not have secured a more coherent or effective policy in the end. But Congress could surely have offered a more credible symbolic gesture. Whatever else it may symbolize, the current 'law' of tax exemptions for private schools also symbolizes the inability of Congress to give clear answers to elemental questions.

Notes

1 U.S. GRANT (1898) 'Seventh Annual Message', 7 December 1875, in J. RICHARDSON *Messages and Papers of the Presidents*, Vol. 7, Washington, D.C., Government Printing Office, p. 334.
2 *Pierce v. Society of Sisters*, 268 US 510 (1925).
3 *Meyer v. Nebraska*, 262 US 390 (1923).
4 *Sherbert v. Verner*, 374 US 398 (1963).
5 *Wisconsin v. Yoder*, 406 US 205 (1972).
6 *Engel v. Vitale*, 370 US 421 (1962); *Abington School Dist. v. Schempp*, 374 US 203 (1963); *Stone v. Graham*, 449 US 39 (1980).
7 *Lemon v. Kurtzman*, 403 US 602 (1971); *Committee for Public Ed. v. Nyquist*, 413 US 756 (1973); *Meek v. Pittenger*, 421 US 349 (1975).
8 *Walz v. Tax Comm'n*, 397 US 664 (1970).
9 Civil Rights Cases, 109 US 3 (1883).
10 *Plessy v. Ferguson*, 163 US 537 (1896).
11 *Burton v. Wilmington Parking Auth.*, 365 US 715 (1961).

12 *Brown v. Board of Educ.*, 347 US 483 (1954).

13 *Green v. County School Bd.*, 391 US 430 (1968).

14 *Swann v. Charlotte Mecklenburg Bd. of Ed.*, 402 US 1 (1971).

15 *Keyes v. School Dist. No. 1, Denver*, 413 US 189 (1973).

16 *Lee v. Macon County Bd. of Educ.*, 267 F. Supp. 458 (M.D. Ala. 1967); *Coffey v. State Ed. Finance Comm'n*, 296 F. Supp. 1389 (S.D. Miss. 1969).

17 *Norwood v. Harrison*, 413 US 455 (1974); compare *Board of Ed. v. Allen*, 392 US 236 (1968).

18 US Commission on Civil Rights (1967) *Southern School Desegregation 1966–67*, p. 73.

19 *Runyon v. McCrary*, 427 US 160 (1976).

20 *Green v. Kennedy*, Complaint filed in US district court, 21 May 1969, pp. 9–10.

21 Act of March 2, 1867, 14 Stat. 475, now codified at 26 U.S.C. § 7421 (a).

22 *Green v. Kennedy*, 309 F. Supp. 1127 (1970).

23 IRS 'News Release', 10 July 1970; reprinted in full in (1979) *Tax Exempt Status of Private Schools*, Hearings before the Subcommittee on Oversight, Committee on Ways and Means, US House of Representatives, 96th Cong., 1st Sess., p. 10.

24 (1970) *Equal Educational Opportunity*, Part 3D, 'Desegregation under Law', Hearings before the Select Committee on Equal Educational Opportunity, US Senate, 91st Cong., 2d Sess. p. 2026.

25 'Defendant's Statement of Genuine Issues', filed 15 March 1970, par. 3.

26 *Green v. Connally*, 330 F. Supp. 1150 (1971).

27 Parents of children in affected private schools did seek to appeal the ruling, but this effort merely yielded a summary affirmance of the lower court ruling: *Colt v. Green*, 404 US 997 (1971). The Supreme Court, itself, subsequently noted that this summary action 'lacks the precedential weight of a case involving a truly adversary controversy' — without explaining whether this meant that the case had not been properly before the Court when it offered its summary judgment, or simply that the Court had not properly considered it. It certainly did not allow oral argument. This cryptic characterization was offered in *Bob Jones Univ. v. Simon*, 416 US 725 (1973) at 740, n. 11.

28 US Commission on Civil Rights (1975) *To Ensure Equal Educational Opportunity*, Vol. 2 of *The Federal Civil Rights Enforcement Effort, 1974*, p. 169.

29 *Ibid.*, n. 439.

30 'Testimony of IRS Commissioner Jerome Kurtz', *Tax Exempt Status of Private Schools*, 1979 House Hearings, pp. 252–3.

31 Rev. Proc. 75–50, C.B. 1975–2, 587 and Rev. Proc. 75–231, C.B. 1975–2, 158.

32 *Wright v. Simon*, 'Complaint for Declaratory and Injunctive Relief', filed 30 July 1976 (C.A. No. 1426–76), signed among others by Drew Days, III, subsequently Assistant Attorney General for Civil Rights in the Carter Justice Department, and by David S. Tatel, subsequently appointed Director of the Office for Civil Rights, in Department of Health, Education and Welfare.

33 43 *Fed. Reg.* 37296 (22 August 1978).

34 See S. Lipset and E. Raab (1981) 'The Election and the Evangelicals', *Commentary*, 71, p. 29; and L. Davis (1980) 'Conservatism in America', *Harpers*, 261, pp. 24–5 on the connection between the tax exemption debate and the subsequent founding of the Moral Majority.

35 For background on the factors encouraging the growth of 'Christian schools', see P. SKERRY (1980) 'Christian Schools versus the I.R.S.', *The Public Interest*, 61, Fall, p.18. See also the presentation of spokesmen for various 'Christian school' associations in *Tax Exempt Status of Private Schools*, 1979 House Hearings.

36 Treasury, Postal Service and General Government Appropriations Act of 1980, P.L. No. 96–74, § 103, 93 Stat. 562 and § 614, 93 Stat. 576 (1979).

37 *Bob Jones Univ. v. Blumenthal*, 468 F. Supp. 890 D.S.C. 1978; *Bob Jones Univ. v. Miller*, 639 F.2d 147 (4th Cir. 1980).

38 *Bob Jones Univ. v. United States*, 461 US 574 (1983). For an account of the very questionable legal status of the case — and of Coleman's role in it — by the time of the Supreme Court's decision, T. McCOY and N. DEVINS (1984) 'Standing and Adverseness on the Issue of Tax Exemptions for Discriminatory Private Schools', *Fordham Law Review*, 52, p. 441.

39 *Allen v. Wright*, 468 US 737 (1984).

40 *Green v. Miller*, Order of 5 May 1980, and 'Order Clarifying and Amending Court's Order and Permanent Injunction of May 5', dated 2 June 1980. The order of 5 May acknowledged that 'the defendants have not violated the order of June 30, 1971', but maintained that 'said order requires supplementation and modification' — because several schools disqualified from participation in a state textbook loan program under the standards announced in *Norwood v. Harrison* were found to be retaining tax-exempt treatment from the IRS. The order was subsequently involved in further inconclusive litigation by private schools claiming religious exemptions — claims that appeared to be settled in the end by the Supreme Court's decision in *Bob Jones*.

41 See generally J. HOCHSCHILD (1984) *The New American Dilemma*, New Haven, Conn., Yale University Press.

42 *Milliken v. Bradley*, 418 US 717 (1974).

43 *Sherbert v. Verner*, 374 US 398 (1963); *Thomas v. Review Bd.*, 450 US 707 (1981).

44 Of 110 schools that had lost their tax-exempt status under the standards in force during the 1970s, only twenty-five changed their policies and had their tax exemptions reinstated, according to figures maintained in the Tax Division of the Justice Department. Some of the others may have ceased to operate, but the precise number is unknown. The federal government maintains no data on the precise number of non-tax-exempt schools still operating at the end of the 1980s.

45 At the outset, the IRS itself had emphasized the limited leverage likely to be gained by threatening to withhold tax-exempt status from such schools. 'Defendant's Answer to Charges', filed 31 July 1969, and 'Defendant's Statements of Genuine Issues', filed 15 May 1970 in *Green v. Kennedy*.

46 *Green v. Kennedy*, 309 F. Supp. 1127 (1970) at 1134.

47 'School Tax Ruling Facing Test', *New York Times*, 10 January 1982, p. 7 (featuring the quoting from Charles Manatt on the continuation at p. 18).

48 See B. BITTKER and K. KAUFMAN (1972) 'Taxes and Civil Rights: Constitutionalizing the Internal Revenue Code', *Yale Law Journal*, 82, p. 51.

49 Even President Grant's formal message to Congress was quite explicit about this concern: see RICHARDSON, *Messages and Papers of the Presidents, op. cit.*,

invoking the specter of a future wholesale confiscation of church property, as in the days of Henry VIII, if the property should accumulate too much due to tax exemption.

50 *Patterson v. McLean Credit Union*, 56 U.S.L.W. 3734, 26 April, 1988.
51 *United States v. Lee*, 455 US 252 (1982).
52 See, e.g., *Roberts v. United States Jaycees*, 468 US 609 (1984).
53 *Tank Truck Rentals v. Commissioner*, 356 US 30 (1958). In a later decision, *Commissioner v. Tellier*, 383 US 687, 691 (1966), the Supreme Court expressly cautioned that the 'public policy' limitation of tax benefits should be applied only 'in extremely limited circumstances', because 'the federal income tax is a tax on net income, not a sanction against wrongdoing.'

Part III
Private Schools and the Pursuit of the Public Good

8
Effective Schools and Equal Opportunity

John E. Chubb and Terry M. Moe

Since the educational inequities suffered by America's racial minorities first received government attention in the early 1950s, the United States has taken many steps to ensure that race does not affect the quality of a child's education. Minorities now have access to schools that would otherwise be attended exclusively by nonminorities, and schools with predominantly minority enrollments now have resources equal to or exceeding those of the proximate schools of nonminorities. Statutory inequities in educational opportunity largely have been erased. But the educational problems of racial minorities, especially those of blacks, largely have not. Minorities have made only modest progress in reducing the yawning gap that separates their academic achievement from that of nonminorities, and they continue to exhibit alarming rates of illiteracy and high school noncompletion.[1]

This continuing struggle exists for many reasons: discouraging economic prospects that depress educational expectations, poorly educated families that do not promote scholastic accomplishment, and no doubt many others. But an important reason is almost certainly the poor quality of many minority schools. Increasing evidence suggests that the kinds of schools that minorities disproportionately attend, particularly urban public schools, are especially unsuccessful. It is not entirely clear why. They do not suffer obvious objective shortcomings such as larger classes, lower per pupil expenditures, or lower teacher salaries.[2] Yet, they seem to lack many of the subjective qualities, such as ambitious goals, strong leadership, cohesive staff, and an academic ethos, that often distinguish successful from unsuccessful schools. This is what we are learning from a promising body of research into the organization and operation of 'effective schools'.[3] Minorities are simply less likely to attend schools that have acquired the requisite attributes for effectiveness.

If correct, this view raises obvious questions about the education of America's racial minorities, as well as other groups stuck in chronically ineffective schools. Why is it that schools especially well organized for high performance seem less likely to develop in many areas where minorities reside? Are government policies aimed at improving the education of minorities and of disadvantaged groups helping their schools develop effective school characteristics? Neither of these questions has been well answered. Research into school effectiveness has been more concerned with identifying the school qualities that enhance performance and less with explaining their origins.[4]

This chapter will argue that it is probably no accident that the schools in which minorities often find themselves are not organized for academic success. In part, this may be because of the academic problems that economically disadvantaged students, such as many minorities, create for educators. However, it may also be because schools are largely products of their environments and thus, above all, of the way in which our system of democratic control operates — intentionally and unintentionally — to shape the organization of schools. To the extent that this is so, ineffective organization is not the fault of the schools or their students, and not a problem they can necessarily do much about. The schools cannot be reformed without making more basic changes in the educational system that governs them, since the system is the source of their ineffectiveness. Fundamental reform of this sort, however, is seldom contemplated. To the contrary, attempts to improve the education of minority students have not only not worked within the existing system, but they have contributed to its size, power, and control.

Real improvements in the educational achievement of minorities, genuine equal opportunity, may demand new approaches altogether. This essay will suggest one approach — ironically modeled after the private systems of education that have often symbolized unequal opportunity. But first it will show why a new approach is needed. That involves a look at extensive new data on the control and organization of a national sample of public and private high schools, and a reconsideration, in the light of that information, of the largest federal education program from which minorities especially benefit, Chapter 1 of the 1981 Educational Consolidation and Improvement Act (formally Title I of the 1965 Elementary and Secondary Education Act).

The Promise and Problems of Research on School Performance

Two different bodies of school research have recently provided promising insights into student achievement. One is concerned with school effectiveness: what are the characteristics of schools that succeed in promoting academic achievement and other educational goals, and how can we institute reforms that encourage existing schools to develop these characteristics? The other is interested in the school sector: are private schools more effective at educating students than public schools are?

Research on school effectiveness has contributed to our understanding of schools in two important respects. First, it is building a consensus on some of the basic characteristics that seem to promote school effectiveness: strong instructional leadership by the principal, clear school goals, rigorous academic requirements, an orderly environment, an integral role for teachers in school decision-making, cooperative principal-teacher relations, high parental involvement and support, and high teacher and principal expectations about student performance.[5] Second, it is establishing the theoretical importance of school organization. What goes on inside a school, something that school research traditionally ignored, appears to play a leading role in explaining school outcomes.[6]

Unfortunately, 'appear' is the watchword of effective schools research. Its conclusions, however reasonable and widely shared, can only be regarded as tentative. Partly, this is a problem of method. Most of the work is based on case studies or qualitative analyses of small numbers of schools that gauge school performance impressionistically (i.e., without measure of student achievement).[7] The main problem, however, is not methodological but conceptual. Effective schools research has produced a lengthy list of things closely associated with good performance, but no cogent explanation of where, why, and when those things are found. School performance is often conceived very narrowly, for example, as a product of how teachers teach or principals lead. Yet, these things and other proximate sources of student achievement, such as homework and discipline, are bound up with each other, and with qualities of the student body and political, administrative, and economic aspects of the school environment. Many of the familiar 'causes' of school effectiveness may therefore be products of more powerful forces that must first be altered if schools are to be lastingly improved. Unfortunately, this is somewhat difficult to determine, for researchers taking this otherwise valuable approach have not brought together systematic data on school environment, organization, and performance.[8]

This uncertainty has been somewhat less of a problem with research comparing public and private schools. That work, including the products of James Coleman and his associates, has demonstrated that school effectiveness depends to some degree on sector. Private schools are evidently more effective than public schools at producing academic achievement gains among comparable students.[9] To be sure, many critics have challenged this claim.[10] But derived, as it is, from the impressive High School and Beyond survey and testing of some 60,000 students, and now buttressed with corroborating evidence from retest data, the claim appears to be secure.[11] This result is important, for it provides the most reliable evidence yet that schools affect student achievement, that schools really matter. It suggests a promising explanation — that the school environment, public or private in this instance, may be closely linked to school organization and, in turn, to performance.

The problem is that the suggestion has not been adequately investigated. The Coleman group demonstrates that many of the differences in public and private school achievement can be accounted for with variables that are logically close to student achievement — coursework, homework, and discipline. But given all that is known about effective schools, it is likely that these things are merely pieces in a large puzzle that only when properly assembled produces a successful school. If reform is to improve school performance, this point must be appreciated. It is unlikely that public schools can be made to perform like private schools simply by mandating more homework and discipline.[12]

An Environmental Perspective on School Performance

It has often been said that schools are products of their environments, that they are 'open systems'.[13] A school, like any organization, survives, grows, and adapts through constant exchanges with an environment — including parents, administrators, politicians, demographic changes, socioeconomic conditions, and a range of other forces that variously generate support, opposition, stress, opportunities for choice, and demands for change. Internally, it has its own distinctive structures and processes, its own culture of norms, beliefs, and values, and its own technology for transforming inputs into outputs. The organization and its environment together constitute an overarching system of behavior in which, as the saying goes, everything is related to everything else. The environment shapes the internal organization, the organization generates outputs, and they in turn have a variety of reciprocal effects on both the organization and its environment.

But precisely what difference does all of this make for students and their achievement? That has never been spelled out, for the open system perspective has never been taken seriously in empirical research on school performance. In the larger project from which this essay derives, we are attempting to investigate the linkages among environments, organization, and achievement.[14] This sort of research requires an unusually comprehensive data set that affords reliable indicators of student achievement and background, school organization and operation, and environment, including the influences of parents, administrators, and politicians. No such data set existed when this project was conceived in 1982, but one came close. The High School and Beyond (HSB) survey, first administered in 1980 and later supplemented by biennial follow-up surveys, provided an excellent database for analyzing student achievement and measuring school performance in the public and private sectors alike. A data set comprising the 1980 and 1982 waves provided measures of actual student achievement for more than 25,000 students in roughly 1000 schools nationwide, and enough information about the 'causes' of that achievement outside schools — e.g., parental and peer influence — to gauge reliably the effectiveness of schools. The only serious problem with the HSB data was that they provided inadequate information about school organization and environment. Principals in the HSB study were surveyed for data available for the most part in school records — e.g., class sizes, course offerings — and teachers were queried only superficially.

It was decided to supplement the HSB surveys with a new survey aimed at organizational and environmental factors. The result is the 'Administrator and Teacher Survey' (ATS), which we designed and directed in collaboration with researchers from Johns Hopkins University, the National Opinion Research Center, Ohio State University, and the University of Wisconsin. Its questionnaires were administered in 1984 to the principal and thirty teachers, among others, in nearly 500 of the HSB schools, including most of the more than 100 private schools.

Some Suggestive Findings

This essay cannot begin to convey all that these data have revealed about the complex relationships among schools, their environments, and their performance. But it can illustrate, using a small portion of the data, a general conclusion about those relationships that also has important implications for the problem of unequal educational opportunity: because of our current system of democratic governance, the public schools may be seriously disadvantaged in their efforts to promote student achievement.

The illustration involves a simple comparison of public and private schools. Since public schools are governed by democratic institutions and private schools are not — they are 'controlled' indirectly by markets rather than directly by politics — a comparision of their organizational features is a nice way of getting at institutional effects. If democratic governance has distinctive consequences for the organization of public schools, they ought to show up when public and private schools are compared. To facilitate the comparison, we will break down the private sector into three types of schools: Catholic, elite (high performance, college prep), and other private (a catch-all category).[15] This breakdown helps to reduce the sector's heterogeneity and clarify the uniformity of the public-private differences.

External Authorities

It is a foregone conclusion that the public governing system will be more complex when it comes to higher levels of political and administrative authority: public schools are part of state and federal governmental systems, and private schools generally are not. But what about immediate outside authorities, those best suited to oversee and constrain the school at the local level?

Not surprisingly, virtually all public schools are subordinate to school boards and to outside administrative superiors. Private schools are far more diverse, regardless of type. Most private schools have a school board of some sort, but may have no accompanying administrative apparatus. Such an apparatus is quite rare among the elite schools; nearly half of the other private schools are similarly unencumbered. It is the Catholic schools that most resemble the public schools in this regard; some two-thirds of them have both school boards and administrative superiors.

Still, these patterns tell us only that private schools are subject to fewer outside authorities. They do not tell us whether the authorities that private schools actually face are any less demanding than those that public schools face. It turns out, however, that they are. On five basic policy dimensions — curriculum, instructional methods, discipline, hiring, and firing — school boards in the public sector appear to have more influence over school policy than they do in the private sector, regardless of the type of private school, and principals, relative to their school boards, have less. When it comes to the influence of administrative superiors, the famed Catholic hierarchy (the only private sector hierarchy worth talking about) plays, by public sector standards, a small role in setting school policy. On all five dimensions, the influence of administrative superiors is far less in Catholic than in public schools, and Catholic principals have more autonomy in setting school policy than public principals do.

These are only simple measures of influence. But the patterns they yield are quite uniform and entirely consistent with the expectation that public schools, by virtue of their reliance on political control, will be subject to greater control by external authorities. The authorities that are so ubiquitous in the democratic context of the public school are often simply absent from private school settings, and even when they are an acknowledged part of the governing apparatus, they are less influential in the determination of school policy. Private schools, it would appear, have more control over their own destinies.

Staffing the Organisation

External authorities are by no means the only constraints on the ability of a school to structure and operate its organization as it sees fit. Two in particular — tenure and unions — restrict a school's freedom to exercise perhaps its most significant form of control: its ability to recruit the kinds of teachers it wants and to get rid of those who do not live up to its standards. Public schools are much more constrained in these regards.

The ATS survey shows that 88 per cent of public schools offer tenure, while only a minority of the private schools do. Among the schools that do offer tenure, moreover, the proportion of teachers who have been awarded it reflects the same asymmetry: 80 per cent of eligible teachers in public schools have tenure, while the figure is some 10 to 16 per cent lower in the private sector. The differences in unionization are even more substantial. The vast majority of public schools are unionized, some 80 per cent; only about 10 per cent of the Catholic schools are unionized; virtually none of the elites and other privates is.

Inherent differences between politics and markets help account for these disparate levels of constraint. Tenure systems in public schools are simply special cases of the civil service systems that exist at all levels of government. Unions are a product, at least in part, of the need among politicians for organization, money, and manpower — real assets in state and local elections where voter turnout is typically low. There is nothing to prevent unions from gaining a foothold in private schools or to keep private schools from adopting tenure and other civil service-like protections; however, there is nothing comparable to government that drives them in that direction. Whether unions and tenure systems take hold in the private sector is determined to a far greater extent by the market.

But do these constraints perceptibly influence school control over important personnel issues? According to the principals in the ATS survey, they certainly do. Public principals claim to face substantially greater obstacles in dismissing a teacher for poor performance than private school principals indicate. The procedures are far more complex, the tenure rules more restrictive, and the preparation and documentation process roughly three times as long. Their complexity and formality make dismissal procedures the highest barrier to firing cited by public school principals. For private school principals, the highest barrier is a personal reluctance to fire.

Even if superintendents and central offices wanted to reduce these obstacles — to delegate greater control over teachers to public school principals — many of these personnel decisions cannot in practice be delegated. In the public sector, tenure protections are usually guaranteed through laws that are written by school boards or state legislatures, and union contracts are typically bargained at the district level. Tenure and unionization tend to settle the question of when and how the basic personnel decisions will be made in the public sector.

Principals

The principal, according to much of the new literature on school effectiveness, holds a key to school success. Excellence in education appears to be promoted by a principal who articulates clear goals, holds high expectations of students and teachers, exercises strong instructional leadership, steers clear of administrative burdens, and effectively extracts resources from the environment. According to our perspective, the principal is also critical. He is responsible for negotiating successfully with the environment — for dealing somehow with demands and pressures from parents, unions, administrators, and school boards.

But this does not mean that schools necessarily will benefit from being headed by an adroit principal. The school environment can have a considerable influence on whether the principal is able to practice the precepts of effective leadership. Effective leadership does not simply inhere in the individual filling the role; it is unavoidably contingent upon the demands, constraints, and resources that the principal must deal with. Depending on the nature and strength of these forces, even the 'best' principal may have only a marginal effect on school performance.

The ATS survey disclosed substantial differences between public and private school principals. To begin with, private school principals have considerably more teaching experience — almost four years more for principals in Catholic schools, and over five years more for those in the elites and other privates. Private school principals also come to their jobs with different motivations than their public counterparts. They are more likely to stress control over school policies, while public school principals place greater emphasis on a preference for administrative responsibilities, a desire to further their careers, and an interest in advancing to higher administrative posts.

These differences in experience and motivation appear to shape the principal's performance as a leader. As judged by their own teachers, private school principals are more effective instructional leaders, and are more likely to exhibit other basic qualities of leadership — knowledge of school problems, openness with the staff, clarity and strength of purpose, and a willingness to innovate.

From the standpoint of politics and markets, these findings make sense. In the public sector, the administrative hierarchy offers an attractive avenue for career advancement. In the private sector, the governing structure offers fewer opportunities. Private school principals consequently stay in teaching longer, and their view of the principalship focuses more on its relation to the school than on its relation to their movement up an educational hierarchy. Of course, these are not the only determinants of leadership. Public school principals are forced to operate in much more complex, conflict filled circumstances in which educational success is more difficult to achieve, regardless of the principal's (perhaps considerable) abilities. If anything, however, the public school principal's lack of teaching expertise and his hierarchic career orientation probably contribute to these leadership problems.

Goals and Policies

Given what we know of their environments, there is every reason to expect that public and private schools should adopt different orientations toward the education of their students. Because public schools must take whoever walks in the door, they do not have the luxury of being able to select the kind of students best suited to organization goals and structure. In practice, this means that the pursuit of educational excellence must compete with much more basic needs — for literacy, for remedial training, for more slowly paced instruction. In addition, the hierarchical structure of democratic control ensures that a range of actors with diverse, often conflicting interests will participate in deciding what the public school ought to pursue and how. Private schools, largely unconstrained by comparison, should find it easier (if they want to do so) to place a high priority on excellence and to choose a set of goals that is clear and consistent, whatever those goals may be.

The results of the ATS survey confirmed these expectations. In terms of general goals, public schools place significantly greater emphasis on basic literacy, citizenship, good work habits, and specific occupational skills, while private schools — regardless of type — are more oriented toward academic excellence, personal growth and fulfillment, and human relations skills. These goals are also upheld by specific policies and clearly discerned by the staff. Private schools have more stringent minimum graduation requirements; their students, regardless of track, must take significantly more English and history, science and math, and foreign language than must public school students in order to graduate. Private schools also have more stringent homework policies. Finally, private teachers uniformly say that school goals are clearer and more clearly communicated by the principal than public teachers report; teachers are also more in agreement among themselves on school priorities.

All these characteristics that private schools possess in greater abundance are stereotypical of effective schools. They are also characteristics that, because of the differential operation of politics and markets, would seem extremely difficult for public schools to develop in the same degree.

Teachers and Teaching

Politics and markets cannot hope to tell us everything we might want to know about organizational structure and process, but they point us in a clear direction. The critical fact about the public school environment is not just that it is complex, but that it imposes decisions about policy, structure, personnel, and procedure on the school. Nowhere is this more apparent than in the control over the most crucial agent of organizational performance: the teacher.

As we have seen, the public school principal is far less able than his private counterpart to staff his organization according to his best judgment. This inability, in turn, should promote differences in staff heterogeneity and conflict. Public school teachers may reject the principal's leadership, dissent from school goals and policies, get along poorly with their colleagues, or fail to perform acceptably in the classroom — but the principal must somehow learn to live with them. When these teachers are represented by unions, as they normally are, leadership difficulties are magnified. Professionalism takes on new meaning: as a demand that decision-making power be transferred from the principal to the teachers.

Private schools are not immune from personnel problems and struggles for power. But the fact that the principal has much greater control over hiring and firing means that he can take steps to recruit the kinds of teachers he wants and weed out those he does not. It also means that teachers have a strong inducement to perform.

By comparison to his public school counterpart, the private school principal is better able to create a team of teachers whose values, skills, and willingness to work together tend to mirror those qualifications he deems conducive to the pursuit of organizational goals. At the same time he is in a position to make teacher professionalism work for rather than against him. Without real threat to his own authority or control, he can encourage teachers to participate in decision-making, extend them substantial autonomy within their own spheres of expertise, and promote a context of interaction, exchange of ideas, and mutual respect.

The data from the ATS survey support this general line of reasoning. Private school principals consistently claim that a larger percentage of their schools' teachers are 'excellent', suggesting that these principals are more confident in the abilities of their staff members than public school principals are in the abilities of theirs. Private sector teachers, in turn, have better relationships with their principals. They are consistently more likely to regard the latter as encouraging, supportive, and reinforcing. Private school teachers also feel more involved and efficacious in important areas of school decision-making that bear on their teaching. They feel more influential over schoolwide policies, and in their classrooms they believe they have more control over most matters that govern their effectiveness.

Relative harmony between private school principals and teachers is matched by relative harmony among the private teachers themselves. On a personal level, relationships are more collegial in the private sector. On a professional level, private school teachers give greater evidence of mutual involvement and support. It should come as no surprise, then, that private school teachers are much more satisfied with their jobs, have better attendance records, and tend to work for less money. Private schools do look more like teams.

School Control and School Organization

Why private schools tend to develop team-like organizations is a question of potentially great import for school improvement. Private schools appear to be more effective than public schools, and the team-like qualities that distinguish private schools — strong leadership, shared goals, cooperative decision-making, collegial relationships, mutual trust, widespread efficacy — are the very qualities that research on school improvement has identified as keys to student achievement. To be sure, private schools may owe some of this organizational *esprit de corps* to the better students and more supportive parents that, on average, they work with, but not all of it. In analyses of the merged HSB-ATS data set, we have found that the school environment is at least as important as the school clientele in determining the organizational climate of the school.[16] Significantly, this conclusion appears to be every bit as true of the shaping of school organizations within the public sector as it is between the public and the private sectors: more complex and straining environments are associated with more troubled school organizations regardless of sector. Still, the differences between the organizations and the environments of public and private schools are so striking that they must be understood — not only for what they may say about the influence of school control but, as we shall see, for what they may disclose about the prospects for school improvement both within and without public education systems.

Above all, it is important to recognize that public schools are captives of democratic politics. They are subordinates in a hierarchical system of control in which myriad interests and actors use the rules, structures, and processes of democracy to impose their preferences on local schools. It is no accident that public schools are lacking in autonomy, that principals are limited in their leadership, and that school goals are heterogeneous, unclear, and undemanding. Nor is it an accident that weak principals and tenured, unionized teachers struggle for power and hold one another in relatively low esteem. These sorts of characteristics constitute an organizational syndrome whose roots are deeply anchored in democratic control as we have come to know it.

Private schools are controlled by society too, but there are few, if any, political or administrative mechanisms to ensure that they respond as they 'should'. They make their own decisions about policy, organization, and personnel subject to market forces that signal how they can best pursue their own goals and prosperity. Given their substantial autonomy, it is not surprising to find that principals are stronger leaders, that they have greater control over hiring and firing, that they and teachers they choose have greater respect for and interaction with one another, and that teachers — without conflict or formal demands — are more integrally involved in school decision-making. As in the public sector, these sorts of organizational characteristics are bound up with one another, and they jointly arise from the surrounding environment. Different environments promote different organizational syndromes.

Politics, Bureaucracy, and Chapter 1

In considering how best to improve the education of racial minorities and other disadvantaged children, it may well be instructive to appreciate how much the experience of Chapter 1 (and Title I), the largest government program attempting such improvement, has been shaped by the dynamic of public control — and how much that dynamic has itself been shaped by Chapter 1.

When Title I was enacted in 1965, it was conceived as a way for the federal government to provide compensatory educational services to disadvantaged children, without becoming involved itself in the delivery of education. As it had in so many other categorical grants-in-aid, the government in Washington would send funds to qualifying lower governments (in this instance, ones with certain concentrations of poor people), on the condition that the funds would be spent for some federally designated purpose. This enabled the federal government to do what it arguably could do best — raise and redistribute revenue — and left the lower governments to exploit their comparative advantage in supplying services to suit local demands. Cumbersome and costly administrative arrangements would be avoided and efficiency enhanced.

Unfortunately, things did not quite work out that way. Federal policy-makers had underestimated the difficulty of accomplishing national goals through subnational governments and agencies. There was often a conflict of interest between the national and the lower governments, as well as a severe asymmetry of information about how policies were being executed and with what consequences. Lower governments did not always agree that federal funds should be spent directly on serving the educationally disadvantaged. Spending on teacher salaries, physical facilities, general school improvements, or even future tax savings were sometimes regarded as more desirable. In addition, because only local governments knew how additional revenues were really being spent, they enjoyed an advantage over federal authorities trying to ensure that national goals were being realized.

The federal authorities faced a classic problem of organizational design, a principal-agent problem.[17] The principal in Washington sought to achieve its own ends through the actions of its agents at the state and local levels, but because of conflict of interest and asymmetric information, control was inherently problematic: the agents had both the incentives and the informational leverage to go their own ways. Washington's task, like that of any principal, was to design a structure that mitigated these difficulties as much as possible, chiefly by monitoring the decision-making and performance of its agents (reducing the information asymmetry), and by trying to alter their incentives to pursue federal goals (reducing the conflict of interest).

Federal policy-makers, alerted by beneficiary groups that Title I funds were not always reaching the disadvantaged, began monitoring state and local educational agencies more carefully in the late 1960s.[18] Their intention was not to tell the agencies precisely how to spend their money, but rather, in the spirit of the policy's initial conception, to ensure that the money was spent on the statute's goal, namely improving the educational experiences of the disadvantaged. Over time, however, the federal government found that it could not afford to supervise directly the behavior of all of the state and local agencies participating in the program (though it did increase its auditing sharply in the early 1970s). Hence, it shifted its approach to one of specifying in ever greater detail the standards that agencies would have to meet to pass occasional federal inspections.[19] These very extensive and explicit regulations − for example, 'supplement not supplant', 'excess costs', and 'comparability' − did not expressly violate the federal government's objective of staying out of local educational processes, but in effect they did.

To make these regulations work with a minimum of direct federal supervision, the federal government had to find some way to get agents at state and local levels to work with them rather than against them. State and local educational authorities, not to mention general governmental authorities, resisted an alliance because their interest was fundamentally in autonomy. So, lacking any ready converts to federal objectives, the national government began paying for the employment of state and local agents it could call its own. Title I allocations included funds to establish and maintain state and local offices of compensatory education, or any other administrative arrangement that would ensure the financial and educational integrity of the program. Once in place, compensatory education agencies had powerful incentives to see to it that Title I funds were properly allocated and spent, and that eligible beneficiaries were actually served: their very existence depended on the maintenance of the program, which ultimately depended on its satisfactory implementation. These agencies were also in excellent positions to carry out their mission. They suffered no informational disadvantages, and in time, they developed the political influence − via beneficiary support and their own organizations − to encourage state and local officials to stay in line.

The federal government cultivated these new allies with more than financial support. It interacted with them regularly, encouraged their participation in intergovernmental associations, and ultimately engendered a sense of professional commitment that united administrators from Washington to the lowest level.[20] By 1980 conflict and suspicion had given way to cooperation and trust — or at least healthy measures of these things — and the spiral of regulation and monitoring could be permitted to stop.[21] An intergovernmental bureaucracy committed to federal purposes had been integrated into state and local educational bureaucracies and was operating relatively smoothly. Federal monies were finally supplementing in significant amounts the education that was being received by the economically and educationally disadvantaged.[22]

The process did not, however, leave subnational educational practices essentially intact or preserve state and local autonomy. To begin with, it contributed to the centralization of school control. While local education agencies — that is, school districts — were designated as the legally responsible officials at the service delivery level, state education agencies were given responsibility for allocating federal funds and for holding local officials accountable. One effect was to draw local districts increasingly under the influence of state authority. But a more important consequence may have been the shift of authority from the individual school to the district. School districts were given the chore of allocating funds among schools and seeing that these funds, in turn, reached eligible students. In practice, this came to mean that schools were less free to choose how best to serve their disadvantaged students, and instead districts were in charge. It also meant that districts had to establish monitoring and reporting procedures and to hire staff, sometimes even create whole offices, to perform these routines. This process was repeated, moreover, for a host of categorical programs besides compensatory education.

How much this centralization contributed to the general process that was already diminishing school autonomy, especially in large metropolitan school systems, is difficult to say. It is true that federal assistance facilitated the overall growth of state and local bureaucracy; however, the connection between federal grants-in-aid and educational centralization has not been well investigated.[23] Still, there is no gainsaying the price in autonomy that has been paid by schools on issues and concerns touched by federal programs. There is little reason to doubt that these losses have been greatest where high concentrations of low income students — and racial minorities — have increased participation in federal programs.

A strong case in point is the uniformity of services now provided by schools to students eligible for compensatory education. From state to state, district to district, and school to school, educators have converged on a relatively small number of approaches to serving the poor. Among the most common are the concentration of services on the lowest grades of school and the provision of supplementary instruction in reading to children removed from their regular classes for just that purpose.[24] While so-called 'pullout' programs may be on the wane, with increasing doubts about their effectiveness, uniformity continues to be the rule. It is important to understand why. It is not because educator after educator has concluded that one approach represents the best way to serve eligible students. It is, rather, because special programs such as 'pullouts' provide the strongest evidence that local authorities can offer to outside authorities that appropriate students are receiving supplementary services.

Even though Chapter 1 has freed lower governments of many of the regulations established under Title I, this has produced little change in the system. The administrative apparatus for carrying out federal purposes is either so entrenched that forces for change are being successfully resisted, or the fear of re-regulation is so great that past routines are being continued out of sheer prudence. Whatever the reason, there is little evidence that increases in administrative flexibility have produced innovations in the services that the disadvantaged are receiving. The program and its central objectives are well institutionalized.

Rethinking Reform

The implementation experience of Title I and Chapter 1 illustrates the potential consequences — often adverse — of trying to improve education through the public system as it is currently constituted. Through an escalating exchange of regulation and resistance between the top of the system and the bottom, a program intended to give resources and discretion to schools with needy children turned into a program delivering highly uniform supplementary services to some of the children in need, but offering precious little to the schools themselves. This outcome, it is important to understand, was not the result of considered decisions by educational professionals about how best to educate the poor, nor was it the result of judgments by politicians about the most effective course of action to take. It was not, however, inadvertent. Federal politicians, under pressure from constituency groups to see that eligible children received compensatory education, reacted in the only way they had at their disposal: by demanding that federal bureaucrats placate those groups. In turn, federal bureaucrats and their subnational allies used the only tools at their disposal — regulation and auditing — to force local education agencies to help the children of the groups that were complaining. Finally, those agencies responded by providing compensatory education in ways that most readily demonstrated their compliance.

Over time, these intergovernmental conflicts have given way to more cooperative implementation routines. But has this adaptive process produced a successful compensatory education policy? This is an important question in thinking about improvement, but it is not the only question, or perhaps even the most important one. We must also ask whether the process that produced the current policy can be relied upon to generate improvements.

The question of Chapter 1's success has been addressed many times and answered in many ways. In recent years, the answers have tended to be positive. It is almost certain that federal spending has increased the resources devoted to educating the poor. Federal aid for poor students is not only proving to be genuinely supplementary; it also seems to be stimulating state and local spending for the same purposes.[25] In addition, there are favorable signs that students receiving compensatory education are achieving more than they would without it — at least during the brief time that they are receiving it.[26]

Still, there is room to question Chapter 1's success and its ultimate desirability. To begin with, many children who are economically and educationally disadvantaged — probably half of the total — do not receive Chapter 1 services, either because they attend schools that have not been designated by their districts to receive compensatory services or, if they attend designated schools, are enrolled in grades that are not receiving services. Second, the schools the Chapter 1 children attend are not demonstrably better off by virtue of offering compensatory services. The children may be, but the schools are not. This dichotomy has repercussions not only for students who are not receiving compensatory services, but also for those who are. If children are benefiting from supplementary services but otherwise suffering from the poor educational environments of their schools, their education remains problematic. Students are better off receiving services than not receiving them, but that is not to say they are being well served.

For one thing, if the centralization process to which compensatory education contributed is in some measure responsible for the deterioration of public education during the time Title I was being implemented, then the compensatory services that some disadvantaged students are receiving may simply be making up for ground that the program itself helped to lose. Be that as it may, there is also a firm basis for questioning the very approach to compensatory education that Chapter 1 has come to embody. Both the literature on effective schools and our own research on public and private schools indicate that school performance has more to do with a complex of factors that characterize schools as total organizations than with any particular programs that schools may provide. Successful schools are distinguished by interdependent qualities — strong leadership, a sense of mission, shared decision-making, relative teacher autonomy — that bind schools together and foster teamwork. This generalization appears to be as true of schools that teach the poor. Compensatory education, as it is currently conceived and implemented, does nothing to nurture these qualities. To the contrary, by increasing the control of the school from the outside, it may discourage their development. The implication for reform is quite plain: if research on school organization and performance is on target, compensatory education might be more successful if aimed at improving the schools that the disadvantaged attend rather than at increasing the services that some of these students receive.

The remaining question, of course, is how this change can be made. How can schools that educate the disadvantaged be encouraged to develop the organizational attributes of effectiveness? If school environments have as much to do with the development of these attributes as the comparative analysis of public and private schools indicates, and as the Title I/Chapter 1 experience suggests, vigorous school organizations may be difficult to cultivate within the current system of public education.

Consider, for example, the expressed desire of the current school reform movement to create such organizations. The rhetoric of reformers is replete with support for greater school autonomy, stronger leadership from principals, and more respect for the professional judgment of teachers. But what reformers fail to appreciate is that these improvements cannot simply be imposed on schools in the public sector. As the compensatory education experience so well illustrates, politicians and administrators have little incentive to support fundamental reform. Their careers are tied to their own control over the schools, and they are unavoidably responsive to interest groups with stakes in the centralized arrangements of the status quo. Reforms that manage to be adopted — for example, tougher graduation requirements and student competency tests — leave the basic structure of the system intact and, in fact, encourage the further regulation and standardization of educational practices within the school.

In time, it is also likely that whatever reforms are adopted will tend to be neutralized and assimilated. Increases in school autonomy are likely to be restricted once school principals take steps and create political difficulties for superintendents or school boards. Reductions in the number of strings attached to compensatory aid are likely to be turned around once interest groups resume complaining that they cannot identify the additional services that schools are providing. Public schools did not lose autonomy or suffer the organizational consequences of that loss by accident or misunderstanding. The newfound wisdom that we may be paying a price for a superfluity of accountability is not likely to change things. The various components of the current system are so closely interconnected, and so driven toward control from the top, that attempts to improve part of the system in isolation from all of the rest — for example, by restructuring Chapter 1 — are likely to set off a series of compensating changes that minimize the impact of the reform.

Where does this conundrum leave the prospects for improvement? In less than good shape — if improvements must be pursued within the existing system. Real improvements may require a different system. It may be necessary to organize the provision of education in some way other than through direct democratic control, as we have come to know it, if the apparent educational problems of centralization, standardization, and routinization are to be avoided. At the very least, the possibility must be entertained.

If schools are to develop the organizational qualities that research now indicates are essential for real educational gains, it may even be necessary to emulate the system of control that governs private schools, where teaching and professional autonomy flourish. Government would still set minimum standards and protect civil liberties, for example, by prohibiting racial discrimination. It would also provide funding, probably in the form of vouchers allocated directly to parents. Students who are difficult to educate, especially the economically disadvantaged, might receive larger vouchers to induce schools to provide for them. But the government, besides providing graduated funding and setting basic standards, would do little else. Virtually all the important decisions about policy, organization, and personnel would be taken out of the hands of politicians and administrators and given to schools and their immediate clients: the students and their parents.

In a system requiring competition for students and resources, schools would have incentives to move toward more efficient and effective forms of organization. Schools that clung to costly bureaucratic methods, that did not attract and utilize talented people, that failed to encourage collegial and productive relationships among their members, or that lacked strong leadership toward clearly defined educational goals would tend to lose support and, finally, go out of business. Effective schools would tend to prosper.

The added virtue of this system for the disadvantaged is that it would provide a way to overcome the considerable professional ignorance about how best to serve those struggling students. Experimentation would be encouraged. Schools and programs that failed to serve the disadvantaged effectively would be weeded out, while those that succeeded would grow. The process would almost certainly move schools away from their current reliance on special classes for the disadvantaged and toward a greater variety of services. But even if it did not, there would at least be reason to believe that the programs in place were justified by their educational merits. Today's programs are justified largely by their political and administrative merits. Some will say that parents, especially of the poor, are not wise enough to make the process of natural selection work. But parental wisdom is not a prerequisite for the process to move forward. Even if many parents continued to send their children to the school closest to their home, that school would probably be a better one: it would have the novel concern that some day parents might find an alternative school more attractive and leave.

Obviously, any change as fundamental as this runs the risk of political infeasibility. Unless the quality or equity of public education declines further, it will be difficult to overcome the opposition of organized groups whose interests are threatened by fundamental reform. Still, there is increasing sympathy among established groups — for example, the National Governors' Association — for the idea of providing schools with greater autonomy in exchange for schools taking greater responsibility for performance. There is even a proposal before Congress to convert Chapter 1 funds to compensatory vouchers. These are significant developments. To be sure, they do not promise enormous improvements. Even the fairly radical idea of providing Chapter 1 vouchers does little more than increase parental choice by a modicum; it does nothing to increase school autonomy. The significance of the ideas is what they signal: serious interest in basic school reform. If schools are indeed products of their environments, and if the way they are organized really shapes their performance, then this approach is vital. Fundamental reform may be the only type of reform that offers genuine hope for school improvement, and through it, greater educational gains for the poor, racial minorities, and others for whom equal opportunity has yet to become a reality.[27]

Notes

1 On racial differences in educational achievement, see especially, Congressional Budget Office (1986) *Trends in Educational Achievement*, April.
2 The voluminous literature on economic or 'objective' determinants of student achievement is probably summarized best in E. HANUSHEK (1986) 'The Economics of Schooling', *Journal of Economic Literature*, 24, pp. 1141–77.
3 While the 'effective schools' literature has considered the performance of schools in all settings, much of it has focused on effective schools for poor — often minority — students in urban settings. Analyses of successful urban schools are provided, for example, in J. CIBULKA, T. O'BRIEN and D. ZEWE, (1982) *Inner City Private Elementary Schools: A Study*, Milwaukee, Wisc., Marquette University Press; R. EDMONDS and J. FREDERICKSEN (1978) *Search*

for Effective Schools: The Identification and Analysis of City Schools That Are Instructionally Effective for Poor Children, Cambridge, Mass., Center for Urban Studies, Harvard University; T. SIZER (1984) *Horace's Compromise: The Dilemma of the American High School*, Boston, Mass., Houghton Mifflin.

4 Research into education policies aimed at the disadvantaged has been more attentive to the impact of programs on students than to their wider effects on schools.

5 The enormous literature on effective schools is thoroughly and critically surveyed in S. PURKEY and M. SMITH (1983) 'Effective Schools: A Review', *Elementary School Journal*, 83, March, pp. 426–52. Original studies of particular note include E. BOYER (1983) *High School: A Report on Secondary Education in America*, New York, Harper and Row; W. BROOKOVER, C. BEADY, P. FLODD, J. SCHWEITZER and J. WISENBAKER (1979) *School Social Systems and Student Achievement: Schools Can Make a Difference*, New York, Praeger; M. Rutter (1983) 'School Effects on Pupil Progress: Research Findings and Policy Implications', in *Child Development*, 54, pp. 1–29; A. POWELL, E. FERRAR and D. COHEN (1986) *The Shopping Mall High School: Winners and Losers in the Educational Marketplace*, New York, Houghton Mifflin.

6 Classic 'input-output' studies, weak on organizations, include J. COLEMAN *et al.* (1966) *Equality of Educational Opportunity*, prepared for US Department of Health, Education and Welfare, Washington, D.C., US Government Printing Office; and C. JENCKS, M. SMITH, H. ACKLAND, M. BANE, D. COHEN, H. GINTIS, B. HEYNES and S. MICHELSON (1972) *Inequality: A Reassessment of the Effect of Family and Schooling in America*, New York, Basic Books.

7 Illustrated most recently by T. SIZER (1984) *Horace's Compromise: The Dilemma of the American High School*, Boston, Mass., Houghton Mifflin; A. POWELL, E. FERRAR and D. COHEN (1986) *The Shopping Mall High School: Winners and Losers in the Educational Marketplace*, New York, Houghton Mifflin.

8 The best survey on school organization, despite being based on an unrepresentative sample, is probably J. GOODLAD (1984) *A Place Called School: Prospects for the Future*, New York, McGraw Hill; however, it lacks data on student achievement. The best current survey of students and their abilities is probably High School and Beyond; however, it is weak on organizational measures.

9 J. COLEMAN, T. HOFFER and S. KILGORE (1982) *High School Achievement: Public, Catholic and Private Schools Compared*, New York, Basic Books.

10 For critiques, see A. BRYK (1981) 'Disciplined Inquiry or Policy Argument?', *Harvard Educational Review*, 51, pp. 497–509; J. GUTHRIE and A. ZUSMAN (1981) 'Unasked Questions', in *Harvard Educational Review*, 51, pp. 515–18; R. MURNANE (1981) 'Evidence, Analysis, and Unanswered Questions', *Harvard Educational Review*, 51, pp. 438–9; A. GOLDBERGER and G. CAIN (1982) 'The Causal Analysis of Cognitive Outcomes in the James S. Coleman, Thomas Hoffer and Sally Kilgore Report', *Sociology of Education*, 55, pp. 102–22; B. HEYNS and T. HILTON (1982) 'The Cognitive Tests for High School and Beyond: An Assessment', in *Sociology of Education*, 55, pp. 89–102.

11 T. HOFFER, A. GREELEY and J. COLEMAN (1985) 'Achievement Growth in Public and Catholic Schools', *Sociology of Education*; 58, 1, pp. 73–97; J.

COLEMAN and T. HOFFER (1987) *Public and Private High Schools: The Impact of Communities*, New York, Basic Books.

12 In their most recent work, Coleman and Hoffer acknowledge this, suggesting that strong 'functional communities' are the key to the development of schools with the requisite practices for success.

13 This perspective is developed in C. BIDWELL (1965) 'The School as a Formal Organization', in J. MARCH (Ed.) *Handbook of Organizations*, Chicago, Ill., Rand McNally College Publishing Co.; K. WEICK (1976) 'Educational Organizations as Loosely Coupled Systems', in *Administrative Science Quarterly*, 21, pp. 1–19; W. SCOTT and J. MEYER (1984) 'Environmental Linkages and Organizational Complexity', Institute for Research on Educational Finance and Governance, Stanford University. Project Report No. 84–A16, July.

14 The comprehensive report of this research is J. CHUBB and T. MOE (1989) *What Price Democracy? Politics, Markets and America's Schools*, Washington, D.C., The Brookings Institution (forthcoming).

15 Portions of the discussion that follow are adapted from J. CHUBB and T. MOE (1986) 'No School Is an Island: Politics, Markets and Education', *The Brookings Review*, 4, pp. 21–8.

16 These results are discussed at length in J. CHUBB and T. MOE (1989) *What Price Democracy? Politics, Markets and America's Schools, op. cit.*

17 This framework is used more formally to evaluate the implementation of Title I in J. CHUBB (1985) 'The Political Economy of Federalism', *American Political Science Review*, 79, pp. 994–1015.

18 On the early implementation experience, see J. MURPHY (1971) 'Title I of ESEA: The Politics of Implementing Federal Education Reform', *Harvard Educational Review*, 41, pp. 35–63; M. MCLAUGHLIN (1975) *Evaluation and Reform: The Elementary and Secondary Education Act of 1965, Title I*, Cambridge, Mass., Balinger.

19 An account of the process is provided in J. CHUBB (1985) 'Excessive Regulation: The Case of Federal Aid to Education', *Political Science Quarterly*, 100, pp. 287–311.

20 This process is emphasized in P. HILL (1979) *Enforcement and Informal Pressure in the Management of Federal Categorical Programs in Education*, Santa Monica, Calif., Rand Corporation.

21 On the evolution of cooperation, see M. KIRST and R. JUNG (1980) 'The Utility of a Longitudinal Perspective in Assessing Implementation: A Thirteen Year View of ESEA, Title I,' *Educational Evaluation and Policy Analysis*, 2, pp. 17–34; P. PETERSON, B. RABE and K. WONG (1986) *When Federalism Works*, Washington, D.C., The Brookings Institution.

22 On the fiscal effectiveness of Title I see J. CHUBB (1985) 'The political economy of federalism', *op. cit.*

23 The impact of federal aid on state and local bureaucracy is discussed and estimated in J. CHUBB (1985) 'Federalism and the Bias for Centralization', in J. CHUBB and P. PETERSON (Eds) *The New Direction in American Politics*, Washington, D.C., The Brookings Institution.

24 M. KENNEDY, R. JUNG and M. ORLAND (1986) *Poverty, Achievement and the Distribution of Compensatory Education Services*, Interim report from the National Assessment of Chapter I, Office of Educational Research and Improvement,

US Department of Education, January; P. PETERSON, B. RABE and K. WONG (1986) *When Federalism Works, op. cit.*

25 The growing fiscal effectiveness of the program can be seen by comparing the estimates of M. FELDSTEIN (1977) 'The Effect of a Differential Add-on Grant: Title I and Local Education Spending', *Journal of Human Resources*, 13, pp. 443–58, and of J. CHUBB (1985) 'The Political Economy of Federalism', *op. cit.* for the period 1965–1979; the period effect is two-thirds higher.

26 Favorable evaluations are reviewed in M. KIRST and R. JUNG (1980) 'The Utility of a Longitudinal Perspective in Assessing Implementation: A Thirteen Year View of ESEA, Title I', *op. cit.*; P. PETERSON, B. RABE and K. WONG (1986) *When Federalism Works, op. cit.*

27 An early version of this paper was prepared for presentation at the Conference on Alternative Strategies in Chapter I, the Compensatory Education Program, Office of Educational Research and Improvement, US Department of Education, Washington, D.C. 18–19 November, 1986.

9
Catholic Schools and Racial Segregation

Robert L. Crain and Christine H. Rossell

The controversy surrounding recent proposals to support private schools through tuition tax credits has prompted renewed interest in the impact of private schooling on racial segregation in education.[1] Thus, it would seem appropriate to reanalyze the issues originally raised by Coleman, Hoffer and Kilgore's report[2] and book[3] on the subject of private and public schools and the effect of the former on the latter. We present our own data on Catholic and public school segregation in 1968 and in the 1980s in three large cities: Chicago, Cleveland, and Boston. The public schools of these cities were racially segregated in 1968, but by the early 1980s all three had instituted school desegregation plans. The parochial schools, by contrast, have the same system of student selection in the 1980s as they had in 1968.

Coleman, Hoffer and Kilgore divide the issue of private schooling and its effect on racial segregation into four questions:

1 Do private schools enroll more or fewer minority students than do public schools?
2 Are the minorities currently attending private schools more racially segregated or integrated than minorities attending public schools?
3 Has the presence of private schools competing with public schools created more or less segregation?
4 If some form of private school subsidy were enacted, would the accelerated transfer of whites and minorities to private schools increase or decrease segregation in education?

Using the 1980 data from the High School and Beyond survey of high school sophomores and seniors, Coleman, Hoffer and Kilgore conclude that although minorities are under-represented in private schools (question 1), they are nevertheless racially balanced there (question 2).

Using a simple accounting model, they conclude that the presence of private schools in the United States has not increased the segregation of black students in American education (question 3). Question 4 requires an exercise in predictive modeling, and is hence the most difficult. Their answer is equivocal.

We will address the first two of these questions by examining the degree of black–white segregation in the Catholic schools of three large cities — Chicago, Cleveland, and Boston. In the latter city, Boston, we also estimate white flights to Catholic schools following desegregation. In each city, the Catholic schools are highly segregated, much more so in the elementary schools than in the high schools — the level examined by Coleman, Hoffer and Kilgore. In the second part of this chapter, we address question 3 by critically analyzing the accounting model used by Coleman, Hoffer and Kilgore. We conclude that the accounting model used to measure the segregative impact of private schools on the combined public and private system of schools is in error. It appears that Catholic schools, the majority of private schools in the US, have created racial segregation in American education. It is very difficult to predict how a subsidy or voucher for parents sending their children to private schools would affect racial segregation, but there is no compelling reason to think that a subsidy would reverse the present pattern, in which the transfer of students to private schools appears to have increased racial segregation.

Measuring Racial Segregation in Private Schools

Coleman, Hoffer and Kilgore used data from eighty-four randomly sampled Catholic high schools and twenty-seven randomly sampled non-Catholic private high schools to compute indices of segregation. They found that the segregation of blacks from (non-Hispanic) whites[4] is lower in either group of private schools than it is in public schools. For Hispanics, the pattern is less clear. They seem less segregated in Catholic schools, more segregated in other private schools.

The index used by Coleman, Hoffer and Kilgore is the relative exposure index. The exposure index is a weighted average, computed across all students of one race, of the percentage of their school which is made up of opposite-race students. If there were no internal segregation within high schools, the percentage of students who are black in the average white student's high school could be thought of as the probability that the student sitting next to any white student is black (with a parallel interpretation for the exposure of black students to whites). When the index compares two groups that make up the universe of students (i.e., nonwhites to whites), it can range from a low of zero to a maximum of the percentage of students of the opposite race in the set of schools as a whole. In other words, if the percentage nonwhite in a school system is 30 per cent, the percentage of nonwhite in the average white child's school cannot be higher than 30 per cent. Although it is possible when comparing two groups that do not constitute the universe of racial or ethnic groups (such as, for example, blacks and whites) to have a percentage white in the average black child's school which is higher than the percentage white in the school system, this situation will not occur under conditions of perfect racial balance.

Under conditions of perfect racial balance, a school district that is 30 per cent black would have an index representing the percentage black in the school attended by the average white student of 0.30. If the district were perfectly segregated, each white would be in a school with no blacks, and the mean percentage black of the schools attended by whites would be zero.

The indices can be used to measure the segregation of any two groups from each other — for example, whites from nonwhites, nonwhites from whites, blacks from Hispanics, blacks from whites, etc. The unstandardized indices are roughly the reciprocal of each other. That is, the percentage black in the average white child's school is the opposite of the percentage white in the average black child's school.[5] When this is standardized, however, the indices of segregation of whites from blacks and of blacks from whites are identical.[6]

The index can be standardized by dividing by the percentage of the entire universe of students which is of the opposite race, and subtracting this from 1.0. This yields an index called the relative exposure index, that ranges from zero, when schools all have the same racial composition, to 100, when they are totally segregated.

Using the relative exposure index, Coleman, Hoffer and Kilgore conclude that in 1980 private high schools were less segregated than public high schools because the relative exposure indices measuring the segregation of blacks from whites were 0.49 for public schools, 0.31 for Catholic schools, and 0.21 for other private schools. There are several problems with this analysis, however.

First, the proportion black in each of these school systems in 1980 differs dramatically: 14 per cent of the students in public high school were black, compared to 6 per cent in Catholic schools, and 3 per cent in other private schools. The unstandardized exposure indices reflect this. In 1980, 7 per cent of the average public high school white student's classmates were black, compared to 4 per cent for a white in a Catholic school, and 2 per cent for a white in another private school. Second, the purpose of a standardized index is to determine the degree to which a school district deviates from a norm of all schools having identical racial composition — typically the school district's racial composition. Unlike public school systems, however, a private school system's minority enrollment is not fixed by geographic boundaries. A private school can recruit more or accept fewer minorities as it wishes. How, then, should one evaluate a private school system that desegregates its minority students, but has very few of them?

Page and Keith argue for an index that penalizes private schools for their small number of black students.[7] One way to do this is to standardize the index of white exposure to blacks, not by the private school percentage black as Coleman, Hoffer and Kilgore did, but by the percentage black of all US high schools, both public and private.[8] Because the percentage black is lower in private schools than in the nation as a whole, private schools appear more segregated than public schools when this version of the relative exposure index is used.

Two very different conclusions can be drawn from the unstandardized indices. On the one hand, whites in private schools have fewer black schoolmates and are in that sense more segregated. On the other hand, blacks have more white schoolmates in private schools and are in that sense less segregated. Which way to look at the problem is mostly a matter of values.

Other Issues in the Coleman, Hoffer and Kilgore Analysis

The choice of which index to use to measure segregation is not the only troublesome issue in the Coleman, Hoffer and Kilgore analysis. Problems of sampling error and the measurement of segregation on a nationwide basis may also cast doubt on the validity of their findings.

With a national sample containing only eighty-four Catholic and twenty-seven non-Catholic private schools, the findings of the Coleman, Hoffer and Kilgore study could very easily be skewed by sampling error. In the report version, Coleman, Hoffer and Kilgore suggest that the high index of segregation for Hispanics in non-Catholic schools may be due to sampling error (64 per cent of the Hispanics in non-Catholic private schools are in a single school).[9] It may well be that a larger sample would show something different. This same possible flaw may also distort the sample of blacks in non-Catholic schools or the samples of blacks and Hispanics in Catholic schools.

Sampling error statistics are not presented for the segregation indices, so it is impossible to say what the confidence interval around each of these figures is, but if the sample of Catholic schools had contained two all-black schools instead of the one that appears to be in the sample, the index of segregation would increase by 0.10. Sampling error affects not only the segregation indices but also the estimates of the number of minority students in private schools. If it is a sampling fluke that caused 64 per cent of the Hispanics to be in a single, predominantly Hispanic school, then that same sampling fluke may have produced an incorrect estimation of the total number and distribution of Hispanics in non-Catholic private schools.

Coleman, Hoffer and Kilgore's analysis of school segregation is unusual in another way. The indices are computed for the entire nation rather than for particular school districts. Typically, segregation indices are computed separately for individual school districts and not for very large units, such as the entire United States. One problem with a national segregation index is that it is impossible to separate the index into the amount contributed by segregative policies and practices in individual school systems and the amount of segregation caused by the uneven distribution of blacks and whites across regions and city types. If many blacks live in New York City and very few live in the Pacific north-west, public schools will have a high standardized segregation index regardless of local public school desegregation policies. Similarly, if private schools tend to be concentrated in areas with differing but homogeneous racial composition, a standardized index will have a very high value even if the private schools in each area work hard to recruit a heterogeneous student body. On the other hand, if the areas where private high schools are located tend to be more heterogeneous in racial mix than the United States as a whole, then it would be possible for a lower segregation index to exist without private schools exerting much effort to desegregate.

Comparing public and private schools in this way is also problematic because the segregation of private schools in individual communities has different causes than the segregation of public schools. The vast majority of public schools, unless under a court order to desegregate, typically assign students on the basis of geography. That is, a school draws all of its students from a single geographic zone surrounding the school. This is sometimes called 'nearest school' or 'neighborhood school' assignment, even though attendance zones are normally drawn to accommodate school needs and student safety, not to conform to 'natural' neighborhoods or send all students to their nearest school.

In desegregated school districts, schools typically also have a geographic assignment policy, but often with two nonadjacent geographic zones, one in a minority neighborhood and the other in a majority neighborhood, sending students to the same school. Only a few school districts have begun experimenting with voluntary desegregation plans, in which students are allowed to attend schools without geographic restriction.

Finally, public schools not only have school attendance zones, but a school district attendance line that cannot be crossed. If a school district is all-white or all-black, there is nothing the district by itself can do about it.

By contrast, Catholic schools almost always have no geographic restriction. Although students often select Catholic schools using proximity as a factor, Catholic schools select students on other criteria, not according to where they live. What impact does this fact have on racial segregation?

We are unlikely to find the definitive answer to this question soon, but we can provide a partial answer by examining school segregation in specific cities. We expect the degree of racial segregation in private school systems to vary with the size of the community being served, its racial and religious mix, and the school assignment policy used by the public schools in the community.

Analysis of Chicago and Cleveland

While data on the racial composition of some private schools are available, they are not assembled into a single source as is the case with public school data in the United States.[10] We have, however, obtained Catholic school data for Chicago, Cleveland, and Boston directly or indirectly from the Catholic school systems themselves.[11]

Table 1 presents the level of black–white segregation in the Catholic schools of Chicago and Cleveland, and compares it to the level of segregation in the public schools in these two cities. (Boston is discussed in the following section.) Black–white segregation is analyzed separately from minority–white segregation because in general the segregation of whites from all other minorities is considerably less than the segregation of whites from blacks only.[12] We used both 1968 and 1982 data for the public schools in order to compare them to parochial schools under two conditions: (1) a strict 'nearest-school' policy, and (2) after the implementation of a court-ordered desegregation. Cleveland desegregated with a mandatory reassignment plan in 1979 while Chicago implemented a magnet-voluntary plan in 1982.

Table 1 includes the three segregation indices mentioned above, the exposure index S_{wb} (the percentage black in the average white child's school), and the two standardized racial balance measures — the relative

Table 1: Black-White Segregation in Public and Catholic School Systems in Chicago and Cleveland

	Chicago			Cleveland		
	Public		Catholic	Public		Catholic
	1968	1982	1981	1968	1982	1981
Elementary Schools (K-8)						
Total enrollment	437,343	313,833	82,968	119,119	60,574	16,351
% black	55.3	60.6	27.9	58.2	67.6	20.4
% other minority	10.1	24.6	20.1	1.6	5.4	5.9
B-W dissimilarity index, D_b	94	86	94	90	21	92
Relative exposure index, R_b	90	70	92	86	5	88
% black in average whites' school, S_{wb}	6.0	18.2	3.9	8.6	64.1	2.5
% of blacks who are in schools less than 50% black	2.3	10.6	4.9	0.8	7.6	11.2
% of whites who are in schools less than 50% white	4.4	39.9	1.5	5.5	98.7	1.6
High Schools						
Total enrollment	136,719	112,695	34,182	35,627	17,467	5,802
% black	46.0	60.4	16.6	47.0	71.7	11.7
% other minority	7.2	19.4	14.2	1.7	5.2	3.5
B-W dissimilarity index, D_b	80	78	73	87	22	53
Relative exposure index, R_b	72	61	63	81	4	18
% black in average whites' school, S_{wb}	14.0	23.7	7.2	9.1	68.6	9.6
% of blacks who are in schools less than 50% black	9.5	14.2	31.0	7.6	0.0	9.6
% of whites who are in schools less than 50% white	9.2	39.0	1.9	5.0	100.0	4.9

exposure index, R_b, and the index of dissimilarity, D_b — multiplied by 100 to produce a percentage.

The index of dissimilarity is based upon the sum across all schools of the difference (in absolute numbers) between the number of whites and the number of blacks in each school building in comparison to the whites and the blacks in the district. Specifically, the formula is:

$$D_b = \frac{\sum_{i=1}^{n} \left| \frac{B_i}{B} - \frac{W_i}{W} \right|}{2}$$

where B_i and W_i are the number of blacks and whites in the ith school, and B and W the number of blacks and whites in the whole district.

Both of the standardized racial balance indices range from zero (perfect desegregation) to 100 (perfect segregation). The dissimilarity index can be interpreted as the sum of the percentage of students of each race who would have to be reassigned for every school in the district to have the same racial mix.

Table 1 shows that the two Catholic school systems differ from their respective public systems and also from each other. The Cleveland Catholic school system is much smaller than the Chicago Catholic school system; both Catholic school systems are substantially smaller than their public school systems. They have proportionately many fewer blacks, but about the same proportion of nonblack minorities.

The racial balance indices show the Chicago and Cleveland Catholic elementary schools to be as highly segregated now, with indices averaging 90, as the public schools were when they were among the most segregated school systems in the north (1968). The unstandardized exposure index shows the same pattern. The average Catholic school white child is in an elementary school that is only 3.9 per cent black in Chicago and 2.5 per cent black in Cleveland. The public elementary schools, by contrast, show less segregation in 1968: 6 per cent black in the average Chicago white student's school and 8.6 per cent black in the average Cleveland white student's school. By 1982, after desegregation, the percentage black in the average white child's school had increased to 18.2 in Chicago and 64.1 in Cleveland, substantially higher than each city's respective parochial schools.

The last two rows of the top panel of Table 1 indicate the extent of segregation in elementary schools in another way. They show that in Chicago Catholic schools only 4.9 per cent of black students are in predominantly white schools and only 1.5 per cent of white students are in predominantly black schools. In 1968 the Chicago public schools had fewer blacks in predominantly white schools (2.3 per cent) but more whites in predominantly black schools (4.4 per cent). In Cleveland, 11.2 per cent of Catholic elementary school black children and 1.6 per cent of Catholic elementary white children are in schools in which they are the minority. The Cleveland public schools in 1968 had substantially fewer (0.8 per cent) blacks and substantially more whites (5.5 per cent) in schools in which they were in the minority. This change reflects in part the fact that the public schools of both cities had fewer predominantly white schools and more predominantly black ones, but it also reflects the rigid geographic school assignment policies then in use. Black students in public schools were not allowed to transfer to predominantly white schools, but white students were likewise rarely allowed to flee from predominantly black schools.

By 1982, 10.6 per cent of blacks and almost 40 per cent of whites were in Chicago public schools in which they were in the minority. Similarly, about 8 per cent of blacks and 99 per cent of whites were in Cleveland public schools in which they were in the minority. Thus, the biggest change has been in the situation of whites. Whereas in 1982 about the same percentage of Catholic school blacks as public school blacks were in schools in which they were in the minority, substantially fewer Catholic school whites than public school whites are in schools in which they are in the minority.

Most measures of segregation (the 1982 dissimilarity index for Chicago is an exception) show Catholic high schools to be less segregated than public high schools were in 1968 under a neighborhood attendance policy, but more segregated than they were in 1982 after court-ordered desegregation.[13] The last two rows of Table 1 show why there is less segregation in Catholic high schools than in Catholic elementary schools. In Chicago, 31 per cent of all black students in Catholic high schools are in predominantly white schools. Because they are older than elementary school students, high school students are apparently more willing to embark on long bus rides to get to a school in a white area. On the other hand, only 1.9 per cent of whites in Chicago Catholic schools go to predominantly black high schools.

The data for Cleveland are more striking because all Catholic high schools are predominantly white. Although blacks are concentrated in four of the seven Catholic schools in Cleveland, there are not enough blacks to make a majority in any of these schools. This yields a very low relative exposure index, although not as low as the Cleveland public schools had in 1982. The dissimilarity index is much higher than the relative exposure index because it is more sensitive to a maldistribution of blacks within these schools and less sensitive to the overall whiteness of the schools.

Table 2 shows the degree of segregation of Hispanics from non-Hispanic whites in Chicago and Cleveland. This table includes the same measures shown in Table 1, but only 1982 public school data are shown because there were very few Hispanics in either city in 1968.

As other research has suggested, Hispanics in both public and Catholic schools are much less segregated from whites than are blacks. As with black–white segregation, however, Hispanic segregation in both cities is slightly higher at the elementary than at the high school level. Hispanics in Catholic schools are also more segregated than Hispanics in public schools, by most measures. The principal difference, however, is the percentage of Hispanics in predominantly white schools. Catholic-school Hispanics are in overwhelmingly white schools. By contrast, only a small percentage of Hispanics in public schools in either city are in

Table 2: Hispanic Segregation in Chicago and Cleveland Catholic Schools and Public Schools

	Chicago		Cleveland	
	Public 1982	Catholic 1981	Public 1982	Catholic 1981
Elementary Schools (K-8)				
Total Hispanics	69,658	13,765	2,569	764
% Hispanics	22.2	16.6	4.2	4.7
Dissimilarity index, D_h	62	68	49	54
Relative exposure index, R_h	−20	49	−0.08	0.4
% Hispanic in school attended by average non-Hispanic white, S_{wh}	26.7	11.9	4.5	4.7
% of Hispanics in predominantly (non-Hispanic) white schools	10.3	43.7	0.3	91.2
% of (non-Hispanic) whites in predominantly Hispanic schools	15.8	3.9	0.0	0.0
High Schools				
Total Hispanics	18,227	4,144	710	141
% Hispanic	16.2	12.1	4.1	2.4
Dissimilarity index D_h	53	44	45	49
Relative exposure index R_h	−20	26	0.0	38
% Hispanic in school attended by average non-Hispanic white, S_{sw}	12.1	11.1	4.2	2.2
% of Hispanics in predominantly (non-Hispanic) white schools	18.3	72.0	0.0	77.3
% of (non-Hispanic) whites in predominantly Hispanic schools	4.9	1.3	0.0	0.0

predominantly white schools, primarily because both cities are predominantly minority. Nevertheless, few whites are in predominantly Hispanic schools.

White Flight to Private Schools

Private schools can also affect the amount of racial segregation in education by providing havens for whites fleeing from desegregated schools. If whites transfer from public schools with more blacks to Catholic schools with fewer blacks, the amount of segregation will increase.

Discussions of white flight to private schools have usually been concerned with flight from newly desegregated public school systems. Few studies have examined the response of the Catholic Church to the implementation of desegregation in the public schools. Rossell found that on the eve of desegregation in ten cities studied, Catholic leaders in *every* city eloquently expounded a policy of not allowing their schools to serve as white flight havens.[14] Nevertheless, the extent of white flight in these cities suggests a divergence between what Catholic leaders said and what local parish priests actually did in the face of intense pressure from parishioners.

Most of the research on white flight from desegregation makes no distinction between flight to private schools and residential relocation. There are, however, nine case studies in eight different school districts that compare the two situations with survey sampling techniques or an analysis of the local housing market and/or private school enrollments. These studies indicate less residential relocation than private school enrollment in most school districts in response to school desegregation.[15] All of the studies, including the five of city school districts, support the theory that whatever the motivating factor, whites calculate the costs and benefits of their actions and tend to choose the course of action with the lowest costs.[16] This is particularly illuminated by the surveys in Louisville[17] and Boston,[18] which found that families who moved to the suburbs were more likely to be renters, young, childless (i.e., those for whom moving was relatively less costly), and more in favor of desegregation than those who transferred to parochial or private schools.

Racially motivated white flight also strikes school systems that have not implemented a desegregation plan. If whites flee the public schools to avoid having their children attend predominantly black schools, then with a neighborhood school policy we should expect flight from predominantly black schools in changing neighborhoods.[19] Becker analyzes growth in private school enrollment for the 1960s, when there was almost no desegregation of northern school districts.[20] He found that the larger the black enrollment in the public schools, the larger the growth of the private schools serving that city. Indeed, this correlation is the single best predictor in his multiple regression equation estimating growth in private school enrollment from a number of demographic factors.

Another case that provides indirect evidence of the use of private schools to avoid desegregation is Jacksonville, where Giles finds a large drop in white enrollment for the middle school grades in which white students are reassigned to schools in black neighborhoods.[21] Thus, whites place their children in private schools during the grades for which they are reassigned, rather than incurring the greater cost of private school for all years or residential relocation beyond the quite large Duval County school district.

In short, private school utilization is an important source of white flight from desegregation. This is particularly true for countrywide school districts and for all districts during the period immediately following implementation.[22]

White Flight in Boston

Boston desegregated in 1974 under a state plan designed solely to meet the limited requirements of the Massachusetts Racial Imbalance Act. The 1974 plan reduced the number of imbalanced schools from sixty-one to forty-two by redistricting, reorganizing, and short-distance busing that paired working class black and white neighborhoods. At the same time that the state plan was being implemented amidst protest and violence, the Boston school desegregation case was being heard in court and publicized in the newspapers. The federal court-ordered plan, implemented the following year in fall 1975, had extensive two-way mandatory reassignments and affected virtually all white students in the school system, except those in East Boston, a noncontiguous area excluded from desegregation.

Boston is the sixteenth largest city in the nation in terms of population, but it has less land area than all but two of the thirty largest cities. One might, therefore, expect most white flight to be to one of the eighty suburban communities within an hour's commute. However, Boston had a well developed Catholic and private school system — 26 per cent of school-age students were in parochial or private schools in 1970, compared to a national average of 10 per cent — and this enrollment had been declining, leaving numerous vacant seats on the eve of desegregation.

Given the availability of suburbs and a parochial school system with surplus capacity, one would expect white flight in Boston to be extreme. The research, however, shows it to be about average for the amount of mandatory white reassignments that occurred, both at the school district level[23] and at the school level.[24] Approximately one-third of all whites reassigned did not show up at the schools to which they were reassigned,[25] and approximately half of the students reassigned to schools that were more than 90 per cent minority before desegregation did not show up.[26] At the school district level, these defections produced a doubling of the normal white enrollment decline in 1974 and 1975.[27]

Where did these students go? Survey research suggests that more than half of them went to Catholic schools.[28] Table 3 compares the public school decline to private and Catholic school enrollment gains in Boston above those predicted by pre-desegregation (1968–73) trends. In 1974, Boston Catholic schools had a gain of 6.2 per cent above the pre-desegregation trend.[29] The public schools, by contrast, lost more than 9.2 per cent in that year, and 17 per cent the following year (1975) as a result of desegregation. The Catholic schools gained 14.1 per cent in 1975 and 23.6 per cent in 1977 above predicted trends.[30] Over the entire period the Catholic/private school gain is an estimated 72 per cent of the public school loss from desegregation.[31]

From 1970 to 1980, the percentage of school-age children enrolled in private schools in Boston increased by 4 percentage points, from 23.3 to 27.7 per cent. In Cleveland, which also desegregated under a mandatory reassignment plan, the percentage of children enrolled in private schools also increased by 4 percentage points, from 17.1 in 1970 to 21.3 per cent in 1980. These gains can be contrasted to Chicago, which had no mandatory reassignments during this period and experienced a decline in the percentage of children enrolled in private schools, from 24.5 per cent in 1970 to 22.6 per cent in 1980, and to the national trend, which shows a decline in the percentage of students enrolled in private schools during this period, from 11.5 per cent in 1970 to 10.3 per cent in 1980. Thus, these data suggest a pattern of flight to private schools from mandatory reassignment desegreation plans.

Segregation in Boston

What is the result of white flight to Catholic schools in Boston? Table 4 compares the level of black–white segregation in the Boston Public

Table 3: Enrollment Change Due to Desegregation in Boston Public, Catholic, and Private Schools, 1974–1977

	N	Phase I (1974-75)		Phase II (1975-76)		Phase III (1977-78)		Total Diff.
		Act-Pred. Diff.	% Diff.	Act-Pred. Diff.	% Diff.	Act-Pred. Diff.	% Diff.	
Boston Public Schools[a]	(187)	−4,646	−9.2	−6,958	−17.0	−1,755	−6.0	−13,906
Catholic Schools[b]	(56)	1,389	6.2	2,959	14.1	4,278	23.6	8,626
Private Schools[b]	(8)	412	37.7	405	40.3	504	58.4	1,321
Total Catholic/Private		1801	7.6	3364	15.2	4782	25.2	9947

Notes: a White enrollment change.
b Total enrollment change.

197

Schools in 1968 and 1986 to the level of segregation in the Catholic schools in 1986.

Despite considerable white flight to Catholic schools, the level of segregation in the Boston public schools has declined dramatically — more than 50 per cent — since desegregation. The Catholic schools are, by contrast, still highly segregated. Indeed, the Catholic schools are as segregated as the public schools were in 1968, when they had a neighborhood school policy. While 44 per cent of blacks are in Catholic elementary schools in which they are in the minority, only 4 per cent of whites are in Catholic schools in which they are in the minority.

Table 4: Black-White Segregation in Boston Public and Catholic Schools

| | Boston | | |
| | Public | | Catholic |
	1968	1986	1986
Elementary Schools (K-8)			
Total enrollment	72,865	41,407	10,837
% black	29.1	47.2	13.3
% other minority	4.5	27.1	7.4
B-W dissimilarity index, D_b	77	35	77
Relative exposure index, R_b	65	15	60
% black in average white child's school, S_{wb}	10.1	40.3	5.3
% of blacks in schools less than 50% black	24.1	33.3	44.2
% of whites in schools less than 50% white	8.4	77.6	4.3
High Schools			
Total enrollment	20,696	18,759	7,071
% black	19.8	48.0	6.7
% other minority	3.5	24.2	3.1
B-W dissimilarity index, D_b	60	35	70
Relative exposure index, R_b	35	16	54
% black in average white child's school, S_{wb}	12.9	40.1	3.1
% of blacks in schools less than 50% black	62.9	31.9	58.8
% of whites in schools less than 50% white	3.1	65.4	3.7

Table 5 makes the comparison for Hispanics and whites. In Catholic schools, Hispanic segregation is less than black–white segregation. The reverse is true in public schools, however. This may be due in part to state and federal bilingual education regulations and Spanish bilingual magnet programs that segregate Hispanics.

Table 5: *Hispanic Segregation in Boston Public and Catholic Schools*

	Boston	
	Public 1986	Catholic 1986
Elementary Schools (K-8)		
Total Hispanics	8,021	618
% Hispanic	19.3	5.7
Dissimilarity index, D_h	49	69
Relative exposure index, R_h	20	45
% Hispanic in school attended by average non-Hispanic whites, S_{wh}	16	3
% of Hispanics in predominantly non-Hispanic white schools	4.7	35.9
% of non-Hispanic whites in predominantly Hispanic schools	2.5	0.0
High Schools		
Total Hispanics	2,739	163
% Hispanic	14.6	2.3
Dissimilarity index, D_h	45	55
Relative exposure index, R_h	22	26
% Hispanic in school attended by average non-Hispanic white, S_{wh}	11.4	1.7
% of Hispanics in predominantly non-Hispanic white schools	8.0	53.9
% of non-Hispanic whites in predominantly Hispanic schools	0.0	0.0

The Relationship between School Segregation and Percentage Black

One would have expected the Catholic elementary schools to show less rather than the same segregation as the public schools of Chicago, Cleveland, and Boston in 1968, because the absolute number of black students enrolled is much smaller in the Catholic schools. In cities with a high level of residential segregation, the amount of public school segregation that occurs under a neighborhood school policy is basically a function of the size of the boundary between blacks and whites (where integrated neighborhood schools might appear) compared to the size of the black residential area. At the extreme, if the black population is not large enough to fill one public elementary school, the public school serving this area under a neighborhood school policy would necessarily have to have an attendance zone large enough to include some whites, thus integrating the school. At the other extreme, where there are very large black residential areas, as is the case with these cities, the number of black students living on the boundary of the black residential area and thus likely to attend an integrated school with whites under a neighborhood school policy is small compared to the total black school age population.

Figure 1 shows the data from public schools supporting the hypothesis that districts with small black populations are less segregated. In this figure we have plotted the 1968 relative exposure indices for elementary and secondary schools combined for the seventy-two largest northern public school districts plotted against the natural log of the total black enrollment in the school districts.

Generally, the fewer blacks in a district, the lower the level of segregation in 1968, when nearly all these public school systems used a simple neighborhood school policy. The Chicago, Cleveland, and

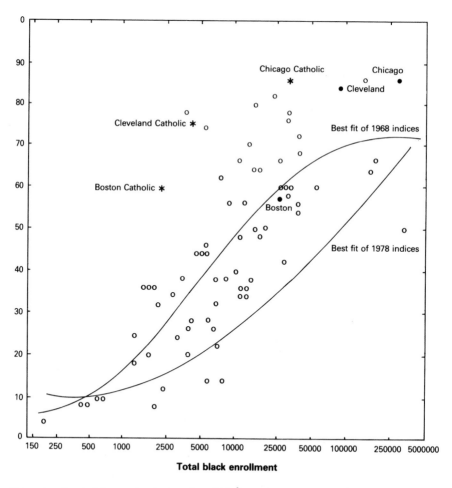

Figure 1. Level of Segregation by Number of Black Students in District, for Seventy-two Cities Using Nearest-School Assignment.

Boston public schools (identified in the figure by a black circle) all show very high levels of segregation, although Boston is the least segregated. The Catholic school systems of these cities (indicated by asterisks) appear to be much more segregated than one would predict on the basis of their relatively small black enrollments. Of the twenty-four school systems with between 2500 and 10,000 black students, the Cleveland Catholic schools are substantially more segregated than all but one of them. Of the thirteen school systems with between 25,000 and 50,000 black students, the Chicago Catholic school system is the most segregated. Of the nine school systems with 1000 to 2000 black students, the Boston Catholic school system is the most segregated.

Figure 1 also indicates that public school districts are likely to have reduced their level of segregation in the decade from 1968 to 1978. A second curve has been drawn to show the relationship of black population size to the 1978 exposure index. This curve is much lower for all districts except those with the very highest and those with the very lowest number of black students. Districts in the bottom left region would benefit little from desegregation because their indexes were already low in 1968, while districts with very large black populations will typically implement very limited plans. Cleveland, however, is an exception to this latter generalization.

One explanation for the high level of elementary school segregation in these Catholic elementary schools and the much lower level of segregation at the high school level is the lack of a neighborhood attendance boundary system in Catholic school systems. At the high school level, more black students may be willing to travel long distances to attend predominantly white high schools, resulting in decreased segregation. For example, in Chicago there are twelve Catholic high schools where blacks outnumber whites. More than 1700 blacks chose not to attend them, however, instead traveling to one of thirty predominantly white high schools, twenty-eight of which are outside the Chicago city limits.

On the other hand, an unrestricted free choice system works to further segregation in an important way. Just as blacks are free to travel to predominantly white schools, so are whites free to avoid predominantly black schools. In Cleveland, only eighty-seven of 12,000 white elementary parochial school students attend predominantly black schools. By comparison, there were nearly 7000 whites in predominantly black public schools in 1968. At the elementary school level, black parents are much less willing to have their children travel long distances; this reluctance is reflected in a much higher level of segregation. In Chicago, there are ninety-five predominantly white Catholic elementary schools that enroll fewer than ten black students — most of them with none. At the same time, freedom of choice does mean that whites are free to avoid predominantly black schools, and they do. The free enrollment policy of the Catholic schools seems to result in a pattern where there is less segregation at the high school level than there would be under a standard 'neighborhood' policy of assigning students on the basis of home residence to a nearer school. At the same time, there appears to be more segregation at the elementary school level than would result from a neighborhood school policy. Figure 1 suggests that the combination of these two factors is a school system that is more segregated than public schools with the same number of black students.

Moreover, although private schools are not permitted to discriminate in their pupil-assignment policy, there has never been an effort to require parochial school systems to adhere to the desegregation policies normally required of public school systems. Certainly, no public school system as large as either the Chicago or Cleveland private school systems, and with as much segregation and so small a number of black students, could avoid being required to desegregate by a court, as indeed occurred in their respective, much larger and more heavily minority, public school systems.

Thus, in all three cities — Chicago, Cleveland, and Boston — the Catholic elementary schools are about as segregated as the public schools were in 1968, and much more segregated than the public schools after court-ordered desegregation. In two of the school districts, Chicago and Cleveland, the Catholic high schools are less segregated than the public high schools in 1968, but more segregated than they were in 1982. In Boston, the Catholic high schools are more segregated than the public high schools both before and after desegregation.

Comparing the three public school systems, we find that Cleveland is the most racially balanced and Chicago the least racially balanced. Chicago is also five times the size of the other school systems, although it is only about ten percentage points more minority than the others. Of the three Catholic school systems, the Boston Catholic schools are by far the most racially balanced, with almost twenty percentage points less segregation than the other two, at least in part because they have a much smaller black enrollment.

The Coleman, Hoffer and Kilgore Model of Flight to Private Schools

Coleman, Hoffer and Kilgore construct an accounting model that leads them to conclude that the existence of private schools does not increase racial segregation in American education. However, their model is based on an erroneous assumption; thus, it seems likely that their conclusions are wrong also.

Coleman, Hoffer and Kilgore argue that one can determine the role of private schools by addressing the question, 'What would happen if all private schools were closed and the students presently enrolled in them were returned to public schools?' If private schools have had a segregative influence in America, then closing them and reassigning all the students to public schools should result in a lower index of segregation. The authors conduct a 'thought experiment', which does exactly this, and conclude that if private schools were closed, the public schools would be no more racially integrated than the present mix of public and private schools are. Hence, the private schools do not have a segregating influence.

The authors assume, however, that when private schools are closed, the white and black students in them will be dispersed into the existing public school systems in an amount proportional to their present white and black enrollment. In other words, each school would increase its tenth grade white enrollment by 7.6 per cent of their present white enrollment, and increase its black enrollment by 2.6 per cent of its present black enrollment.[32]

Such a model may seem reasonable at first glance, but a hypothetical example immediately reveals the problem. The model assumes that *all* white schools experience the same 7.6 per cent increase in enrollment, in other words, that the students left these public schools, or chose not to attend them, in a manner that bears no correlation with the racial composition of the schools. Furthermore, as shown in Table 6, using Chicago's 1968 public high school data, their model projects that only 4859 whites returned to public schools, even though there were 23,634 whites enrolled in Catholic schools in 1980, and that nearly all the whites attending Catholic schools lived in areas served by predominantly white schools.

As shown in the next to last column in Table 6, only twenty-one Catholic school whites are assumed to live in areas served by the twenty-three Chicago high schools that were 95 per cent or more black. Overall, the model assumes that only 10 per cent of the total Catholic student population live in areas that have high schools greater than 50 per cent black. This assumption is contradicted by all the research on white flight and ecological succession, including Coleman's own, which indicates that whites are more likely to withdraw from the public schools to attend private schools if they are assigned to schools with large numbers of black students.[33] In other words, this model assumes that there is no 'white flight' from public to private schools because of race, a thesis Coleman

Table 6: Application of the Coleman-Hoffer-Kilgore Accounting Model to
the Chicago Public High Schools

Racial Mix* of high school	Number of schools	Public schools before closing Catholic schools		Public schools after closing Catholic schools	
		Number of whites	Number of blacks	Increases in number of whites (7.6%)	Increases in number of blacks (2.6%)
0 – 5% black	20	31380	306	2385	8
5 – 20% black	12	19050	2472	1448	64
20 – 50% black	7	6602	3233	502	84
50 – 80% black	10	6624	11917	503	310
80 – 95% black	0	0	0	0	0
95 – 100% black	23	280	45007	21	1170
Total each race	72	63936	63005	4859	1636
Total white + black		126,941		6,495	

Note: *Non-black minorities excluded.

has spent a decade rebutting in his writings, paper presentations, and court testimony.

Of course, if there were no white flight for racial reasons, then there would be no reason to assume that the movement from public schools to private schools created segregation. Although we do not know the extent of white flight, there is certainly no reason to assume a hypothesis that runs directly contrary to all the existing evidence, including our data on Chicago, Cleveland, and Boston. Much of the movement in those cities from public to private schools consisted of blacks leaving segregated public schools to attend segregated private schools, while whites left a mixture of segregated and integrated schools to attend private schools which were overwhelmingly white.

Another problem with the Coleman, Hoffer and Kilgore accounting model is that it is based exclusively on high school data. If Cleveland, Chicago, and Boston are representative of other cities, there is a good deal more segregation in private schools at the elementary school level than at the high school level.

The Other Side of the Argument: What Private Schools May Be Doing to Help Desegregation

The role of private schools in racial segregation in American education is not simply one-sided. Private schools may also work to integrate American schools, or at least to integrate the neighborhoods these schools serve. This result can occur in three ways. First, Rossell has shown that the white flight due solely to desegregation is greatest in the first few years of desegregation.[34] By approximately the fourth year of a desegregation plan, the rate of white loss in some countywide school systems appears to be less than would have occurred had there been no desegregation (although the implementation year losses may not be recovered).[35] One reason for this may be that many families withdraw their children not by moving to the suburbs but by enrolling them in private schools within the school district. These families are more likely to return their children to public schools after desegregation, particularly if there is a change in the plan, than those who have moved to the suburbs. If whites must flee from desegregation, we think it is preferable for them to remain in the city, sending their children to private schools, than for them to move to the suburbs. On the other hand, it is quite possible that some families would leave their children in the public school and not move to the suburbs if no private schools existed.

The same argument applies to white flight from school systems that have never implemented a desegregation plan. In segregated school systems, it is often the case that a changing neighborhood is served by an all-black elementary school long before the neighborhood itself loses its last white family. This situation occurs for four reasons. First, blacks typically have larger families than whites; thus, there will be more blacks than whites in a neighborhood elementary school even if the neighborhood is equally divided among the two races. Second, many of the whites in older, changing neighborhoods are themselves older, with children who have finished school. Third, many of the whites with school-age children will place them in parochial schools for both racial and nonracial reasons. Finally, black families moving into integrated neighborhoods often move there in order to locate a good public school for their children. For this reason, a neighborhood may be racially mixed, but have a school that is overwhelmingly black, hence unacceptable to many white families. In this situation, a private school alternative may enable some families to remain living in an integrated neighborhood rather than moving out and contributing to the process of residential transition.[36]

On the other hand, public schools can provide the same sort of opportunity for integrated or changing neighborhoods. Racially balanced magnet schools have been created as alternatives to the neighborhood school for white families in neighborhoods with overwhelmingly black schools. One of the best ways to stabilize integrated neighborhoods is to adopt a districtwide desegregation plan that guarantees that residents of neighborhoods in transition will have integrated options for the indefinite future.[37] In the absence of such a plan, however, a private school system may serve to slow a neighborhood change by providing a 'haven' for white school children whose parents would move out otherwise.

Sometimes a predominantly white private school system provides an opportunity for voluntary integration for some black students. In cities like Chicago and Cleveland, the Catholic school system serves as a last resort for black families concerned about what they see as the low quality of education and serious discipline problems in inner-city public schools. Even if all whites in Chicago Catholic schools returned to public schools, the public schools would still be less than 30 per cent white. Thus, if there were no Catholic schools, many black students would be trapped in segregated inner-city public schools without a desegregated alternative.

Whether the transfer of black students from public schools to private schools creates desegregation for them depends on whether the private school systems are segregated. In the three large cities we have studied, Catholic elementary school systems are so highly segregated there is not much chance that a minority elementary student enrolling in them will be attending a desegregated school. At the high school level in Cleveland, however, where there are no predominantly black or predominantly Hispanic Catholic high schools, minorities in private schools will be desegregated. Similarly, in Boston, where all but two Catholic high schools are predominantly white, the chances are good that a black or Hispanic in a Catholic school will be desegregated. This is not the case for Chicago, however, and for many other large school systems.

The public schools in large metropolitan areas with large black school enrollments could themselves provide an alternative to segregated education for black or Hispanic students by negotiating interdistrict transfer plans. In the St Louis metropolitan area, almost 10,000 black students assigned to segregated schools in the city of St Louis are taking advantage of the opportunity to transfer to white suburban public schools under a federal court order. Milwaukee and Indianapolis are two other cities where thousands of inner-city black students are permitted to attend suburban schools. In Cleveland and Chicago, many segregated black students could be desegregated if they were allowed to attend suburban school systems, but there is no provision for transfer across district lines in these metropolitan areas.

Thus, a private school system or the suburban public schools can provide an opportunity for desegregation and improved education not otherwise available. Even this option is a double-edged sword, however, because it amounts to a kind of tracking, in which the children from highly motivated families are allowed to segregate themselves into schools that in many cases are selective, excluding students with academic or behavior problems. The public schools thus become a sort of lower track. Evidence from studies of tracked schools indicates that students in the lower tracks learn less than they would if they were in heterogeneously grouped classrooms.[38] Thus, the operation of two school systems may function to make inner-city, low-income schools worse than they would otherwise be.[39]

Private schools thus have both benefits and costs. On the one hand, they encourage the racial integration of central city neighborhoods and provide a desegregated education for some black students. On the other hand, they serve as white flight havens destabilizing desegregated central-city school systems and creating segregated public schools. We do not have all of the data necessary to balance these competing processes, though what we have presented thus far indicates that the parochial schools may cause more segregation than they prevent.

The Educational Effects of Attending Desegregated Private Schools

Coleman, Hoffer and Kilgore, as well as Greeley and Cibulka, O'Brien, and Zewe, argue that parochial schools provide educational benefits to minority students superior to those provided by the public schools.[40] Both view the parochial school as a 'common school' that is better able to serve the needs of a wide range of students than is the public school system. Greeley makes this argument explicit, saying that the Catholic schools have had a tradition of educating immigrants entering the United States, and are, therefore, almost instinctively oriented toward providing avenues for upward mobility for persons outside the mainstream of society.

It is clearly the case that the black students in private schools in the Coleman, Hoffer and Kilgore (High School and Beyond) sample score much higher on standardized achievement tests than do blacks attending public school. There are two alternative arguments to the common school thesis, however. First, private schools are highly selective and only admit the brighter minority students (or conversely, only the brighter, higher socioeconomic status minority students apply). Second, private schools are educationally superior for minority students because they have a higher proportion white than do the public schools. Research has indicated that the higher the percentage white in the schools attended by black students, the higher their achievement. In Cleveland and Chicago, black students who transfer from public schools to private schools are not very likely to receive a desegregated education, at least at the elementary school level, so there is not much chance of an educational benefit being derived from minority enrollment in the Catholic schools of these cities. In Boston, on the other hand, black students who leave segregated inner-city schools have a good chance of attending predominantly white Catholic schools; hence, we would expect their education to improve.

The greater segregation in Catholic schools at the elementary school level than at the high school level ultimately reduces the chance of an achievement gain for a minority student enrolling in Catholic schools. A recent review of the literature on desegregation and minority achievement by Crain and Mahard concludes that not only do minority students in desegregated schools score higher on standardized achievement tests than they would if they were in segregated schools, but this effect is greater for those desegregated in the early grades.[41] The Crain and Mahard review identified twenty-three studies, with forty-five samples of students involved in nineteen desegregation plans; that compared black students who had been desegregated since first grade to black students in segregated schools or to black students in the same grade and school district before desegregation. Of the forty-five samples, forty show positive effects. Among those for which an effect size could be estimated, desegregation appeared to raise achievement by a quarter of a standard deviation — the equivalent of twenty-five points on the SAT verbal or quantitative test.[42]

Thus, it is quite possible that in some cities a private school system provides an opportunity for desegregation and improved education not otherwise available. Even this alternative can be viewed as problematic, however, because it amounts to the kind of tracking described above in relation to city-suburban transfer plans. The public schools become a sort of lower track, and the operation of the two school systems may function to make inner-city, low-income schools worse than they otherwise would be.

Will Private School Subsidies Lead to Desegregation?

The last question asked by Coleman, Kilgore and Hoffer is whether any sort of subsidy to private schools would increase or decrease segregation. They use a simple model, in which they liken a subsidy to a general increase in affluence, and conclude that the students on the margin, those most likely to shift as a result of a voucher, will include enough minorities so that the difference in racial mix between public and private schools will decline. The model has been severely criticized by several analysts,[43] and we will not do so again, except to note that their model shows the most segregated and deprived sector of the population, low-income blacks, *least* likely to transfer to private schools.

In fact, the effect on segregation of a subsidy plan will depend on the specifics of the plan. The voucher plan proposed in California, for example, has strict controls designed to encourage desegregation and the participation of low-income families. On the other hand, a tuition tax credit would clearly not encourage low-income families to transfer because the attractiveness of reimbursement would be dependent on having an income high enough to pay a substantial amount of taxes.

Of course, any subsidy plan could contain specific requirements for desegregation of private schools either imposed by law or required by a court's interpretation of the Constitution. For example, subsidy legislation (or a court order) might require that transportation be provided so minority students could attend desegregated private schools. Thus, it is easy to imagine a private school subsidy plan that would enable more low-income minority students to gain a desegregated education. But it is useless to speculate on the abstract, because so much depends on the specifics of any legislation.

Conclusion

The optimistic conclusions drawn by Coleman, Hoffer and Kilgore are not supported by the data from the three large cities studied here. The Catholic schools in these three cities — Chicago, Cleveland, and Boston — are, on average, much more segregated than the public schools. This was true at the elementary school level when the public schools had a neighborhood assignment policy, and it is true at both the elementary and high school levels now that the public schools have been desegregated. In general, the Catholic schools are much more segregated than one would predict from their small black enrollment. Thus, these data give us little reason to believe that the impact of private schools is simply benign. At the same time, we do not have enough data available to draw the more complicated conclusion which we suspect is the correct one: namely, that private schools further the segregation of schools under certain conditions, and encourage racial integration of schools or residential neighborhoods under others.

Notes

1 W. BENNETT (1986) *First Lessons: A Report on Elementary Education in America*, Washington, D.C., US Office of Education.
2 J. COLEMAN, T. HOFFER and S. KILGORE (1981) *Public and Private Schools*, Final report to National Center for Educational Statistics, Washington, D.C.
3 J. COLEMAN, T. HOFFER and S. KILGORE (1982) *High School Achievement*, New York, Basic Books.
4 In this paper, 'whites' always means 'non-Hispanic whites'.
5 The formula for Sbw — the percentage of white in the average black child's school — is:

$$S_{bw} = \frac{\sum\limits_{k=1}^{n} N_{kb} P_{kw}}{\sum\limits_{k=1}^{n} N_{kb}}$$

This has been used to measure the 'net benefit' or interracial exposure of desegregation plans after white reassignments and white flight. See, for example, C. ROSSELL (1985) 'Estimating the Net Benefit of School Desegregation Reassignments', *Educational Evaluation and Policy Analysis*, 7, 3, pp. 217–28, and C. ROSSELL and R. CLARKE (1987) *The Carrot or the Stick in School Desegregation Policy?*, A report to the National Institute of Education, Washington, D.C., Grant NIE-G-83-0019, March 1987. Swb can be converted to Sbw by the following formula:

$$Sbw = \frac{Swb \text{ (white enrollment)}}{\text{black enrollment}}$$

and Sbw can be converted into Swb by:

$$Swb = \frac{Sbw \text{ (black enrollment)}}{\text{white enrollment}}$$

6 The formula for Swb — the percentage black in the average white child's school is:

$$S_{wb} = \frac{\sum\limits_{k=1}^{n} N_{kw} P_{kb}}{\sum\limits_{k=1}^{n} N_{kw}}$$

The formulae for the indices are:
(i) standardized (relative):

$$R_b = 1 - \frac{S_{wb}}{P_b}$$

or

(ii) standardized (relative):

$$R_b = 1 - \frac{S_{bw}}{P_w}$$

where N_{kw} is the number of whites in the kth school, P_{kb} is the percentage black of the kth school, P_b is the percentage black of the entire school system, and P_w is the percentage white of the entire school system. An alternative formula for R_b is:

$$R_b = \frac{P_b - S_{wb}}{P_b}$$

or

$$R_b = \frac{P_w - S_{bw}}{P_w}$$

7 E. PAGE and T. KEITH (1981) 'Effect of U.S. Private Schools: A Technical Analysis of Two Recent Claims', *Educational Researcher*, 10, 7, pp. 7–17.

8 Furthermore, standardization does not completely control for the small percentage black in private schools. Taeuber and James note that, of several indices available, the relative exposure index, which they call the variance ratio index, is most sensitive to the racial mix of the schools. K. TAEUBER and O. JAMES (1982) 'Racial Segregation among Public and Private Schools', *Sociology of Education*, 55, 2–3, pp. 133–43. They compute a dissimilarity index, and find segregation levels of public and private schools to be more similar — with public 0.70 and private 0.63.

Which standardized index is chosen is a matter of values; there is no compelling reason for using either the relative exposure index or the dissimilarity index. Both measures have problems when used to evaluate segregation in private schools.

9 COLEMAN *et al., Public and Private Schools, op.cit.*

10 Since 1967, the United States Government has collected data on the racial composition of all schools in virtually all but the smallest school districts. After 1974, the data were collected only in the even numbered years. These data are on computer tape, as well as in bound volumes in the even numbered years.

11 The data for Chicago were provided by Joe T. Darden, Urban Affairs Program, Michigan State University; the data for Cleveland were provided by Richard Overmanns of the Cuyahoga Plan of Cleveland, a group concerned with housing segregation issues. The data for Boston Catholic schools were provided by the Boston Archdiocese directly.

12 R. FARLEY (1981) Final Report, NIE Grant G-79–0151, Population Studies Center, The University of Michigan, Ann Arbor, Michigan.

13 Since 1982 was the first year of Chicago's magnet-voluntary plan, this comparison somewhat disadvantages Chicago. In each year since 1982, racial imbalance has declined by an additional small amount.

14 C. ROSSELL (1978) 'The Effect of Community Leadership and the Mass Media on Public Behavior', *Theory Into Practice*, 17, 2, pp. 131–9.

15 J. LORD (1975) 'School Busing and White Abandonment of Public Schools', *Southeastern Geographer*, 15, 2, pp. 81–92; J. McCONAHAY and W. HAWLEY (1977) *Attitudes of Louisville and Jefferson County Citizens toward Busing for Public School Desegregation: Results from the Second Year*, Durham, N.C., Duke University, Institute of Policy Sciences and Public Affairs; K. TAEUBER and F. WILSON (1978) 'The Demographic Impact of School Desegregation Policy', in M. KRAFT and M. SCHNEIDER (Eds) *Population Policy Analysis*, Lexington, Mass., Lexington Books; G. ORFIELD (1978) Report to the Superior Court of the State of California for the County of Los Angeles,

Mary Ellen Crawford et al. vs. Board of Education of the City of Los Angeles; G. CUNNINGHAM and W. HUSK (1979) 'A Metropolitan Desegregation Plan: Where the White Students Went', Paper presented at the annual meeting of the American Educational Research Association, San Francisco; L. ESTABROOK (1980) 'The Effect of Desegregation on Parents' Evaluation of Schools', PhD dissertation, Boston University; J. ROSS (1981) Testimony prepared for the Senate Judiciary Committee, Subcommittee on the Separation of Powers, (J–97–29) 97th Congress, 1st Session, 30 September; E. CATALDO (1982) *Enrollment Decline and School Desegregation in Cleveland: An Analysis of Trends and Causes*, Cleveland, Ohio, Office of School Monitoring and Community Relations; R. HULA (1984) 'Housing Market Effects of Public School Desegregation: The Case of Dallas, Texas', *Urban Affairs Quarterly*, 19, 3, pp. 409–23.

16 J. ROSS (1981) Testimony prepared for the Senate Judiciary Committee, Subcommittee on the Separation of Powers, (J–97–29) 97th Congress, 1st Session, 30 September [Boston]; L. ESTABROOK (1980) 'The Effect of Desegregation on Parents' Evaluation of Schools', PhD dissertation, Boston University; G. ORFIELD (1978) Report to the Superior Court of the State of California for the County of Los Angeles, *Mary Ellen Crawford et al. vs. Board of Education of the City of Los Angeles*; E. CATALDO (1982) *Enrollment Decline and School Desegregation in Cleveland: An Analysis of Trends and Causes*, Cleveland, Ohio, Office of School Monitoring and Community Relations; R. HULA (1984) 'Housing Market Effects of Public School Desegregation: The Case of Dallas, Texas', *Urban Affairs Quarterly*, 19, 3, pp. 409–23.

17 J. McCONAHAY and W. HAWLEY (1977) *Attitudes of Louisville and Jefferson County Citizens toward Busing for Public School Desegregation: Results from the Second Year*, Durham, N.C., Duke University, Institute of Policy Sciences and Public Affairs; G. CUNNINGHAM and W. HUSK (1979) 'A Metropolitan Desegregation Plan: Where the White Students Went', Paper presented at the annual meeting of the American Educational Research Association, San Francisco.

18 L. ESTABROOK (1980) 'The Effect of Desegregation on Parents' Evaluation of Schools', PhD dissertation, Boston University; J. ROSS (1981) Testimony prepared for the Senate Judiciary Committee, Subcommittee on the Separation of Powers, (J–97–29) 97th Congress, 1st Session, 30 September.

19 C. ROSSELL (1983) 'Desegregation Plans, Racial Isolation, White Flight, and Community Response', in C. ROSSELL and W. HAWLEY (Eds) *The Consequences of School Desegregation*, Philadelphia, Pa., Temple University Press.

20 H. BECKER (1978) *The Impact of Racial Composition and Public School Desegregation on Changes in Non-Public School Enrollment*, Baltimore, Md., Center for Social Organization of Schools, Johns Hopkins University, Report 252.

21 M. GILES (1977) 'Racial Stability and Urban School Desegregation', *Urban Affairs Quarterly*, 12, 4, pp. 499–510.

22 After the implementation period, nonentrance may become a more important factor than exit.

23 C. ROSSELL (1977) 'Boston's Desegregation and White Flight', *Integrated Education*, 15, 1, pp. 36p; C. ROSSELL (1978) *Assessing the Unintended Impact of Public Policy: School Desegregation and Resegregation*, A report to the National

Institute of Education, Washington, D.C.

24 C. ROSSELL (1988) 'Is it the Buging or the Blacks?' *Urban Affairs Quarterly*, 24, 1, pp. 138–48.

25 C. ROSSELL and J. ROSS (1979) 'The Long-Term Effect of Court-Ordered Desegregation on Student Enrollment in Central City School Systems: The Case of Boston 1974–1979', Boston, Mass., Sociology Department, Boston University.

26 C. ROSSELL and R. CLARKE (1987) *The Carrot or the Stick in School Desegregation Policy?*, A report to the National Institute of Education, Washington, D.C., Grant NIE-G-83-0019, March.

27 C. ROSSELL (1977) 'Boston's Desegregation and White Flight', *Integrated Education*, 15, 1, pp. 36–9; C. ROSSELL (1978) *Assessing the Unintended Impact of Public Policy: School Desegregation and Resegregation*, A report to the National Institute of Education, Washington, D.C.

28 L. ESTABROOK (1980) 'The Effect of Desegregation on Parents' Evaluation of Schools', PhD dissertation, Boston University; J. ROSS (1981) Testimony prepared for the Senate Judiciary Committee, Subcommittee on the Separation of Powers, (J-97-29) 97th Congress, 1st Session, 30 September.

29 This is calculated as the enrollment difference − actual minus predicted − divided by the predicted enrollment multiplied by 100.

30 Reliable Catholic and private school enrollment data are unavailable for 1976 or 1978.

31 The 13,906 estimate of white public school loss as a result of desegregation is very close to the estimate of 14,546 white enrollment loss from desegregation that can be derived from Rossell's figures; see C. ROSSELL (1978) *Assessing the Unintended Impacts of Public Policy: School Desegregation and Resegregation*, A report to the National Institute of Education, Washington, D.C., but much lower than Armor's (1978) estimate of 16,000. ARMOR, DAVID J. (1978) 'White flight, demographic transition and the future of school desegregation', paper presented at the American Sociological Association Meetings, San Francisco, CA. It should be remembered that the nonpublic enrollment gain includes all races. If we assume white enrollment is 90 per cent of this figure, then the 10,000 enrollment gain is two-thirds of the public school white enrollment loss. It should also be remembered that although these data show an increasingly larger gain over time above what would be predicted from the pre-desegregation trend, it would be unwarranted to conclude that white flight is increasing. The farther one gets from the trend used for prediction (e.g., the pre-desegregation trend), the less accurate the comparisons over time become. Assuming all categories will suffer from this problem equally, the comparisons between groups should still be accurate.

32 These percentages are derived as follows. The number of tenth grade students of each race in Catholic schools is divided by the number of tenth grade students of each race in public schools as obtained from Table 3–1 in COLEMAN, HOFFER and KILGORE, *High School Achievement, op.cit.* When this is done, Catholic school white enrollment is 7.6 per cent of public school white enrollment, and Catholic school black enrollment is 2.6 per cent of public school black enrollment.

33 J. COLEMAN, S. KELLY and J. MOORE (1975) *Trends in Segregation, 1968–1973*, Washington, D.C., Urban Institute. A similar argument has been made in

K. Taeuber and D. James (1982) 'Racial Segregation among Public and Private Schools', *Sociology of Education*, 55, 2–3, pp. 133–43, and R. Crain (1981) 'Initial Comments' in School Research Forum in *Coleman Report on Public and Private Schools*, Arlington, Va., Educational Research Service.

34 C. Rossell (1983) 'Desegregation Plans, Racial Isolation, White Flight, and Community Response', in C. Rossell and W. Hawley (Eds) *The Consequences of School Desegregation*, Philadelphia, Pa., Temple University Press.

35 This may, however, be an artifact of the much larger loss rates in city school districts both pre- and post-desegregation and the inability of the regression analysis to adequately control for the pre-desegregation loss rate in the countywide school districts when comparing them to the numerically superior (about three-quarters of the sample) city school districts.

36 H. Aldrich (1978) 'Ecological Succession in Racially Changing Neighborhoods: A Review of the literature', *Urban Affairs Quarterly*, 10, 3, pp. 327–48.

37 D. Pearce, R. Crain and F. Reynolds (1984) *Lessons Not Lost: The Effect of School Desegregation on the Rate of Residential Desegregation in Large Central Cities*, Washington, D.C., Center for National Policy Review; D. Pearce (1980) *Breaking Down Barriers: New Evidence on the Impact of Metropolitan School Desegregation on Housing Patterns*, Washington, D.C., Report to the National Institute of Education.

38 R. Slavin (1986) *Ability Grouping and Student Achievement in Elementary Schools: A Best Evidence Synthesis*, Baltimore, Md., Center for Social Organization of Schools, Johns Hopkins University, Report No. 1.

39 For a discussion of the public-private schools as a 'tracked' system, see J. McPartland and E. McDill (1982) 'Control and Differentiation in the Structure of American Education', *Sociology of Education*, 55, 2–3, pp. 77–88.

40 A. Greeley (1982) *Catholic High Schools and Minority Students*, New Brunswick, N.J., Transaction Books; J. Cibulka, T. O'Brien and D. Zewe (1982) *Inner-City Private Elementary Schools: A Study*, Milwaukee, Wisc., Marquette University Press.

41 R. Crain and R. Mahard (1983) 'The Effects of Research Methodology on Desegregation-Achievement Studies: A Meta-Analysis', *American Journal of Sociology*, 88, 5, pp. 839–54.

42 In 1982, the National Institute of Education, under the Reagan administration, organized a 'bi-partisan' panel of experts to critique the Crain and Mahard review. After discarding twenty-one of the twenty-three studies of students desegregated since first grade because they did not have a pre-test, the panelists still concluded that desegregation raised achievement but that the effects were smaller than those found by Crain and Mahard. See T. Cook, D. Armor, R. Crain, N. Miller, W. Stephan, H. Walberg and P. Wortman (1984) *School Desegregation and Black Achievement*, Washington, D.C., National Institute of Education. Clearly, the failure to have a control group is a serious problem, but it poses a conundrum for education research. Educational theory suggests that any educational intervention will have its greatest effect on younger children, but these children will almost always be lacking a pre-test by which to assess accurately the extent of improvement.

43 R. Crain and W. Hawley (1982) 'Standards of Research', *Society*, 19, 12, pp. 14–21.

10
Education as a Public and Private Good

Henry M. Levin

In the general debate over the private provision of public services, schools and education have been central topics. There are several reasons for this. First, many of the recent national reports on elementary and secondary education have suggested deep concerns about present educational standards and the ability of the schools to meet future challenges.[1] Increased reliance on the private sector represents one alternative for meeting schooling needs.

Second, a recent set of studies has argued that student achievement is higher in private schools than in public ones, even when differences in student characteristics between the two sectors are held constant.[2] Although the methods used to reach these conclusions have been hotly contested,[3] the studies have drawn attention to private schools as a model for thinking about school improvement.

Third, there is a relatively long history of debate on educational vouchers, a method for creating an educational marketplace through public funding. Under such a plan, parents would be provided with a certificate or voucher that could be used for tuition at any 'approved' school. Schools would meet standards set out by the states in order to be eligible to redeem vouchers and compete for students. Although the voucher approach goes back at least to Tom Paine,[4] its current form was proposed more recently by Milton Friedman.[5] Current initiatives to provide tuition tax credits for households with children in private schools have been proposed in several states and in the US Congress.[6]

Finally, any successful movement towards greater privatization of educational services would be significant in both symbolic and real terms for the overall privatization movement. In 1983, about 45 million children were attending elementary and secondary schools, and almost 6 million were in private schools.[7] Direct expenditures on elementary and secondary schools were estimated at about $160 billion in 1986,[8] and public school expenditures constitute the most important single budgetary component at state and local levels.

Most of the discussions of privatization in education pay little attention to education as a social good. They view education primarily as a private good that focuses on student achievement and reinforcement or extension of family values. To the degree that social benefits are deemed important, they are often viewed as the sum of the private benefits and their distribution.

Some argue that privately and publicly sponsored schools in a competitive marketplace will necessarily create a more efficient educational solution by raising student achievement and by providing parental choice in the types of values or pedagogy to which children are exposed. I will contend in this chapter that (1) the problem of reconciling private needs and social needs in education has always created a dilemma, (2) the social goods aspects of education are not merely the sum of the private benefits produced, (3) the production of those social goods through a regulated private market is problematic, and (4) public choice arrangements seem to come closer to a practical solution.

A major difference between this essay and those proposals that argue for greater participation of private schools, including the essays in this book by authors such as Arons or Chubb and Moe, is a fundamentally different assumption about the nature of educational production. Private school advocates assert that such schools are able to produce greater student acheivement than public schools produce, and at lower cost. I will show that the evidence does not support such claims, and the cost data that are marshaled in their defense are particularly biased in the direction of the authors' conclusions.

Another difference relates to the public purposes of schooling. Some private school advocates do not accept the existence of public goals of schooling, raising questions why they would wish to argue for public support for private schools. But even those who do accept the public goals of schooling assume that any public role can be imparted by meeting minimal curriculum or subject-matter guidelines. I will show that even if the authors assume that the public objectives of schooling can simply be 'added-on' to the private ones, a serious problem of monitoring and regulation arises, a problem that is likely to be costly and intrusive. More to the point, the notion that educational experiences supporting public goals can be glued on to a core of activities on behalf of private ones is particularly naive in a situation where the composition of students and the nature of their participation in the educational process are important determinants of educational outcomes.

Even more ominous is the likelihood that the whole notion of a competitive market of private schools will necessarily undermine the public goals of creating a society based upon the common literacy, knowledge, and values required for democratic functioning. Such a view requires schools with common features drawing students from a reasonable cross-section of different social, racial, and political backgrounds. But the very appeal of private schools will be to provide the narrower values, philosophies, and orientations that are considered important by families in their private domains. That is, schools will seek to succeed in particular market niches by specializing in those areas that will attract a particular clientele with similar values and viewpoints. Product differentiation is a natural market response to a non-homogeneous clientele. Thus, the very nature of the private school market will tend to undermine the commonalities that spokesmen like Milton Friedman view as necessary for the stable and democratic society.

This presentation will be limited only to elementary and secondary schooling. Although similar issues arise in postsecondary and other forms of education, the differences in those arenas are substantial and would merit special treatment.

Public and Private Benefits of Schooling

Public education stands at the intersection of two legitimate rights. The first is the right of a democratic society to assure its reproduction and continuous democratic functioning through providing a common set of values and knowledge. The other involves the right of families to decide the ways in which their children will be molded and the types of influences to which their children will be exposed.[9] To the degree that families have different political, social, and religious beliefs and values, a basic incompatibility may exist between their private concerns and the public functions of schooling.

Schooling as a Private Good

Families will desire schooling for their children in order to reap the many private benefits associated with it. It has long been established that schooling enhances individual productivity and earnings.[10] But, in addition, schooling seems to increase trainability, health, efficiency in consumption, access to information, and a wide variety of other private outcomes.[11] Beyond these, evidence suggests that education contributes to political participation and the inculcation of civic values.[12] Finally, schooling can contribute to social status, technical and cultural literacy, and promotion of family values. The private benefits of schooling are substantial and provide strong incentives for a private schooling market, even in the absence of public intervention.

Schooling as a Public Good

Schooling serves not only private ends in improving the lives of children and their families who participate.[13] It also serves the nation, region, and community by addressing a variety of social needs.[14]

Schools provide students with a common set of values and knowledge to create citizens who can function democratically. Schools contribute to equality of social, economic, and political opportunities among persons from different racial and social origins. Schools are expected to play a major role in contributing to economic growth and full employment for the nation and its regions. Schooling also is viewed as a major contributor to cultural and scientific progress and to the defense of the nation. These represent some of the areas in which education must be perceived as a social good, beyond any contribution it makes to fulfilling private needs.

The Nexus between Public and Private Goods

That schools are expected to provide both public and private benefits raises a potential dilemma. In the happy case where public benefits are simply equal to the sum of private benefits, only two challenges arise: whether enough education is produced, and whether the distribution of education can adequately capture the social benefits, because many require widespread participation. At one extreme, one can argue that private gains in individual productivity and earnings from schooling can be aggregated to produce social gains of full employment and economic growth. At the other extreme, one can argue that a particular type of schooling that yields private benefits — for example, that which advocates authoritarian values and governance — can be injurious to the establishment of democratic social processes. In this case, public and private benefits would not be compatible.

Of course, the true situation lies somewhere between these two extremes. This necessary middle ground was recognized in the establishment of public schools subject to compulsory attendance laws and some uniformity. The common experience considered crucial to producing the social or public benefits of education would have been difficult to capture in a private schooling market. Some persons would not have been able to obtain schooling for their children at all; others would have sought schooling that reinforced narrow, religious, political, ethnic, or cultural ends; yet others would have found schooling for their offspring that would have set them apart through elite practices.

Schooling would have been sought for its limited 'private' benefits by families considering only their own personal interests rather than those of the larger society. Accordingly, the concept of the common school required compulsory participation in an institution that provided a shared experience, rather than one based upon the more idiosyncratic elements of choice.

But in all other elements of child rearing, parents were able to decide the ways in which they would influence their children's development. Thus, a basic right of parents conflicted with the compulsory and uniform intent of the common schools. This conflict was resolved by political compromise that combined elements of choice and diversity with uniformity into a system of public schools.

First, families could send their children to private schools if they had the resources. Such children simply were not required to participate in common schools where they would be exposed to a 'democratic' education. Second, in the spirit of participatory democracy, the schools were treated as local institutions that served local communities, although legally established by the constitutional authority of the states. Because individual communities were often relatively homogeneous in terms of occupation, wealth, income, race, ethnicity, politics, and religion, the schools also reflected those attributes. Hiring patterns, curricula, religious practices, political content, and values in local schools mirrored the surrounding community.[15] Local financing also meant the amount spent on schools closely reflected differences in state and local wealth, as well as social and racial discrimination against schools attended by nonwhites and the poor.

The conflict between the private interests of citizens and the public interest of the commonwealth was resolved through a compromise. Private differences were permitted in an overall system of common schools established within a broad institutional structure of formal education and compulsory attendance requirements.

Legal and political challenges to these practices in the twentieth century — and particularly after World War II — narrowed differences considerably. These challenges were mounted through social movements that attempted to increase democratic participation, equality, and greater extension of constitutional rights into the public schools.[16]

Private schools faced early attacks on their legitimacy in meeting the compulsory attendance requirements of the states. These disputes were ultimately resolved in 1925 by the decision of the Supreme Court in *Pierce v. Society of Sisters*, which ensured the freedom of citizens to send their children to schools outside the public system. But within the public system, movement towards equality and uniformity proceeded apace in response to the democratic imperative.

The last thirty years witnessed the following changes:[17] reductions in spending disparities among localities as states more nearly equalized educational expenditures; proscription of religious practices from public schools; protection of teachers and students from dismissal or suspension for exercising their rights to freedom of expression; new laws and funding on behalf of female, handicapped, bilingual, and economically disadvantaged students; affirmative action in admissions to special programs and in hiring; and a legal attack on racial segregation.

The increased uniformity and egalitarianism in public schools often occurred at the expense of private privilege. This loss was greatest among those with the highest incomes, social status, and political resources, as well as among those with strong political and religious views who had taken for granted the ability to foster their views in the schools. These groups are largely at the forefront of recent quests for the expansion of public support for private schooling.

Recasting the Issue

The term 'privatization of education' generally denotes a shift towards greater private production of public services. But at the heart of the previous discussion was the distinction between schooling as a public good and as a private good, not the distinction between public and private schools. Surely all private schools produce some social goods, and all public schools produce some private goods in the sense that we have defined those goods.[18] But the larger issue is how to organize schooling to produce the highest level of social welfare that combines the production of public and private goods.

As the public schools have increasingly become characterized by uniformity of financing, proscription of religion and politics, and equalization of opportunities for those who had formerly been neglected (girls, minorities, disadvantaged, bilingual, and handicapped), certain populations have perceived a loss of private goods in the public schools. These are the groups that are pushing hardest for increased educational choice, whether through public sector reforms or expansion of publicly supported private options.

Privatization of education can be viewed as an increase in the production of private educational outputs, those that respond to the private tastes of households for educational services. It is generally considered a basic parental right to control the types of experiences that will influence the upbringing of their children. Parents who feel that they have relinquished these rights wish to recapture them, while pro-family political and religious movements wish to expand generally the private choice aspects of the schools their children attend.

At first glance, one could argue that such movements are against the public interest because of their willingness to sacrifice important public outputs of schooling in order to obtain increased private outputs. But at least some possibility exists that more private goods can be obtained without reducing public ones through reorganization of educational financing and producing. This result can be accomplished in at least two ways. First, by increasing efficiency through shifting to a competitive system of market choices, while restricting such choices to those that maintain (or even increase) social outputs; second, by increasing the production of private goods within existing public schools, while maintaining (or expanding) the level of production of social goods.

Expanded Private Provision of Schooling

One alternative for increasing private choice is using financing mechanisms, such as vouchers or tuition tax credits, to expand the role of private schools in producing education. In this section, I examine two aspects of that alternative: efficiency in the production of schooling, and effects on public goods production.

Efficiency

One of the most compelling reasons for increasing the private production of schooling is its claim of greater efficiency. Milton Friedman makes efficiency a central part of his argument for educational vouchers. From an economic perspective, efficiency refers to obtaining the largest contribution to social welfare for any particular use of resources. Friedman believes that a voucher scheme will do this through market competition and by increasing parental choice.

In essence, Friedman asserts that a combination of choice and competitive incentives created by an educational marketplace will automatically provide a more efficient solution than an educational 'monopoly'. Many advocates of private schools believe that because existing private schools must compete for students, they are more efficient than public schools. One type of evidence repeatedly cited as proof is that private schools have considerably lower expenditures — on average — than public schools.[19]

These comparisons tend to understate drastically the costs of private schools *vis-à-vis* comparable public schools.[20] Such comparisons usually compare per-student expenditures in public schools with tuition charges in Catholic schools. But tuition reflects only a portion of expenditures for Catholic schools. Extensive fund raising and periodic fees are used to supplement tuition, and many other resources are donated or subsidized.[21] For example, Catholic parochial schools often rely heavily upon teaching clergy whose salaries understate substantially their market value. The church often provides facilities that are not charged to the school. As a result, much of the apparent disparity in costs is due to massive gaps in cost accounting in private school data rather than to real cost differences.

But beyond this difference, the service mix is quite different for public and private schools.[22] Public schools must provide many mandated services and educate 'high-cost' students who are often excluded from private schools. Although public schools are required to provide expensive services for handicapped students,[23] private schools are not, and few provide them. The same applies to vocational education, which is considerably more costly than the other secondary tracks.[24] The result is that public schools must provide more services and more of the high-cost services than must private schools. Thus, the present evidence on so-called cost differences is not adequate for comparing efficiency of public and private schools.[25]

Yet, recent studies have suggested that at least for one output — student achievement — private secondary schools are superior to public ones. In cross-sectional regressions comparing achievement between public and private schools, while adjusting for student race and socioeconomic background, Coleman, Hoffer and Kilgore found that students in private schools had between a 0.12 to 0.29 standard deviation advantage in achievement.[26] Their results were criticized as overstatements of private school effects because of the treatment of tracking, inadequate controls for self-selection — that is, families with a stronger taste for education within race and socioeconomic background who choose private schools — and other flaws in the statistical design.[27] Adjustments for some of these problems considerably reduced or eliminated estimated private school advantages.[28]

Longitudinal results based on sophomore-to-senior changes found even smaller estimated private school effects.[29] Depending upon the statistical model, the maximum private school advantage varied from nothing to about 0.1 standard deviations. Even if we accept the upper part of this range, it is useful to explore the social implications for efficiency.

As Alexander and Pallas note,[30] students in Catholic schools would score about 2 percentile points more (52nd percentile) on mathematics and reading tests relative to public school students (50th percentile). The distributions of achievement between the public and private sector overlap so substantially that 48 per cent of private school students score below the average for public schools, despite the putative emphasis on achievement and unadjusted selection advantages for private schools. We should bear in mind that some analyses found no statistical differences; even this advantage, therefore, may be overstated.[31]

But how powerful is a 0.1 standard deviation advantage in student achievement in social terms, for instance, in gaining admission to a selective college, increasing earnings, or reducing the probability of unemployment? Such a gain on the Scholastic Aptitude Test amounts to about ten points on a scale where the average score is between 450 and 500, and the range is 200–800. Elite colleges show median test scores of about 700; the best public universities show medians of about 600; and somewhat selective public and private universities and colleges show median SAT scores of about 500. Clearly, a ten point advantage is unlikely to make much difference in college admissions.

Such an achievement advantage also would appear to have an anemic effect on increasing the employment of high school graduates and upon their wages. Meyer and Wise estimated earnings and employment functions for high school graduates in the four years following graduation for a national sample representing the high school class of 1972.[32] According to their results, a 0.1 standard deviation increase in achievement would increase employment by less than one day out of an average of about ten weeks of annual unemployment for this cohort.

A standard deviation increase in student achievement was associated with an increase of only about 3 per cent in wage rates or considerably less than 1 per cent for a 0.1 standard deviation advantage. Given an average wage of even $5.00 an hour, the maximum estimated achievement advantage attributed to private schooling would be associated with less than five cents an hour in additional pay.

Public Goods Production

Even when we do not take into account the differences in public goods production between public and private schools, there is little evidence to suggest substantial efficiency gains through private sector production of schooling. It is important, however, to consider the capacity of private schools for public goods production as well when considering overall efficiency.

At least two authors have asserted that it is unimportant to take account of public goods in education, even though both favor public support for private schools. On the basis of evidence for nineteenth century England, West has passionately argued that no public goods are produced in education that are independent of those produced by the aggregation of private goods.[33] His arguments are long on ideology, short on evidence, and run counter to even Friedman's reasoning on the subject. Coons and Sugarman agree that there is a public interest in schooling, but they maintain that its concrete nature is far from unanimous and is continuously contested.[34] They argue that, in the absence of consensus, the decision should be left to the private marketplace, with parents deciding for themselves the types of schools to which they send their children. They predicate their view upon the rather extreme contention that total consensus is required for democratic institutions as they are presently constituted. Both of these theories are fundamentally flawed in a democratic, capitalist society, and the dilemma on how to obtain balance between the production of public and private educational benefits persists.

One way of exploring its solution is to consider the capacity of private schools to meet public goods requirements, under different assumptions about the joint production of public and private goods. Public and private goods might be related in production through several different linkages. First, the output of public goods might be a function of the overall level of educational output. Musgrave suggests that education is a merit good because it would be underproduced in the market relative to its social merits.[35] Therefore, society finds it meritorious to expand educational output beyond the market equilibrium to capture the social benefits.

Friedman advocates a similar theory. He argues that 'a stable and democratic society is impossible without a minimum degree of literacy and knowledge on the part of most citizens and without widespread acceptance of some common set of values.'[36] He suggests that social benefits can be obtained by mandating a minimum level of schooling of a specified kind for all. Beyond this level, the benefits are mostly or exclusively private ones. In this first case, it is only necessary to expand the output and distribution of education to that level and population coverage which will capture the social benefits. Presumably, beyond that level the marginal social benefits approach zero, and only private benefits can be obtained. Friedman would, therefore, provide a minimum voucher at public expense, beyond which parents could add to the voucher to reflect their preferences for education.

A second view suggests that at any level of schooling investment, the output mix can be altered between and among public and private goods. Friedman recommends the establishment of 'certain minimum standards, such as the inclusion of a minimum common content in their programs.'[37] This view implies that government must regulate private schools to assure that they meet at least the minimum requirements for satisfying the social benefits.

At the heart of this view is a substantial involvement of the state in private education to meet the public interest. Somehow the state must assure that at least a minimum set of public outputs is produced. Whether this can be done through mandating minimum personnel, curriculum, or output requirements is problematic. Surely personnel must be competent to impart the values and knowledge to produce public benefits efficiently, the curriculum must include the subjects and experiences that will contribute to this end, and the result must be reflected in the outputs of the schools.

Yet, to assure that this is so would require an unusual amount of regulation, and would be costly, cumbersome,[38] and probably unconstitutional to the degree that the state would need to become entangled in religion when evaluating whether schools meet these regulations.[39] Furthermore, it is not clear that many of the public benefits of schooling can be measured for purposes of public accountability. Testing of values and attitudes is still a primitive art rather than a science. It should be noted that, in the past, government subsidies to the private sector have invariably resulted in increased monitoring and regulation of those private activities.[40]

Beyond the problematic issue of regulation, the second case assumes that public and private outputs are largely separable in production. That is, different compositions of public and private outputs can be produced by shifting resources among production activities in response to government regulations. But a third case suggests that some important public goods produced by education are inextricably related to the choice of educational process, and that the process itself will be affected by the fact of public or private sponsorship of schooling.

For example, effective participation in a democracy requires a willingness to tolerate diversity. This process must acknowledge the existence of different views on a subject, and accept a set of procedures for resolving differences among those views in reaching social decisions. This requirement suggests that schooling for democracy must ensure exposure to different views in controversial areas, a discourse among those views, and the acceptance of a mechanism for reconciling the debate. Research on political socialization has shown that tolerance for diversity is related to the degree to which different children are exposed to different viewpoints on controversial subjects in both the home and the school.[41]

A major advantage of a private market for schooling is the ability of families to choose the type of schooling that reflects their political and religious values. It would be unrealistic to expect that Catholic schools will expose their students to both sides of the abortion issue; that evangelical schools would provide a disinterested comparison of creation and evolution; that military academies would debate disarmament; that leftist schools would provide a balanced presentation of the capitalist system; or that white academies would explore different views towards race in the US. Their curriculum and faculty would be selected to make them efficient competitors in a differentiated market for students in which the view of parents would be reinforced and others excluded or derided. Precisely this interpretation of 'family choice' is at the heart of much of the privatization quest.[42]

Obviously, this raises a dilemma regarding the role of private schools with narrow political and religious sponsorship to provide important social benefits. If these schools fail to produce important public goods, such as citizen training for democracy, to what degree is the overall functioning of the society impaired? The answer, in general, is that as long as the numbers of persons lacking those orientations are relatively small, little problem exists. The analogy can be found in immunization for disease, where each additional person immunized also reduces the risk to susceptibles who are not immunized. Although 90 per cent of a society must be immunized against smallpox to control the disease, only 70 per cent must be immunized against diphtheria.[43]

Thus, not all of the population needs adequate training in democratic participation and behavior to assure that nondemocratic epidemic threats do not arise. At present, about 11 per cent of elementary and secondary students attend private schools, and some of these schools probably do provide adequate democratic training. But a vast expansion of private schools along religious, political, and ethnic lines could easily change this pattern so that the overall criterion is not met.

Expanding the Output of Public and Private Goods

At the heart of improving educational policy must be a consideration of how to expand the output of private goods, while maintaining public goods or increasing them for any given resource commitment. At least two available mechanisms can be used to accomplish this expansion. First, it is possible to expand the role of the private sector through the use of such funding mechanisms as educational vouchers or tuition tax credits. Second, it is possible to expand the role of public choice within the public sector. Each of these approaches could increase privatization of educational services as defined by an increase in choice of private educational goods available to families and communities.

Expansion of the private sector through public funding for schools is problematic for a number of reasons. Despite rhetorical claims that private schools can more efficiently produce such important private and public goods as student achievement, only meager evidence supports this claim. At the same time, there are inherent obstacles to the production of certain public goods by private schools in a market that provides incentives for product differentiation and appeals to a distinct and narrow clientele. Furthermore, major problems arise in regulating either the production or output mix of private schools. Outputs are largely psychological and thus not easily measurable, and transaction costs of measurement and regulation loom large in both resource terms[44] and in challenges to First Amendment nonentanglement of the state in religion.

Public Choice Approaches

The use of public options as an alternative to private ones in expanding the privatization of educational services finds support in an empirical study showing that the larger the range of public educational choices in a geographical area, the smaller the number of private enrollments, *ceteris paribus*.[45] This correlation suggests that expanded public choice can be an effective substitute for private schooling in the quest for private educational services.

The public choice approach to increased privatization of educational services must be guided by two principles. First, a common core of experiences must be maintained that will meet the requirements of preparing the young for economic and social participation and democratic life in the US, and helping to attain other pertinent social benefits. Second, options must be established for parents and students that will provide choices among schools, programs, and educational philosophies within the common core experience.

Among the goals of a common core ought to be the provision of equal and appropriate educational opportunities for all children; exposure to ideas, values, political views, and individuals from backgrounds and cultures other than their own; fulfillment of basic requirements in a common language; familiarity with major technological issues; capability in numerical calculations and reasoning; understanding of our system of government and the rights and responsibilities of individuals; an appreciation of the fine arts and music; and an understanding of the functioning of the economy, as well as preparation for direct access to jobs or to further education and training. The detailed goals will be derived through democratic processes as they have been in the past.

Beyond the existence of this core, educational options can be expanded through a variety of political and organizational arrangements.[46] Among them are the following.

School-Site Governance. One way of making schools more responsive is to create governance around smaller schooling units, such as individual schools, rather than around school districts. The decentralization of governance would place many school decisions closer to the families who are affected by them, and permit families to have more influence on the schooling of their children in areas outside the common core.

Open Enrollment. Permitting open enrollment both within and among school districts is an effective way of increasing parental choice. It would be most effective in an urban setting, with many school districts in a compact geographical area where inexpensive public transportation exists.

Schools of Choice. A more elaborate method of developing choice is to provide a system of schools within a district that specialize in particular themes.[47] Each school would attempt to satisfy the common core requirements, as well as offering a particular orientation to meet parental demands. For example, specialization in 'basics', art, music, science, or cultural enrichment would be major candidates. Individual schools that were too large could be divided into several minischools, each with its own appeal.[48]

Using Post-Secondary Options. The availability of public four-year and community colleges in proximity to most communities suggests that secondary school students be given study options in those institutions. Particularly in sparsely populated areas with small secondary schools, curriculum offerings might be enhanced by providing access to courses in post-secondary institutions (as is presently being done in Minnesota).

Minivouchers. Minivouchers are certificates that students can use for a selected range of educational services beyond the common educational core. These options might be limited to 'enrichment areas', such as creative writing, computer programming, and specialized scientific and artistic subjects; they might also be used for ancillary educational services, such as those for handicapped, disadvantaged, and bilingual students. (In 1985 the US Department of Education proposed such federally funded minivouchers for services for the disadvantaged. From an efficiency perspective, however, the plan is rather weak because equal vouchers would be mandated for all disadvantaged students regardless of the modesty or severity of their needs.)

Private Contractors. A final way of establishing more alternatives is to contract out various parts of the educational program beyond the common core. For example, private contractors could be enlisted to provide instruction in specified subjects as alternatives to parents who were not satisfied with the progress of their students in regular classes.[49] To the degree that the purposes of such schooling could be captured in standard tests of achievement or other measurable outcomes, it might be possible to make arrangements in which payment would be made according to results.[50]

Conclusion

In summary, a private market would face intrinsic barriers in producing the public outputs of education so fundamental to US democratic society. In contrast, a public choice approach could yield greater private benefits, while not undermining the public ones. This discussion has not addressed methods of increasing the effectiveness of public schools, an issue that is especially important for those schools that educate disadvantaged youngsters in America.[51] Even accepting the maximum estimates of private school effects, one can hardly conclude that private schools have the answer to the educational challenge of the disadvantaged. A major challenge is the design of new approaches, with appropriate incentives and accountability mechanisms to address the educational needs of a rising population of disadvantaged students.[52]

Notes

1 See, for example, National Commission on Excellence in Education (1983) *A Nation at Risk*, Washington, D.C., US Department of Education; and Task Force on Education for Economic Growth (1983) *Action for Excellence*, Denver, Colo., Education Commission of the States.

2 J.S. COLEMAN, T. HOFFER, T. and S. KILGORE (1982) *High School Achievement: Public, Catholic, and Private Schools Compared*, New York, Basic Books; T.

HOFFER, A. GREELEY and J.S. COLEMAN (1985) 'Achievement Growth in Public and Catholic Schools', *Sociology of Education*, 58, April, pp. 74–97.

3 K.L. ALEXANDER and A.M. PALLAS (1985) 'School Sector and Cognitive Performance: When Is a Little a Little?', *Sociology of Education*, 58, 2, pp. 115–28; A.S. GOLDBERGER and G.G. CAIN (1982) 'The Causal Analysis of Cognitive Outcomes in the Coleman, Hoffer, and Kilgore Report', *Sociology of Education*, 55, April–July, pp. 103–22; J.D. WILLMS (1985) 'Catholic School Effects on Academic Achievement: New Evidence from the High School and Beyond Follow-up Study', *Sociology of Education*, 58, 2, pp. 98–114.

4 E.G. WEST (1967) 'Tom Paine's Voucher Scheme for Public Education', *Southern Economic Journal*, 33, January pp. 378–82.

5 M. FRIEDMAN (1962) 'The Role of Government in Education', *Capitalism and Freedom*, Chicago, Ill., University of Chicago Press, Ch. 6.

6 T. JAMES and H.M. LEVIN (Eds) (1983) *Public Dollars for Private Schools*, Philadelphia, Pa., Temple University Press.

7 V.W. PLISKO and J.D. STERN (1985) *The Condition of Education*, Washington, D.C., US Government Printing Office, p. 18.

8 US DEPARTMENT OF COMMERCE, BUREAU OF THE CENSUS (1985) *Statistical Abstract of the United States 1986*, 106th ed., Washington, D.C., US Government Printing Office, p. 128.

9 H.M. LEVIN (1983) 'Educational Choice and the Pains of Democracy', in JAMES and LEVIN, *op.cit.*, Ch. 1.

10 G.S. BECKER (1964) *Human Capital*, New York, Columbia University Press.

11 R.H. HAVEMAN and B.L. WOLFE (1984) 'Schooling and Economic Well-Being: The Role of Nonmarket Effects', *Journal of Human Resources*, 19, Summer, pp. 377–407.

12 See A. CAMPBELL (1964) 'The Passive Citizen', *Acta Sociologica*, 6, facs. 1–2, pp. 1–21; and J. TORNEY-PURTA and J. SCHWILLE (1986) 'Civil Values Learned in School: Policy and Practice in Industrialized Nations', *Comparative Education Review*, 30, February, pp. 30–49.

13 R.F. BUTTS (1978) *Public Education in the United States*, New York, Holt, Rinehart and Winston; B.A. WEISBROD (1964) *External Benefits of Public Education*, Princeton, N.J., Industrial Relations Section, Department of Economics, Princeton University.

14 H.M. LEVIN (1985) 'Are Block Grants the Answer to the Federal Role in Education?', *Economics of Education Review*, 4, 3, pp. 261–9.

15 D.B. TYACK (1974) *The One Best System: A History of American Urban Education*, Cambridge, Mass., Harvard University Press, pp. 104–9; M. KATZ (1971) *Class, Bureaucracy and Schools*, New York, Praeger.

16 M. CARNOY and H.M. LEVIN (1985) *Schooling and Work in the Democratic State*, Stanford, Calif., Stanford University Press.

17 H.M. LEVIN in JAMES and LEVIN, *op.cit.*

18 T. JAMES 'Questions about Educational Choice: An Argument from History', in JAMES and LEVIN, *op.cit.*, Ch. 3.

19 See, for example, AMERICAN ENTERPRISE INSTITUTE (1978) *Tuition Tax Credits and Alternatives*, Washington, D.C., AEI, p. 28; and E.G. WEST (1981) *The Economics of Education Tax Credits*, Washington, D.C., The Heritage Foundation, p.28.

20 D.J. SULLIVAN (1983) 'Comparing Efficiency between Public and Private Schools', TTC-15, Stanford, Calif., Stanford University Institute for Research on Educational Finance and Governance.

21 E. BARTELL (1968) *Costs and Benefits of Catholic Elementary and Secondary Schools*, South Bend, Ind., Notre Dame University Press.

22 SULLIVAN, *op.cit.*

23 J.S. KAKALIK, W.S. FURRY, M.A. THOMAS and M.F. CARNEY (1981) *The Cost of Special Education*, Santa Monica, Calif., Rand Corporation.

24 T. HU and E.W. STROMSDORFER (1979) 'Cost-Benefit Analysis of Vocational Education', in T. ABRAMSON, C.K. TITTLE and L. COHEN *Handbook of Vocational Education Evaluation*, Beverly Hills, Calif., Sage, Ch. 8.

25 Chambers found that teacher compensation was lower in private than in public schools. But much of the difference was found to be due to differences in teacher qualifications, and it was not possible to adjust salaries for the work demands of different student and service mixes between the two sectors. See J.G. CHAMBERS (1985) 'Patterns of Compensation of Public and Private School Teachers', *Economics of Education Review*, 4, 4, pp. 291–310.

26 COLEMAN, HOFFER and KILGORE, *op.cit.*

27 GOLDBLERGER and CAIN, *op.cit.*

28 WILLMS (1983), *op.cit.*

29 ALEXANDER and PALLAS, *op.cit.*; HOFFER, GREELEY and COLEMAN, *op.cit.*; WILLMS (1985), *op.cit.*

30 ALEXANDER and PALLAS, *op.cit.*

31 WILLMS (1985), *op.cit.*

32 R. MEYER and D. WISE (1982) 'High School Preparation and Early Labor Force Experience', in R.B. FREEMAN and D. WISE (Eds) *The Youth Labor Market Problem: Its Nature, Causes and Consequences*, Chicago, Ill., University of Chicago Press, Ch. 9.

33 E.G. WEST (1965) *Education and the State: A Study in Political Economy*, London, Institute of Economic Affairs.

34 J.E. COONS and S.D. SUGARMAN (1978) *Education by Choice*, Berkeley, Calif., University of California Press.

35 R.A. MUSGRAVE (1959) *The Theory of Public Finance*, New York, McGraw Hill, pp. 13–14.

36 FRIEDMAN, *op.cit.*, p. 86.

37 *Ibid.*, p. 89.

38 R.J. MURNANE (1986) 'Comparisons of Private and Public Schools: The Critical Role of Regulations', in D.C. LEVY (Ed.) *Private Education: Studies in Choice and Public Policy*, New York, Oxford University Press, Ch. 5.

39 *Lemon v. Kurtzman*, 403 US 602, 619 (1971).

40 D.J. ENCARNATION 'Public Finance and Regulation of Nonpublic Education: Retrospect and Prospect', in JAMES and LEVIN, *op.cit.*, Ch. 10.

41 J. TORNEY-PURTA 'Political Socialization and Policy: The United States in a Cross-National Context', in H. STEVENSON and A. SIEGELF (Eds) (1984) *Child Development Research and Social Policy*, Chicago, Ill., University of Chicago Press.

42 COONS and SUGARMAN, *op.cit.*

43 J.S. MAUSNER and A.K. BAHN (1974) *Epidemiology: An Introductory Text*, Philadelphia, Pa., W.B. Saunders.

44 These issues are reviewed in detail for a specific voucher proposal in H.M. LEVIN (1980) 'Educational Vouchers and Social Policy', in R. HASKINS and J.J. GALLAGHER (Eds) (1980) *Care and Education in America*, Norwood, N.J., Ablex, Ch. 5.

45 J. MARTINEZ-VAZQUEZ and B. SEAMAN (1985) 'Private Schooling and the Tiebout Hypothesis', *Public Finance Quarterly*, 13, July, pp. 293–318. Research on the demand for private schooling also supports this notion of substitutability.

46 M.A. RAYWID (1985) 'Family Choice Arrangements in Public Schools: A Review of the Literature', *Review of Educational Research*, 55, 4, pp. 435–67.

47 G.V. BASS (1978) *A Study of Alternatives in American Education, Vol. 1: District Policies and the Implementation of Change*, R2170/1-NIE, Santa Monica, Calif., Rand Corporation.

48 D. WEILER *et al.* (1974) *A Public School Voucher Demonstration: The First Year at Alum Rock*, Santa Monica, Calif., Rand Corporation.

49 J.S. COLEMAN (1967) 'Towards Open Schools', *The Public Interest*, 9, Fall, pp. 20–7.

50 L. LESSINGER (1970) *Every Kid a Winner: Accountability in Education*, New York, Simon and Schuster.

51 H.M. LEVIN (1987) 'Accelerated Schools for Disadvantaged Students', *Educational Leadership*, 44, 6, pp. 22–3.

52 Substantial portions of this essay were first published in *Journal of Policy Analysis and Management*, 1987, 6, 4, pp. 628–41.

Part IV
Prospects for Reform

11
Education and the Power of the State: Reconceiving Some Problems and Their Solutions

John Lachs and Shirley M. Lachs

Introduction

The Growth of State Power

The twentieth century has seen a vast increase in the scope of state power. The expectation of government solutions to a broad range of problems has been both a cause and an effect of this development. Through legislation and the activity of the courts, the federal and state governments have come to regulate such previously autonomous interactions as those between employers and workers. They have interposed themselves between interested parties in a variety of hitherto private areas of concern, such as life-and-death treatment decisions that had been the exclusive province of physicians, patients, and their families.

A governmental presence in nearly all areas of life tends to obliterate the realms of what is private and what, though social, used to be immune from the power of the state. As a result, nearly everything becomes a public good and we lose sight of any clear limits on regulations imposed in the name of the public interest. This entails a significant loss both of freedom and, because not all activities are equally well suited for regulation, of efficiency. Nevertheless, the growth in the number of people and in the complexity of their interactions exerts steady pressure for extensive and uniform rules centrally administered.

Although education in the United States has so far escaped the monolithic state control we find in many European countries, it has become subject to a growing variety of federal demands. To many, it is of special concern that these rules and requirements are aimed at private schools no less than at public. The debate about the appropriateness of such an extension of central power is conducted in terms typically of the right of individuals to raise their children as they see fit and the right of society — and of the government as its agent — to set limits to and place conditions on this liberty.

Reconceiving the Problem

The terms of the discussion are natural and inevitable so long as the issue is primarily the power of one side or the other to do what it desires. But conceiving the problem in this way does little to advance our grasp of the changing conditions of social life that render the conflict acute and frequently fails to provide a generally acceptable solution. For groups that challenge state intervention, the use of this conceptual framework constitutes, moreover, an acceptance through its terms of what they want to reject in substance. For the very language of rights, requiring adjudication in the courts, concedes that government control is a politico-legal issue and thereby invites invocation of the public interest.

We shall altogether sidestep the formulation of the problem of the relation of the state to the schools in the currently popular terms of individual rights and legitimate government power. Political solutions presuppose social problems; only by understanding these can we assess the adequacy of the remedy. There are at least two major problems we face with respect to education. In general terms, they are the desperate need to improve teaching and learning, and the continuing requirement not to let the schools contribute to injustice and discrimination in our society. We cannot devise effective solutions to these problems without understanding the social conditions that obtain in a populous and thoroughly institutionalized community.

Accordingly, we shall attempt to provide an account of the structural problems that beset our educational systems. Not surprisingly, these difficulties are for the most part the same as the problems we face in society at large. They arise out of the growth of specialization and widespread loss of immediacy that characterize our interactions. As a result of their ubiquity in our social life, they infect private educational institutions no less than large public school systems. If this analysis is accurate, it has profound implications for how to improve the educational experience of young people. It also bears direct relevance to the socially desirable limits of politico-legal conflict resolution and to the manner in which laws are to be made, interpreted, and administered.

The Need for Immediacy

The Nature of Education

Except for sex, education is the most intimate of human contacts. Other than marriage, it is the most loving and momentous of personal relations. The comparison with sex and marriage is not gratuitous. Education is essentially parenting: the begetting of human beings or the transformation of suitable biological organisms into socialized individuals.

This activity, poorly understood even today, displays immense complexities. It includes, among other elements, conveying a certain amount of information, helping to develop necessary skills, fostering important social attitudes and establishing vital values. The means used to accomplish these ends are both deliberate and discursive — as we find in overt attempts to teach — and subtle, unspoken, and surprising — as when young people learn by imitation and example. The ultimate aim of education consists in the development of persons who are both self-determining and respectful of the self-determination of others, both individuals and supportive of a shared social life.

This intensely personal interaction is organized and governed, in the modern world, by large, impersonal institutions. Legislatures have wrested control over and parents have, for the most part, surrendered responsibility for the education of children. Only lately have sperm banks and surrogate motherhood enabled us to have biological offspring by proxy. But the day care center, the school system, and Sunday School have for a long time made it possible for us to raise our children by proxy: to retire from lovingly teaching them ourselves and to delegate the task of endowing them with personality to strangers. These people, presumably experts at the art of person-making, operate under the constraints imposed by the institutions that employ them. The creation of the next generation ceases, in this way, to be self-improvement through cultural self-reproduction and becomes, instead, a bureaucratic job.

The Institutional Context

Large institutions inevitably suffer from certain structural problems. They consist of chains of individuals interacting in complex patterns. The tasks accomplished are broken into their constituent elements and each of these is executed by a different person or group within the chain. In this way, momentous acts can be performed, and the need for collaboration greatly enhances our social, cooperative tendencies. But there are also costs, many of them due to the fragmentation of tasks and the attendant growth of specialization.

The natural pattern of an integrated human action includes intention, execution, and the enjoyment or suffering of consequences. In large-scale social acts performed by institutional chains, these functions are separated and assigned to different individuals. Some people plan and administer, while others carry out directives or man operations. Those primarily affected by the actions constitute a separate group from either of these two; they are customers or clients or, in unfortunate cases, victims of the institution. The division of tasks places the three groups at a psychological, and frequently at a physical, distance from one another. The result is ignorance by each of the purposes and activities of the others and inability by persons in every section of the chain to view their own actions as parts of a complete and significant human act.

A pervasive sense of meaninglessness, lack of control over one's own contribution, frustration at the insensitivity of the institution, and the fear that all its functionaries are manipulated manipulators conspire to create an atmosphere of uncaring irresponsibility. In such structures, it is natural to retreat within the narrowest parameters of one's job; since we feel that it is beyond our power to change the system we tend to disclaim responsibility for what it causes. Surprisingly, even expertise fosters cold indifference: primary allegiance to professional standards narrows the scope of caring and shifts its focus from people to the quality of one's performance.

These general problems of large-scale institutions now pervade education throughout our land.[1] The image of the small country schoolhouse with a loving teacher beckons only as the symbol of a simpler and better past. The sheer size of the task of instructing the next generation presents problems: many teachers see hundreds of young people in their classes, and school boards deal with tens of thousands of students. The press of numbers eliminates the possibility of sustained contact and personal relationships between teachers and students. Education then becomes a product whose uniform quality must be assured by a multitude of rules and regulations. Administrators are the creators and enforcers of these rules, and teachers learn to herd their charges through a body of material in accordance with them. Young people know little of the reason for the regulations and the institution is in no hurry to justify or explain them. The result is that students view the educational system as an alien machine to which they must submit on account of its enormous power.

Students, however, are not alone in regarding the educational Leviathan with suspicion. The initial pleasure of parents in having their children taken off their hands tends to be followed by repeated encounters with an unaccommodating bureaucracy. Teachers themselves feel their autonomy threatened and their lives consumed by the petty demands of functionaries. School administrators find themselves in a hierarchical system hemmed in by parents, taxpayers, and politicians at the one end, and the shoulder-shrugging incompetence of coaches and assistant principals at the other.

This lumbering institution consumes the good intentions and the energy of all who join it for idealistic reasons, without yielding significant improvement in return. Astoundingly, none who comes in contact with it does what he or she wants: constraint and compromise remove both the joy of learning and the special pleasures of intergenerational communication. The prevailing experience in the educational system is frustration, and the universal reality in it is that anything out of the ordinary requires backbreaking effort. Openness to change and to reason, the very spirit of experimentation that we think should characterize the enterprise of spreading knowledge, appear to be altogether gone.

This litany of the current ills of education is not meant to deny the efficiency, enthusiasm, and inventiveness of isolated individuals or groups. There is no doubt, moreover, that in spite of its problems the system manages to do a great deal of good by socializing young people, teaching them useful skills, and transmitting vast amounts of information. But the accomplishments of individual teachers and administrators occur too often in spite of rather than because of the existing structure. What education achieves pales by comparison with its ideals and its possibilities.

Not all the problems of education are due to its institutional shape. But many are, and those are the ones we wish to discuss here. They are not normally seen to be related, much less to have a single cause. Our analysis offers a unitary explanation of widely diverse phenomena and, through identification of the source of the difficulties, promises the possibility of intelligent remedial action.

Loss of Immediacy

The central reality on which we must focus is the loss of immediacy and, through that, the loss of intimacy in the educational process. There is some forfeiture of immediacy in every institution. But when the social structure is small, the loss is relatively minor or easily counteracted. In a single, small, autonomous school, for example, teachers are in continuing contact with one another, and the administrator can readily acquaint her staff with the constraints under which she operates and the issues she faces. In the small community this small school serves, teachers and parents are neighbors; their direct, daily contact gives each side a living grasp of the concerns and practices of the other. It is not, of course, that such communities are free of conflict. But whatever difficulties may beset them arise not from suspicion, people's ignorance of each other, and nameless irresponsibility. Teachers see and know their students not only in the classroom but throughout the activities of daily life, so that the enterprise of learning comes naturally to be conceived as a necessary and perhaps even exciting partnership.

The growth in the size of institutions is proportional to the decline of immediacy in them. In large schools, there is little educationally significant interaction among teachers. They tend to deal with their classroom problems as best they can, in isolation from one another. It is considered unwise to share difficulties with the administration: the principal may well regard trouble as the result of teacher incompetence rather than welcoming its discussion as the salutary effort to bring social experience to bear on its resolution. Administrators, in turn, think it best to keep teachers in the dark about the details and even about the procedures of their work. But the issue is even deeper than the intentions of people. The institution requires a division of labor; once individuals develop the narrow skills necessary to occupy specialized roles, others simply fail to see or to understand the precise nature of what they do. Psychic distance from each other — ignorance of the feelings and actions of others — becomes in this way endemic to the institution.

Immediacy between teachers and students may appear to be unaffected by the size of the educational system. Audiovisual aids, computers, and teaching machines have not, after all, replaced the person who enters the classroom to instruct. But this appearance is deceptive: direct contact in classrooms is a sharply circumscribed and relatively impotent affair. Teachers and students are strangers to each other when they meet; their brief time together, focused on the mastery of a body of material, is inadequate to bring them to the point of friendship and sharing and trust. The very roles they fill make a close relation difficult. Education is supposed to be a one-way flow of knowledge that can be turned on at the beginning of the hour and turned off at the end. The asymmetry between the teacher, acting like spigot, and the students, expected to be empty bottles ready to be filled, is so great that the group can never constitute itself as a community of inquiry exploring matters of mutual interest.

Classroom immediacy is, moreover, meant to be all business. Personal relations are unnecessary for and may, in fact, place obstacles in the way of learning. With large classes and a limited teaching time, instructors find that there is simply no possibility of taking a direct interest in their charges. There is not even time to explore the relevance of what is learned to the students' lives; everything is centered on covering and remembering material, and compliance is assured by the threat of grades. The encounter in the classroom, though it appears to be between persons in fact lacks all personal elements: it is bereft of unity of purpose, long-term caring, and mutual respect. It is not surprising that teaching machines can readily replace human instructors in many fields. Once the deeply personal nurturing aspect of teaching is lost, flesh-and-blood instructors themselves become mechanical.

Expertise and Professionalization

The growth of expertise in society, and with it the professionalization of teaching, naturally lead to narrow but exclusive social roles. The jobs that must be done require both specialized knowledge and the freedom to perform them without interference from unskilled outsiders. The educational establishment developed and acquired its monopoly power by insisting on this liberty: professionals, it was frequently affirmed, must not be subjected to the standards and the review of those who are not experts in the field. This understandable, and in some respects even salutary, insistence on professional self-determination has essentially eliminated immediacy between teachers and the society they serve. What happens in the classroom has become, in this way, a secret if not mysterious ritual. Parents feel ill at ease to say anything about it, even when their deepest instincts tell them that their children are poorly served. There is a similar reluctance on the part of the public to deal with bothersome aspects of school administration: ignorance of both how things are run and how they ought to be effectively stills external criticism. It is not that parents surrender dissatisfaction when they cede the right to object. If anything, their frustration increases with the perception that the system for which they pay appears unintelligible and remains unresponsive to their concerns.

When the sense of parental impotence reaches a peak, the political and the judicial systems are enlisted to bring the educational establishment to heel. Although sometimes this is effective, it further reduces immediacy. For the attempt to resolve problems face to face is then altogether abandoned and new mediators are interposed between the community and its schools. The intermediaries themselves are in a difficult position: judges and politicians find themselves as ignorant of what goes on in the educational system as the rest of the society whose interests they try to represent. How best to represent the interests of the community is also not without problems. The educational establishment defends itself by seeking access to courts and legislatures in order to convince them that students will be best served if it is left alone. Legislatures, in particular, are accustomed to being used to consolidate the power of professional educators: they rarely balk even at such absurdities as putting the force of law behind the number of hours students must spend in school.

Parties to conflicts, many of which result from the loss of open and direct contact between the schools and the community, then attempt to resolve their differences by having even less immediacy. Issues may be settled this way, but only because decreed or legislated solutions are supported by the coercive power of the state. The relation of the schools to the community is rarely improved and the quality of education is not affected much or for very long. In the nature of the case, no distant institution can sensitize or vitalize another. Once a social structure rigidifies and forces its members into narrow roles, nothing less than a threat to its existence can restore its responsiveness and life. The reason for this resides, once again, in the nature of the social structure.

Attempts to Revitalize Institutionalized Education

At times of business-as-usual, no one in the institution actually understands all its work and no one controls it. Superintendents know little of what transpires in their classrooms. Classroom teachers, in turn, have little influence on and even less concrete grasp of management decisions by the leadership. In no single human mind is there a clear and detailed idea of both rules and their implementation, of both design and execution. Location in a complex chain of agents limits everyone's vision; although people in executive positions tend to see more than others, even they do not see it all. Since they utilize established channels of communication, they may come to believe that they know what happens in the far reaches of their institutional world. This is a mistake partly because it is in the interest of employees to inform their superiors selectively and to present events in the best possible light. But even the most accurate report is inadequate by comparison with direct experience, and it is precisely this immediate encounter with how things really work that leaders lack.

To revitalize an institution, someone must realize that all is not well. The recognition may come as a result of external criticism or threat, but the ultimate motive power for change must spring from direct acquaintance with the ways in which the institution fails. It is not, of course, that people always make a constructive response to the perception of problems; it is possible to shut one's eyes or to present excuses. But firsthand grasp of a situation offers knowledge that is vivid and detailed and that tends to motivate the will. The palpable experience of cruelty or wickedness is more likely to engage our active parts than a description or a distant report of it.

Re-establishing Immediacy in the Public Schools

Immediacy serves not only as a spur to reform, but also as a major part of the cure for our ills. In order to reverse the passivity, manipulativeness, and irresponsibility that attend large-scale mediation, we must re-establish a measure of immediacy throughout the educational system. Since this involves openness, trust, and the unhindered flow of information among the participants in the process of nurturing young people, it requires the sincere and sustained efforts of them all.

School Officials and Administrators

The school system must find ways to ensure that education is near the center of the public's agenda at all times, and not only when the need for increased appropriations becomes intense. To accomplish this, school boards must consist of individuals elected in campaigns that include an informed and detailed debate on educational problems. The meetings of school boards must be open to the public, and the media must be invited to provide helpful and responsible coverage. School administrators must make extraordinary efforts to acquaint the public, and especially parents, with the rules and procedures and the reasons for the rules and procedures in accordance with which their institutions operate. Such openness through unforced disclosure and the repeated invitation of public comment is admittedly bothersome and time-consuming. But, in the long run, schools that adhere to it encounter fewer problems and enjoy not only greater community support but, in the case of mistakes, more ready understanding and forgiveness.

School administrators must supplement such unrestricted flow of information toward the general public with even greater receptivity to the cognitive needs of teachers and students. A secretive, unapproachable principal can have a ruinous effect on the learning environment in an entire school. Arbitrariness and injustice destroy morale. Unless there is forthright communication about administrative decisions, arbitrariness and the appearance of it cannot be distinguished, and both students and teachers fall into the habit of suspecting favoritism and skulduggery. An open-door policy is not enough to combat such natural alienation: the power of their position keeps administrators from receiving casual visits, searching questions, and timely complaints. Leaders must take active steps to learn about problems and to disseminate information: they must initiate contacts with those committed to their care and discuss common concerns in a frank and detailed way. This does not mean that they should engage in a public relations effort to gain approval of their views. Although we would all like to have things our way, few people are so naive as to suppose that the world will play by their rules. Most of us are perfectly content to let the leaders lead, so long as we understand the reasons for their actions and feel that our voices have been heard. Within the school, this demand for respect, for the sense that what students and teachers think and what they say matter is best met if the administrator seeks regular, informal contact with each group in its own world.

Teachers

The same immediacy that needs to pervade the world of school boards and administrators must also surround teachers in their official capacity. That this openness be expected of instructors and that it become a natural part of their exertions is of central significance. Some teachers take a personal interest in their students and handle their tasks as if they constituted a calling and not a job. Unfortunately, however, such individuals are rare, and our system, viewing their devotion as something beyond what their job description demands, offers them few rewards. We operate on the assumption that it is enough for employees in large institutions to fulfill their narrow, and impersonal, role responsibilities. This may work well in factories where we deal with metals and plastic, but it can lead to disaster when the primary objects of our activity are young human beings. We must, therefore, revise the very criteria by which we judge teacher performance, to include not only professional competence but also human caring and the readiness to sustain a broad spectrum of personal relations.

This means that in interacting with students, teachers must be direct and approachable. They must show themselves as stable, predictable, and fair persons, and embed their professional activities in the context of humane relations. They must be sensitive to the fact that we teach more by example than by words and that, for this reason, the instructor's character, attitudes, and actions must be worthy of imitation. Accordingly, they need to demonstrate a vivid interest in their students and an abiding readiness to aid in their development. They must, in short, resist the natural tendency to view students as their relatively helpless charges, or as savage strangers, and assume the nurturing activity of parents.

The immediate and friendly contact teachers should seek must extend beyond the classroom. Instructors can take care of the needs of young people only if they establish an effective partnership with their parents. The occasional parent-teacher conference is altogether inadequate to accomplish this. Teachers must institute extensive and continuing direct communication with the home, acting as if parents were their primary and immediate employers. They must also achieve daily personal contact with administrators and sufficient identity in the eyes of school board members to permit significant conversations when these seem appropriate. The entire educational system revolves around the work of teachers. What they do, therefore, both in and out of the classroom, carries momentous weight. A commitment by them to human caring, open communication, and enhanced immediacy would go a long way toward overcoming the alienation in our schools.

Parents

In its attitudes and actions toward the schools, the community must reciprocate the forthright partnership that should be offered by professional educators. Teachers and principals must be viewed as trusted friends and advisors, instead of busy functionaries who are not to be approached. Many adults find it difficult to rid themselves of their childhood perceptions: instead of considering them equals, they look upon teachers with trepidation. The friendliest gestures by school staff cannot serve as more than an invitation to such people. To develop genuine cooperation, parents must avail themselves of the opportunity to discuss shared problems and to develop mutually satisfactory solutions. They need to spend time in the school and to get to know the teachers of their children as parents themselves or at least as kindred human beings.

One way to foster this exchange is by exploding the myth that only certified instructors have anything to teach young people. Individuals whose acquaintance with social conditions, political activities, economic enterprises, or varied professional skills is direct exude a scent of reality. They have much to teach our children not only on account of their fund of learning and experience, but also because of their instant credibility with them. An incidental benefit of bringing such people to the classroom is that the sharp contrast between school and 'real life' tends to disappear.

Direct contact with teachers on the basis of equality enables parents to view the task of education as a genuine partnership.

For the partnership to be effective, parents must retain or regain immediacy with their children. The popular distinction between quantity and quality of time spent with the people we brought into the world serves as a transparent self-justification on the part of those who wish to abandon a major parental responsibility. It is always desirable, of course, that the activities parents and children share be of the highest quality. But such richness and diversity are difficult to develop without a significant commitment of time. Even the best activities performed at white heat are inadequate to meet the extensive and intensely personal needs of a growing human being. In fact, quiet activities and sustained presence are as important as roaring fun and frequently serve as its indispensable conditions. Intense moments of tenderness and self-revelation cannot be precipitated at will and then quickly pushed aside to meet one's next appointment. We cannot be our children's parents and friends without a vast investment of time, emotion, and energy.

This means that parents cannot cease being their children's teachers. Bringing young souls into the world has a price in terms of lost liberties and unavoidable obligations. The anguished, 'All I do with my education is raise children!' can be understood as the sentiment of a woman trapped in early marriage. But on the intellectual side, it represents a profound set of mistakes about the function of education, the value of nurturing children, and the proper priorities in the lives of parents. Education is, after all, not primarily preparation for employment, and it is difficult to conceive an end more worthy of the efforts of an educated person than that of guiding the growth, creating the habits, and shaping the personality of another human being.

Students

The sustained interest of parents in the progress of their children must be matched by a suitable level of helpful exertion on the part of students. In some ways, this may be the most difficult task to accomplish. Young people go through periods of extensive and painful adjustment. Organic changes distract their attention and challenge their precariously established beliefs. Their environment presents opportunities for confusion and disaster that, if left to their own devices they may be unable to resist. The position of students in the school, moreover, leaves them vulnerable and passive. Viewed as immature and transitional members of the community, they tend to be given little say in its affairs. The resulting asymmetry between the power of school employees and of students is so great that it becomes difficult to see the enterprise of teaching and learning as a partnership.

The initiating steps toward breaking up this system of disempowerment must come from teachers and administrators. Since they hold essentially all the power in the school, only they are in a position to invite others to share it. Here again, immediate and forthright communication with students may convince officials that learning can be mutual. Those in the classroom know more about the quality of teaching than anyone else; they also know, from firsthand experience, the obstacles to learning that exist in certain places in the school. There is not much principals could do to gain a keener insight into their institutions than listen to the perceptive and the articulate among their students. There is no doubt that the single most significant reform immediately available is selective action on the suggestions and complaints of those being educated. This does not suppose that students are infallible or all-knowing, only that direct perceptions are often accurate, and that without taking the experience of clients into account, no service can be meaningfully improved.

Private Schools for All?

What we have said about the need for immediacy may be taken as an argument for the privatization of our entire educational system. Do private schools not already manifest the intimacy in size and human contacts that we think essential? Would the dismantling of large-scale public education, perhaps through a voucher system, not therefore establish the cooperative and open interaction of teachers, students, parents, and administrators?

Those who are inclined to answer such questions in the affirmative tend to take a romantic view of private schools. To them, these institutions are pristine islands in a polluted stream, small enclaves of righteousness and enduring values in a world that has abandoned the good and the true. In fact, of course, no part of society is immune to the problems that beset the whole: the mediation-shaped attitudes and character of people are not left behind at the schoolhouse door. Accordingly, even though system size is not a problem in private schools, they suffer from the lack of certain forms and important conditions of immediacy.

A relatively small number of students in a classroom does not guarantee immediacy. The direct exposure necessary for successful education is personal: it takes the form of sustained interest in each others' perceptions, feelings, problems, and pleasures. This caring beyond the confines of official roles is precisely what standards of professional competence disregard or even discourage. Private day-school teachers have as little contact with the personal lives of their students as their public school colleagues. In residential institutions, where constant interaction is possible, the context is artificially impoverished: distance from family, and many of the pressures of social life, minimize opportunities for immediacy about matters of significance to young people.

Some private institutions, especially religious ones, make a great show of taking a personal interest in students. But the concern is quickly recognized as tendentious, aimed at saving souls, establishing approved habits, or assuring proper behavior. This destroys the openness necessary for meaningful and reciprocal immediacy. The lack of mutuality is an endemic problem in private schools. Secrecy, unbending commitment to hierarchical structure, and a general resistance to sharing power render them incapable of offering parents and students genuine partnership. Immediacy cannot thrive in authoritarian settings. Imbalances of power, manipulativeness, and claims of expertise are hallmarks of the mediated world; that is the region where nearly all our institutions, including private schools, now belong.

This perspective also sheds new light on the reasons for desegregating the schools. Although the official justification for integration was phrased in terms of justice, rights, and the public good, a major — though perhaps unarticulated — motive was the recognition of the need for immediacy. Peace and justice cannot reign in a pluralistic society, it was thought, unless widely divergent groups of citizens have direct contact with each other. The earlier in the life of young people such immediacy is established, the better the chances for ethnic, class, racial, and religious understanding. It is blatantly false that separate must always be unequal, but it is always uncommunal.

The desperate need for desegregation first became clear to us when a young friend of our children innocently remarked that she thought all blacks were cleaning ladies. Nothing combats such devastating stereotypes better than early exposure to the full humanity of others, with all the friendship, or at least understanding tolerance, that involves. Without it, we cannot even be sure that we can raise wise judges, fair policemen, or business people who understand the need for equal opportunity. If individuals will not, the courts — acting on behalf of society — must combat this threat to the welfare of citizens and, in the long run, to the stability of the entire social order.

Private schools cannot exempt themselves from such last-resort regulation. Lack of immediacy, when it reaches sufficient magnitude, makes it impossible for members of a society to share values. The resultant loss of community leads to disorder and to strife. At such times, private schools, defined by their own exclusiveness as obstacles to immediacy, are naturally and appropriately required by government to share the burdens of social reconciliation.

Conclusion: The Reach of the State

Debate about the proper limits of state control over the schools is inevitably cast in terms of the conflict of individual rights with the public good. The principle of the power of courts and legislatures over significant aspects of public education is well established. But many people think that private schools should be immune from such interference, for they are an expression of the liberty of individuals to pass on their beliefs, their values, and their way of life to their children. Those committed to a measure of central control invoke the notion of the public good. Education, they argue, is essential for empowerment which, in turn, is an indispensable condition of equality. Without equality, at least of opportunity, no society can be just and perhaps even universally free.

We have proposed to replace this conceptual framework with one less adversarial and more useful. In our terms, the question is not whether government has a right to impose its will on the private schools, but rather what we must do to enjoy the benefits of immediacy. Without such sustained, open, and mutual contact between segments of the population, it is impossible to have a peaceful democratic society. In accordance with our deepest values, this immediacy is for individuals to achieve and to foster. Only when they fail at the task, and thereby endanger the entire project of our communal life can government step in.

But we must move with great caution here. The idea of such distant mediating agencies as Congress and the courts demanding immediacy appears anomalous. Those that mandate open and direct contact must strive to achieve it themselves. Yet the salutary order to establish immediacy in the schools has not been matched by the efforts of the courts to attain it in their own operations: the legal system continues to function at a remove from ordinary life, and judges often lack immediate experience of the problems they address. Open interchange is always educational in character and leads, at its best, to action on the basis of consensus. Enforcing the rights of one group involves restricting the freedom of some other. The limitation becomes less odious, may in fact altogether lose its objectionable feel, if it is freely adopted. Convincing people to change their ways retains respect for their autonomy; the application of force not only degrades them to the level of manipulable objects, but also engenders resistance and resentment. In spite of this, legislators and our judicial system tend to substitute compulsory solutions for voluntary compliance achieved by persuasion.

This tendency reveals a fundamental misunderstanding of the role of government in a society of free individuals. The central function of government is neither control over the behavior of people nor promotion of their welfare. It is, instead, educational in the broadest and finest sense of the term. That education leads to intelligent adjustments in how we act and promotes human welfare is, of course, true. But these are secondary consequences of the successful pursuit of the primary good, which is the development of fully socialized, yet self-determining, human beings. Such character formation is a lifelong activity: government must envelop the work of the schools in a broader and richer educational effort. The application of force can be only the last resort and a temporary expedient in the enterprise of creating free and mature individuals.

Our proposed reconception places education at the center of government action and immediacy at the pivot of education. Immediacy is the frank and cooperative way in which people can *be* together in a pluralistic democracy. The stress on such direct contact and shared decision-making converts schooling into a partnership of the young and the mature. The first great success of education is the conviction that no one in the community can be left out of this partnership.

Note

1 For a full treatment of these problems, see J. Lachs (1981) *Intermediate Man*, Indianapolis, Ind., Hackett.

12
State Control of the Private School's Curriculum: An Essay in Law, Jurisprudence, and Political Philosophy

Tyll van Geel

In the State of Defiance parents motivated by religious and other concerns have established a large number of private schools. Their dominant purpose is teaching students that blacks are mentally and morally inferior to whites. Deeply troubled by this development, the Defiance legislature has moved against these schools by directly prohibiting parents from sending their children to schools that teach racism.[1]

Regulations such as Defiance's are usually justified as serving either or both of two general purposes: first, the protection of the government and/or polity; second, the protection of the child against negligent, incompetent, or even venal parents. (The distinction between the two types of regulation may simultaneously protect child and policy.)[2] I assume in this discussion that Defiance's interest in adopting its regulation is to protect the polity and/or government. I imagine the state defending its regulation along the following lines. First, racist teaching is false, and its very utterance inflicts a harm on a racial group. It promotes no social good. Second, the program of instruction in these private schools attacks the basic principle of a just, democratic society: that all people are to be treated with equal dignity and respect. Third, instruction in racism reproduces racists, and a society populated with racists is a society that will be riven with oppression and violence, ultimately undermining that society and its government.

Though there are powerful reasons in support of Defiance's regulation we must still ask whether the regulation is constitutionally permissible. I will argue that there is no right answer to the question of the constitutionality of Defiance's regulation. Relevant judicial precedent and political and moral philosophical considerations are sufficiently ambiguous and in conflict as to preclude an obvious and easily decided answer to the question of the regulation's constitutionality. As a consequence, any answer the Supreme Court might adopt in resolving a constitutional challenge to Defiance's regulation must inevitably be arbitrary and simply a matter of which answer garners the most votes among the justices.

In advancing this thesis, I hope to accomplish two additional tasks. First I will seek to illuminate the real philosophical and legal difficulties raised by the State of Defiance's efforts to regulate its private schools. Second, I seek to demonstrate that Dworkin, who argues that there is always a 'single right answer', even to hard cases such as this one, is not correct in this instance.[3] I will accomplish these objectives by following the analytical steps that Dworkin says courts should and, in fact, do follow in deciding hard cases.

Judicial Precedent

According to Dworkin, a judge must begin his or her analysis with precedent and seek to discover some coherent theory, some principle, that explains the precedent.[4] This already difficult task is made more complex if the body of precedent is not easily reconciled, because different sets of cases point toward different principles. When this happens, the question of 'fit' — the question of what principle best explains most of the precedent — no longer will play a useful role in deciding the new case before the court. Thus the second step the judge must take is to choose among those principles, each of which explains perhaps only a portion of the precedent. To make this choice, the judge must ask which principle 'shows the legal record to the best it can be from the standpoint of substantive political morality'.[5] I shall say more about this second step later, but first we need to examine legal precedent to see if there is a single principle that explains precedent and provides a starting point for addressing our problem.

We are confronted with five different strands or themes in the precedent, each suggestive of a different approach. Furthermore, none of these approaches yields a definitive answer to our problem. The five categories of precedent are: (1) suppression of speech based on disagreement with the viewpoint expressed; (2) control of speech in order to preserve community; (3) government as 'educator'; (4) government as protector of children; and (5) religious freedom.

First, we can approach Defiance's regulation as an effort to control racist instruction because of government's disagreement with the viewpoint expressed. An important body of cases can be cited in support of the proposition that governmental suppression of speech because of disagreement with the viewpoint and fear of the consequences is permissible only if certain extremely stiff tests are met. For example, according to a significant number of cases, even speech advocating violence may not be prohibited unless the advocacy is directed to inciting or producing imminent lawless action and is likely to produce such actions.[6] Viewed in this manner, a substantial portion, but not the entire corpus, of Supreme Court cases points us toward the unconstitutionality of the regulation. That the court itself might approach the case in this way is underscored by dictum in one case stating that, although private schools may not discriminate on the basis of race in their admissions policies, parents and children have a constitutional right to attend schools that advocate segregation.[7] But as extensive as the list of precedent is in support of the proposition that Defiance's regulation is unconstitutional, other precedent suggests that speech may be suppressed where the speech is foisted upon a captive audience, such as the children in private schools.[8]

If the Defiance regulation is viewed differently — as a regulation intended to preserve community, to suppress only special categories of speech, obscenity and libel, and to maintain values and morality — then a different body of precedent becomes relevant. Most relevant by way of analogy is the Supreme Court's decision upholding a group libel law prohibiting the publishing, selling, or exhibition of any publication degrading a class of citizens, of any race, color, creed, or religion.[9] Moving somewhat wider afield, a judge might consider the Supreme Court's decisions upholding laws controlling the sale and distribution of obscenity. These cases could be cited to support the proposition that constitutional doctrine permits government to regulate speech in order to maintain the tone of the society, to maintain its moral fabric.[10]

Other precedents point to a different set of conclusions. The decision in *New York Times Co. v. Sullivan*[11] could support the claim that government efforts to regulate group libel would today no longer receive judicial approval. We also can anticipate that the opponent of Defiance's regulation would seek to distinguish the obscenity decisions and argue their irrelevance to the problem at hand.

A third way to look at Defiance's regulation makes yet another body of cases relevant. When the state acts as 'educator', the scope of its power is broader than when it simply seeks to control the flow of communication among adults. In support of this proposition, opinions can be cited supporting the proposition that the state may properly inculcate fundamental values necessary to the maintenance of a democratic political system.[12] If the state may aggressively inculcate students, it may also protect them from inculcation with the wrong values. This line of argument can be buttressed with the claim that the Supreme Court has embraced the proposition that private schools may be subject to reasonable state regulations.[13]

As we have come to expect, this line of argument itself can be countered with other opinions — thrust, counter-thrust. As noted earlier, the Court has said that parents have a right to send their children to schools which advocate racism. Furthermore, all previous efforts to control the private school curriculum, even in the name of preserving community, society, and democracy, have not survived judicial review.[14] Furthermore, other precedent supports the proposition that children have constitutional rights of autonomy with which *government* — as opposed to parents — may not interfere.[15] This line of cases suggests that governmental efforts to control the ideological beliefs of students are at least suspect and probably unconstitutional.

Additionally, we can view regulation as an exercise of government's power to protect children. Viewed in this way, a body of precedent supports the principle that government's authority to protect children is broader than its authority to protect adults. Hence government may take action toward children that it may not toward adults.[16] Countering this approach is another significant body of precedent supporting the proposition that the right of parents to control the upbringing of their children imposes a significant limit on government's authority to control the educational program of the child.[17]

Finally, mention should be made of the probability that no matter what reasons are put forth by Defiance, parents who send their children to religious schools advocating racism would invoke the free exercise clause of the First Amendment as a shield against enforcement of the regulation. Assuming that these parents would be able to establish, as they must in order to be successful, that theirs is a religiously-based claim to an exemption, that their claim is sincerely made, and that enforcement of the regulation would have a severe impact on the free exercise of their religious beliefs, the burden would be placed on government to convince the court that continued uniform enforcement of the regulation was a necessary, a least restrictive means for achieving a compelling state interest.[18] But again precedent points in two directions, with the Court in one case upholding the denial of tax-exempt status to a religious school that discriminated on the basis of race, and in another case the Court, in dictum, saying parents have a right to send their children to private schools that promote a belief in segregation.[19]

Precedent thus offers no solution to our problem, and we are forced to resort to the second step of Dworkin's approach for adjudicating hard cases. We need to examine which of these approaches and their associated principles, or perhaps some other principles, is best from a perspective of abstract justice, as well as which should be followed as a matter of political fairness — which approach best conforms to the moral convictions shared by a substantial portion of the public.[20] I thus turn to an examination of political philosophy and morality.

Describing the different political philosophies with adherents in the American political scene and a claim to embodying a plausible principle of justice is a treacherous task; I make no claim that the scheme outlined here fully captures our social reality. For these purposes, I think it useful to think of American political philosophies as ranging along two dimensions standing in an orthogonal relationship. On one dimension, these philosophies range from those with little or no concern with social and economic equalities (i.e., which make efficiency a primary value) to those which make inequalities in the distribution of wealth and status central to their concerns. On the second dimension, these philosophies vary from those which stress political and other forms of individualism to those which stress the importance of community. When these dimensions are combined, we arrive at four major political philosophies: (1) libertarianism — a philosophy with no concern for economic-social inequalities but which places great stress on certain individual rights and efficiency; (2) liberalism — a philosophy that at its root is also individualistic but places considerable stress on different aspects of social-economic inequalities; (3) communitarianism without egalitarianism — a philosophy that stresses a particular form of community but with only a modest concern for social-economic inequalities; (4) communitarian liberalism — a philosophy that endorses a concept of community combined with a strong concern for social and economic inequalities.

In the four sections that follow I describe and analyze each ideology and discuss whether or not adherents to that ideology would accept or reject Defiance's regulation. A court that finds no sure guidance from precedent would be forced to consider these ideologies: however, as we shall learn, turning to political philosophy and ideology also provides no easily found answer to the permissibility of the regulation.

Libertarianism

For the libertarian interested in dismantling our extensive system of governments, Defiance's step is 180 degrees in the wrong direction.[21]

Yet the libertarian response to this regulation may not be as automatic as it at first might seem.

The libertarian ideology begins with the recognition that while individual people are real and have separate lives, collective entities such as the 'group', 'society', 'community', and 'government' are but intellectually created abstractions. The individual and his or her interests are prior to 'society' and prior to 'dialogue'. Thus social and political philosophy must speak in terms of individual humans and their separate and conflicting interests. A central libertarian position is the assumption that individuals own and have a right to their own bodies, talents, labor, and the fruits of their labor. Ownership in unowned things is acquired by mixing one's labor with it, and it is the owner who may do with his or her property as he wishes — keep it, trade it, sell it, give it away, or even destroy it. Property rights is one of the two key principles of libertarian philosophy. More specifically, central components of the libertarian view are the two principles for the acquisition and transfer of property. A third and closely related, central principle is the principle of liberty. Liberty in the libertarian lexicon is conceived of as negative liberty — freedom from force, coercion or the threat of coercion regarding economic and other matters, such as freedom of speech, religion, sexual relations, and even the use of drugs. Relying on these sets of rights, the libertarian concludes that however people pursue their goals they may not do so by the use of force or coercion against each other. Force is only permissible in self-defense. Because individuals may not use force against each other except in self-defense, they may not delegate even to a police force the authority to use force except to prevent or punish the use of force.

The libertarian takes the view that government has no greater rights or authority than does the individual. To the extent that any government may exist, its functions must be limited to protection against force, fraud, theft, and enforcement of contracts, unless unanimous consent is given to a broader range of coercive actions. An important conclusion that follows from these principles is that individuals may not be 'sacrificed' or be forced by government to serve or benefit another without their express consent. The forcible taking from the well-off (through a scheme of taxation) to meet even the basic nutritional needs of others is an immoral act even when done by government.

While the libertarian disfavors government, the free market stands at the top of the list of favored institutions because voluntary exchange perfectly satisfies the libertarian principles of property, liberty, and noncoercion. The libertarian shares with economists the faith that free markets yield enormous benefits in the general improvement of wealth.

As Adam Smith wrote, 'Every individual intends only his own gain, and he is in this as in so many other cases, led by an invisible hand to promote an end which was not part of his intention.'[22]

Libertarian views on the relationship between the child, parent, and state are not clearly settled. Most libertarians would oppose compulsory education laws,[23] others may accept such laws for practical reasons.[24] A truly hard-headed libertarian would also oppose taxation to support education simply because all taxation is immoral. Yet others in the minimalist government camp would support taxation for a system of private schools — not public schools.[25] Libertarians would also agree that parents may initiate force against their children to prevent them from harming themselves, others, or property. It is far less clear how far libertarians would let parents go in using force to coerce children to learn. Perhaps we can assume that some libertarians would permit such force under some notion of paternalism, whereas others might insist that the education of children must be nondirective and noncoercive.[26] Thus libertarians of the latter kind might approve of the Defiance regulation and argue that it does not go far enough to protect children from their parents' coercion. On the other hand, the paternalistic-libertarian would reject Defiance's regulation as an improper use of governmental coercion, because the parents' educational efforts may not properly be understood as the initiation of force against which the use of governmental action is justified. In sum, the Defiance regulation is improper, not because freedom of speech is given a special place above other liberties, but because all liberties are absolutely protected in the libertarian world.

There are some things, however, that our paternalistic and non-paternalistic libertarians would have in common. They both would reject all three of Defiance's arguments in support of its regulation. Neither would be concerned with the group libel argument, because in the libertarian world, only the initiation of force itself is an evil with which government should deal. Similarly, the concern that racist instruction attacks the premises of society would appeal to the libertarian only if the racist teaching urged that blacks, because of their supposed inferiority, did not have a right to property and liberty and should be enslaved. Racist teaching falling short of such an extreme position would not be seen as an attack on fundamentals.

This position on racist instruction is best understood as part of the more general attitude of libertarians toward racism. Based on a deeply held distrust of government, a favorable view of the market, and the rejection of force, except in self-defense, it also follows that in the libertarian world, while racial discrimination may be irrational and immoral, it is a practice that may not be stopped by force or coercion.

The houseowner, shop owner, and employer may refuse anyone an invitation to his or her home, prohibit anyone in his or her store, and hire whom he or she pleases, even if these decisions are based on race. Government efforts to prevent discrimination would be the illegitimate use of force, hence anti–discrimination laws would themselves be unjust. Now the libertarian relieves the harsh outlines of this position by arguing that the free market will itself naturally deal with racism. Employers, for example, will in time discover an economic advantage in hiring competent blacks and providing their services to black customers.

What should now be clear is that libertarianism considers almost everything that people do a private affair, not properly the subject of collective concern. This principle would extend to private education as well. Governmental action is viewed as an external intrusion into this private process and presumed to be impermissible, unless it can be shown to deal with the initiation of force, theft, fraud, or the enforcement of contracts. By placing primary value on property rights and liberty, libertarianism avoids engaging in the balancing of interests, or attempting to realize the 'mirage of social justice'.[27] The libertarian is not concerned with activities that take place within the constraints imposed by these rights, even if they produce consequences that some may say are harmful — some people may end up with very few resources. Libertarians refuse to speak the language of 'the public good', or 'the public interest', and instead insist that such talk is the talk of myths. The libertarian conception of the 'good citizen' is limited to avoiding the initiation of force, engaging in fraud, theft, or the breach of contracts. The notion of citizenship is a 'thin' concept in libertarianism. The need for 'consensus' is reduced to a consensus on property rights and liberty. (New research even suggests that consensus on basic values is not a necessary condition for the emergence of cooperation, even among self–interested individuals.)[28]

Liberalism

The liberal response to Defiance's regulation is even less predictable than the libertarian response. Even when we seek to limit our attempt to a description and explication of liberalism as it appears in the contemporary American scene, putting aside a historical and/or international perspective, the task of defining liberalism and its response to our hypothetical regulation is fraught with difficulties. Liberalism is less a coherent philosophy than a loosely connected set of goals, fears, and general principles, with a longstanding debate among those who count themselves as liberals as to how those principles and values are to be defined, rank-ordered, grounded, and justified. The strategy I will follow in describing liberalism is to describe common features of some versions of liberalism developed by a variety of philosophers, and then turn to the different ways these versions of liberalism might respond to Defiance's regulation of private schools.

The avoiding of a war of all against all and a desire for prosperity have from the start of liberalism been among the central concerns thought best addressed by the formation of a government that gained its legitimacy from the voluntary consent of those subject to it.[29] Although Hobbes argued that people would or have consented to a government of unlimited power and authority, the liberal dominant persuasion has walked a thin line between the anarchy of libertarianism and the Hobbesian leviathan, by arguing that people have and would consent to a government of greater powers than the nightwatchman state, but with less authority than Hobbes' leviathan. Liberals accept a limited democratic government as legitimate so long as it does not violate certain individual rights retained by each person. Liberals as a group tend to embrace a principle of liberty, or at least a belief in the importance of a certain set of liberties; a principle of property rights (in some version); and, significant for modern liberalism and the role of government, a principle of equality, which in some versions requires the extensive and continuous redistribution of wealth.[30] In sum, liberals favor liberty, but not to the extent libertarians do; support property rights, but not in the absolute way libertarians do; support some notion of equality, in a way very different from libertarians, and in a way that can and does come into conflict with some liberties; and yet liberals tend not to presume the need for or to promote community in the deep ways the more communitarian philosophies discussed later do. Compared to the communitarians, liberals give more scope to a private life, privately pursued; but at the same time, in contrast to the libertarians, liberals seek to check or ameliorate, through governmental intervention, certain consequences of individual actions that liberals define as harms, but which libertarians would accept as inevitable and natural consequences not properly the subject of governmental attention.

Based on such principles, liberals of all kinds have supported the provision of a public system of education, merely tolerated in the name of a principle of freedom a system of private education, and supported strong anti-discrimination laws directed at a variety of forms of discrimination, but most importantly, race-based discrimination. Liberals also accept a definition of a collective good that is broader than that of libertarians. Thus, for example, liberals may accept the proposition that a sense of justice, an individual's belief in the liberal principles of justice, is a collective good — a good that provides benefits to all members of the society, benefits that would be impossible to exclude from given members of the society by any known technology, by any morally acceptable method, or at an acceptable cost. As a collective good, it is a subject government may properly consider promoting.[31]

I turn now to how various liberals might respond to the Defiance regulation. This regulation raises a problem analogous to reconciling the liberal principles of property and equality. In this case, the conflict is between a principle of liberty (including a right to freedom of speech, and a parental right to control the upbringing of the child) and a principle of equality. More specifically, because the Defiance regulation promotes equality among the races, it establishes a confrontation between the principle of equality and the negative liberty of parents to be free of state regulation.[32] There may be at least six different liberal responses to the Defiance regulation: (1) placing primacy upon a broad conception of the principle of freedom of speech; (2) placing an absolute value on a narrow concept of the principle of freedom of speech; (3) approaching the problem of balancing the interest in freedom of speech against the interests in regulation; (4) placing a strong priority on a broad concept of equality; (5) stressing the importance of the autonomy of the child; and (6) stressing the child's right to a certain kind of education.

Some liberals place such a high value on freedom of speech that only the most obvious, extreme, and likely harms would provide a basis for restriction. For example, Emerson argues that freedom of speech is so valuable in assuring individual self-fulfillment, advancing the frontiers of knowledge, making possible self-government, and achieving a more stable society that government should not be allowed to seek such ends as virtue, justice, or equality by suppressing the expression of beliefs or opinions.[33] More generally, free expression may not be restricted as a method of obtaining other social objectives.[34] Attempts to restrict group libel therefore are impermissible. Richards has argued that governmental regulation of even racist speech (group libel) violates the basic moral principle of a right to conscience, the integrity of our moral judgment, the people's right to retain the moral power of judgment of the government, and the corollary principle of freedom of expression.[35] Free speech accordingly may only be restricted when speech directly threatens basic harm, such as falsely shouting 'Fire!' in a crowded theater, or when an individual's dignity or rational autonomy is attacked through slander knowingly uttered, or privacy is invaded by the revealing of intimate details about another person's life against his wishes.[36] In effect, speech may not be suppressed merely because of disagreement with the viewpoint expressed. To warrant suppression, there must first be substantial proof of an inevitable serious harm to specific individuals; failing this, speech must not be restricted. Under these principles, of course, Defiance's regulation would not survive judicial scrutiny.

Meiklejohn has argued that the principle of freedom of speech springs simply and solely from the necessities of self-government. The principle is deduced from the other principle that public issues are to be decided by universal suffrage. If that decision-making process is to be well-informed, the free flow of information should not be constrained.[37] Consequently, Defiance's regulation would be morally permissible because the speech being regulated would not be speech directly related to the political decision-making process.[38]

It is more difficult to anticipate the response of advocates of the need to balance the interests served by freedom of speech against the harms associated with unregulated speech.[39] Depending on how they define and weigh the harms they assume might be caused by the regulation compared to the harms they assume might occur without the regulation, advocates of balancing, such as Redish, may or may not approve of Defiance's regulation. On the other hand, Redish embraces the principle of free speech because it serves individual self-realization; thus, he may view the parent's educational program as a threat to the child's interest in self-realization, and accordingly favor Defiance's regulation for reasons very different from those put forward by the state itself.

Others may approve of Defiance's regulation because they place so much weight upon a principle of equality, see the kind of education Defiance seeks to prohibit as a direct attack upon that principle, and agree with the state that racist education fosters racial inequality, the subordinate position of blacks, and racially motivated violence against blacks.[40] This argument may itself be buttressed by arguing that a nonracist education is a public good, or at least a merit good, and as such, there is warrant for governmental efforts to see to its provision.

Others may emphasize a concern for the autonomy of the child and support regulation of private education to protect that autonomy. For example, although Ackerman would reject Defiance's regulation, he would approve of a state regulation that imposed upon parents a duty to provide their children access to a wide range of cultural materials, which the children might find useful in developing their own moral ideas and patterns of life.[41] Parents, according to this view, are not to be given the exclusive voice in shaping the educational program of their children because such exclusive control runs the danger of violating the child's right to decide for himself which communications are most profitable to believe and follow.

Other liberals, such as Rawls, may take a somewhat different approach by stressing the existence of a child's right to a certain kind of education — and this right to an education may, in turn, justify 'state regulation of private and public education to the extent that such regulation provides the best guarantee in all children of an education adequate to full and equal citizenship.'[42] Under this approach, the liberal may reject Defiance's particular regulation as deficient for not adequately protecting the child's right to an appropriately defined education. For example, under one interpretation of Rawls' theory of justice, children have a right not just to an education, but to an education that cultivates their capacity for moral reasoning.[43] Under this theory, the state might justifiably regulate parents' educational choice to protect the child's right, but in this case, Defiance's regulation would be seen as only partially adequate in protecting the child's right. Others, such as Gutmann, would go further, arguing that the state must regulate private education to assure, among other things, that children in private schools are taught 'mutual respect among the races'.[44] She argues that in a democratic society committed to 'conscious social reproduction' through 'collective' decision-making, children must be educated so they will develop 'the capacity to deliberate among alternative ways of personal and political life.'[45] Given this goal, educators should teach children that racial and religious bigotry is wrong. 'The justification for teaching these virtues is that they constitute the kind of character necessary to create a society committed to conscious social reproduction.'[46]

In sum, there is no single liberal response to Defiance's regulation. In this connection, one need only recall that Rawls' theory was used above both to suggest a reason why Defiance's regulation, indeed any such regulation, was without moral warrant and why that regulation did not go far enough in protecting the child.

Community without Egalitarianism

In the eyes of some, libertarianism and liberalism turn people toward narrow self-interest, creating competitive and adversarial relationships that lead to the destruction of community and relationships based on benevolence.[47] The resulting anomic society is ripe for take-over by a charismatic demogogue such as Hitler who promises a return to community, a sense of belonging.

But the criticism goes deeper. Under liberalism, community is reduced to merely one goal that individuals may or may not seek to realize within the framework of principles established by liberalism and libertarianism, instead of being received as a 'rival account of' liberalism and libertarianism itself.[48] At the heart of this alternative view is the principle that a community is 'an ingredient or constituent of' the identity of people as such.[49] The self is not prior to community, community is prior to the self. We belong to tradition, history, and language before they belong to us.[50] Interests do not precede community, and self-recognition can only occur through interaction with others. People are shaped by their histories, conditioned by their social context, and stand in a reciprocal relationship with that context. It is my attachments and commitments that partly define the person I am.[51] Thus liberalism and libertarianism are said to be mortally flawed in resting upon the erroneous conception of the unencumbered self. Furthermore, liberalism has gone astray by asserting that 'the good' is a matter of choice for this encumbered self, by embracing the notion that the 'right' precedes the good.[52] The good becomes wholly subjective in the liberal world; thus the notion of right itself is drained of any foundation and meaning.

The critics of liberalism and libertarianism assert that not only *is* community necessary to become human, to develop an identity, but also that being in and part of a community is a fundamental need, a desire, a good and central purpose of humans. Accordingly, the self is not beyond politics and is the proper object of continuing attention and concern. The self is an achievement of politics and one of its most aspiring possibilities.[53] Therefore, government has a role, with a long history behind it, in pursuit of this important human good. In the phrase of George F. Will, statecraft is properly soulcraft.

At a minimum, government may and should seek to foster social bonds, consensus, a set of common purposes, a self-understanding according to which people define themselves in terms of being part of the community, and perhaps also the nation. A revised self-understanding that comprehends a subject wider than the individual, whether family, tribe, city, class, or nation, is to be fostered. Government may even aspire to improving our 'cognitive access to others' so that the reach of our understanding of others is not as bounded as under liberalism and libertarianism. Government has a role in promoting a 'common vocabulary of discourse and background of implicit practices and understanding within which the capacity of the participants is reduced if never finally dissolved.'[54] If we know each other better, perhaps the need for the rather abstract and legalistic principles of justice will be lessened. Some critics of liberalism and libertarianism move off at this point toward a Burkean-like conservativism, extolling the need to work with and within tradition.[55] Others embrace a moralistic idealism, while others take a different road leading toward utopianism.

At this point, we reach a dividing point in the literature. I will at this point concentrate on the moralistic idealist branch and turn to utopianism in the next section. These moral idealists place a special interpretation on their version of community by stressing that forging community is but part of realizing a more perfect humanity. That is, people can be lifted from 'degradation', and their 'better halves' made to flourish.[56] The proper measure of government is not the gross national product, but the kind of people it nourishes.[57] For some, government's proper moral agenda merely includes the promotion of certain virtues such as temperance, farsightedness, civic virtue, patriotism, and moral neighborliness. More hard-edged moral idealists also embrace the need for government to combat pornography, sexual promiscuity, and homosexuality, while promoting marriage, family, church, and union with God.

Given these concerns, it is not surprising that moral idealists see an important role for government in the education of children. Will, for example, sees public education as central to government's proper role in society and only tolerates private education as a necessary competitive spur for the properly dominant public school system.[58]

Although government has a legitimate and extensive role in education, its function to ameliorate the social and economic inequalities of the free market is smaller. Consequently, moral idealists argue, despite continued class divisions society will hold together because of the overriding sense of community, a sense of shared participation in a joint enterprise, a shared recognition that all are at least equal as citizens. A sense of a common good provides social cement. Thus hierarchy and inequalities are accepted features of social life and, according to the moral idealist, would also be to the citizens living in a world of the moral idealists' making.

I turn now to the question of how the moral idealist might respond to Defiance's regulation. It is not difficult to imagine a moral idealist taking the following position. Free speech is a valuable principle but only up to a point. Civic virtue, the maintaining of a certain moral tone, assuring that people are more than animals, the avoidance of corruption, the cultivation of self-restraint, and the cabining of desire are all important too.[59] For these reasons, freedom of speech does not encompass im-moral speech such as obscenity. Racist teaching is also an immoral form of speech and also undermines public civility and civic virtue, hence it also may properly be suppressed.[60] On the other hand, one can imagine the moral idealist arguing that if racist teaching is based on religious convictions, then it may not be regulated.[61] Religion being so central to the realization of the moral ideal, government may not properly play any role in restricting religious freedom.

Brief mention should also be made of those communitarians who have made racism the center piece of their international, domestic, and educational policies, the fascists. Not only would the fascist permit private instruction in racism; it also seems that the fascist would require all children to be so instructed.[62]

Communitarianism with Egalitarianism

The communitarian vision without egalitarianism is suggestive of a feudal society with hierarchy, roles, socially defined purposes and virtues associated with those roles, and even an overall discoverable higher good that binds the social classes together.[63] Traditional institutions such as the family and friendship are extolled as the proper models for society in general.

But because the family has itself been associated with, and seen as symptomatic of, inequality and domination, critics of these communitarians have themselves sought to move toward communitarianism with egalitarianism and without domination and exploitation by either the state or economic men.[54] In the hands of some of these political and social philosophers, this new version evokes the themes of older utopian thinkers and dreamers:[65] harmony, mutuality of interests, mutual caring, the absence of conflict and competition; material and psychological conditions conducive to safety, security, and self-realization; an end to alienation, loneliness, and social isolation; a renewal of public spirit, a sense of the common good, and civic virtue; a re-creation of a lost unity.

The policy implications to be drawn from this ambitious hope include assuring equal participation in politics, a redistribution of wealth to end poverty, efforts to end unemployment, and the democratization of the workplace and economic relationships.[66] Politics is to become part of the process of the search for a meaningful life. In Sandel's phrase, 'when politics goes well, we can know a common good that we cannot know alone.'[67] Not all goods we value can somehow be the product of arms-length bargaining between isolated individuals situated in a market; thus we need to seek a new way of communal life. But if we are going to achieve the new politics, we also need an educational program designed to promote civic virtue, sympathy, mutual caring, respect, and the realization of the value of community and our mutual interdependence. The education program should renew the older, richer, notion of citizenship as a way of life that changes the person entering it and abandon the liberal vision of politics as impersonal mechanism of profit and loss for people with interests established antecedently to society. The proper object of moral education is to be this new, yet old, conception of citizenship.

The priority given by communal egalitarians to harmony, trust, dignity, and justice points to a willingness to assure that community is preserved and protected from activities, especially misguided education, that directly attack the basis of the hoped-for new society. Indeed, it is not inconceivable that while communal egalitarians might tolerate the espousing of racist doctrine, they would not show the same toleration toward these views when part of an education program. Moral education of the right kind is so central to the realization of the utopian vision of the communal egalitarian that it is unlikely, even were private schooling a permissible option, that private education programs that preached a politics of exclusion, domination, and exploitation would be tolerated. Something like Defiance's regulation would be accepted, if not forgone in favor of a more sweeping requirement that private schools teach the dignity and worth of all. These conclusions would sit comfortably with many communitarian egalitarians because they would not be troubled by the thought that such policies harm individual rights. The very notions of 'rights' and the associated 'rights consciousness' are themselves rejected as inherently implying the necessity for social antagonism and excluding the possibility of conceiving human freedom as self-realization and growth within and through community.[68]

Is There a Right Answer?

Having found precedent in deep conflict and having had to turn to moral and political philosophy to determine the best constructive interpretation of past legal decisions, the court must now decide the case. The central problem the court faces is whether it is even feasible to arrive at a coherent best interpretation in this case. The task before the court is formidable: precedent points in many directions; there are at least four basic ideologies reflecting different conceptions of social justice; these ideologies are themselves internally in conflict and can be intepreted as responding to our problem in different ways; and no meta-ethic or Archimedean point by which these ideologies can be weighed and ranked establishes priorities among the competing principles found in the precedent. Worse still, the four ideologies themselves are incompatible visions of humanity, society, and justice, and although exponents can be found in large numbers for each viewpoint, the viewpoints cannot intellectually be reconciled. Nor is there a meta-ethic for choosing which of these ideologies is to be preferred, which is the 'best'. In short, the legal culture — our body of precedent and background principles and ideologies — is not amenable to a uniform and coherent interpretation and justification.

More generally, the body of law and principle relevant to our problem shares the characteristics a growing number of legal scholars have found to exist in other parts of the law.[69] No precedent directly addresses the problem, the precedent and related principles are ambiguous, the law is infused with contradictory values, and the conflicting and irreconcilable ideologies of political life are replicated in the law. Law is not an objective thing or 'brute data' waiting to be discovered; thus judges must unavoidably choose the law, and choosing the law is not a value-free or ideology-free enterprise.

At this point, we come to another fork in the intellectual road. The crucial question is how are the values, biases, and prejudices of the judge related to the legal and ideological materials before him or her. One theory argues that so deep and so many are the contradictions in the law and its background principles that the situation allows and forces judges to read their own favored theory into the law. 'Judges holding to virtually any ideology which is of significance in the American political arena, will simply read their favored ideology into the settled law as its soundest theory. This can be and is done, even by the most conscientious judge, because each view on the political spectrum is embodied in some substantial portion of the authoritative materials.'[70] One works under an illusion if one thinks the law and its background principles constrain the choice of judges.

Dworkin has chosen to offer a different response to the subjectivist claim that the goal of finding a right answer is impossible and the noble dream of the right answer actually a nightmare of nihilism.[71] He writes that the skeptic's argument is powerful, but only if the skeptic has looked for a less skeptical interpretation and failed. To be convincing, the skeptic 'must show that the flawed and contradictory account is the only one available.'[72] This move by Dworkin to place the burden of persuasion on his critics is clever, but begs the question why it is not he who should have the burden of showing that it is possible to 'impose order over doctrine.'[73] Supposing that, with extensive further analysis, some order or coherence could be imposed on the materials we have reviewed, it seems clear that Dworkin has chosen the correct word when he speaks of 'imposing' an order. It may be that an order can be imposed and a 'right' answer developed, but it also is clear that there is a high probability that this would be an arbitrary order that cannot be proved correct. Though a judge can adopt some universal principle or base his or her decision on some notion of rights, the choice of these principles and rights, the choice of the premises for the crucial syllogism, is a matter of personal discretion. We should stop believing and hoping that it can be otherwise. Adjudication is not and cannot be separate from politics; it is politics carried out in a certain style.

My claim is that, although judges may, at bottom, when all the arguments have ceased, be arbitrary, they are not necessarily capricious. Working with that distinction, I conclude that at least 'judicial reason' has not been ruled out. Thus the hope remains for a nontyrannical adjudication based on a process of conversation (argument) and the recognition of reason as well as the unavoidability of choice.[74]

Finally, the need for this conversation seems to be especially acute when coming to an understanding of the proper relationship among child, parent, state. The single hypothetical dealt with here is but one small part of the intricately intertwined issues in this area, an area in which there is both little social consensus and little understanding of precisely what the issues are and how the many issues link up and relate to each other. On the question of the relationship among child, parent, and state, both law and political philosophy are in a state of incoherence and confusion. Do children have a right to an education vis-à-vis their parents? The state? A right to what sort of education? Do children have a right to freedom of belief and autonomy vis-à-vis their parents? Vis-à-vis the state? What authority does the state have to impose upon parent and child to protect the state? To protect the child? The questions pile up; the effort to understand them is, despite its ancient lineage, still in its infancy.[75]

There is an additional question which highlights the theme of this chapter. We live in a time of conflicting and perhaps irreconcilable educational ideologies. To what extent should children be taught to enhance their autonomy and capacity for self-definition and choice and to what extent ought children be educated to believe in and adhere to certain virtues? Not only might we expect a different answer to this question from a libertarian than from the two kinds of communitarians discussed in this chapter, but we also find those who would call themselves liberals, concerned specifically with the education of children within and for a democratic society, profoundly disagreeing. Gutmann, who advocates development of a capacity in children for critical evaluation, also asks, 'Why must freedom be the sole end of education, given that most of us value things that conflict with freedom...? Why prevent teachers from cultivating moral character by biasing the choices of children toward good lives and, if necessary, by constraining the range of life that children are capable of choosing when they mature.'[76] But Feinberg argues that children have a right to an open future.[77] Scheffler says that children should be educated to be rational and critical even if this runs risks that Gutmann says we need not and should not run.[78] Scheffler writes,

Such a direction in schooling is fraught with risk, for it means entrusting our current conceptions to the judgment of our pupils. In exposing these conceptions to their rational evaluation we are inviting them to see for themselves whether our conceptions are adequate, proper, fair. Such a risk is central to scientific education, where we deliberately subject our current theories to the test of continuous evaluation by future generations of our students-scientists. It is central to our moral code, *insofar as* we ourselves take the moral point of view toward this code. And, finally, it is central to the democratic commitment which holds social policies to be continually open to free and public review. In sum, rationality liberates, but there is not liberty without risk.[79]

Given this background of philosophical indeterminacy on this crucial point, it seems clear that we are likely to continue to have legal conflict over such additional questions as the authority of public school officials to select and remove text and library books, or even such apparently 'easier' issues as the scope of free speech rights of students in public schools.[80]

Notes

1 Compare *Bob Jones University v. United States*, 461 US 574 (1983). The Supreme Court upheld against constitutional challenge the authority of the federal government to withhold tax-exempt status from private religious schools that *practiced* racial discrimination by forbidding interracial marriage or dating or by following a racially discriminatory admissions policy. In *Runyon v. McCrary*, 427 US 160 (1976), the Court upheld enforcement of a federal statute that prohibited racial discrimination in the making of contracts against a private school which had a racially discriminatory admissions policy. In dictum in that case, the Court said that parents had a right to send their children to private schools which promoted the belief that racial segregation is desirable, and that the children had an equal right to attend such institutions. But it did not follow, said the Court, that these schools had a constitutional right to practice racial exclusion.
2 For example, a regulation seeking to ensure that children are taught a certain minimum level of math and science may serve to protect the interest of the child in an open future, while also protecting the polity by ensuring an adequate supply of educated, economically protected people. Sometimes these purposes can be in conflict. For example, seeing that children are inculcated in the democratic creed may serve the purpose of protecting the polity, but may not serve the interest of the child in learning skills of critical thinking.
3 A. ALTMAN (1986) 'Legal Realism, Critical Legal Studies, and Dworkin', *Philosophy and Public Affairs*, 15, pp. 205–35.

4 R. DWORKIN (1986) *Law's Empire*, Cambridge, Mass., Harvard University Press, p. 240.

5 DWORKIN, *op. cit.*, p. 248.

6 *Brandenburg v. Ohio*, 395 US 444 (1969). See also, *New York Times Co. v. United States*, 403 US 713 (1971); *Keyishian v. Board of Regents*, 385 US 589 (1967); *Wood v. Georgia*, 370 US 375 (1962); *Watts v. United States*, 394 US 705 (1969); *Yates v. United States*, 354 US 298 (1957); *Near v. Minnesota*, 283 US 697 (1931); *American Booksellers Ass'n v. Hudnut*, 771 F.2d 323 (7th Cir. 1985).

7 *Runyon v. McCrary*, 427 US 160, 176 (1976) (upholding the use of 42 U.S.C. § 1981 (1982) to prohibit private schools from denying admission of qualified children solely on the basis of race).

8 *Bethel School Dist. No. 403 v. Fraser*, 106 S. Ct. 3159 (1986); *Lehman v. Shaker Heights*, 418 US 298 (1974); *Public Utilities Comm'n v. Pollak*, 343 US 451 (1952).

9 *Beauharnais v. Illinois*, 343 US 250 (1952). Also see *Smith v. Collins*, 436 US 953 (1978).

10 *Young v. American Mini Theaters*, 427 US 50 (1976); *Paris Adult Theatre v. Slaton*, 413 US 49 (1973).

11 376 US 254 (1964) (striking down an Alabama law, as applied to public officials, that declared a publication libelous per se if the words tended to injure a person [in] his reputation or to bring him into public contempt).

12 *Board of Educ. v. Pico*, 457 US 853 (1982); *Ambach v. Norwick*, 441 US 68 (1979). See also the plurality opinion in *Board of Educ. v. Pico*, 457 US 853 (1982).

13 *Pierce v. Society of Sisters*, 268 US 510 (1925). Radio and television may also be regulated to protect children; see *FCC v. Pacifica Foundation*, 438 US 726 (1978).

14 *Farrington v. Tokushige*, 273 US 284 (1927); *Meyer v. Nebraska*, 262 US 390 (1923).

15 *Bellotti v. Baird*, 443 US 622 (1979); *Carey v. Population Services Int.*, 431 US 678 (1977); *Board of Educ. v. Barnett*, 319 US 624 (1943).

16 *Bethel School Dist. No. 403 v. Fraser*, 106 S. Ct. 3159 (1986); *New York v. Ferber*, 458 US 747 (1982); *FCC v. Pacifica Foundation*, 438 US 726 (1978); *Ginsberg v. New York*, 390 US 629 (1968).

17 *Wisconsin v. Yoder*, 406 US 205 (1972); *Farrington v. Tokushige*, 273 US 284 (1927); *Pierce v. Society of Sisters*, 268 US 510 (1925); *Meyer v. Nebraska*, 262 US 390 (1923). See also *Parham v. J.R.*, 442 US 584 (1979); *Runyon v. McCrary*, ,427 US 160, 176 (1976).

18 *Wisconsin v. Yoder*, 406 US 205 (1972).

19 See cases cited in note 1.

20 DWORKIN, *op. cit.*, p. 249.

21 This section on libertarianism rests on several sources: R. NOZICK (1974) *Anarchy, State and Utopia*, New York, Basic Books; W. BURRIS (1983) *A Liberty Primer*, 2nd ed., Rochester, N.Y., Society for Individual Liberty; F. HAYEK (1960) *The Constitution of Liberty*, Chicago, Ill., University of Chicago Press; M. ROTHBARD (1973) *For a New Liberty*, New York, Macmillan Company; D. FRIEDMAN (1973) *The Machinery of Freedom*, New York, Harper Colophon Books, M. FRIEDMAN (1962) *Capitalism and Freedom*, Chicago, Ill., University of Chicago Press.

22 As quoted in NOZICK, *supra*, p. 18.

23 E. WEST (1970) *Education and the State*, 2nd ed., London, Institute of Economic Affairs.

24 HAYEK, *op.cit.*, p. 377.

25 *Ibid.*, p. 381; FRIEDMAN, *op.cit.*, generally.

26 J. HOLT (1972) *Freedom and Beyond*, New York, Dell Publishing Company.

27 F. HAYEK (1976) *The Mirage of Social Justice*, Chicago, Ill., University of Chicago Press.

28 An emerging body of literature suggests that engaging in a policy of tit-for-tat (doing harm to someone once after they have done harm to you, and then waiting to see if they harm you again before harming them) encourages cooperation over a period of time. R. AXELROD (1984) *The Evolution of Cooperation*, New York, Basic Books.

29 T. SPRAGENS (1976) *Understanding Political Theory*, New York, St Martin's Press, pp. 31–4.

30 D. BELL (1972) 'On Meritocracy and Equality', *The Public Interest*, 29, pp. 26–68; RAWLS, *op.cit.*; B. ACKERMAN (1980) *Social Justice in the Liberal State*, New Haven, Conn., Yale University Press; A. GEWIRTH (1978) *Reason and Morality*, Chicago, Ill., University of Chicago Press.

31 T. VAN GEEL (1976) 'John Rawls and Educational Policy', in S. GOVE and F. WIRT (Eds) *Political Science and School Politics*, Lexington, Mass., Lexington Books, D.C. Heath and Company, pp. 121–43.

32 For a general review of different models of the child-parent-state relationship, see T. VAN GEEL (1986) 'The Constitution and the Child's Right to Freedom from Political Indoctrination', in D. MOSHMAN (Ed.) *Children's Intellectual Rights*, San Francisco, Calif., Jossey-Bass, pp. 7–23.

33 T. EMERSON (1970) *The System of Freedom of Expression*, New York, Vintage Books, pp. 6–8.

34 T. EMERSON (1963) 'Toward a General Theory of the First Amendment', *Yale Law Journal*, 72, pp. 877–955.

35 D. RICHARDS (1986) *Toleration and the Constitution*, New York, Oxford University Press, pp. 79–84, 100–1, 168–72, 183, 191. A similar approach to providing a rationale for freedom of speech appears in S. SMITH (1987) 'Skepticism, Tolerance, and Truth in the Theory of Free Expression', *Southern California Law Review*, 60, pp. 649–731.

36 GEWIRTH, *op.cit.*, pp. 325–6.

37 R. BORK (1971) 'Neutral Principles and Some First Amendment Problems', *Indiana Law Journal*, 47, pp. 1–35. Also see L. BEVIER (1978) 'The First Amendment and Political Speech: An Inquiry into the Substance and Limits of Principle', *Stanford Law Review*, 30, pp. 299–358.

39 M. REDISH (1984) *Freedom of Expression: A Critical Analysis*, Charlottesville, Va., The Michie Company, pp. 9–86.

40 Compare C. MACKINNON (1985) 'Pornography, Civil Rights, and Speech', *Harvard Civil Rights — Civil Liberties Law Review*, 20, pp. 1–70; H. ARKES (1974) 'Civility and the Restriction of Speech: Rediscovering the Defamation of Groups', in P. KURLAND et al. (Eds) *Supreme Court Review*, Chicago, Ill., University of Chicago Press, pp. 281–335.

41 ACKERMAN, *op.cit.*, pp. 155–6. John Rawls' theory of justice is sufficiently open to interpretation to make it possible that, contrary to the interpretation of his work adopted by Richards, Rawls would agree with Ackerman on

this point; see VAN GEEL, 'John Rawls and Educational Policy', *op.cit.* for a further elaboration of the notion of child's right to freedom of belief and the implications for the public school curriculum, see T. VAN GEEL (1983) 'The Search for Constitutional Limits on Governmental Authority to Inculcate', *Texas Law Review*, 62, pp. 197–297. Also see T. McLaughlin (1984) 'Parental Rights and the Religious Upbringing of Children', *Journal of Philosophy of Education*, 18, pp. 75–83; D. Richards (1960) 'The Individual, the Family and the Constitution: A Jurisprudential Perspective', *New York University Law Review*, 55, pp. 1–62.

42 A. Gutmann, (1980) 'Children, Paternalism, and Education', *Philosophy and Public Affairs*, 9, pp. 338, 351. For different but excellent treatment, see J. Feinberg (1980) 'The Child's Right to an Open Future', in W. Aiken and H. LaFollette, *Whose Child?*, Totowa, N.J., Littlefield, Adams and Co., pp. 124–53; F. Olafson (1973) 'Rights and Duties in Education', in J. Doyle (Ed.) *Educational Judgments*, London, Routledge and Kegan Paul, pp. 173–95.

43 VAN GEEL, 'John Rawls and Educational Policy', *op.cit.* pp. 134–9.

44 A. Gutmann (1987) *Democratic Education*, Princeton, N.J., Princeton University Press, p. 118.

45 *Ibid.*, pp. 39, 40.

46 *Ibid.*

47 The discussion in this section is based on several works: G. Will (1983) *Statecraft as Soulcraft*, New York, Simon and Schuster; M. Sandel (1982) *Liberalism and the Limits of Justice*, Cambridge, Cambridge University Press; A. Vincent and R. Plant (1985) *Philosophy, Politics and Citizenship*, Oxford, Basil Blackwell; W. Sullivan (1986) *Reconstructing Public Philosophy*, Berkeley, Calif., University of California Press; R. Nisbet (1986) *Conservatism*, Minneapolis, Minn., University of Minnesota Press; C. Rossiter (1962) *Conservatism in America*, 2nd ed. revised, New York, Vantage Books.

48 Sandel, *op.cit.*, p. 64.

49 *Ibid.*; A. MacIntyre (1981) *After Virtue*, South Bend, Ind., University of Notre Dame Press.

50 R. Bernstein (1983) *Beyond Objectivism and Relativism*, Philadelphia, Pa., University of Pennsylvania Press, p. 167.

51 *Ibid.*, p. 179.

52 MacIntyre, *op.cit.*, generally.

53 *Ibid.*, p. 183.

54 *Ibid.*, pp. 172–3.

55 *Ibid.*, p. 207. Nisbet, *op.cit.* Michael Walzer, a liberal, also stresses the unavoidability of working with and within tradition: M. Walzer (1983) *Spheres of Justice*, New York, Basic Books.

56 Vincent and Plant, *op.cit.*, p. 60.

57 Will, *op.cit.*, pp. 85, 135.

58 *Ibid.*, p. 130.

59 W. Berns (1976) *The First Amendment and the Future of American Democracy*, New York, Basic Books, pp. 205–25; M. Sandel (1984) 'Morality and the Liberal Ideal', *The New Republic*, May 7, pp. 15–17.

60 Arkes, *op.cit.*, generally.

61 WALTER, *op.cit.*, pp. 1–32, 146.
62 G. MOSSE (1966) *Nazi Culture*, New York, Grosset and Dunlap, pp. 283–4; H. KOCH (1975) *The Hitler Youth*, New York, Stein and Day.
63 MACINTYRE, *op.cit.*, generally.
64 A. GUTMANN (1985) 'Communitarian Critics of Liberalism', *Philosophy and Public Affairs*, 14, pp. 308–22.
65 R. KANTER (1972) *Committment and Community*, Cambridge, Mass., Harvard University Press.
66 The comments in this paragraph are based on SULLIVAN *op.cit.*
67 SANDEL, *op.cit.*, p. 183.
68 Professor Michelman summarizes the recent attack on the notion of rights in F. MICHELMAN (1985) 'Justification (and Justifiability) of Law in a Contradictory World', in J. PENNOCK and J. CHAPMAN (Eds) *Justification*, New York, New York University Press, pp. 71–99.
69 See, for example, J. SINGER (1984) 'The Player and the Cards: Nihilism and Legal Theory', *Yale Law Journal*, 94, pp. 1–70; R. UNGER (1983) 'The Critical Legal Studies Movement', *Harvard Law Review*, 96, pp. 561–675; D. KENNEDY (1976) 'Form and Substance in Private Law Adjudication', *Harvard Law Review*, 89, pp. 1685–778.
70 ALTMAN, *op.cit.*, p. 231.
71 H. HART (1977) 'American Jurisprudence through English Eyes: The Nightmare and the Noble Dream', *Georgia Law Review*, 11, p. 969.
72 DWORKIN, *op.cit.*, p. 274.
73 *Ibid.*, p. 273.
74 MICHELMAN, *op.cit.*, p. 90.
75 I have been working on these sets of problems for a number of years: VAN GEEL, 'John Rawls and Educational Policy', *op.cit.*; VAN GEEL, 'The Constitution and the Child's Right to Freedom from Political Indoctrination', *op.cit.*; VAN GEEL, 'The Search for Constitutional Limits on Governmental Authority to Inculcate', *op.cit.*.
76 GUTMANN, *Democratic Education*, *op.cit.*, p. 37.
77 FEINBERG, *op.cit.*, generally.
78 I. SCHEFFLER (1973) 'Moral Education and the Democratic Ideal', in I. SCHEFFLER, *Reason and Teaching*, Indianapolis, Ind., Bobbs-Merrill Co., pp. 134, 140.
79 SCHEFFLER, *op.cit.*, p. 143.
80 Cf. *Bethel School District No. 403 v. Fraser*, 106 S.Ct. 3159 (1986).

13
The Constitution and Private Schools

Erwin Chemerinsky

The state action doctrine is one of the most important limits on the Constitution's protection of individual liberties. Simply stated, the Constitution restricts government conduct; private institution and individual actions are not proscribed by constitutional limitations. State action doctrine draws a rigid distinction between society's public and private realms. The public sector — government at all levels and its officers — must operate within constitutional guidelines and may be sued for infringing individual constitutional rights. The private sector is immune from constitutional control or review.

Undoubtedly, the state action doctrine has particular importance in the area of education. The Fourteenth Amendment of the Constitution guarantees all persons equal protection of the laws and prevents government from discriminating in providing education, but that Amendment does not prevent private school discrimination. The ability of parents to send children to segregated private schools has been responsible for a perpetuation and intensification of segregation in many public school systems.[1] Teachers in public schools have First Amendment rights and generally may not be disciplined for their speech; but the First Amendment provides no such protection for teachers in private schools.[2] Public schools must provide procedural due process — notice and hearing — in many cases before firing teachers or disciplining students.[3] Private schools, however, are under no such obligation.

Given education's importance in American society, courts and commentators have been troubled by the ability of private schools to disregard basic constitutional values and even to undermine important social objectives such as school desegregation. Therefore, the Supreme Court has developed a number of methods for expanding the Constitution's protections to many private school actions. I contend, however, that even these constitutional restrictions of private schools do not go far enough. All schools — public and private — perform an essential public function. All should be obligated to follow the United States Constitution.

The first part of this chapter describes the state action doctrine. The problems with private school immunity from constitutional scrutiny are discussed in the second part. In particular, private schools have become havens for white students fleeing school desegregation, perpetuating segregated schools in most urban areas. The steps taken by the Supreme Court to limit discrimination by private schools are summarized in the third part. Finally, I argue for further extension of the Constitution's protections of individual liberties.

The State Action Doctrine: The General Inapplicability of the Constitution to Private Schools

It is firmly established that the Constitution only applies to government conduct, usually referred to as 'state action'.[4] The behavior of private citizens and corporations is controlled by common law rules, such as tort and contract law, and by statutes, but not by the Constitution. In 1879, not long after the ratification of the Fourteenth Amendment, the Supreme Court declared that the 'provisions of the Fourteenth Amendment...all have reference to state action exclusively, and not to any action of private individuals.'[5] Similarly, in the *Civil Rights Cases*, in 1883, the Court held that 'it is state action of a particular character that is prohibited. Individual invasion of individual rights is not the subject-matter of the amendment.'[6]

These holdings remain undisturbed. The Constitution does not prohibit private deprivations of constitutional rights. Private behavior need comply with the Constitution only if the state is so intimately involved in the conduct — if the nexus to the state is so great — that the state can be held responsible for the activity. Therefore, courts are powerless to halt private infringements of even the most basic constitutional values. The Supreme Court repeatedly has stated that the Constitution offers no shield against 'private conduct however discriminatory or wrongful.'[7]

The term 'state action' refers to conduct by any level of government — local, state, or federal. It includes actions by individual government officers. Thus, the Constitution prevents a public school, but not private schools, from discriminating against black and Hispanic students.

Why does the Constitution apply only to government? After all, why should society tolerate infringements of basic values — equality, freedom of expression, privacy — just because the violator is private rather than public? Speech can be chilled and lost as much by private sanctions as public ones. Private discrimination causes and perpetuates social inequalities at least as pernicious as those caused by government action.

Traditionally, two major justifications are offered for the state action doctrine. One is that the state action requirement protects individual freedom by defining a zone of private conduct beyond the Constitution's reach. The Supreme Court has observed that limiting the Constitution to government conduct 'preserves an area of individual freedom by limiting the reach of federal law and federal judicial power.'[8] Of course, even if the Constitution applied to private conduct, that would not mean that private parties always would be held to the same standards as government. Often there might be justifications for private behavior, such as privacy and freedom of association, that would not sanction government actions. Arguably, however, without a state action doctrine, individuals could be called into court to justify any behavior that interferes with another person's rights. Thus, it is claimed that the state action doctrine is useful because it creates a zone of private activity about which the government may not even inquire.[9]

A second justification for the state action doctrine is its preservation of state sovereignty, and thus federalism.[10] The *Civil Rights Cases* held that federal constitutional rights do not govern individual behavior and, furthermore, that Congress lacks authority to apply them to private conduct.[11] Structuring the legal relationships of private citizens is for state, not national, government. As such, the state action doctrine protects state sovereignty by leaving governance of individual behavior to state political processes.

Between World War II and 1969, the first year of the Burger Court, the Supreme Court had an easier time finding that the government was so entangled with private conduct, the nexus to the government was so great, that the Constitution applied. Especially in cases involving claims of racial discrimination, the Court liberalized the state action requirement, making it much easier to prevent private discrimination.

Specifically, the Court identified two important situations in which the Constitution regulates private conduct. Each of these potentially can be used to justify applying the Constitution to private schools. More recent decisions of the Burger Court, however, dramatically limit the scope of these exceptions.

First, the Court found that if private parties perform a public function, they are held to the standards of the Constitution. In *Marsh v. Alabama*, the Court held that a company that owned a town had to comply with the First Amendment and permit distribution of leaflets.[12] The Court said that the company, by governing a city, was performing a public function. Similarly, in a series of cases, the Court invalidated political primaries, conducted by private groups, that excluded racial minorities.[13] The Court concluded that holding elections is a traditional public function and that a state cannot escape the Constitution's strictures by delegating the task to private parties.[14] Thus, 'when private entities have been allowed to perform functions ordinarily undertaken by the state government, they are treated as agents of the state for constitutional purposes.'[15]

In the light of these decisions, several commentators argued that private schools perform a public function and therefore should be compelled to comply with the Constitution. Education obviously is a service traditionally provided by the state. Moreover, as the Supreme Court recognized in *Brown v. Board of Education*, education is so fundamentally important to society that it properly can be viewed as perhaps the most essential government activity.[16] Judge Skelly Wright, speaking of private colleges, explained why private education should be viewed as a public function and therefore governed by the Constitution:

> One may question whether any school or college can ever be so 'private' as to escape the reach of the Fourteenth Amendment....Institutions of learning are not things of purely private concern....Clearly the administrators of a private college are performing a public function. They do the work of the state, often in the place of the state. Does it not follow that they stand in the state's shoes? And, if so, are they not then agents of the state, subject to the constitutional restraints on governmental action, to the same extent as private persons who govern a company town...or control a political party?[17]

The Burger Court, however, recoiled from such expansive applications of the Constitution. In *Jackson v. Metropolitan Edison Co.*, the Court refused to find state action in the conduct of a privately owned utility company that had a state-granted monopoly in the provision of electricity.[18] In *Jackson*, the Court, in an opinion by Justice Rehnquist, stated that a public function is an activity that 'traditionally exclusively [had been] reserved to the State[s].'[19] This obviously is a difficult test. The very fact that the challenged activity is being performed by a private party is evidence that it is not 'exclusively' done by government.

In terms of private schools, the provision of education is not something 'traditionally exclusively' provided by the government. Non-public schools long have existed in the United States. In fact, more than sixty years ago the Supreme Court declared that parents have a constitutionally protected right to send their children to parochial schools.[20] Under the Burger Court's definition, an activity is not a public function because of its social importance. Thus, under current law, private education is not a public function and not obligated to comply with the Constitution.

A second means by which the Supreme Court has held private conduct to be state action is finding a substantial government entanglement with the private parties. For example, in *Shelley v. Kramer*, the Supreme Court held that court enforcement of racially restrictive private covenants constitutes state action.[21] Previously, courts repeatedly held that enforcement of purely private agreements did not involve state action. When courts uphold agreements such as those challenged in *Shelley*, they do so because the common law of contracts does not forbid racially restrictive covenants. However, the common law is created and applied by the courts, an arm of the state. Thus, state courts are integral to the discriminatory act. Hence, the Court concluded that there is government action in the enforcement of a racially restrictive covenant.[22]

Another example of a sufficient nexus between the government and a private party is *Burton v. Wilmington Parking Authority*.[23] In *Burton*, the Supreme Court found state action when a private restaurant, which leased its premises from the state, discriminated against blacks. The Court stated:

> In its lease with Eagle [the private restaurant] the Authority could have affirmatively required Eagle to discharge the responsibilities...imposed upon the private enterprise as a consequence of state participation. But no state may effectively abdicate its responsibilities by either ignoring them or by merely failing to discharge them whatever the motive may be. By its inaction, the Authority, and through it the State, has not only made itself a party to the refusal of service, but has elected to place its power, property and prestige behind the admitted discrimination.[24]

Commentators argued that these cases provide a basis for applying the Constitution to private schools. All discrimination and violation of rights by private schools occurs because the state tolerates it. Just as the state could have prevented discrimination in its lease with the restaurant in *Burton*, so could the state insist that private schools comply with the Constitution.[25] Just as inaction did not excuse the state in *Burton*, nor should it permit constitutional violations by private schools.[26]

Moreover, private schools are highly regulated by the government. The state prescribes numerous aspects of policy for all elementary and secondary schools, including attendance requirements, curriculum, and teacher qualifications. In the light of *Shelley* and *Burton*, this state involvement is arguably so great and continuous as to justify the application of the Constitution to private education.[27]

Once again, however, the Burger Court greatly narrowed the circumstances under which state regulation or involvement creates state action. In *Jackson v. Metropolitan Edison Co.*, the Court found that pervasive regulation of a utility company by the state was insufficient to create state action.[28] In *Moose Lodge No. 107 v. Irvis*, the Court held that there is no state action when a private club with a state liquor license discriminates on the basis of race.[29] The Court concluded that the state had no obligation to insist, as a condition for receipt of the license, that there be no discrimination on the premises. In *Blum v. Yaretsky*, the Court found no state action, even though a nursing home received substantial government funding and was highly regulated by the government.[30]

Given these decisions, it appears quite unlikely that private schools will be required to comply with the Constitution because of government toleration of discrimination and rights violations or because of government regulation. In fact, in *Rendell-Baker v. Kohn*, the Supreme Court explicitly refused to find state action in the conduct of a state subsidized private school.[31] In this case, a teacher claimed that her firing was in retaliation for her speaking out in favor of more rights for students. She argued that she deserved First Amendment protection because the private school where she worked was an arm of the state. The school specialized in teaching students who had experienced difficulties in the public schools, including many students with drug, alcohol, or behavior problems.

The school received almost all its students from referrals from the public school system. Additionally, it received between 90 and 99 per cent of its money from government agencies.[32] Nonetheless, the Supreme Court held that there was no state action; thus, the Constitution provided the teacher with no protection.

The Court observed that the school cannot be said to perform a public function simply because it performs a public service; because education is not 'traditionally the *exclusive* prerogative of the state', the Constitution cannot be applied on that basis.[33] Nor is there state action, the Court said, because there is state regulation, even if the state involvement is 'extensive and detailed'.[34] The fact that the school receives almost all its funding from the state was deemed irrelevant for state action purposes. The Court declared:

> The school...is not fundamentally different from many private corporations whose business depends primarily on contracts to

build roads, bridges, dams, ships, or submarines for the
government. Acts of such private contractors do not become
acts of the government by reason of their significant or even
total engagement in performing public contracts.[35]

Unless the teacher could demonstrate that the state itself was substantially
involved in her firing, she could not allege state action or apply the
Constitution to the private school.

The conclusion that emerges is that the state action doctrine is alive
and well. The Supreme Court is unlikely to hold that private schools
are obligated to comply with the Constitution either on the grounds that
they perform a public function or because of substantial state
entanglement.

Private Schools and the Constitution: Why Private Schools Should Not Be Exempt from Constitutional Protections

Substantial ill effects arise from immunizing private schools from
constitutional regulation. First and perhaps most important, because the
Fourteenth Amendment does not apply to private schools, they are
permitted to discriminate against blacks and thus become havens for white
students fleeing desegregated public schools. Even before substantial
efforts at school desegregation, far more white students attended private
schools than did minority students. For example, in 1960, 39 per cent
of white elementary school students attended nonpublic schools,
compared with only 6 per cent of minority students.[36] Court-imposed
school desegregation only intensified this disparity. White flight from
public schools has been a national phenomenon. The more aggressive
the desegregation efforts, the greater the flight to private schools. For
example, the 'estimated enrollment in Southern private schools organized
or expanded in response to desegregation increased from roughly 25,000
in 1966 to approximately 535,000 by 1972.'[37]

Although the exact number of white students who have left the public
schools to avoid desegregation is not known,[38] white flight to private
schools has substantially undermined desegregation efforts, and even has
increased segregation in public schools. As one commentator observed,
'in many areas of the South, efforts to eliminate segregation in public
education have been nullified by the massive withdrawal of white children
from the public schools and the concomitant establishment of a "private"
school system.'[39] Especially when combined with white flight from
cities to predominantly white suburbs, the effect has been largely to
prevent effective school desegregation.[40]

The massive withdrawal of students from the public schools has decreased the willingness of parents and government to spend money on public school education. As whites have been withdrawn from public schools, tax rates for school funding also have been cut. Typical cuts occurred in Sumter County, Georgia, where the rate of taxes for schools was cut from 20 to 12 per cent between 1970 and 1972, a time of substantial efforts at school desegregation.[41] Likewise, local electorates 'have increasingly refused to approve new [school] bond issues and issues approved before desegregation have not been funded.'[42]

The result is that less is spent on education for pupils, often mostly from minority groups, who remain in the public schools. The effect is that American education is separate and unequal. In 1980, '63 per cent of black students and 66 per cent of hispanics were in segregated schools, that is, schools with more than half minority enrollment.'[43] The statistics for specific cities are even more startling. In Chicago, in 1981, whites comprised only 17 per cent of students in the public school system.[44] In Washington, D.C., the public schools are more than 96 per cent black.[45] In Baltimore, Dallas, Detroit, Houston, Los Angeles, Miami, Memphis, New York, and Philadelphia, whites constitute less than one-third of the students enrolled in public schools.[46] Moreover, in the United States, 20 per cent more is spent on the average white student's elementary and secondary education than on the average black child's schooling.[47] The promise of *Brown v. Board of Education* is unfulfilled: education is separate and unequal.

Second, even apart from these effects of private schools, society should not tolerate important institutions violating such fundamental values as freedom of expression, privacy, and equality.[48] Especially if one believes that schools inculcate values in children, then it is undesirable for students to observe teachers fired for their speech, students and teachers disciplined without due process, and discrimination.

Furthermore, the traditional justifications for the state action doctrine have little merit in the context of private schools. Although the state action doctrine may be desirable in preserving a zone of *individual* freedom exempt from government control, there is no reason why an *institution*, such as a private school, should have such immunity. The primary argument advanced for allowing private schools to discriminate is freedom of association — that white parents should have the right to have their children only associate with white students. Yet, the Supreme Court has forcefully rejected this argument, explaining that the freedom of whites does not justify allowing them to impose harm on blacks. In *Norwood v. Harrison*, the Supreme Court declared, 'Invidious private discrimination may be characterized as a form of exercising freedom of association protected by the First Amendment, but it has never been accorded affirmative constitutional protections.'[49] At the very least, the state has a compelling interest in school desegregation that justifies infringing any associational rights that might exist.

Nor does state sovereignty justify applying the state action doctrine to private schools. States should not have the discretion to tolerate discrimination or violations of fundamental rights. Hence, even assuming state sovereignty to be of value, applying the Constitution to private schools has at most a marginal effect on the states.

Thus, in the context of education, the state action doctrine is pernicious and undesirable. The doctrine should not be allowed to shield private schools from the obligation to adhere to constitutional principles of equal protection.

The Supreme Court and Private Schools

The Supreme Court has recognized two major limits on the ability of private schools to discriminate against blacks and other minorities. First, the Court has held that a school that discriminates is ineligible for government assistance. *Norwood v. Harrison* was a challenge to a Mississippi statute that authorized the state to provide textbooks to all schools, private or public, regardless of whether the school had racially discriminatory policies.[50] In *Norwood*, the Court noted that the marked growth in the number of private schools in Mississippi was coincident with major efforts to desegregate public schools. The Court observed that in 1963–64, Mississippi had seventeen private, non–Catholic schools; by 1970, this number had increased to 155, with a population of 42,000 students.[51]

The Court, however, made it clear that the issue in *Norwood* was a narrow one. The Court did not rule that private school discrimination is impermissible. Rather, the sole issue was the ability of the state to provide textbooks to schools that discriminate. The Court concluded:

> This Court has consistently affirmed decisions enjoining state tuition grants to students attending racially discriminatory private schools. A textbook lending program is not legally distinguishable from the forms of state assistance foreclosed by the private cases....[T]he constitutional infirmity of the Mississippi textbook program is that it significantly aids the organization and continuation of a separate system of private schools which...may discriminate if they so desire. A State's constitutional obligation requires it to steer clear, not only of

operating the old dual system of racially segregated schools, but also of giving significant aid to institutions that practice racial or other invidious discrimination.[52]

Thus, under *Norwood*, discriminatory private schools may exist, but they may not receive substantial assistance, such as textbooks, from the state government. Following similar reasoning, in *Gilmore v. City of Montgomery*, the Supreme Court held that Montgomery, Alabama, could not constitutionally allow private segregated schools to use the municipal stadium and other city facilities for athletic events.[53]

In *Bob Jones University v. United States*, the Supreme Court held that the United States Internal Revenue Service could deny tax-exempt status to schools, including religious schools, that discriminate on the basis of race.[54] Bob Jones University permitted unmarried black students to enroll, but denied admission to applicants who were part of interracial marriages or who advocated interracial marriage and dating. Goldsboro Christian Schools, also a petitioner before the Supreme Court, maintained a racially discriminatory admissions policy. Both of these schools based their policies on an interpretation of the Bible that requires separation of the races.

The Internal Revenue Service revoked the tax-exempt status of the schools because of their racial discrimination. The schools argued that their First Amendment right to free exercise of religion was infringed because the admissions policy under attack was based on religious beliefs. After discussing the importance of education to society, the Supreme Court concluded that the state has a compelling interest in preventing discrimination in education, including discrimination by private schools. The Court held:

> The governmental interest at stake here is compelling....[T]he government has a fundamental, overriding interest in eradicating racial discrimination in education — discrimination that prevailed, with official approval, for the first 165 years of this Nation's constitutional history. That governmental interest substantially outweighs whatever burden denial of tax benefits places on petitioners' exercise of their religious beliefs.[55]

The Court, however, did not rule in *Bob Jones* that the Constitution prohibited the government from granting tax benefits to schools that discriminate. Instead, the ruling was confined to the limited holding that the Internal Revenue Service constitutionally may deny tax benefits to schools with racially discriminatory admissions policies. Although several lower courts have ruled that private schools that discriminate may not receive tax advantages from the government, the issue remains unsettled.[56]

Additionally, lower courts have greatly limited the ability of government to enter into transactions with private schools that discriminate. For instance, in *United States v. Mississippi*, the United States Court of Appeals for the Fifth Circuit held it unconstitutional for a county to lease property to a racially discriminatory private school.[57] In other cases, the Fifth Circuit held that 'if a state actually sells property knowing that the property will be used for the establishment of a segregated academy or the sale actually interferes with the desegregation of the public school system, then the sale must be set aside.'[58]

Again, however, these cases only serve to limit private school discrimination indirectly by restricting government involvement with private schools. They do not, even implicitly, apply constitutional provisions to the schools or prevent private schools from discriminating on the basis of race.

The second way in which the Supreme Court has protected civil rights from infringement by private schools is by application of the civil rights statutes to private schools. Following the Civil War, the Thirteenth Amendment was promptly ratified, prohibiting slavery or involuntary servitude in the United States. Section two of the Amendment states that 'Congress shall have power to enforce this article by appropriate legislation.' The Thirteenth Amendment is unique in that it regulates private behavior, eliminating slavery, and is not confined to government actions. Soon after the Amendment's ratification, Congress adopted several civil rights statutes prohibiting many types of private and public racial discrimination.

In the *Civil Rights Cases*, however, the Supreme Court narrowly construed Congress' powers to enact legislation under the Thirteenth Amendment.[59] Although recognizing that the Thirteenth Amendment applies to private conduct, the Court held that Congress could not proscribe private racial discrimination as a method to eradicate badges of slavery. The Court emphasized that it 'would be running the slavery argument into the ground to make it apply to every act of discrimination which a person may see fit to make as to the guests he will entertain, or as to the people he will take into his coach, or cab or car, or to admit to his concert or theatre, or deal with in other matters of intercourse or business.'[60]

Thus, the *Civil Rights Cases* were a major restriction on the reach of the post-Civil War Amendments and on Congress' power to use them to eliminate private racial discrimination. In subsequent cases, the Court reiterated this limited view. For example, in *Hodges v. United States*, the

Supreme Court concluded that Congress could prohibit only those private activities that create a 'state of entire subjection of one person to the will of another.'[61] Similarly, in other decisions, the Court held that the Thirteenth Amendment does not authorize Congress to prohibit private racial discrimination.[62]

In a dramatic departure from precedent, however, the Supreme Court, in *Jones v. Alfred H. Mayer Co.*, held that a civil rights statute adopted under the Thirteenth Amendment soon after the Civil War, 42 U.S.C. § 1982, could be applied to prevent private racial discrimination in the sale or leasing of housing.[63] Section 1982 guarantees to all citizens 'the same right, in every State and Territory, as is enjoyed by white citizens thereof to inherit, purchase, lease, sell, hold and convey real and personal property.' In *Jones*, the Court concluded that the 'Act was designed to do just what its terms suggest: to prohibit all racial discrimination, whether or not under color of law, with respect to the rights...to purchase or lease property.'[64]

In *Runyon v. McCrary*, the Court explicitly relied on *Jones* and held that a companion statute, 42 U.S.C. § 1981, could be applied to prevent racial discrimination by private schools.[65] Section 1981 states that 'all persons within the jurisdiction of the United States shall have the same right...to make and enforce contracts, to sue, be parties, give evidence, and to the full and equal benefit of the laws and proceedings for the security of persons and property as is enjoyed by white citizens.' In *Runyon*, the Court concluded that Section 1981 prohibited a private, commercially operated, nonsectarian school from denying admission to prospective students because of their race. The Court observed that the open policy of racial discrimination maintained by the schools was 'a classic violation of Section 1981.'[66]

Runyon involved two private schools in northern Virginia that regularly advertised for applicants, neither of which had ever admitted a black student. In response to brochures they received in the mail and advertisements found in the Yellow Pages, two black families submitted applications for their children. After the children were denied admission because of their race, the parents filed suit pursuant to Section 1981. The Supreme Court affirmed lower court rulings in favor of the plaintiffs, holding that Section 1981 prevents a private, nonsectarian school from discriminating against prospective students on account of their race.

As in earlier decisions, the Court summarily rejected the schools' claim that white parents and children had a constitutional right to freedom of association that justified permitting discriminatory school policies.[67] The Court once again made it clear that there is no constitutional right to discriminate.

Runyon, therefore, is a powerful tool to eliminate discrimination by private schools. Although it does not apply the Constitution to private schools, the effect of using the civil rights statutes is much the same in prohibiting discrimination. Children denied admission to private schools on account of their race have a cause of action under the federal civil rights law, 42 U.S.C. § 1981.

The Next Step: Apply the Constitution to Private Schools

Although the Supreme Court has made substantial progress in limiting discrimination by private schools, more needs to be done to apply the Constitution to private schools. All of the Supreme Court's decisions have been in the context of race and equal protection. None of the decisions has applied other constitutional protections, such as the First Amendment or due process, to private schools. Just as private schools should not be allowed to discriminate, nor should they be able to discipline students or teachers in violation of the First Amendment or without procedural due process.

The reach of *Runyon v. McCrary* in preventing discrimination by private schools is uncertain. In *Runyon*, the schools had advertised widely and solicited applicants. Also, the schools were nonsectarian. The application of *Runyon* to less commercially visible or sectarian schools is unclear.[68]

Therefore, I contend that the appropriate step is to declare that private schools perform an essential public function and must comply with the Constitution. I am not arguing for abolition of parochial schools. Nor do I believe that applying the Constitution to private education would have such an effect. At minimum, the Court could justify the existence of nondiscriminatory parochial schools based on the compelling interest in assuring free exercise of religion and providing parents the right to direct their children's upbringing.[69] No constitutional right is absolute. Hence, even if parochial schools were violating the establishment clause, allowing private schools is a compelling interest.

Nor would applying the Constitution to nonpublic schools substantially undermine private or religious education. Schools generally still could determine the content of their curriculum and their rules and policies, consistent, of course, with existing state laws. In this chapter I have identified three important areas where the schools' decisions must give way to the compelling government interests represented in the Constitution: ending discrimination against racial minorities, preventing punishment on the basis of constitutionally protected speech, and assuring due process. None of these areas would change the fundamental content of private education; even if it did, there is a sufficiently important social interest in assuring protection of these fundamental values.

Undoubtedly, application of the Constitution to private schools will pose difficult questions in the future. For example, could private schools discriminate on the basis of gender? Are they allowed, in their curriculum, to advocate segregation? These questions, however, are not fundamentally different from the kinds of issues always confronting courts in constitutional cases. The judiciary will need to balance society's interests, as reflected in the Constitution's values, against the interests asserted by the private schools.

Overall, society gains little by allowing private schools to discriminate or violate basic rights. The Supreme Court correctly has rejected claims that freedom of association or freedom of religion justify private school autonomy from the Constitution. The state action doctrine provides immunity for activities — discrimination, violation of basic rights — that should not be tolerated. Finally, 200 years after the adoption of the Constitution, 119 years after the ratification of the Fourteenth Amendment, and thirty-four years after the landmark decision in *Brown v. Board of Education*, it is time to stop constitutional violations by private schools.[70]

Notes

1 See, e.g., Note (1968) 'The Wall of Racial Separation: The Role of Private and Parochial Schools in Racial Integration', *New York University Law Review*, 43, p. 516 ('Private and parochial school enrollment, which is overwhelmingly white...is a significant factor in the increasing separation of white and Negro school children'); N. Dorsen (1967) 'Racial Discrimination in Private Schools', *William and Mary Law Rev.*, 9, pp. 49–50.
2 See, e.g., *Rendell-Baker v. Kohn*, 457 US 830 (1982) (firing of teacher for her speech by school receiving 99 per cent of its funds from the state is not unconstitutional because there is no state action).
3 See, e.g., *Goss v. Lopez*, 419 US 565 (1975) (procedural due process requirements before a student can be disciplined in public schools).
4 For a background general discussion of the state action doctrine, see E. Chemerinsky (1985) 'Rethinking State Action', *Northwestern University Law Review*, 80, p. 503; M. Phillips (1984) 'The Inevitable Incoherence of the Modern State Action Doctrine', *St Louis University Law Journal*, 28, p. 683; (1982) 'A Symposium: The Public/Private Distinction', *University of Pennsylvania Law Review*, 130; C. Black (1967) 'Foreword: State Action, Equal Protection, and California's Proposition 14', *Harvard Law Review*, 81, p. 69.
5 *Virginia v. Rives*, 100 US 313, 318 (1879).

6 109 US 3, 11 (1883).
7 *Jackson v. Metropolitan Edison Co.*, 419 US 345, 349 (1974).
8 *Lugar v. Edmondson Oil Co.*, 457 US 922, 936 (1982).
9 W. MARSHALL (1985) 'Diluting Constitutional Rights: Rethinking "Rethinking State Action"', *Northwestern University Law Review*, 80, pp. 561–2.
10 See *Lugar v. Edmondson Oil Co.*, 457 US 922, 936 (1982).
11 109 US 3 (1883); see W. BURKE and D. REBER (1973) 'State Action, Congressional Power and Creditors' Rights: An Essay on the Fourteenth Amendment' (pt. 1), *Southern California Law Review*, 46, pp. 1012–18 (state action doctrine preserves state sovereignty).
12 *Marsh v. Alabama*, 326 US 501 (1946).
13 See, e.g., *Terry v. Adams*, 345 US 461 (1953).
14 See Note (1973) 'Segregation Academies and State Action', *Yale Law Journal*, 82, pp. 1454–5 ('it is impermissible for the state to avoid the constitutional standards applied to its functions by permitting those duties to be assumed by nominally private groups').
15 Note, 'The Wall of Racial Separation', *supra*, p. 518.
16 347 US 483, 493 (1954); Note, 'The Wall of Racial Separation', *supra*, p. 520.
17 *Guillory v. Administrators of Tulane Univ.*, 203 F. Supp. 855, 858–59 (E.D. La. 1962).
18 419 US 345 (1974).
19 *Id.* at 352; see J. NOWAK, R. ROTUNDA and J. YOUNG (1986) *Constitutional Law*, 3rd ed., St Paul, Minn., West, p. 430 (difficulty of finding activities to be public functions under the Burger Court's test).
20 *Pierce v. Society of Sisters*, 268 US 510, 535 (1925).
21 334 US 1 (1948).
22 The literature discussing *Shelley v. Kramer* is voluminous. See, e.g., Note (1948) 'Racial Discrimination in Housing', *Yale Law Journal*, 57, p. 426; J. FRANK (1948) 'The United States Supreme Court: 1947–48', *University of Chicago Law Review*, 16, p. 1; W. MING (1949) 'Racial Restrictions and the Fourteenth Amendment: The Restrictive Covenant Cases', *University of Chicago Law Review*, 16, p. 203; W. VAN ALSTYNE and K. KARST (1961) 'State Action', *Stanford Law Review*, 14, p. 3.
23 365 US 715 (1961).
24 365 US at 725.
25 The Supreme Court has made it clear that private schools do not have a constitutional right to discriminate based on freedom of association. See *Norwood v. Harrison*, 413 US 455, 469 (1973).
26 Note, 'The Wall of Racial Separation', *supra*, pp. 423–4 (discrimination by private schools occurs because the state tolerates it).
27 See A. MILLER (1957) 'Racial Discrimination and Private Schools', *Minnesota Law Review*, 41, pp. 262–3.
28 419 US 345 (1974).
29 407 US 163 (1972).
30 457 US 991 (1982).
31 457 US 830 (1982).
32 *Id.* at 832.
33 *Id.* at 842.

34 *Id.* at 841.

35 *Id.* at 840–41.

36 Note, 'The Wall of Racial Separation', *supra,* pp. 516; 1 US Commission of Civil Rights (1967) *Racial Isolation in the Public Schools,* p. 7; Note, 'Segregation Academies and State Action', *supra.*

37 Note, 'Segregation Academies', *supra,* pp. 1441.

38 Dorsen, *supra,* p. 46.

39 Note, 'Segregation Academies', *supra,* p. 1436.

40 See E. CHEMERINSKY, (1982) 'Ending the Dual System of American Public Educaction: The Urgent Need for Legislative Action', in 32, *DePaul L. Rev.,* p. 77 (hereinafter 'Ending the Dual System') (describing the effects of white flight to suburbs and its effects on school segregation).

41 C. BROWN and M. PROVIZER (1972) 'The New South's New Dual School System: A Case Study', in *New South,* 4, pp. 59–72.

42 Note, 'Segregation Academies', *supra,* p. 1452.

43 CHEMERINSKY, 'Ending the Dual System' *supra,* p. 82.

44 Chicago Public Schools, Racial/Ethnic Survey, (1981), p. 2.

45 United States Dept. of Housing and Urban Dev. (1989) *The President's National Urban Policy Report,* pp. 10–12.

46 J. ZIEMBA 'School Desegregation Called Key to City', *Chicago Tribune,* 8 February, p. 3, col. 1.

47 E. CHEMERINSKY *supra,* pp. 77–8; C. JENCKS (1972) *Inequality,* New York, Basic Books, p. 28.

48 I develop this argument at length in E. CHEMERINSKY *Rethinking State Action, supra.*

49 413 US 455, 470 (1973).

50 413 US 455 (1973).

51 *Id.* at 457.

52 *Id.* at 463, 467.

53 417 US 556 (1974).

54 461 US 574 (1983).

55 *Id.* at 604.

56 See, e.g., *Green v. Kennedy,* 309 F. Supp. 1127, *appeal dismissed sub. nom., Cannon v. Green,* 398 US 956 (1970); *Pitts v. Department of Revenue,* 333 F. Supp. 662 (E.D. Wis. 1971). See C. GALVIN and N. DEVINS (1983) 'A Tax Policy Analysis of Bob Jones University v. United States', *Vanderbilt Law Review,* 36, pp. 1377–9.

57 499 F.2d 425 (5th Cir. 1974).

58 *Id.* at 432; *McNeal v. Tate County School Dist.,* 460 F.2d 568 (5th Cir. 1972); *Wright v. City of Brighton,* 441 F.2d 447 (5th Cir. 1971).

59 109 US 3 (1883).

60 *Id.* at 24–5.

61 203 US 1, 17 (1906).

62 *Corrigan v. Buckley,* 271 US 323, 330–31 (1926); *Hurd v. Hodge,* 334 US 24, 31 (1948) (Thirteenth Amendment does not authorize Congress to prohibit private racially restrictive covenants).

63 392 US 409 (1968).

64 *Id.* at 436.

65 427 US 160 (1976).

66 *Id.* at 172.
67 *Id.* at 166.
68 See J. NOWAK *et al.*, *supra*, pp. 818–19.
69 *Pierce v. Society of Sisters*, 268 US 510, 535 (1925).
70 I want to thank Penny Alexander for her excellent research assistance.

Notes on Contributors

Stephen Arons is a professor of legal studies at the University of Massachusetts at Amherst and was previously a senior staff attorney at the Harvard Center for Law and Education. He is the author of numerous books and articles in the area of law and education, including *Compelling Belief: The Culture of American Schooling*.

Joanne C. Brant is an associate at Thompson, Hine and Florey, a Cleveland law firm. Her interests include labor law and First Amendment topics.

Erwin Chemerinsky is a professor of law at the University of Southern California Law Center. He has published many articles on constitutional law in publications such as *The Boston University Law Review*, *The Michigan Law Review*, *The Northwestern Law Review*, and *The UCLA Law Review*. He also is the author of *Interpreting the Constitution* and *Federal Jurisdiction*.

John E. Chubb is a senior fellow in the Governmental Studies Program at The Brookings Institution specializing in the study of bureaucracy and public policy. His most recent books include *Can the Government Govern?* (co-authored with Paul E. Peterson) and *What Price Democracy? Politics, Markets and America's Schools* (co-authored with Terry M. Moe).

Robert L. Crain is a professor of sociology and education at Teachers College, Columbia University. His research interests include educational policy and school desegregation and its effect on academic achievement and life chances. He has written numerous books and articles, including *The Politics of School Desegregation* and *Strategies for Effective Desegregation* (co-authored with Christine Rossell and others).

Neal E. Devins is an assistant professor of law at the Marshall-Wythe School of Law, College of William and Mary and a Research Fellow at the school's Institute of Bill of Rights Law. Professor Devins has previously served as Assistant General Counsel, US Commission on Civil Rights and as a Project Director at the Center for Education Policy, Vanderbilt Institute for Public Policy Studies. He is the author of over two dozen articles on constitutional, civil rights, and education topics. His work has appeared in *The Public Interest*, *The Stanford Law Review*, *The Columbia Law Review*, *The California Law Review*, and *The Duke Law Journal*.

Carl H. Esbeck is a professor of law at the University of Missouri-Columbia. He is an editor of the *Religious Freedom Reporter* and a member of the executive committee of the Center for Church/State Studies. He has authored several articles concerning church-state relations. His work has appeared in the *Washington and Lee Law Review*, the *Brigham Young University Law Review*, and other law journals.

Robert K. Fullinwider is a research scholar at the Institute for Philosophy and Public Policy, University of Maryland. He is the author of numerous books and articles, including *The Reverse Discrimination Controversy: A Moral and Legal Analysis* and *The Moral Foundations of Civil Rights* (co-edited with Claudia Mills). He currently works in the areas of civic and moral education.

John Lachs is a professor of philosophy at Vanderbilt University. He is the author of numerous books and articles on a range of philosophical topics. His most recent books include *Intermediate Man, The Human Search*, and *Minds and Philosophers*.

Shirley M. Lachs lives in Nashville, Tennessee. Her research interests include ethics and public policy topics. She is co-editor of *Physical Order and Moral Liberty* (with John Lachs).

Henry M. Levin is a professor of education and economics at Stanford University specializing in the economics of human resources. He is the author of numerous books and articles, including *Comparing Public and Private Schools* (co-edited with Edward Haertel and Thomas James) and *Schooling and Work in the Democratic State* (co-authored with Martin Carnoy).

William P. Marshall is a professor of law at the Case Western Reserve University Law School. He is the author of numerous articles on First Amendment and federal jurisdiction topics. His work has appeared in *The Supreme Court Review*, *The Northwestern University Law Review*, and *The University of Chicago Law Review*.

Terry M. Moe is an associate professor of political science at Stanford University, and was previously a Senior Fellow in the Governmental Studies Program at The Brookings Institution. His fields of expertise include regulation and organization theory, in which he has written many articles for professional journals and books. He is also co-author of *What Price Democracy?*.

Jeremy A. Rabkin is an associate professor of government at Cornell University. He is author of *Judicial Compulsions, How Public Law Distorts Public Policy*, and of numerous articles on public law and government regulation in such publications as *The Public Interest* and *The Stanford Law Review*. He is a contributing editor to *Regulation* and *The American Spectator*.

Michael A. Rebell is a partner at Rebell and Katzive, a New York law firm, and a visiting lecturer at the Yale Law School. He is the author of numerous books and articles on a wide range of education topics, including *Educational Policy Making and the Courts: An Empirical Study on Judicial Activism* and *Equality and Education* (both co-authored with Arthur Block).

Christine H. Rossell is an associate professor of political science at Boston University. Her research interests include school desegregation, bilingual education, and educational policy. She has written numerous books and articles on white flight, community reaction to school desegregation, magnet schools, and bilingual education. She is a co-author of *Strategies for Effective Desegregation* and co-editor of *The Consequences of School Desegregation* (with Willis D. Hawley).

Tyll van Geel is a professor of education in the Graduate School of Education and Human Development and Chairman of the Social Context Area at the University of Rochester. He is the author of numerous books and articles on a wide range of education topics, including *Educational Policy and the Law* (co-authored with David Kirp, Mark Yudof, and Betsy Levin) and *The Courts and American Education Law*.

Index